CASE STUDIES IN PALEOETHNOBOTANY

Case Studies in Paleoethnobotany focuses on interpretation in paleoethnobotany. In it the reader is guided through the process of analyzing archaeobotanical data and of using that data to address research questions. Part I introduces archaeobotanical remains and how they are deposited, preserved, sampled, recovered, and analyzed. Five issue-oriented case studies make up Part II and illustrate paleoethnobotanical inference and applications. A recurrent theme is the strength of using multiple lines of evidence to address issues of significance.

This book is unique in its explicit focus on interpretation for "consumers" of paleoethnobotanical knowledge. Paleoethnobotanical inference is increasingly sophisticated and contributes to our understanding of the past in ways that may not be apparent outside the field or to all practitioners. The case study format allows in-depth exploration of the process of interpretation in the context of significant issues that will engage readers. No other work introduces paleoethnobotany and illustrates its application in this way.

This book will appeal to students interested in ancient plant–people interrelationships, as well as archaeologists, paleoethnobotanists, and paleoecologists. The short methods chapters and topical case studies are ideal for instructors of classes in archaeological methods, environmental archaeology, and ethnobiology.

Deborah M. Pearsall is Professor Emeritus at the University of Missouri, having retired in 2013 after 35 years. She holds a BA from the University of Michigan and an MA and PhD from the University of Illinois, all of which are in the subject of Anthropology. Her interests within this discipline center on South American archaeology and paleoethnobotany: the study of plant–people interrelationships through the archaeological record. She has conducted paleoethnobotanical research in numerous locations in the Americas. Her research has two broad themes: the origins and spread of agriculture in the lowland Neotropics, and methods and approaches in paleoethnobotany. She is the author of three books: *Paleoethnobotany: A Handbook of Procedures*; *Plants and People in Ancient Ecuador: The Ethnobotany of the Jama River Valley*; and, with D. R. Piperno, *The Origins of Agriculture in the Lowland Neotropics*. She was also the general editor of Academic Press's 2008 *Encyclopedia of Archaeology* and has published in numerous professional journals and edited collections.

CASE STUDIES IN PALEOETHNOBOTANY

Understanding Ancient Lifeways Through the Study of Phytoliths, Starch, Macroremains, and Pollen

Deborah M. Pearsall

 Routledge
Taylor & Francis Group

NEW YORK AND LONDON

First published 2019
by Routledge
711 Third Avenue, New York, NY 10017

and by Routledge
2 Park Square, Milton Park, Abingdon, Oxon, OX14 4RN

Routledge is an imprint of the Taylor & Francis Group, an informa business

Library of Congress Cataloging-in-Publication Data
A catalog record for this title has been requested

ISBN: 978-1-138-54471-0 (hbk)
ISBN: 978-1-611-32296-5 (pbk)
ISBN: 978-1-351-00968-3 (ebk)

Typeset in Bembo
by Apex CoVantage, LLC

CV 01.11.2019 1625

For my students, lab assistants, and the visitors who passed through the MU lab, 1979–2013: thanks for making my work possible and fun; For archaeology students curious about ancient plant remains; For my husband, Mike, for your loving support.

CONTENTS

FIGURES

TABLES

PREFACE

I wrote the original version of *Paleoethnobotany: A Handbook of Procedures* (1989, Academic Press) following the outline of a class I taught every other year or so at the University of Missouri. The class was not just aimed at aspiring paleoethnobotanists, but at a more general audience of students interested in learning about ancient plant use. In time the class became one of the methods offerings for majors, and I added readings from the literature that illustrated how macroremains, pollen, phytoliths, and, eventually, starch could be used to address interesting research questions. Those readings were often challenging, but it became clear to me that students who put the effort into reading the graphs and tables and who thought about whether the conclusions made sense from those data not only learned something about past plant–people interrelationships, but about the process of drawing robust inferences as well.

My goal in this book, *Case Studies in Paleoethnobotany: Understanding Ancient Lifeways Through the Study of Phytoliths, Starch, Macroremains, and Pollen*, is to focus explicitly on the process of interpretation in paleoethnobotany—in essence, guiding students, practicing archaeologists, and paleoethnobotanists alike through the process of reading those graphs and tables and evaluating those research results. Paleoethnobotanical inference is increasingly sophisticated and contributes to our understanding of the past in ways that may not be apparent outside the field or to all practitioners. I will illustrate some of these contributions through five issue-oriented case studies that feature robust and innovative approaches to interpreting past plant–people interrelationships. A theme that runs through all the case studies is the strength of using multiple lines of evidence to address issues of significance.

To set the stage for the case studies, the book begins in Part I with an introduction to paleoethnobotany, the study of plant–people interrelationships through the archaeological record. In Chapter 1 the reader is introduced to the paleoethnobotanical approach and to the major kinds of archaeobotanical remains—macroremains (seeds, fruits, underground storage organs, wood), pollen, phytoliths, and starch grains—and how they are studied. Chapter 2 discusses how these plant remains become deposited and preserved in archaeological sites and environmental contexts like lake sediments. Chapter 3 covers the basics of taking samples in the field, discusses sampling strategies, and describes flotation, a common method for recovering macroremains often carried out by field archaeologists. Chapter 4 describes the ways in which paleoethnobotanists examine and draw inferences from the results of their studies of macroremains, pollen, phytoliths, and starch. The reader is also guided through how to read a standard stratigraphic diagram, a common format for presenting pollen and phytolith results from environmental cores.

Part II focuses on how archaeobotanical data are interpreted and used to address research questions of interest to archaeologists, paleoethnobotanists, and other researchers. Five case studies illustrate how paleoethnobotanical data are interpreted and integrated:

Chapter 5: Investigating Neanderthal Lifeways Through Paleoethnobotany
Chapter 6: The Paleoethnobotany of Maize: Understanding Domestication and Agriculture
Chapter 7: Archaeobotany and Insights Into Social Relationships at Cahokia
Chapter 8: An Individual's Relationship to the Natural World: Ötzi, the Tyrolean Iceman
Chapter 9: Plants and Healing/Health

I selected these case studies to illustrate the diversity of issues and questions that can be illuminated through an understanding of plant–people interrelationships. The cases range widely in time, geography, and the types of data used to investigate the issues. In each case the reader will be introduced to the issues and questions, provided necessary background information, and then presented the key findings and a sample of actual data relevant to the case. Chapter 10 presents some final thoughts on investigating ancient lifeways through paleoethnobotany.

ACKNOWLEDGMENTS

Special thanks to retired professional photographer Howard Wilson, who reproduced the figures from *Paleoethnobotany: A Handbook of Procedures* used in Part I and prepared all the tables and figures reproduced from published works for inclusion in this book. Howard also composed Figures 1.7, 1.9, 1.10, 2.2, 2.3, and 6.1.

I thank the following for creating original art that first appeared in *Paleoethnobotany: A Handbook of Procedures*: Elizabeth Dinan, Figures 3.1, 3.2, and 3.3 and Lisa Harrison, Figures 1.1, 1.2, 1.3, 1.4, 1.5, and 1.6.

The author photo was taken by Gina Beckley.

Sources of tables and figures reproduced from published works are listed in the captions of the images; I thank the publishers and authors for granting permission to use these works.

PART I

The Nature and Study of Paleoethnobotanical Remains

1

PALEOETHNOBOTANICAL REMAINS

Glossary

dichotomous key   a tool that helps the user identify an unknown organism or other entity, such as a pollen grain or wood specimen. A dichotomous key is composed of a series of statements consisting of two choices (different characteristics of the entity) that lead the user to the correct identification.

Introduction: The Paleoethnobotanical Approach

Paleoethnobotany is the study of the interrelationships between humans and plants through the archaeological record. In this chapter I describe the paleoethnobotanical approach and introduce the major kinds of archaeobotanical remains—macroremains (seeds, fruits, underground storage organs, wood), pollen, phytoliths, and starch grains—and discuss how they are studied.

Paleoethnobotany is essentially an archaeological approach, and many paleoethnobotanists are trained as archaeologists. Plant remains, the primary research materials of paleoethnobotany, must be recovered from sites and identified. Human interactions with the plant world—for example, cultivation and consumption of domesticated plants—result in the deposition and preservation of four primary kinds of plant remains. *Macroremains* are larger plant tissues that are visible to the naked eye. Often, plant tissues preserve by becoming charred, for instance, in a cooking accident. Food preparation may also result in the deposition of *starch* on grinding stones and in cooking pots, where it may be preserved in crevices or food crusts. Decay or burning of plant tissues such as leaves, stems, and fruits releases *phytoliths* (plant opal silica bodies) into site sediments. Certain kinds of cooking techniques may also result in phytolith deposition in vessels or ovens. In the process of creating gardens, people cut down and weed out some plants and cultivate and encourage others. This changes the mixture of *pollen* that is deposited over the landscape. Pollen deposited and preserved in lake sediments records the history of human–plant interrelationships on local and regional scales; phytoliths that wash into lakes with eroding soil also reflect past vegetation. Pollen may also be ingested, for example, in a tea made from flowers, and preserved in human fecal remains (coprolites) with other plant and animal tissues. It is not uncommon for plants to be represented in the archaeological record in multiple ways.

The nature of these diverse archaeobotanical materials also demands expertise in botany. Archaeologically trained paleoethnobotanists must learn plant taxonomy, anatomy, and laboratory skills necessary to recover and identify plant remains. Even paleoethnobotanists whose primary training is in botany must adapt their skills to deal with fragmentary materials and the incomplete archaeological record.

As a field, paleoethnobotany has its roots in the early to mid-nineteenth century, when well-preserved plant remains from Egyptian tombs, lakeside Swiss villages, and Peruvian mummy bundles were studied by botanists. Study of macroremains continued in the late nineteenth and first half of the twentieth centuries in Europe, the Mediterranean region, and coastal Peru.

Pollen and phytoliths also began to be studied systematically at that time. The real potential of fossil pollen studies was realized in 1916 when Lennart von Post presented the first modern percentage pollen analysis. This approach permitted direct quantitative description of past vegetation composition. Another early application of pollen analysis was determining relative dating of archaeological sites by comparing pollen assemblages from sites to a sequence of vegetation changes during the late Pleistocene and Holocene epochs established from studies of peat bog and lake deposits. Early twentieth-century applications of phytolith analysis focused on identifying cultivated grasses of the Near East.

In spite of early studies of well-preserved plant remains from Peru by European and Latin American scholars, American archaeologists and botanists did not show much interest in archaeological plant remains until after 1930. A similar situation existed for pollen analysis, with early research largely limited to the arid southwestern United States. In North America phytoliths were mostly of interest to botanists and soil scientists, and starch to food scientists.

Analyses by Gilmore (1931) and Jones (1936) of desiccated plant remains from rock shelters in the United States helped fuel interest in paleoethnobotany in North America, and publication of *Excavations at Star Carr* by British archaeologist J.G.D. Clark (1954) convinced many of the importance of biological remains for archaeological interpretation. With increased interest in American archaeology on reconstructing subsistence and paleoenvironment, greater emphasis was put during the late 1950s and 1960s on recovering and analyzing macroremains and pollen. After Struever (1968) described flotation, archaeologists began to recover macroremains from a diversity of sites, not just those in which dry or waterlogged conditions preserved quantities of material. By the 1970s, pollen analysis was incorporated into archaeological investigations in many regions of the United States, Canada, and Latin America.

The development of phytolith analysis in archaeology was tied to two research foci of the 1970s and 1980s: the origins and intensification of agriculture, and reconstructing past environments. The potential of starch analysis was first recognized through study of organic residues on stone tools, which began in the late 1970s and early 1980s in Oceania and North America. These studies revealed that organic residues, including identifiable starch, survived more often than expected (i.e., not just in arid sites). By 2006, when *Ancient Starch Research* (Torrence and Barton, eds.) was published, it had become apparent that starch was surprisingly common in the archaeological record.

Paleoethnobotanical research has diversified and grown exponentially in the last three decades. Among the research topics that have been addressed through the study of archaeobotanical remains: identification of domesticated plants, agricultural practices, and agricultural intensification; reconstructing diet and subsistence; prehistory of beer and wine making; use of wild foods by agriculturalists; wood acquisition, use, and environmental impact; plants and political complexity, social status, and social change; plants as indicators of ethnicity; identification of fiber and wooden artifacts; prehistory of spices; plants in ritual and medicine; plants in economic systems; human environmental impacts, management, and land use; study of living conditions of prehistoric populations; tracing the settlement by humans of remote regions, such as Polynesia; investigating diet and health through study of coprolites; study of agricultural fields and gardens; plants in human evolution; spatial and activity analysis; and diet of living and extinct primates.

Paleoethnobotanical Data and Their Study

Macroremains

Macroremains are larger plant tissues visible to the naked eye. They include seeds, fruits, nuts (all plant reproductive structures), wood, roots and tubers, and other vegetative materials. The last named will not be covered here. Table 1.1 lists the scientific names of plants mentioned in the text.

Seeds

A seed is a reproductive structure composed of a protected embryonic plant (Shackley 1981). In the major group of seed-bearing plants, the angiosperms, seeds develop in the ovary, the basal portion of the female part of the flower. The ovary and seeds develop into the fruit. Angiosperm seeds have three major parts: embryo, endosperm, and seed coat (testa) (Figure 1.1). The embryo is composed of the first "true" leaves, the primary root, and the

TABLE 1.1 Scientific names of plants mentioned in text

arrowroot family	Marantaceae
banana family	Musaceae
bird-of-paradise family	Heliconiaceae
canna family	Cannaceae
carrot	*Daucus carota*
cotton	*Gossypium*
daisy family	Asteraceae
grass family	Poaceae or Gramineae
ginger family	Zingiberaceae
gourd	*Lagenaria siceraria*
hickory family	Juglandaceae
legume or bean family	Fabaceae or Leguminosae
maize	*Zea mays*
palm family	Arecaceae or Palmae
peach	*Prunus persica*
sedge family	Cyperaceae
Squash	*Cucurbita*
sweet potato	*Ipomoea batatas*

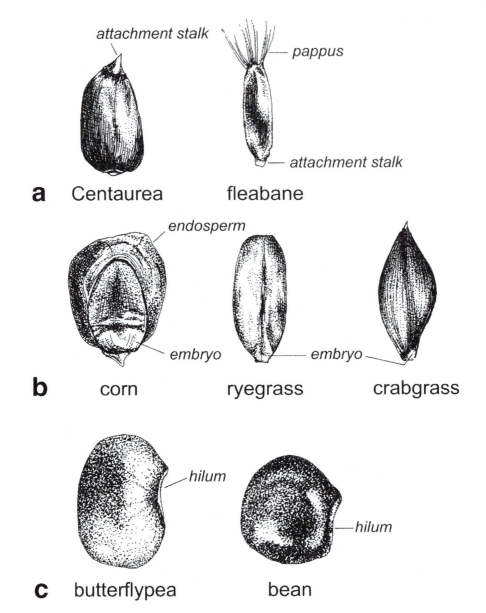

a Centaurea   fleabane

b corn   ryegrass   crabgrass

c butterflypea   bean

FIGURE 1.1   Examples of angiosperm seeds, illustrating characteristics that aid identification: (a) Asteraceae (daisy family); seeds are often oblong and sometimes ridged; a pappus (ring of hairs or scales) may be present; an attachment stalk (remains of funiculus) is often prominent; (b) Poaceae (grass family) seeds have a lateral or basal-lateral embryo; endosperm tends to be abundant; some grasses have elongated, grooved seeds (e.g., ryegrass); others have seeds that are flattened and lightly ridged (e.g., crabgrass); (c) Fabaceae (bean family); many legumes are beanlike, with a notched attachment area or hilum; the seed coat is usually smooth; seed interior consists mostly of two broad, thick cotyledons, with little or no endosperm. Not to scale.

cotyledon or "seed" leaf (Evert 2006). Dicotyledons have two "seed" leaves, monocotyledons one. In some plants, such as legumes, cotyledons are large and contain stored nutrients to nourish the seedling. Seeds of other plants contain specialized tissue, the endosperm, which provides these nutrients. The amount of endosperm and its position in the seed relative to the embryo differ among plant groups and are important traits in seed identification. Embryo and endosperm, if present, are protected by the seed coat, a one- or two-layer outer covering. Seeds coats may have distinctive coloration, texture, or surface features that can be important distinguishing characteristics. The point where the seed was attached to the ovary is the hilum, or attachment scar.

Not all distinguishing characteristics may be preserved in archaeological seeds. Size and shape may be distorted by charring, for instance, or seeds may be broken. The seed coat is an important source of diagnostic characteristics, including color for uncharred seeds, texture (whether the testa is smooth or has a raised pattern), attachments, and scars like the hilum. If the seed coat is lost during charring or badly eroded in desiccated materials, identifiability decreases markedly. Waterlogged seeds may also lose their outer layers and suffer cell distortion.

Accurate identification of archaeological seeds to botanical taxon is largely a matter of practice, and is grounded in comparing archaeological specimens to known kinds of seeds. Photographs and line drawings are helpful visual aids, but are no substitute for identified examples. Study of comparative seed specimens helps the novice learn the diagnostic features of each kind of seed, how it appears when broken or charred, and how it can be distinguished from similar seeds.

Fruits and Nuts

A fruit is a ripened ovary and its adhering parts—the seed-bearing organ of the plant. The ovary wall, or pericarp, can be soft and fleshy, leathery, hard, or thin and paperlike, depending on the form of the fruit (Figure 1.2). Internal arrangement of seeds in the fruit is also variable. Some fruits have only one seed, which is fused to the ovary wall; other fruits have several seeds. Although whole fruits are sometimes found archaeologically, it is more common to find fragments of inedible fruit parts. Very large seeds, such as palm and other tropical fruit seeds, often produce macroremains that are more similar in size and appearance to fruit fragments than to small seeds.

Nuts are indehiscent (not splitting open to release seeds when ripe), usually one-seeded, hard and bony fruits. Some nuts, such as those in the hickory family, are covered with a leathery husk. Fragments of husk, nut shell (hard pericarp), and nut meats (embryo) may all be found archaeologically. There are two major types of succulent fruits: drupes and berries. Drupes are fleshy fruits with one or more seeds enclosed in a hard, stony portion of endocarp, such as the peach pit illustrated in Figure 1.2. Berries are similar to drupes, but their seeds are surrounded only by a hardened seed coat. Legumes are dry fruits that open along two sutures, releasing the mature seeds. The cotton fruit shown in Figure 1.2 is an example of a capsule, a multichambered fruit that opens along one or more sutures.

Identifying fragmented fruit and nut remains presents the analyst with a set of problems somewhat different from those encountered in seed identification. Published manuals or drawings are less useful as identification aids, because fragmented remains do not resemble illustrated whole specimens. Photographs or drawings often do not illustrate internal portions

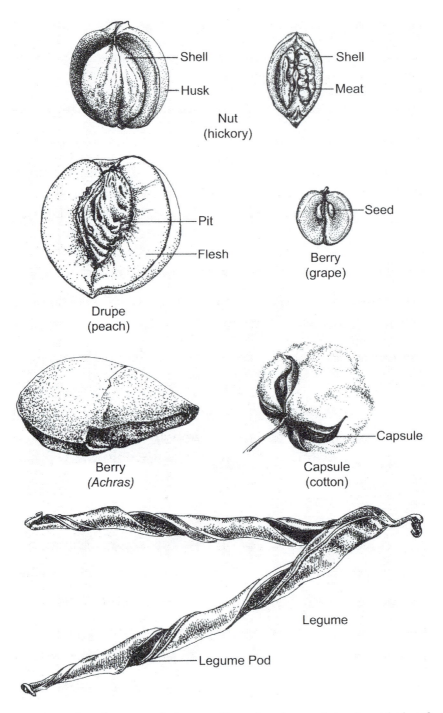

FIGURE 1.2 Examples of common fruit types, illustrating characteristics that aid identification. Not to scale.

of fruit, the nature of tissues, or details of attachment areas. A comparative collection thus becomes of primary importance for correct identification of such remains. Large seeds present similar difficulties, because they are often recovered in fragmented form. For identifying charred specimens, comparative materials should be charred and broken up into pieces like the archaeological materials, and distinctive features of the various tissues described. It may be useful to compile this information into a desktop identification aid (card file), database, or formal dichotomous key.

Wood

Fragments of charred wood are often the most abundant macroremains recovered archaeologically. Wood is xylem tissue (tissue that conducts water and nutrients) of the secondarily thickened plant. The term "wood" is used broadly here to include all plant tissues found in secondarily thickened stems. A number of texts describe the structure of wood in detail; the basic reference used here was Panshin and de Zeeuw (1980).

Features of wood commonly used for identification are illustrated in Figure 1.3 and Figure 1.4 and include vessels and their arrangement; size and arrangement of rays; and abundance and nature of parenchyma. Physical characteristics, such as color, texture, and hardness, and certain microanatomical features can also be useful. Features of wood can be viewed from three different planes or sections: the transverse or cross-section (plane across the stem), the radial longitudinal section (plane paralleling a radius of the stem), and the tangential longitudinal section (plane at a right angle to a radius of the stem).

The nature and arrangement of vessels—linear arrangements of specialized cells that conduct water and dissolved salts—as viewed in transverse section are key features for distinguishing woods. Presence or absence of vessels, for example, can be used to distinguish softwoods

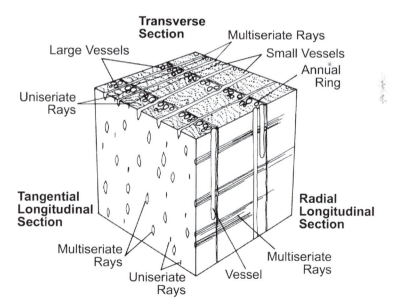

FIGURE 1.3   Transverse, tangential, and radial sections of a typical hardwood, showing vessels (large, small) and their arrangement into annual rings and rays (uniseriate, multiseriate).

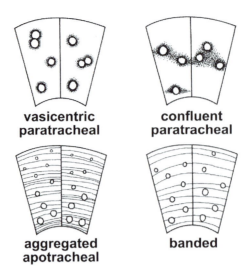

vasicentric
paratracheal

confluent
paratracheal

aggregated
apotracheal

banded

FIGURE 1.4   Some common arrangements of parenchyma tissue. Paratracheal parenchyma is depicted by black dots; aggregated apotracheal and banded are depicted by thin lines.

(conifers) from most hardwoods (angiosperms). One of the easiest features to recognize is the annual growth ring: if vessels formed during spring growth of the tree (early wood) are larger than those formed during the summer growth period (late wood), the wood is called ring porous; if vessels formed during growth of early and late wood are the same size, wood is classified as diffuse porous. Vessels may occur singly, in groups, or in chains and may be sparse or quite numerous in relation to other tissues.

Size and arrangement of rays, which are composed of parenchyma tissue (storage cells with undifferentiated walls) and tracheids (a type of water-conducting cell) are additional features useful for wood identification. Viewed from the transverse section, rays appear like spokes of a wheel, radiating out from the center of the stem. Using this section, size and arrangement of rays can be described as they appear when "sliced" through one horizontal plane: in some taxa all rays are very narrow (uniseriate); in others rays appear variable in width (multiseriate). Rays also differ in height and overall spacing and abundance.

Abundance and nature of parenchyma tissue are the third set of features commonly used for wood identification. As mentioned earlier, parenchyma cells make up much of the tissue of rays. Parenchyma also occurs in strands running longitudinally through wood. The arrangement of this kind of parenchyma, illustrated in Figure 1.4, can be useful in identification.

Identifying charred wood is a task undertaken by many paleoethnobotanists. Charring eliminates a number of features useful for identifying fresh wood, such as color and odor, and alters others. Charred wood is usually examined by snapping the specimen or cutting it with a sharp razor blade to create a fresh transverse surface. Viewed under low magnification (15–30 ×) with a dissecting microscope and obliquely angled top lighting, characteristics such as arrangement, abundance, and size of vessels and spacing and abundance of rays can be observed. Parenchyma characteristics and ray widths typically require higher magnification. Snapping or cutting radial longitudinal and tangential longitudinal sections gives additional views of rays. Dried or waterlogged wood may be too fragile to examine this way and require embedding and sectioning (see Pearsall 2015 for details).

As in identifying seeds, nuts, and fruits, a comparative collection is essential for wood identification. I found it useful to make an index card for each charred comparative specimen that included a description of the features of the wood, sketches of sections, and notes on characteristics that distinguished the specimen from similar ones. Published wood identification keys can also be adapted for use with charred specimens.

Roots and Tubers

In spite of the important role roots and tubers likely played in prehistoric subsistence, macroremains of underground storage organs (USOs) are often sparse in the archaeobotanical record. Fleshy USOs can be divided into two types: those originating in stem tissue and those that are actually roots (Figure 1.5). When stems occur underground, they retain anatomical structures of leaf-bearing organs: nodes (areas that bear leaves), buds, and sometimes remnant, scalelike leaves. By contrast, roots do not have nodes, internodes (portions of stem between two nodes), or remnant leaves. Crops with storage organs that are true roots include carrots and sweet potatoes. There are a variety of fleshy underground storage organs that originate in stem tissue; they occur in both monocotyledon and dicotyledon families. Common types are rhizomes, corms, bulbs, and tubers (Figure 1.6).

Although there is sufficient variation in form and structure of many roots and tubers to permit identification, success may be limited by the state of preservation of macroremain USOs, including their degree of fragmentation. Often, the only part of a USO that remains after use is the peel. Although some USO peelings are tough and fibrous, others have thin

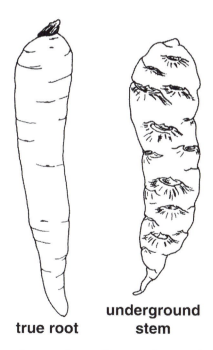

true root   **underground stem**

FIGURE 1.5   True root and underground stem. In an underground stem such as *mashua*, shown here, leaf nodes—the "eyes" of the tuber—indicate its origin as stem tissue. The carrot, a true root, has no eyes, only inconspicuous root scars.

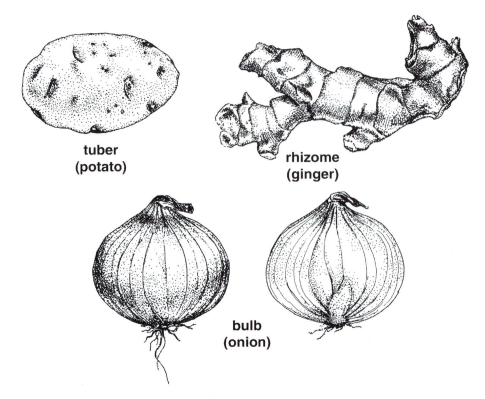

FIGURE 1.6 Various types of underground stems.

peels that quickly decay or may be eaten with the fleshy part of the USO. When preservation is through charring, recovering tuber or root peelings is very unlikely, because such remains are quite fragile. Finds do occur in dry and waterlogged preservation settings, however.

If USOs are fairly complete, the first step in identification is to sort remains into like groups based on gross morphology, for example, presence or absence of leaf nodes (true root vs. rhizome or tuber). Other useful anatomical characteristics include the size, shape, wall characteristics, and patterning of cavities; the organization of vascular tissues; the characteristics of parenchymous and mechanical (sclerenchymous) tissues; and the color, luster, and hardness of charcoal (Hather 1991, 1993).

The following websites host databases and/or images of macroremains of seeds, fruits, wood, or USOs:

International Work Group for Palaeoethnobotany, Institute for Prehistory and Archaeological Science, IPAS, Basel University. This site has many helpful links to research and databases, www.archaeobotany.org/links.php

George Pitt-Rivers Laboratory for Bioarchaeology, Cambridge University. This site has many helpful links to research and databases, www.arch.cam.ac.uk/pittrivers/links.html

Washington University, St. Louis, Laboratory Guide to Archaeological Plant Remains From Eastern North America, http://artsci.wustl.edu/~gjfritz/

Microscopic Wood Anatomy of Central European Species, a web-based identification key with images, www.woodanatomy.ch/

George Willcox Archaeobotany, an atlas of images of charred archaeobotanical finds, http://g.willcox.pagesperso-orange.fr/

Paleobot.org, a collaborative open-access web resource (macroremains, pollen, phytoliths, starch, isotopes), www.paleobot.org/

Department of Horticulture and Crop Science, The Ohio State University, Seed ID Workshop, www.oardc.ohio-state.edu/seedid/search.asp

Pollen

Pollen grains are formed in the anther, the male portion of a flower. On maturity, the wall of the anther breaks, releasing pollen for transfer to the female portion of the flower. The mechanism for this transfer differs among plants and influences both the abundance of pollen produced and its form (Faegri et al. 1989).

There are four major pollination mechanisms in higher plants: wind pollination, pollination by animal vector, water pollination, and self-pollination (Faegri et al. 1989). Wind-pollinated plants produce the greatest quantity of pollen of any group of plants, generally 10,000 to 70,000 grains per anther. Many wind-pollinated plants have smooth pollen grains with little sculpturing. Grains also tend to be dry and nonclumping. These characteristics make pollen of wind-pollinated plants very aerodynamic, aiding in their dispersal and large contribution to pollen deposited over the landscape, or the pollen rain. By contrast, zoophilous taxa, plants whose pollen is dispersed by animals, tend to produce fewer pollen grains, in the range of 1,000 or less per anther. Pollen grains of zoophilous taxa are often covered with sticky oils or are highly sculpted so they adhere to the pollinating animal. These characteristics result in little zoophilous pollen becoming part of pollen rain. Water pollination and self-pollination typically also lead to poor representation of plant taxa in pollen rain.

Most pollen grains are elliptical in shape and symmetrical around an axis (Figure 1.7). Triangular forms and irregular types, often with attachments, also occur. Pollen grains range in size from 5 microns to more than 200 microns. Shape and size can be important characteristics for distinguishing among taxa.

A pollen grain consists of several layers. The outermost, the exine, is composed largely of sporopollenin, one of the most resistant natural organic substances. The exine is the portion of the grain preserved in fossil pollen. Sporopollenin is susceptible to oxidation, however, and to destruction by mechanical degradation and biological agents. Fossil pollen is identified largely by the structure and sculpturing of the exine and by the form of the openings, or apertures, in it.

Faegri et al. (1989) present a detailed discussion of terminology used to describe structure, sculpturing, and apertures of the exine; familiarity with terms such as "tectate," "echinate," "rugulate," and "colpate" are necessary to use pollen keys like Kapp (1969; Kapp et al. 2000) and Moore et al. (1991). Although the actual number of pollen types encountered in archaeological samples is often fairly low, lake core samples may contain a rich assemblage of taxa. Recognition of types requires a comprehensive pollen comparative collection, as well as experience in keying.

Pollen is studied by viewing its surface and internal components using a transmitted light research microscope. The surface (exine) has a number of features used to distinguish pollen

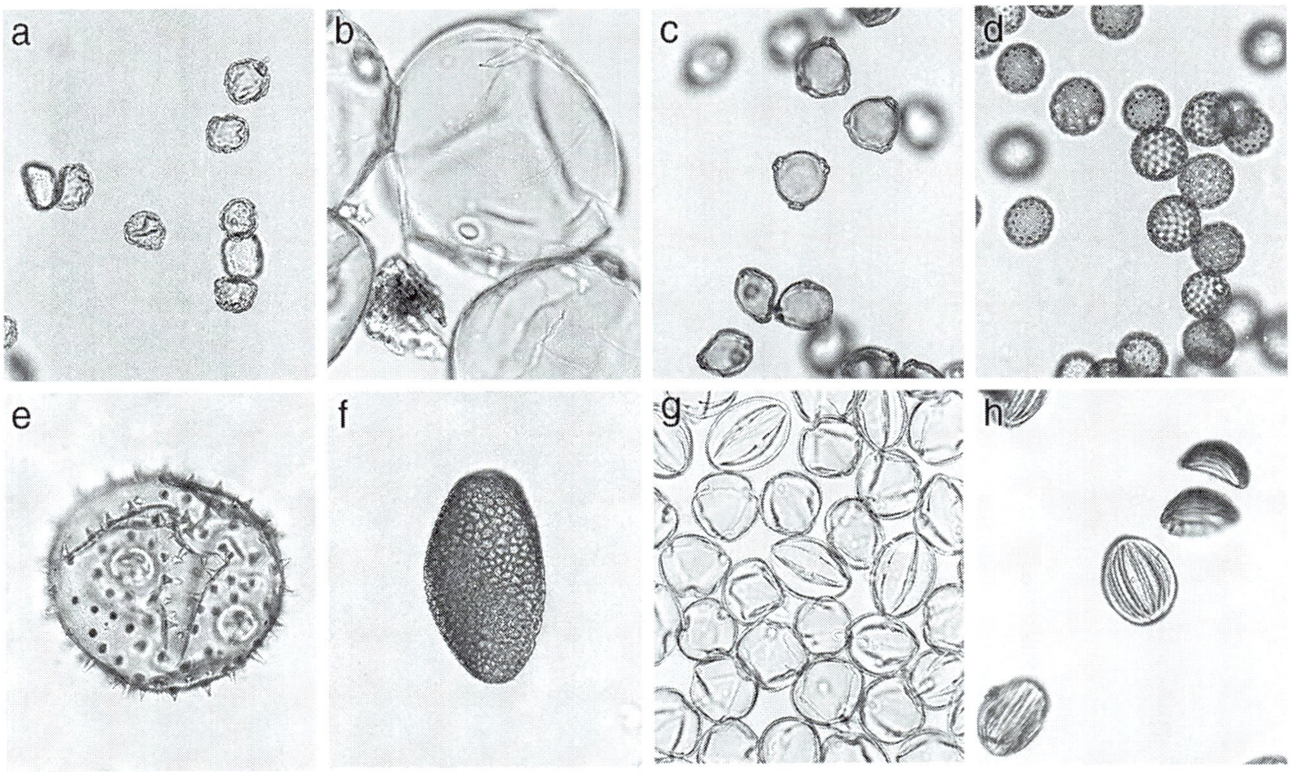

FIGURE 1.7 Micrographs illustrating some of the range of variation in pollen grains. Terms in parentheses refer to characteristics of the grain surface and the form of openings in it; see Pearsall (2015) for details: (a) *Populus nigra* (inaperturate, densely verrucate, or scabrate); (b) *Zea mays* (monoporate, large, faintly granular); (c) *Betula papyrifea* (triporate, psilate); (d) *Chenopodium album* (periporate, 70–75 pores); (e) *Cucurbita foetidissima* (periporate, 15–20 pores); (f) *Agave* sp. (monocolpate, exine perforate tectate); (g) *Prosopis* sp. (tricolporate, psilate); (h) *Ephedra* sp. (polyplicate, 11–15 ridges).

Images courtesy of Dr. Peter Warnock.

of different taxa. A basic distinction is whether the outermost surface, the tectum (Latin "roof"), is fused into a continuous surface, is discontinuous (i.e., a "roof" with holes), or is absent. If the tectum is discontinuous, the columellae ("pillars" holding up the "roof") and foot layer may be visible through the openings. If the tectum is absent, the columellae will also be lacking. Patterning produced by the form and surface visibility of these elements contributes to the distinctive character of the exine. In some pollen, the tectum is covered with projections, which may be connected to form surface patterns known as sculpturing.

Apertures open into the interior of the grain, permitting shrinking and swelling of it and providing an avenue for emergence of the pollen tube. There are two types of apertures: pores and furrows. Pores are usually round but can be somewhat elongated with rounded ends. Furrows are elongated with pointed ends. The location of pores or furrows on the grain and the number of apertures present are characteristics useful for separating pollen types.

As will be discussed in Chapter 2, a number of factors determine whether pollen grains are preserved over time. The forces that affect pollen preservation can also render surviving pollen grains difficult to identify. Exine surfaces can become abraded by soil particles, for example, which eventually leads to the breakup of grains, and loss of sculpturing detail can make damaged grains less identifiable. Successful pollen identification comes with practice, guidance from published sources and experienced researchers, and study of comparative collections. Some types are very distinctive and readily recognizable; for others, only the major group to which it belongs can be determined (e.g., Kapp 1969:21–27, picture key to major spore and pollen groups).

The following is a list of some websites on which are posted databases and images of pollen:

University of Arizona Catalog of Internet Pollen and Spore Images. A site with links to many of the databases listed here. Includes an index of all images on linked sites organized by botanical family and species. Many images can be accessed from the site, www.geo.arizona.edu/palynology/polonweb.html. See also University of Arizona SEM pollen images, www.geo.arizona.edu/palynology/sem/semuofa.html

Australian National University, Australasian Pollen and Spore Atlas, http://apsa.anu.edu.au/

The African Pollen Database, developed and maintained by Medias-France, http://medias3.mediasfrance.org/apd/accueil.htm

USDA, Areawide Pest Management Research Unit (APMRU), Pollen Reference Collection, http://pollen.usda.gov/index.htm

Pollen key for selected plants of the San Francisco Estuary region. University of California, Berkeley, http://oldweb.geog.berkeley.edu/ProjectsResources/PollenKey/byFamiliesAll-in-1.html

The Newcastle Pollen Collection, mirrored on the University of Arizona Department of Geosciences server, www.geo.arizona.edu/palynology/nsw/index.html

Society for the Promotion of Palynological Research in Austria. PalDat—Palyological database, www.paldat.org/

Phytoliths

Phytoliths are inorganic inclusions that occur in stems, leaves, roots, and inflorescences (flowering and fruiting structures) of plants, formed when plants take up silica in groundwater and deposit it in epidermal and other cells. In many plant taxa, distinctive forms that retain cell shape after organic tissue has decayed or burned are formed. In general, families and orders of plants show strong tendencies to silicify or not silicify their tissues, and production of many kinds of phytoliths is consistent within the same taxon growing under different environmental conditions. Distinctive phytoliths are produced in many plant families; genus-level diagnostics are common; species-level identification is possible for many plants (Pearsall 2015; Piperno 2006).

Diagnostic phytoliths are identified by their shape (three-dimensional morphology), surface texture and/or ornamentation, outline, symmetrical features, morphometric data (size measurements), and anatomical origin, if known. In recent years standard terms have been established for describing features useful for characterizing phytoliths and naming diagnostic forms (e.g., Bowdery et al. 2001; Madella et al. 2005). Some common types of phytoliths are illustrated in Figure 1.8 and Figure 1.9. These examples come from the MU Phytolith database, which is composed largely of plants from the lowland Neotropics.

Grass phytoliths are often encountered in archaeological samples and environmental cores. Grasses are abundant phytolith producers and silicify a broad array of tissues, as illustrated in Figure 1.8. Short cell shape can be used to distinguish among grass subfamilies (i.e., festucoid, chloridoid, panicoid, bambusoid, and arundinoid groups), and genus- and species-level diagnostics have been developed for economically important taxa, including cereals.

Spherical (globular) to spheroidal phytoliths with surface projections, folds, or facets may also be common components of archaeological and environmental samples. Surface features are important for correct classification of spherical phytoliths to plant taxon; some common types are illustrated in Figure 1.9, a–g. Among the plant groups that produce spherical

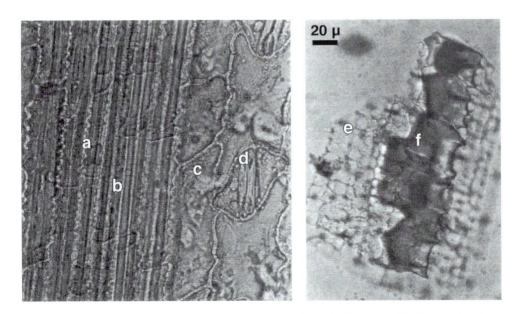

FIGURE 1.8   Cells of the grass epidermis that become silicified: (a) short cells, (b) vascular tissue, (c) long cells, and (d) stomata (illustrated using maize); (e) long cells and (f) bulliform cells (illustrated using an unknown grass from a surface sample from Yap). Silicified tissues are often found disarticulated in sediment samples.

phytoliths are some woody dicots, palms, the arrowroot, ginger, and canna families, as well as squashes and gourds.

Well-silicified cylindrical to cuboid phytoliths with single, distinctive indentations ("troughs") are produced in the leaves of members of the banana and bird-of-paradise families (Figure 1.9, h, i). Detailed study of these forms, using attributes like base length and shape, indentation depth and position, and cone shape, can help distinguish between some banana taxa (Lentfer 2009).

In the sedge family distinctive epidermal cells with conical projections are silicified in leaves and inflorescences (Figure 1.9, j, k). Overall shape and surface decoration on sedge inflorescence phytoliths permit genus-level identification (Piperno 1989). Leaf epidermal cells with sinuous outlines and conical projections are produced in some species of *Celtis* in the Ulmaceae (Figure 1.9, l).

Distinctive kinds of silicified epidermal cells are also used to identify dicots as a general group (anticlinal and polyhedral cells, Figure 1.9, m, n), the daisy family (black, perforated

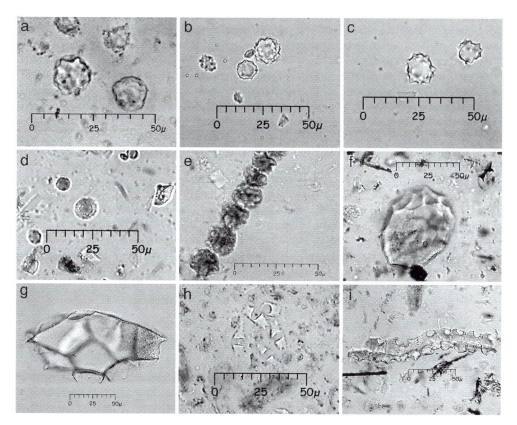

FIGURE 1.9   Distinctive phytoliths from some nongrasses: (a) rugulose sphere (right, above scale), irregularly angled/folded sphere (left); (b) nodular sphere (right, above scale), Marantaceae conical (left); (c) spinulose sphere; (d) Arecaceae conical; (e) irregularly angled/folded sphere; (f) faceted sphere; (g) faceted hemisphere; (h) *Heliconia* troughed; (i) *Musa* troughed. (Figure continues.)

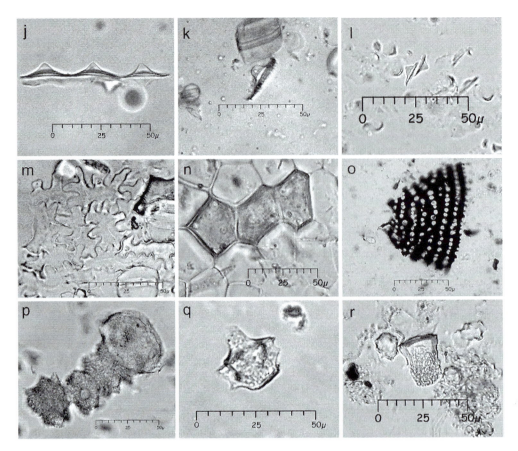

FIGURE 1.9 (Continued) (j) Cyperaceae leaf conical; (k) *Cyperus* inflorescence conical; (l) *Celtis* conical; (m) anticlinal epidermis; (n) polyhedral epidermis; (o) Asteraceae epidermis; (p) *Calathea allouia* seed cylinder; (q) *Maranta arundinacea* seed cylinder; (r) *Calathea* rhizome cylinder. (Figure continues.)

epidermal cells, Figure 1.9, o), seeds and roots of the arrowroot family (Figure 1.9, p, q, r), and a number of families and genera of dicot trees (Figure 1.9, s, t, u), among other examples.

In dicot families that silicify tissues, striking examples of silicified hairs and conjoined basal cells may be observed in comparative specimens, such as those illustrated in Figure 1.9, v–y). Unfortunately, these phytoliths are often lightly silicified and fragile and are rarely encountered in archaeological or geological sediments. If preserved in protected contexts, characteristics that are useful in identifying hairs to taxon include whether they are simple (unicellular, Figure 1.9, v) or composed of multiple cells (Figure 1.9, w, x), smooth or armed (with surface projections) (Figure 1.9, w, x), and whether tips are straight or curved, among other features.

Silicified sclereids, cells with thick, lignified walls that provide support to plant tissues (Figure 1.9, z), may be a common component of archaeological sediments to which woody plants contributed. Parenchyma cells (thin-walled ground, or fundamental cells) and transport tissues (xylem, phloem) (Figure 1.9, aa, ab) may become lightly silicified in some plants and tissues and preserved in protected contexts like stone tool surfaces (Chandler-Ezell et al. 2006).

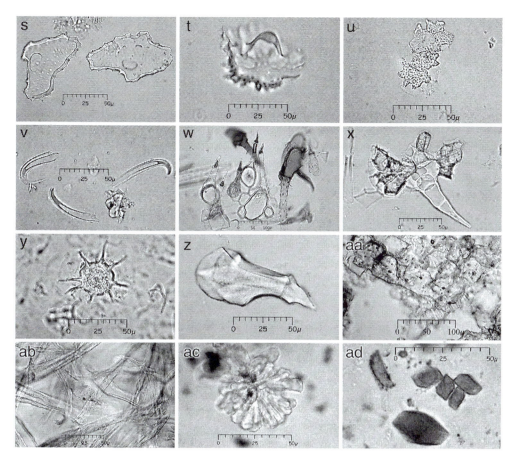

FIGURE 1.9   (Continued) (s) Burseraceae seed epidermis; (t) Burseraceae seed epidermis; (u) *Celtis shippii* seed epidermis; (v) *Phaseolus* simple hair; (w) multicellular armed hair; (x) multicellular smooth hair, complex base; (y) simple hair base; (z) sclereid; (aa) parenchyma; (ab) transport tissues; (ac) cystolith; (ad) tabular crystal.

Plant crystals may form from minerals other than silica. Cystoliths are calcium carbonate concretions that form in epidermal cells of some plants, often arboreal taxa. They are spheroidal to elongated (Figure 1.9, ac). Other kinds of calcium carbonate concretions occur in wood, such as the tabular crystals from *Guazuma ulmifolia* shown in Figure 1.9, ad.

The following is a list of some websites on which are posted databases and images of phytoliths:

www.homepages.ucl.ac.uk/~tcrndfu/phytoliths.html (Dorian Fuller, Old World reference phytoliths)

http://web.stcloudstate.edu/msblinnikov/phd/phyt.html (Mikhail Blinnikov, Pacific Northwest)

http://phytolith.missouri.edu/Welcome.html (Deborah Pearsall, lowland Neotropics)

http://research.history.org/archaeological_research/collections/collarchaeobot/phytolith Search.cfm (Colonial Williamsburg, New and Old World)

www.archeoscience.com (Phytolith Online Database, Phytcore [GEPEG]; register at archeo-
science website, access catalog through Phytolith DP; open to researchers, institutions, and
research groups to add databases)

www.wits.ac.za/academic/science/geosciences/bpi/research/6593/wopd.html (Lucille Pereira,
University of the Witwatersrand, Johannesburg. Wits Online Phytolith Database)

Starch

The terms *starch grain* and *starch granule* are often used interchangeably. Following usage in
Torrence and Barton (2006), in this discussion I use the term *starch granule* to refer to recognizable starch bodies and *starch* as a broader category that includes recognizable granules,
damaged granules, gelatinized masses, and so on.

Starch granules are composed of two kinds of polymers (large molecules made up of many
repeated subunits): amylose (a linear polymer) and amylopectin (a very large branched polymer). Granules form by accretion of layers (lamellae) of these polymers, beginning at a point
called the hilum, which may remain visible on the granule. The ratio of amylose and amylopectin within a given kind of starch affects granule morphology, as well as starch functionality
in foods. Starch granules can be simple or compound. Starch is semicrystalline and exhibits
strong birefringence, that is, under polarized light unmodified starch appears white against
the black background and an extinction cross, a dark cross centered on the hilum ("Maltese
cross"), is visible (Figure 1.10).

Starch serves a vital function in living plants as the primary energy storage mechanism.
Some starch is transitory—consisting of small granules formed in green stems and leaves during daylight hours and converted back to sugar at night. Other starch serves the function of
long-term energy storage. It is this storage starch that humans target for food. It is produced in
seeds and underground storage organs, as well as some other tissues. Formation of starch granules is under genetic control, and distinctive granule shape, location and shape of the hilum
region, and other traits produce diagnostic granules in many species, such as those illustrated
in Figure 1.10. Among the features used to identify different types of starch are characteristics
of the extinction cross, edge (angularity), hilum, fissures, surface, protuberances, and outer
wall; granule size and shape; presence and nature of lamellae; and whether starch is simple or
compound. The International Code for Starch Nomenclature (ICSN 2011; available at www.
fossilfarm.org/ICSN/Code.html) includes a list of definitions of basic starch terminology.

Not all starch granules encountered in archaeological contexts exhibit features as well preserved
as those illustrated in Figure 1.10. Pounding, cutting, and cooking can alter starch and make it difficult to identify; for example, pounding and grinding abrade surfaces and enlarge fissures, which
in turn alter or eliminate the extinction cross. Starch swells in water, a change that is reversible at
low temperatures. When heat is applied with water, a point is reached—gelatinization—at which
irreversible changes in starch occur, eventually producing amorphous masses.

Studying Archaeobotanical Remains

Given the differences in the nature of the common types of archaeobotanical remains,
somewhat different approaches are taken in studying macroremains, pollen, phytoliths,
and starch.

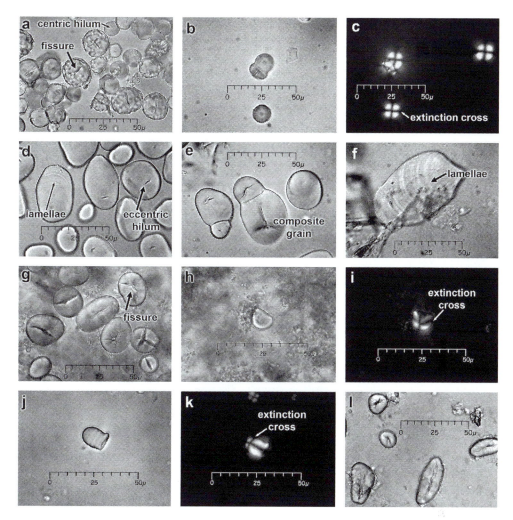

FIGURE 1.10 Examples of distinctive starch grains of some economic plants, with features discussed in the text labeled: (a) maize; (b, c) manioc, shown in transmitted and polarized light; (d) arrowroot; (e) llerén; (f) canna; (g) common bean; (h, i) chili pepper, transmitted and polarized light; (j, k) squash, transmitted and polarized light; (l) achiote

The most common ways of recovering macroremains are through flotation or fine sieving; these techniques are described in Chapter 3. Both concentrate macroremains present in site sediments. Charred, waterlogged, or desiccated ancient materials are usually mixed with rootlets and other modern organic debris in processed flotation and fine sieve samples. Although it is generally not too difficult to determine which organic materials are ancient, separating these from the rest is time consuming. Hand-sorting samples to remove macroremains is typically the first step in a study.

Although the aim of sorting macroremain samples is simple, there are steps that make this process easier and the end results more comparable to other studies. After the weight of the entire processed sample is determined, samples can be divided into size fractions, or splits. This allows the analyst to examine particles of approximately equal size. Creating two splits with a 2.0-mm geological sieve is a common approach; creating more size fractions may facilitate sorting of dried or waterlogged samples. Larger splits can usually be sorted by the naked eye or with an illuminated magnifier, whereas finer splits are examined under a dissecting microscope. Different classes of materials may be removed from each split; one approach is to remove all ancient materials from larger splits, but only small seeds from finer splits. In the case of flotation-recovered macroremains, both buoyant and nonbuoyant materials are studied. Depending on the experience of the sorter, seeds, nuts, and so on may be identified to plant taxon and counted as they are removed from samples, or final identifications and tallies may be made during a second examination of the sorted sample.

Although volume of sediment floated or fine sieved can be adjusted to produce macroremain samples of a sufficient yet manageable size, samples sometimes turn out to be larger than necessary. In this case a randomly selected subsample may be studied. See Chapter 3 for a discussion of determining adequate sample sizes for archaeobotanical analysis.

Pollen, phytoliths, and starch grains are recovered from archaeological sediments, artifact residues, and environmental core samples using specialized procedures in a laboratory setting. These procedures will not be discussed here; see Pearsall (2015) for details on how each type of microfossil is recovered. Basically, procedures have been developed to release microfossils from chemical bonds holding them in the sediment or residue matrix, to concentrate them, and to remove them from the sample without damaging them.

Once pollen, phytoliths, or starch grains have been extracted from a sample, slide mounts are made so that the microfossils can be examined microscopically. Different mounting media are used depending on the microfossil (i.e., to give the best contrast for viewing and to minimize damage). Often the analyst uses a standard amount of extract for each slide; creating a standard mount allows informal comparisons in microfossil densities to be made among samples, that is, by noting how many fields or rows were needed to reach a predetermined count or by estimating total granules per slide mount. Unless all available extract is mounted, it is important that a representative sample is used to make slides.

Slide-mounted pollen, phytolith, or starch samples are typically examined microscopically, or scanned, at 250 to 400 × (or higher) magnification. Scanning is a systematic process whereby the analyst searches the slide for the target microfossils. The scan may cover the entire slide, or it may be randomly sampled in some way. As pollen, phytoliths, or starch grains are encountered, they are examined (including in different rotations), drawn and/or photographed, and measured. A check-off form may be used to note features important for establishing the identification and to record measurements. As discussed earlier, microfossil identification is done by comparison to known examples (i.e., a comparative collection) and using published descriptions, photographs, and keys.

Microfossil scanning involves counting as well as identification. If microfossils are relatively scarce, all encountered on the slide mount are tabulated by plant taxon. It is often the case, however, that many thousands of pollen grains or phytoliths are present on a slide. A sample can be counted using a standard sum (i.e., the first 200 pollen grains/diagnostic phytoliths/starch grains encountered are tallied). If counting is to proceed to a standard sum, the analyst may include all types of pollen/phytoliths/starch grains encountered in the sum, or may establish a target list of plants to include, for instance, economic species or arboreal taxa. Counting to a standard sum produces relative counts, that is, the quantity of each taxon is expressed as a percentage of the whole. Absolute counts can be made by counting the entire slide (and extrapolating to the total extract) or by adding a known quantity of marker micro-fossils to the sample. See Pearsall (2015) for details.

The Comparative Collection

Accurate identification of archaeobotanical remains requires one-to-one comparisons between unknown archaeological materials and known plant specimens. Photographs, keys, or descriptions are each useful, but are no substitute for a comparative collection. Because macroremains are often fragmented or otherwise altered from their fresh condition, comparative specimens are most useful if reduced to a similar state. Pollen, phytoliths, and starch must be extracted from plant tissues. In many cases, this precludes the use of material collected for other purposes (e.g., specimens housed in an herbarium, a depository of dried plant specimens), and it falls to the paleoethnobotanist to build his or her own laboratory collection. It is also the case, however, that seeds, fragments of wood, or slide mounts of pollen do not in themselves form a complete comparative collection. All such "working" specimens must be backed up by identified voucher specimens: dried, identified examples of complete plants.

Collecting plants for comparative study serves a second important purpose, that of providing information on vegetation of the study area. Data on plant associations, seasonality and abundance of resources, and distribution of resources can be gathered as plants are collected.

Plant taxonomy textbooks usually include a section on field and herbarium techniques, and the websites of major herbaria often have plant-collecting instructions among their offerings, including information on how to press and dry voucher specimens. See those sources and Pearsall (2015) for equipment lists and details on how to collect good usable specimens. Each specimen in a comparative collection must fill three different requirements. It must be identifiable (the portion collected must be adequate to make a precise scientific determination), it must be usable (the collection must include seeds, fruits, and wood; flowers for pollen; leaves, fruits, and roots for phytoliths and starch), and it must be representative of a population (plants should be selected to represent both average and range for species).

Collecting identifiable specimens means collecting examples in flower, in fruit, or both. Good flowering specimens are needed for identifying the plant, even if flowers are not needed for the comparative collection. If plants are not in flower, then fruiting specimens should be collected. Plants not in flower or fruit are quite difficult to identify without the help of a botanist familiar with the flora. Properly pressed and dried specimens also facilitate identification; whenever possible, the entire plant (root, stem, leaves, inflorescence) should be pressed in one newspaper page, overlapping leaves trimmed off (leaving basal portions), and flowers pressed open to show the arrangement of flower parts. Drying pressed voucher specimens can be completed with or without an artificial heat source, although drying with heat is more common. Each specimen should be clearly labeled with its collection number and should include typed labels with full provenience and collection information.

Making sure that plant collections will be of use in identifying archaeological plant remains means careful attention to collecting potentially useful parts of plants and anatomically different parts of the same useful plant. In wood, for example, twigs, branches, trunk, and roots vary in the number of growth rings and abundance of support tissue. If possible, collecting should follow some preliminary analysis of archaeological botanical remains, or at least familiarization with types of materials found in previous studies. Compiling a list of useful plants from ethnographic or ethnohistoric sources is another way of making collecting time more productive. For wood collecting, it is useful to focus first on dominant, common trees and those trees and shrubs said to be good for firewood or construction, rather than attempting to collect all taxa in a diverse forest environment. Getting at least dominant species from all environmental zones in the study area is also important. For seeds and fruits, collections should include weedy annuals as well as berry- and nut-producing taxa. If tuber or root remains are anticipated, collecting should not neglect these plant parts. In short, the more precollection time spent making lists of useful plants (and what parts are used), studying reports of prior paleoethnobotanical analyses from the region, talking with local people about traditional uses of plants, and thinking about the ways the collection will be used, the more productive collecting time can be.

Because identifications of archaeological materials are based in large part on the comparative collection, it is vital that specimens representative of the species be collected. Diseased or insect-damaged plants should be avoided, as should individuals much smaller or much larger than the population as a whole. Range of variation should be noted, however. If possible, fruits should be collected from a variety of different plants so that the collection represents the natural variation in the population. Wood samples should not be collected from obviously stressed trees.

Before doing any plant collecting, get permission to collect from landowners and, if required, the government. Most countries require that foreign botanists obtain collecting permits, deposit examples of some or all plants collected, obey regulations on collecting endangered species, and obtain permission to export collections. Determine whether a permit is required to import dried, pest-free specimens for scientific use into your home country (none is required for the United States). Information on prohibited taxa and importing live plants is generally available from the government agency regulating agriculture. Applications for soil importation permits are also typically made to agricultural agencies.

The final step in building a comparative botanical collection is to prepare and organize collected materials into easily used, hands-on collections. In the case of macroremains, this usually involves charring comparative materials to render them more directly comparable to archaeological remains. For the analyst working with waterlogged materials, it is useful to "age" fresh seeds by soaking them in water or dilute acid so that outer layers can be removed. Uncharred examples of all materials should be retained for use in identifying uncharred remains and replacing lost charred materials. To build a comparative collection of pollen, phytoliths, and starch, these microfossils must first be extracted from the appropriate plant tissues. In the case of pollen and phytoliths, extraction involves chemical processing, following which slide mounts are made; see Pearsall (2015) for details. For starch, starchy tissues are first separated from nonstarchy tissues, such as seed coats, then crushed to produce a fine powder of starch granules that can be slide-mounted. Fresh starchy tissues, such as roots or tubers, can be scraped and smeared onto a microscope slide. Vials or boxes of comparative macroremains and collections of slide-mounted microfossils are then arranged so that it is easy to find and compare specimens. Photographs, drawings, and written descriptions of key characteristics of specimens also facilitate their use.

An electronic database of the comparative collection facilitates its management and makes it even more useful (Nesbitt et al. 2003). Participants of a 2000 workshop that explored database standards for seed reference collections recommended 18 "core fields" that contain essential information on specimens, and that can be used to generate labels. Among other fields, these include family and genus names, species epithet, kind of collection, country of origin, collector, and information on who determined the specimens (Nesbitt et al. 2003). See also chapters in Salick (2014) on database standards, curation of digital images, and the importance of having an inventory of biocultural collections in electronic form. The better organized and curated a comparative collection is, the more useful it is, both for the researcher(s) who created it and for a future paleoethnobotanist who may inherit or adopt it.

Online reference collections (i.e., open-access digital images of reference materials) provide a potentially valuable resource for preliminary identifications of archaeobotanical materials (Warinner et al. 2011). A number of web-based resources are currently available (see list in this section and earlier), but most are closed access (i.e., images are limited to those uploaded by the website's creators). Warinner and colleagues developed paleobot.org (www.paleobot.org) as an open-access site that allows researchers to share reference collection images and data and post unknowns on a free platform. The website includes clear copyright and fair use guidelines, and all users retain copyright for images they upload to the site.

References

Bowdery, Doreen, Diane M. Hart, Carol Lentfer and Lynley A. Wallis 2001 A universal phytolith key. In *Phytoliths: Applications in Earth Sciences and Human History*, edited by J. D. Meunier and F. Collin, pp. 267–278. A. A. Balkema, Lisse.

Chandler-Ezell, Karol, Deborah M. Pearsall and James A. Zeidler 2006 Root and tuber phytoliths and starch grains document manioc (*Manihot esculenta*), arrowroot (*Maranta arundinacea*), and llerén (*Calathea* sp.) at the Real Alto site, Ecuador. *Economic Botany* 60(2):103–120.

Clark, J. G. D. 1954 *Excavations at Star Carr: An Early Mesolithic Site at Seamer, Near Scarborough, Yorkshire*. Cambridge University Press, London.

Evert, Ray F. 2006 *Esau's Plant Anatomy: Meristems, Cells, and Tissues of the Plant Body: Their Structure, Function, and Development*. Wiley-Interscience, Hoboken, NJ.

Faegri, Knut, Peter Emil Kaland and Knut Krzywinski 1989 *Textbook of Pollen Analysis by Knut Faegri and Johs Iversen*. Fourth ed. John Wiley and Sons, Chichester, England.

Gilmore, Melvin R. 1931 Vegetal remains of the Ozark Bluff-Dweller culture. *Papers of the Michigan Academy of Science, Arts, and Letters* 14:83–102.

Hather, Jon G. 1991 The identification of charred archaeological remains of vegetative parenchymous tissue. *Journal of Archaeological Science* 18(6):661–675.

——— 1993 *An Archaeobotanical Guide to Root and Tuber Identification: Volume 1: Europe and South West Asia*. Oxbow Monograph 28, Oxbow Books, Oxford.

Jones, Volney H. 1936 The vegetal remains of Newt Kash Hollow shelter. In *Rock Shelters in Menifee County, Kentucky*, edited by W. S. Webb and W. D. Funkhouser, pp. 147–167. University of Kentucky Reports in Archaeology and Anthropology, Vol. 3(4).

Kapp, Ronald O. 1969 *How To Know Pollen and Spores*. William C. Brown, Dubuque, Iowa.

Kapp, Ronald O., Owen K. Davis and James E. King 2000 *Ronald O. Kapp's Pollen and Spores*. Second ed. American Association of Stratigraphic Palynologists Foundation, College Station, Texas.

Lentfer, C. J. 2009 Tracing domestication and cultivation of bananas from phytoliths: An update from Papua New Guinea. *Ethnobotany Research and Applications* 7:247–270.

Madella, M., A. Alexandre and T. Ball 2005 International code for phytolith nomenclature 1.0. *Annals of Botany* 96(2):253–260.

Moore, P. D., J. A. Webb and M. E. Collinson 1991 *Pollen Analysis*. Second ed. (reprinted in 1999) Blackwell Scientific Publications, Oxford.

Nesbitt, Mark, Sue Colledge and Mary Anne Murray 2003 Organisation and management of seed reference collections. *Environmental Archaeology* 8:77–84.

Panshin, A. J. and Carl de Zeeuw 1980 *Textbook of Wood Technology*. Fourth ed. McGraw-Hill, New York.

Pearsall, Deborah M. 2015 *Paleoethnobotany: A Handbook of Procedures*. Third ed. Routledge, New York.

Piperno, Dolores R. 1989 The occurrence of phytoliths in the reproductive structures of selected tropical angiosperms and their significance in tropical paleoecology, paleoethnobotany, and systematics. *Review of Palaeobotany and Palynology* 61:147–173.

———— 2006 *Phytoliths: A Comprehensive Guide for Archaeologists and Paleoecologists*. AltaMira Press, Lanham, MD.

Salick, Jan (editor) 2014 *Curating Biocultural Collections: A Handbook*. Kew Press, London.

Shackley, Myra 1981 *Environmental Archaeology*. Allen and Unwin, London.

Struever, Stuart 1968 Flotation techniques for the recovery of small-scale archaeological remains. *American Antiquity* 33:353–362.

Torrence, Robin and Huw Barton (editors) 2006 *Ancient Starch Research*. Left Coast Press, Walnut Creek, CA.

Warinner, C., J. D. Guedes and D. Goode 2011 Paleobot.org: Establishing open-access online reference collections for archaeobotanical research. *Vegetation History and Archaeobotany* 20(3):241–244.

2

DEPOSITION AND PRESERVATION OF PALEOETHNOBOTANICAL REMAINS

Glossary

primary depositional context   an archaeological context/situation where it can be inferred that materials (such as plant remains) recovered there were deposited as a result of activities carried out in/associated with the context. For example, a grinding stone with cereal grain starch embedded in its crevices (inference: processing of starchy tissues using the artifact).

secondary depositional context   an archaeological context/situation where it can be inferred that materials (such as plant remains) recovered there were redeposited from activities carried out elsewhere. For example, a sediment-filled pit containing charred nut hulls, broken pottery, and animal bone (inference: redeposition of debris from food preparation, pottery use/production, and butchery activities carried out elsewhere).

Introduction

Determining what kind(s) of human behaviors and natural processes resulted in deposition and preservation of plant tissues in archaeological sites is the interpretive challenge at the heart of paleoethnobotany. This issue cross-cuts the kinds of materials being studied, or the geographic or topical focus of research. In essence interpretation is the drawing of convincing inferences about human behaviors from plants present at sites and from the combinations in which they occur and the contexts in which they are found. Fundamentally, this means inferring the processes and pathways through which the remains of plants, of whatever kinds, became deposited and preserved in the sites and contexts we are studying. In this chapter I discuss some of the ways plant remains come into sites and summarize the conditions that lead to their preservation (or destruction).

In Pearsall (2015) I developed a series of models for the deposition and preservation of archaeobotanical materials that illustrated how integrating multiple biological indicators allows us to draw strong inferences of past plant–people interrelationships. These models were built in part on my own thinking on this topic, for example, this model from Pearsall (1983) of two pathways for preservation of macroremains through charring (Figure 2.1), and also on the work of others, only some of which can be mentioned here.

Plant remains become deposited in locations that will become archaeological sites in many ways. Sometimes it is straightforward to determine the source of material. For instance, it is usually easy to distinguish modern and ancient plant tissues when only preservation of charred materials is expected (i.e., when conditions lead to quick decay of organic materials). Microfossils embedded in the crevices of a grinding stone likely represent the remains of foods. Charred wood recovered from a hearth likely represents fuel. Comparing archaeological plant assemblages to modern surface vegetation also provides insights for interpretation in settings where ancient seeds are dried or waterlogged and not readily distinguishable from modern seeds. This approach also facilitates interpretation of pollen and phytolith data.

Ethnographic observation and ethnoarchaeology (studying the material remains of a society) are valuable sources of information on potential uses of plants. For example, it is possible to determine the types of plant remains likely to be recovered from various crop-processing activities by sampling such activity areas in a traditional farming village. Similarly, experimental studies can reveal the likely remains from such activities as burning animal dung fuel in a hearth, parching cereal grains, or firing a garbage midden. Scrutiny of the contexts in which remains occur (for example, inside versus outside structures) is critical in differentiating among depositional pathways. Micromorphological analysis provides insights into the formation of complex deposits (Box 2.1).

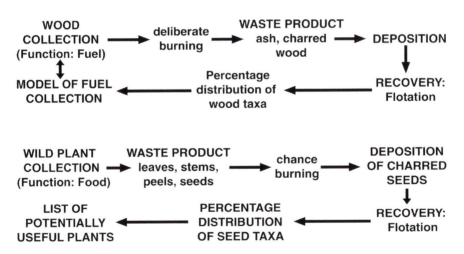

FIGURE 2.1   Two pathways for charred preservation: deliberate burning (upper loop) characterizes fuels such as wood and dung; chance or accidental burning (lower loop) characterizes foods, medicines, and other nonfuels. (Figure 1 from Pearsall, Deborah M. 1983. Evaluating the stability of subsistence strategies by use of paleoethnobotanical data. *Journal of Ethnobiology* 3(2):121–137.)

BOX 2.1 MICROMORPHOLOGICAL ANALYSIS

A valuable approach for understanding formation processes of the archaeobotanical record is through micromorphological analysis. Micromorphological analysis is the study of diverse sediment, bioarchaeological, and microartifactual components in situ in large-format thin sections, which provide insights into formation processes of complex deposits, for example, urban sites (Matthews 2010), rock shelters (Diaz and Eraso 2010), and lakeside settlements (Ismail-Meyer et al. 2013). Large-format thin sections preserve the structure of fragile plant remains, which might otherwise be destroyed by sieving or flotation. In a review of case studies of early urban sites in the Near East, Matthews (2010) illustrated how micromorphometric analysis led to the identification of post-depositional alterations to plant remains, for example, compaction of articulated remains, secondary burning, and fragmentation from bioturbation. Impressions of tissues that decayed away were preserved, as were articulated phytoliths of seed pericarps and leaves. Localized preservation conditions—for example, waterlogging— could be identified, as could animal dung, and its importance as a fuel evaluated (Matthews 2010).

Similarly, Díaz and Eraso (2010) utilized micromorphometric analysis to compare post-depositional alterations in deposits at two rock shelters in Spain, both of which had been used to stable animals. Post-depositional features common to both sites included truncated microfacies (microscopic features) from cleaning, trampling, and bioturbation. However, in one shelter the sequence was well preserved and included features resulting from human activities. In the other shelter, a spring at the rear resulted in mixing and truncation of microfacies, among other environmental effects. Micromorphometric analysis played an important role in understanding the complex taphonomy of these stabling deposits (Díaz and Eraso 2010).

Natural and anthropogenic site formation processes also interact in complex ways in waterlogged sites. For example, whereas well-preserved organic materials recovered from Swiss lake dwellings offer excellent research opportunities, hiatuses in deposits caused by the dynamic nature of the lakeshore environment can hinder high-resolution study of site stratigraphy (Ismail-Meyer et al. 2013). Micromorphological studies have contributed significantly to understanding such depositional environments, for example, in identifying the effects of erosion and reworking on accumulated cultural debris.

Through these and related approaches, much has been learned about processes of deposition and preservation of macroremains, phytoliths, starch, and pollen, making it possible to model how these plant remains come to form part of the archaeological and geological records. Figure 2.2 illustrates such a model for macroremains, and Figure 2.3 for phytoliths. In these models I propose what kinds of activities or processes likely acted as primary (horizontal lines) and secondary (vertical lines) pathways leading to the deposition of remains, and the potential of each activity or process for deposition and/or preservation of remains (dotted,

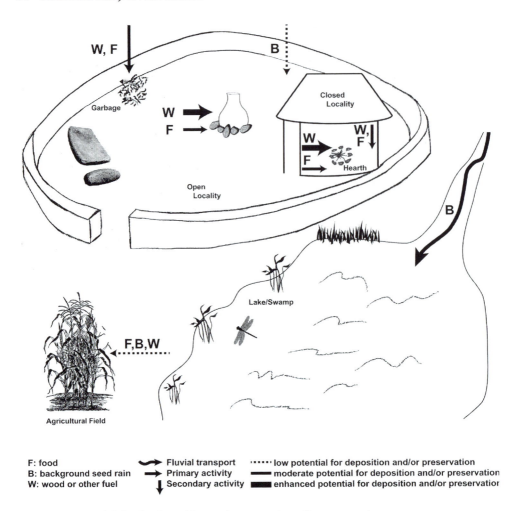

FIGURE 2.2 Model for the deposition and preservation of macroremains.

thin, and thick lines for low, moderate, and enhanced potential). Three contexts were modeled: an occupation area (with house, open courtyard, hearths, garbage midden, grinding area), an agricultural field, and lake/swamp sediments. For these two examples, notice the similarities and differences in the ways macroremains and phytoliths came to be deposited and preserved in the contexts illustrated.

It is beyond the scope of this review to discuss these models in further detail, so after summarizing key points concerning deposition and preservation of each kind of archaeobotanical data, I present one hypothetical example—that of a ground stone tool recovered in situ in the deposits of a house floor—to illustrate differences in pathways of deposition and preservation among the four primary kinds of archaeological plant remains. We will make three assumptions for that example: that macroremains were preserved by charring; that floor sediments were intact, primary deposits; and that the floor was covered by a roof.

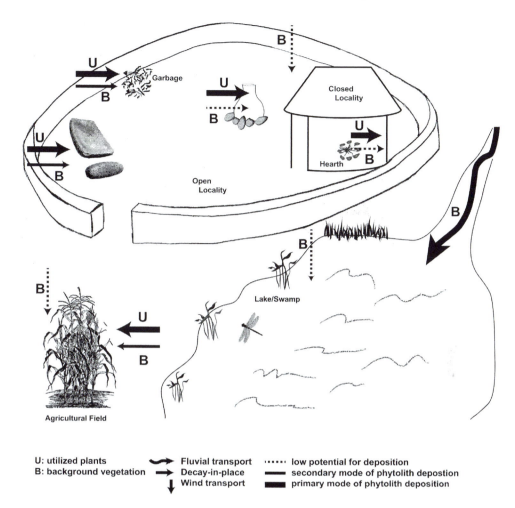

U: utilized plants   → Fluvial transport   ⋯⋯ low potential for deposition
B: background vegetation   → Decay-in-place   ━━ secondary mode of phytolith depostion
                            ↓ Wind transport   ━━ primary mode of phytolith deposition

FIGURE 2.3   Model for the deposition and preservation of phytoliths.

Macroremain Deposition and Preservation

Summary

Deposition

With the exceptions of severely bioturbated sediments and the potential for heavy modern seed rain in the upper levels of sites, human actions are the main vectors of deposition of macroremains in most site contexts: wood was brought into a house and burned as fuel in a hearth; vegetables were cleaned and the debris thrown on a garbage heap; mats were woven and used as floor coverings. Determining what kind(s) of human actions led to deposition of plant tissues is the interpretive challenge. As mentioned earlier, ethnographic, experimental, and ethnoarchaeological studies provide data for modeling behaviors involving plants, which can then be compared to archaeological botanical assemblages. For archaeologists and paleoeth-nobotanists working on sites of agro-pastoralists, habitual burning of dung fuel in cooking fires provides an additional interpretive challenge: seeds present in dung must be distinguished from those deposited through cooking accidents.

Preservation

Differential preservation can have a major impact on understanding plant–people interrelationships through study of macroremains. This is most notably the case for the most common mode of preservation, charring—that is, when regular wetting and drying of site sediments leads to decay of organic materials, and only plant tissues burned in a reducing atmosphere survive. There are a great many variables affecting which plant species and tissues survive charring, burial, and recovery, making it difficult to compare occurrences of plants that are subject to very different preservation biases (for example, tubers—rarely preserved charred—and robust seeds or fruit fragments—more often preserved charred). Although there are specialized techniques that aid in identifying extremely fragmented remains, these only help if some material was charred and preserved to start with: plant tissues not exposed to fire will not be preserved. The presence of a small amount of "low-probability" material scattered over a site may be as strong an indication of importance as large quantities of "high-probability" plants. As will be discussed further in Chapter 3, this is the rationale for using percentage presence, or ubiquity, to describe the occurrence of macroremains.

It may be helpful to categorize plant taxa and tissues by the likelihood of their being charred and preserved in recognizable form and then to use this "preservation factor" to temper interpretations. For example, when discussing sitewide plant occurrences, one can suggest which taxa are probably underrepresented and how this affects ratios or other measures of abundance. I do not recommend trying to "correct" abundances of underrepresented taxa quantitatively, however. Even if a portion of the site in question was subject to desiccated or waterlogged preservation conditions, relative abundances of remains there may not reflect abundances in other parts of the site.

As ethnographic, ethnoarchaeological, and experimental studies provide insights into behaviors that bring plants into the archaeological record, they are also valuable sources for understanding which species and tissues are likely to be preserved as macroremains and which are unlikely to enter the record in this form (but perhaps will be represented in the pollen, phytolith, or starch records). Ethnographic observations, especially coupled with study of modern samples of plant products and residues associated with those observations, can help the researcher develop models for interpreting macroremains that are regionally and culturally relevant.

Waterlogged and desiccated site conditions that retard organic decay lead to greatly enhanced preservation of macroremains, although plant tissues are not unchanged by these processes, and sorting through multiple potential pathways of deposition can be a formidable interpretive challenge.

Grinding Stone Example

In a setting in which uncharred plant tissues quickly decay, seed grinding would not result in the preservation of macroremains on grinding stone surfaces (Table 2.1). Grinding per se is not associated with heating, so no macroremains would be expected from the decay-in-place

TABLE 2.1 Example of grinding stone in house floor: predictions about deposition and preservation of macroremains and phytoliths. For macroremains, preservation is by charring

	Macroremains	*Phytoliths*
Grinding stone	NONE associated with grinding stone	PRESENT if phytolith-producing tissues processed OR ABSENT if not a phytolith producer
Floor sediments	NONE from decay-in-place in floor of processing residues OR PRESENT if sediments heated by an overlying hearth or structure fire	PRESENT from decay-in-place in floor of processing residues, foods if a phytolith producer PRESENT from bedding, roofing material if producers

of processing residues or foods deposited in the sediments around the grinding feature. However, if the area around the grinding feature was subsequently overlain by a hearth, experiments by Sievers and Wadley (2008) indicated that buried plant materials (i.e., those not yet decayed) could become charred. In their study seeds and fruits tossed into the experimental fires did not become charred, only those buried under the area that was fired. Experiments by Gustafsson (2000) and Guarino and Sciarrillo (2004) also indicated that burial enhances seed survival in hearths; in their studies some unburied seeds did survive "accidental" charring. These authors found considerable variation in seed survival among botanical families. Experimental house firings produced a very complex preservation situation, but did lead to enhanced seed preservation in some circumstances.

Phytolith Deposition and Preservation

Summary

Deposition

Phytoliths do not have a dispersal mechanism; they become incorporated into soils and sediments through the decay, burning, or digestion of plant tissues. Individual phytoliths are not "loose" in soil, but bound up in its organic and inorganic components. Movement of soil—by wind, water, or animal burrowing—results in phytolith movement. It is important, therefore, to examine soil and sediment profiles for evidence of bioturbation and to avoid sampling within such contexts. Although an unknown proportion of phytoliths in archaeological deposits may be the result of regional transport via soil movement, these are likely to be in the minority in most cases, as compared to phytoliths released from plants brought onto the site and used and discarded by people (or in some cases domestic animals, via their dung). Sampling within structures, pits, or other protected contexts further enhances the recovery of phytoliths resulting from human activities. The pathways through which phytoliths become deposited on or in artifacts are through human actions involving plant tissues that contain phytoliths (e.g., cooking, pounding, grinding, cutting, brewing, storage) and incidental exposure of artifacts to sediments that contain phytoliths. The major mode of deposition of phytoliths into lake and swamp sediments is fluvial, via soil that is washed in from the watershed.

Preservation

Phytoliths, being inorganic, are not subject to decay, but this does not mean they are indestructible. Acidic contexts result in better preservation than very alkaline; drier conditions (even if high pH) enhance preservation; larger phytoliths, especially if less well silicified, may be more subject to loss than smaller. Because chemical processing can have a detrimental effect on some more lightly silicified phytoliths, standardization in procedures is essential for drawing comparisons among samples. Phytoliths have the potential to survive in contexts in which organic preservation is poor and can contribute substantially to understanding past plant–people interrelationships.

Grinding Stone Example

Phytoliths would become deposited on a grinding stone if the tissues being processed contained them, but would not be expected if the food or tissues were not phytolith producers (Table 2.1). Sometimes phytoliths occurring in closely associated tissues may become deposited on artifacts. For example, maize kernels lack phytoliths, but the soft glumes from the cob contain them. Cob phytoliths (and maize starch) were recovered from grinding stones from the Real Alto site, Ecuador, for example (Pearsall et al. 2004). Raviele's (2011) experimental study of phytoliths in cooking residues found that cooking of green corn on the cob created cooking residues high in phytoliths.

   Because phytoliths are released through decay, burning, or digestion of plant tissues, a large proportion of phytoliths represents in situ deposition (the decay-in-place model). In closed localities, like the floor sediments of the grinding stone example, deposition of phytoliths from culturally selected plants would dominate. Cabanes et al. (2010) examined phytolith concentrations across units at Esquilleu Cave, a Neanderthal site in Spain, and compared them to modern control samples. They were able to interpret phytolith accumulations as decay from grass bedding and activities related to fire. For crops that are heavy phytolith producers, distinctive phytolith patterns may characterize different agricultural practices. Harvey and Fuller (2005) demonstrated this for rice, for example.

Starch Deposition and Preservation

Summary

Deposition

Like phytoliths, starch does not have a natural dispersal mechanism. Its deposition in soils and sediments is inferred to be decay-in-place. Research by Lentfer et al. (2002) in Papua New Guinea, for example, demonstrated that starch recovered from top soils could be used to discriminate among modern environments, such as between cultivated and noncultivated areas. The primary mode of deposition of starch in the archaeological record (e.g., on artifact surfaces, in food crusts, in site sediments), and often the environmental record (e.g., in agricultural field and garden sediments), is through the use and discard of starch-rich plant tissues by people. Experiments, although limited, indicate very little movement of starch within soils (in the absence of bioturbation or soil movement) or between soils and buried artifacts.

Incidental deposition of starch on artifacts or contamination from soil can be distinguished from use-related deposition by starch abundance, patterned occurrence (i.e., in association with areas of the tool demonstrating wear from use), context, or comparisons between artifact and soil starch assemblages and quantities. Starch deposition was likely commonplace on ancient tools and in house middens, former crop fields, and plant processing areas.

Preservation

Factors that influence starch survival in archaeological contexts are complex and incompletely understood. Research suggests that, for the most part, starch residues that are buried, even shallowly, survive better than those exposed to rain, heat, and wind. Enhanced protection can be provided by burial in caves or rock shelters (dry environments) and in permanently waterlogged sites. Any given site is likely to have microhabitats detrimental to starch preservation, such as around hearths (i.e., exposed to heat), and those that may enhance the chances of recovery, such as places in which refuse accumulates and activities involving plants were common, and protected areas (under flagstones, overturned pottery vessels, near metal artifacts, and the like). Artifact surfaces and food residues (foodcrusts) can provide environments conducive to starch preservation: starch becomes embedded and sealed within crevices or organic residues, and is then protected to some extent from further exposure to moisture, heat, or abrasion. Food processing damages starch, but often leaves identifiable granules. Ethnohistoric and ethnobotanical sources may provide considerable insights into the range of foods and food processing techniques that may produce the starch records we recover from artifacts. These sources can also guide the selection of artifacts for study.

Grinding Stone Example

Starch would very likely become deposited on the grinding stone through direct contact between the artifact and starch-rich tissues (Table 2.2). Grinding/milling damages starch, but often leaves identifiable granules, as Babot (2003) observed for maize. Starch would be protected within the crevices of the grinding stone, and preservation further enhanced by the fact that the grinding stone was used in an enclosed area (inside a house) and eventually buried.

TABLE 2.2 Example of grinding stone in house floor: predictions about deposition and preservation of starch and pollen

	Starch	*Pollen*
Grinding stone	PRESENT if starchy tissues processed	PRESENT if pollen-bearing tissues processed OR ABSENT if such tissues removed prior to food processing
Floor sediments	PRESENT if large quantities deposited; if protected by an artifact, stone slab, rapid burial; when starch-destroying enzymes inhibited	PRESENT if pollen-bearing tissues deposited AND PRESENT if protected by an artifact, stone slab, rapid burial; mechanical, chemical, biological destruction inhibited

Starchy residues were also likely deposited in the floor sediments around the grinding stone. As Haslam (2004) has discussed, exposure to starch-degrading enzymes leads to rapid decomposition of starch, and such enzymes are present in all soils. Whether starch survived in this hypothetical case would depend on the sheer numbers of granules deposited and whether burial afforded sufficient protection from starch-degrading enzymes. Sampling the sediments *under* the grinding stone might well be productive, as the stone would afford additional protection.

Pollen Deposition and Preservation

Summary

Deposition

A major pathway of pollen deposition over the landscape—including localities that will become archaeological sites—is through pollen rain, the mixture of pollen from wind-pollinated plants. In open-air settings, pollen rain from the surrounding vegetation mixes with pollen deposited through human activities involving plants, such as seed grinding or refuse disposal. Because deposition of pollen from background wind-pollinated plants is limited inside closed locations, like structures, finding high concentrations of such pollen in a closed context may indicate human behavior. Pollen from animal-pollinated plants is not typically represented in the pollen rain, so the presence of such pollen in closed or open contexts can be used to infer human behavior. Pollen becomes deposited onto the surfaces of artifacts through several pathways, including exposure to pollen rain—both during artifact use lives and after discard—and through processing of pollen-bearing tissues using the artifact. Another pathway by which pollen from both wind- and animal-pollinated plants can enter the archaeological record is by its incorporation into the human digestive system. The major source of pollen in lake and swamp sediments is pollen rain.

Preservation

Pollen representation in archaeological sediments is in many cases a matter of preservation: site conditions may expose pollen to mechanical degradation, chemical destruction, and action of biological agents, forces that act alone or together to reduce pollen survival. If pollen is differentially preserved across a site, for example, only under flagstones, artifacts, mounds, or in waterlogged areas, or only in more deeply buried deposits, this is a complicating factor in inferring spatial or temporal patterning in plant use using pollen data. Assessing the quality of preservation is vital; comparisons may be limited to contexts in which pollen is equally well preserved. Damage or destruction of pollen is reduced in arid or waterlogged soils and in deposits covered by acid peat because of lower microbial activity. When ancient pollen is well preserved, understanding the pollination biology of plants potentially targeted by humans is an essential part of interpretation. Sampling within closed or otherwise protected localities maximizes recovery of pollen of utilized plants and minimizes the contribution from pollen rain. Under these circumstances, spatial patterning of different human activities involving plants may be revealed. Permanently waterlogged swamp and lake sediments are environments in which biological decomposition, including of pollen, is inhibited. As long as lake or swamp sediments do not dry up, preservation has relatively little impact on pollen representation in these contexts.

Grinding Stone Example

Pollen would become deposited on the grinding stone during seed processing if pollen-bearing tissues were associated with seeds, but would not be expected if such tissues were removed prior to seed grinding (Table 2.2). Geib and Smith (2008), for example, conducted grinding and wash experiments using maize and wild plants from the Colorado Plateau and found that recovered concentrations of pollen varied among species, in part due to pollination biology, but also according to whether it was possible to remove tissues that held pollen (e.g., grass glumes, maize husks) prior to processing. Like starch, pollen would be afforded protection by being embedded in crevices in the grinding stone and by rapid burial of the artifact in the house floor.

Similarly, pollen would become incorporated into the house floor deposits if pollen-bearing tissues were associated with the seeds being ground or if the seeds were also cleaned in that locality. In this hypothetical case, the floor (and the grinding stone) was inside a house and so was not subject to pollen rain, except near the doorway. Finding high concentrations of pollen from wind-pollinated plants in such a closed context can indicate human behavior. Kelso et al. (2006) demonstrated, for example, that pollen from utilized plants was incorporated into floor deposits in a nineteenth-century barn in significantly higher quantities than occurrence of the same pollen in background vegetation. Whether pollen survived in floor deposits would depend on the extent to which it was subjected to mechanical abrasion, alternating wetting and drying, and attack by fungi and bacteria. As was the case for starch, it might be productive to sample sediments beneath the grinding stone for pollen.

In summary, what are some of the key factors for understanding representation of archaeobotanical remains, and what are the implications of these factors for interpreting archaeobotanical data, such as our hypothetical example of macroremains, pollen, phytoliths, and starch recovered on and around a grinding stone found in an earthen house floor?

In the case of macroremains, understanding how plant tissues become charred and how they survive after charring are key factors for understanding representation for this mode of macroremain preservation. In the grinding stone example, charred macroremains of the foods being processed using the artifact may be completely absent in the context because processing did not involve fire. If we found charred grain in the floor sediments, it could represent secondary deposition (e.g., spreading of ashy debris on the floor) or a burning event unrelated to use of the tool (e.g., a structure fire that burned grain stored in the area or later use of the area for burning activity). A discovery of charred grain would allow us to identify the presence of a potential food in the house, but would not necessarily provide a direct link between the plant and the food-processing context.

In the case of pollen, representation in archaeological sediments is often a matter of preservation: site conditions are often not ideal for pollen survival. This would likely have been the case in the grinding stone example, because the site was not arid or waterlogged. However, if pollen–bearing tissues were associated with the food being processed, pollen might have survived in the crevices of the grinding stone and in the floor sediments underneath it or other artifacts in the floor. Because milling was taking place in an enclosed space, pollen recovered on and around the stone would have had minimal input from pollen rain (i.e., would be more likely to originate from plants processed on the tool).

In the case of phytoliths, their representation in archaeological sediments and on artifacts is chiefly a matter of phytolith production patterns in utilized plants and plant tissues. In the grinding stone example, if grains were being milled, we would expect to find phytoliths on or around the artifact: grasses are known silica accumulators, including in chaff associated with grains. Sampling in an enclosed locality would minimize the contribution of phytoliths from background plants, such as weedy grasses growing around the settlement. One potential interpretive challenge: grass phytoliths introduced into the floor sediments from decay of grass mats or roofing materials.

Finally, in the case of starch, the factors affecting its survival in archaeological sediments are equally as complex as for pollen, and our experience is much more limited. Starch residues that are buried, even shallowly, survive better than those exposed to rain, heat, and wind. Artifact surfaces and food residues often provide environments conducive to starch preservation. In the grinding stone example, conditions would likely have been favorable for recovering starch from whatever was being processed using the artifact, providing a direct link between the plant and the food-processing activity.

Conclusion: Deposition and Preservation of Paleoethnobotanical Remains

At times it is straightforward to model the processes and pathways that brought plant remains into sites and led to their preservation. For instance, it is usually easy to distinguish modern and ancient plant tissues when site conditions were not conducive to preservation of uncharred materials. Microfossils embedded within burned vessel residues likely represented the remains of foods. Charred wood recovered from a hearth likely represented fuel. Comparing archaeological plant assemblages to modern surface vegetation provides insights for drawing inferences in more complex situations, for example, when ancient seeds were dried or waterlogged and not as easily distinguishable from modern seeds. This approach also facilitates interpretation of pollen and phytolith data. Ethnographic observation, ethnoarchaeology, and experimental studies provide valuable insights into how plant tissues are transformed through cultural practices and potentially deposited and preserved. For example, it may be possible to infer the types of residues likely (and unlikely) to be recovered from a pit-roasting locality or area around a milling stone through study of traditional practices or the re-creation of them.

Through these and related approaches, much has been learned about processes of deposition and preservation of paleoethnobotanical remains, making it possible to model how different kinds of plant remains are represented in the archaeological record (Pearsall 2015). In general, the key factors for understanding representation of remains differ by type: preservation and pollination biology for pollen, preservation and food processing technology for starch, production patterns in plants and tissues for phytoliths, and preservation and fire technology for macroremains. These understandings underpin inferences of human behavior drawn from the archaeobotanical record. For example, if our research question requires data on the consumption of food or drink in specific types of contexts, understanding how food and drink are potentially represented as pollen, starch, phytoliths, or macroremains in such contexts is essential for identifying the actions. Similarly, if we are interested in food production, tasks centered around a grinding stone might be more productively approached through a different set of indicators than those centered on tuber pit roasting or beer brewing. Although generalized models of representation, such as those illustrated in Figure 2.2, may point us toward productive kinds of data to incorporate into our studies, I believe that the strongest inferences are those grounded in ethnographic observations, ethnoarchaeology, or experimental studies of human behaviors surrounding plants, and in a sound understanding of the archaeological contexts of samples.

Finally, an obvious but important point about deposition of archaeobotanical remains: there is nothing we can do about utilized plants that do not make it into the archaeological record (i.e., trail foods and the like). This is nonrandom data loss for which there is no correction. Such "depositional" bias is part of every analysis, making interpretation of absence all but impossible: the archaeological record can never be considered complete.

References

Babot, María del Pilar 2003 Starch grain damage as an indicator of food processing. In *Phytolith and Starch Research in the Australian-Pacific-Asian Regions: The State of the Art*, edited by D. M. Hart and L. A. Wallis, pp. 69–81. Terra Australis 19, Pandanus Books, Research School of Pacific and Asian Studies, The Australian National University, Canberra, Australia.

Cabanes, Dan, Carolina Mollol, Isabel Expósito and Javier Baena 2010 Phytolith evidence for hearths and beds in the late Mousterian occupations of Esquilleu cave (Cantabria, Spain). *Journal of Archaeological Science* 37:2847–2957.

Díaz, A. P. and J. F. Eraso 2010 Same anthropogenic activity, different taphonomic processes: A comparison of deposits from Los Husos I & II (Upper Ebro Basin, Spain). *Quaternary International* 214(1–2):82–97.

Geib, Phil R. and Susan J. Smith 2008 Palynology and archaeological inference: Bridging the gap between pollen washes and past behavior. *Journal of Archaeological Science* 35:2085–2101.

Guarino, C. and R. Sciarrillo 2004 Carbonized seeds in a protohistoric house: Results of hearth and house experiments. *Vegetation History and Archaeobotany* 13(1):65–70.

Gustafsson, S. 2000 Carbonized cereal grains and weed seeds in prehistoric houses—An experimental perspective. *Journal of Archaeological Science* 27(1):65–70.

Harvey, Emma L. and Dorian Q. Fuller 2005 Investigating crop processing using phytolith analysis: The example of rice and millets. *Journal of Archaeological Science* 32:739–752.

Haslam, M. 2004 The decomposition of starch grains in soils: Implications for archaeological residue analyses. *Journal of Archaeological Science* 31(12):1715–1734.

Ismail-Meyer, K., P. Rentzel and P. Wiemann 2013 Neolithic lakeshore settlements in Switzerland: New insights on site formation processes from micromorphology. *Geoarchaeology* 28(4):317–339.

Kelso, Gerald K., Frederica R. Dimmick, David H. Dimmick and Tonya B. Largy 2006 An ethnopalynological test of task-specific area analysis: Bay View Stable, Cataumet, Massachusetts. *Journal of Archaeological Science* 33:953–960.

Lentfer, C. J., M. Therin and R. Torrence 2002 Starch grains and environmental reconstruction: A modern test case from west New Britain, Papua New Guinea. *Journal of Archaeological Science* 29(7):687–698.

Matthews, Wendy 2010 Geoarchaeology and taphonomy of plant remains and microarchaeological residues in early urban environments in the Ancient Near East. *Quaternary International* 214:98–113.

Pearsall, Deborah M. 1983 Evaluating the stability of subsistence strategies by use of paleoethnobotanical data. *Journal of Ethnobiology* 3(2):121–137.

———— 2015 *Paleoethnobotany: A Handbook of Procedures*. Third ed. Routledge, New York.

Pearsall, Deborah M., Karol Chandler-Ezell and James A. Zeidler 2004 Maize in ancient Ecuador: Results of residue analysis of stone tools from the Real Alto site. *Journal of Archaeological Science* 31:423–442.

Raviele, Maria E. 2011 Experimental assessment of maize phytolith and starch taphonomy in carbonized cooking residues. *Journal of Archaeological Science* 38:2708–2713.

Sievers, Christine and Lyn Wadley 2008 Going underground: Experimental carbonization of fruiting structures under hearths. *Journal of Archaeological Science* 35:2909–2917.

3
FIELD SAMPLING AND RECOVERY

Introduction

In this chapter I describe the basics of taking archaeobotanical samples in the field, discuss sampling strategies, describe flotation—a technique for recovering macroremains that is often carried out by field archaeologists—and present guidelines for selecting artifacts for residue analysis and field-sampling them.

The recovery and study of macroremains—botanical materials visible to the naked eye and identifiable at low-power magnification—is a common and important part of paleoethnobotany. In this chapter I discuss recovering macroremains in some detail, because this step is usually carried out by field archaeologists: they collect plant remains in situ during excavation, pull them from excavation screens, and process subsamples of the site matrix by flotation or fine sieving, techniques developed to recover a representative sample of all sizes of macroremains.

Pollen grains, phytoliths, and starch grains are too small to be visible in site sediments; they are recovered from subsamples of the site matrix using specialized techniques in a clean laboratory setting. I will not describe how microfossils are extracted here; see Pearsall (2015) for procedures for recovering pollen, phytoliths, and starch. Artifacts may be sampled in the field for later microfossil study, however, as described later.

Pollen, phytoliths, and particulate charcoal deposited in lake or swamp sediments preserve evidence for plant–people interrelationships on the scale of the landscape. In Chapter 4 I describe how to read and interpret the results of such studies as presented in standard stratigraphic diagrams, but we will not cover how cores are taken in the field.

Before I describe the mechanics of flotation or how samples for microfossil analysis are taken, we need to consider a more fundamental question: How should a site be sampled for paleoethnobotanical data so our research questions can be investigated?

Strategies and Techniques for Sampling

As mentioned earlier, macroremains may be recovered in situ during excavation or in screens set up to recover artifacts from sediments. These finds are typically of larger plant tissues; tiny seeds are not visible in situ and pass through the large mesh often used in excavation screens. It is usually impractical to recover all size classes of macroremains from every cubic meter of sediment removed from a site; even bulk sieving using 1.0 mm or 1/16" mesh will lead to loss of small remains. Bulk sieving is also time consuming and may produce more material than can ever be analyzed. Collecting *samples* of excavated sediments for flotation or fine sieving is a practical alternative to bulk sieving for all size grades of macroremains. Sampling produces fewer samples for analysis and speeds processing, because small sediment volumes (rather than entire contexts) are processed. Sampling and processing of small-volume samples is also the approach used to recover plant microfossils, in addition to processing artifact residues (discussed later).

I recommend a *blanket sampling strategy* for archaeobotanical sampling: collect sediments for flotation/sieving and microfossil recovery from all excavation contexts. There are practical reasons for this strategy, but it also has advantages for later analysis of materials.

During the course of excavation, it is often impossible to predict which contexts (i.e., site areas, feature classes, sediment types, cultural components) contain archaeobotanical remains. For macroremains this is especially true if only charred remains are preserved, because these are difficult to see during excavation. Because charring occurs through deliberate or accidental burning, collecting samples only from contexts with evidence of burning may seem a viable strategy. In practice, however, sampling only in hearths or obvious ashy deposits does not always lead to recovery of a representative sample of macroremains. Hearth samples often contain little more than charred wood, because repeated use of a hearth destroys fragile remains such as seeds or tubers. Such material may be more abundant on the floor around the hearth or in a garbage pit. Hearths may be periodically cleaned, further limiting their usefulness. Once charred material is spread around (i.e., moved from primary to secondary depositional contexts), it is difficult to see and therefore difficult to sample. Routinely sampling all contexts avoids the problem of predicting where macroremains will occur. And microfossils are, of course, not visible at all. For these reasons I recommend a field sampling strategy that results in flotation/fine-sieve samples *and* samples for microfossil extractions from all archaeological contexts.

Another practical advantage of blanket sampling is that it is an easy strategy to carry out in the field. Excavation crews are simply instructed to take archaeobotanical samples from every level in each unit and from all features. Taking sediment samples becomes routine; variation in sample taking among individuals is minimized.

From the perspective of later analysis of materials, blanket sampling gives the analyst maximum flexibility. If, for example, a site has several temporal components, a subsample of sediment samples can be chosen for analysis to maximize temporal contrasts. One might compare assemblages from all hearth features or floor samples through time, for example. For single-component sites, samples might be chosen to give the greatest information on differential use of space. In short, it is easier to choose a subsample for analysis from a large population of samples (perhaps analyzing 25 percent or less of total samples) than to predict the best contexts for sampling while excavation is proceeding. See Pearsall (2015) for discussion of other sampling strategies.

There are three commonly used techniques for taking archaeobotanical samples: "pinch" or composite sampling, column sampling, and point sampling. Sampling for flotation/fine-sieving is described first; additional steps/considerations for microfossil sampling are then discussed.

Composite, or pinch, sampling is appropriate for many sampling situations. A composite sample (referred to as a scatter sample by Lennstrom and Hastorf 1992) is made up of small amounts of sediment gathered from all over a context combined in one sample bag. In the hypothetical excavation illustrated in Figure 3.1, for example, a house floor has been exposed in eight excavation units (a–h). A number of features have been defined (1–5). Each section of floor (unit) and each feature can be considered a separate context for sampling, yielding 13 samples per level excavated. To collect composite flotation samples for one level of such a house floor, label flotation bags with provenience information for each context. Fill each bag with small scoops of sediment from all around the context. Sediment may be taken toward the

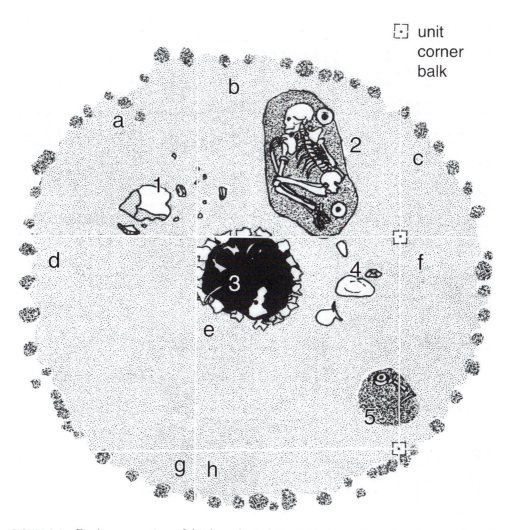

FIGURE 3.1   During excavation of this hypothetical Neolithic house floor, flotation samples will be taken from each discrete archaeological context. First composite samples will be taken from each excavation square (a–h), then each feature will be sampled: (1) stone tool manufacturing area; (2) burial pit; (3) hearth; (4) milling area; (5) trash pit.

bottom of a level, in the upper part of the level, or little by little throughout. The important point is that sediment be collected widely over each context so that the sample represents the area as a whole. Cultural levels in middens, sublevels in large features, and arbitrary fill levels are other appropriate contexts for composite sampling. Composite samples should always be taken from the area around features so that feature fill may be compared to a general unit fill. A standard soil volume should be collected whenever possible.

Flotation samples for a sequence of fill layers or floors can also be taken from one area selected at random for sampling purposes. This is column sampling. In Figure 3.2, a sampling column has been left in one unit until excavation is completed. Each natural level of floor

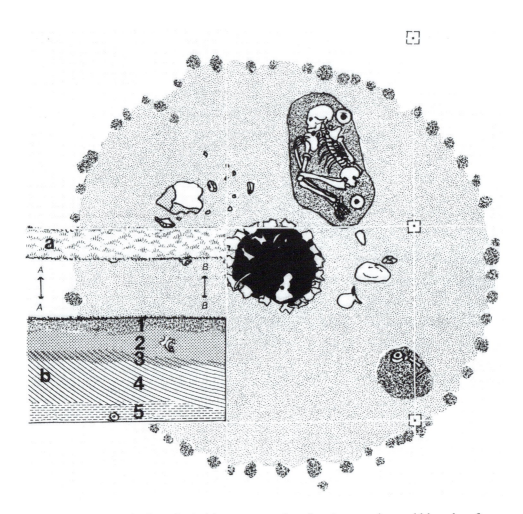

FIGURE 3.2 During the hypothetical house excavation, flotation samples could be taken from a single sediment column rather than by composite sampling. A sediment balk (a) is left in one excavation square; (b) shows the balk in profile. Archaeobotanical samples are taken from each stratigraphic level (1–5) of the balk. Note that a number of features are not represented in this column. These would be sampled separately as they were encountered, as in composite sampling.

(1–5) is to be sampled separately. More than one balk can be left for sampling purposes. The advantages of column sampling are that samples can be left in place until the unit is finished; each level is clearly visible in profile for precise sampling; and all bagging, labeling, and note taking can be done at once. The major disadvantage is that samples represent only remains present in part of the excavation. This is a valid subsample, but of a different kind than a composite sample. When using the column sampling approach, be sure to sample features or distinct strata that do not occur in the column as they are encountered.

There are a number of situations in which sampling small, precisely located areas provides useful information. I refer to this as point sampling; Lennstrom and Hastorf (1992) use the term *bulk sample*. Figure 3.3 illustrates how one unit of the hypothetical house floor could be

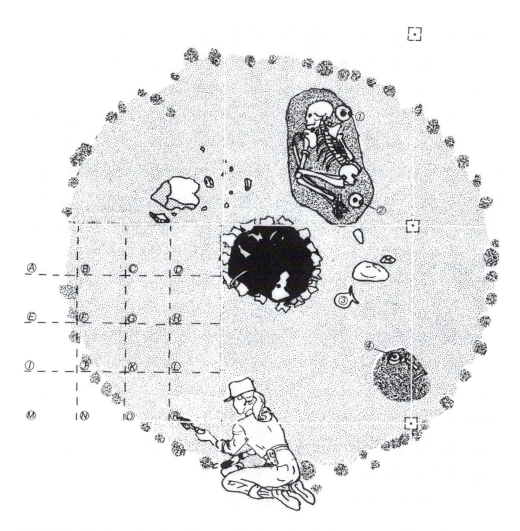

FIGURE 3.3   Point sampling in a 50-cm grid: the archaeologist places a grid in each square to facilitate taking samples (A-P). The interiors of four ceramic vessels (1–4) will also be sampled.

sampled in a 50 × 50-cm grid to obtain detailed information on activity areas. Sampling small features and the soil inside or under ceramic vessels are other examples of point sampling. Soil volume should always be measured, and do not let sample sizes fluctuate dramatically among contexts, as this could affect comparability of rarer remains.

How does one decide whether to take composite or point samples for macroremain recovery? An important point to consider is whether the higher effort and cost of taking more samples per unit area—in essence, this is what point sampling means—overrides the ease of composite sampling. In my view, the key is the importance of spatial data. In other words, if excavation involves opening up horizontally complex areas and context-specific botanical data are important, then samples should be taken at closer intervals and from more closely circumscribed areas. It is important that sampling be responsive to changes in excavation strategy or circumstances. Finally, I would not recommend composite sampling over more than a 1 × 1-m area; if units are larger, then they should be subdivided.

Small sediment samples for pollen, phytolith, and starch analyses can be taken using the three approaches just discussed, with extra precautions to avoid contamination. For starters, *no* eating or drinking in the area while sampling is ongoing; wash hands or wear starch-free gloves (also wash hands after donning gloves); store supplies and tools for microfossil sampling away from food and drink; use only new plastic bags or containers that have been stored closed. For sampling a horizontal surface, such as the house floor in our hypothetical excavation, by composite or point sampling, sample unit by unit across the floor. Scrape each unit just before sampling to guard against transfer of sediments between units, to prevent contamination with sediment on shoes or clothing, and to remove sediments exposed to modern pollen rain. Although it may be impossible to avoid walking on floor deposits during sampling, one can minimize disturbance by working from the perimeter across the floor (i.e., clean the surfaces in front of you, sample, and move to the next sector). Place each sediment sample into a new plastic bag; close immediately and label with provenience information (grid number and so on). Clean the sampling tool (trowel or the like) between samples. Within each sampling unit, care should be taken to cut into the floor to a uniform depth while sampling (i.e., not to cut into a lower stratum). For features such as storage pits, although sampling pit fill may give data on garbage thrown into the pit after it was no longer used for storage, only samples scraped carefully from the bottom and sides of the pit may reflect its original function. Even these samples may be contaminated by microfossils from later fill, unless a clear boundary is visible between the fill and residue of the original contents. Excavating large pit features in sections, so that profiles can be studied to guide sampling, improves chances of obtaining botanical samples representing the original function.

In the case of sampling a profile, whether within a feature or a standing balk such as illustrated in Figure 3.2, for pollen, phytolith, and starch samples, contamination can be minimized by (1) cleaning the surface of the profile immediately prior to sampling; (2) using a clean trowel or other sampling tool and a new container to hold the sample; (3) sampling starting at the bottom and working toward the top, so that material falling from the upper samples does not contaminate the lower samples; and (4) moving the trowel laterally, following the plane of the stratum (Bryant and Holloway 1983). Samples should not cross stratum boundaries, but rather sample above and below the boundary. In general, use smaller rather than larger sampling intervals in microfossil sampling, and take large enough samples (or multiple samples) so that additional extractions or other analyses can be performed (Lentfer 2006). Sketches and photographs of the sampled profile will provide valuable information about sample locations.

In summary, here are some hints for good archaeobotanical sampling:

(1) Collect standard-sized samples of sediment for flotation/fine-sieving. As discussed in Chapter 4, it is important not only that the analyst knows how much sediment was processed to produce an assemblage of macroremains, but also that sample sizes do not fluctuate dramatically among contexts. Sample size fluctuation can affect comparability of rarer remains. It may not always be possible to take a standard-sized sample, for instance, from a small feature. This is why I recommend that sample volume or weight be measured again before flotation/fine-sieving (see later).

  The only way to choose an appropriate sample size is by experimentation and prior experience. Start by floating/sieving several 10-L samples collected from different contexts and evaluate the quantity of material recovered. Although there are formulas for calculating optimal sample sizes for assemblages of macroremains, a useful rule of thumb is a minimum of 20 pieces of wood. If enough soil is floated to concentrate wood to that extent, chances are that sufficient numbers of seeds are also present. If test samples consistently contain few seeds, however, sample size should be increased even if wood is abundant. It is also difficult to generalize about sample sizes for pollen, phytolith, and starch samples, as microfossil densities can vary widely in different kinds of sediments and archaeological contexts. If possible, run test samples to assess microfossil preservation and abundance. My recommendation is to begin with 100-g samples (per microfossil), which should provide ample sediment to run tests and have sediment in reserve.

(2) Treat sediment collected for flotation or fine sieving gently. If you must collect samples from sediment that has first passed through bulk screens, take care that the sediment is not mashed through the screen. Remember that larger botanical remains and faunal materials will be separated from the rest of the sample if sediments are screened; this will bias results later in the analysis. Do not pack sediment tightly into sample bags, and be careful not to put heavy artifact bags on top of sediment bags or stack too many bags on top of each other.

(3) Double-tag sediment bags. Paper tags placed inside flotation sample bags disintegrate rapidly in moist sediment. Provenience information written with an ink marker on the outside of plastic bags fades quickly in sunlight. String tags can be pulled off when bags are moved. Double-tagging all bags for flotation or fine sieving (one label inside the bag, one outside) maximizes chances that provenience information will stay with the sample until it is processed. For inside labels, use aluminum or plastic tags. Alternatively, double-bag samples, placing the internal tag between inner and outer bags, or write directly on the inner bag with indelible ink. That is also the best way to double-tag microfossil samples; to avoid contamination, tags should not be placed inside bags. I recommend that all provenience data and sample numbers be written in full on both tags. Detailed labeling takes a little longer, but it gives the flotation crew an original tag to put with each flotation fraction (light and heavy) or the microfossil analyst two opportunities to decipher poor handwriting or smeared ink.

(4) Evaluate the condition of the sediments. If flotation samples are wet, plastic bags should be left open for sediments to dry while awaiting processing. It may be necessary to spread out large wet samples or to process those by water sieving. If samples are waterlogged and wet sieving is planned, be sure sample bags are tightly closed and sediments do not dry out. It is also a good idea to close tightly samples containing desiccated remains;

otherwise, dry sediments may pick up moisture from the air, which can lead to mold growth. Moist pollen samples should be stored at 5°C or colder or dried. Oven drying at 90 to 100°C is the safest practice, although sun drying can be used if precautions are taken to avoid contamination. Higher temperatures should be avoided, because distortion of pollen grains can occur. Alternatively, a few drops of fungicide or alcohol (ethanol or rubbing alcohol) can be added to pollen samples to prevent microbial activity that can destroy pollen. Starch grains can be damaged by heat (especially moist heat): store sediment samples for starch analysis in a cool, dry place. Phytoliths are not affected by sediment moisture or temperature.

(5) Float or fine sieve sediment samples with the goal of keeping pace with fieldwork. Although macroremain recovery invariably runs behind excavation, beginning sediment processing early in the field season, rather than leaving it all for the end, allows feedback on recovery to guide sampling, both in size and in location of samples. Early in the field season test a diverse set of samples—from different cultural contexts and sediment types—for pollen, phytolith, and starch to evaluate deposition and preservation of each type of microfossil.

Flotation and Fine-Sieving

As mentioned earlier, macroremains can be recovered from archaeological sites in three ways: in situ during excavation, in excavation screens, and by use of water recovery techniques (flotation) or fine-sieving. For recovering all size classes of macroremains from sediments, flotation and fine-sieving (dry or wet) are the best approaches. The impact on archaeology of the application of flotation to recover small botanical and faunal materials in quantity can hardly be overstated. See Pearsall (2015) for a detailed discussion of how to choose among the options for flotation and approaches to fine-sieving.

Water flotation is a recovery technique that utilizes differences in density of organic and inorganic material to achieve separation of organic remains from archaeological sediments. Basically, a sediment sample is poured into a container of water and agitated (either manually or by water flow), which results in lighter organic materials being released from the inorganic component of the sediments and floating to the surface, where the organics are skimmed or poured off. Flotation can be contrasted to sieving, in which sediment is washed or shaken through one or more sieves, with material remaining in the sieves removed for study. In sieving, recovery of macroremains is dependent on the size of the mesh of the sieve; in flotation, recovery of all size classes of macroremains is possible.

Briefly, there are three kinds of flotation systems: manual flotation and two types of machine-assisted systems (water separator/SMAP systems and froth flotation). Each has drawbacks and advantages. As the names imply, in manual flotation, the operator provides the agitation that separates botanical materials from sediments; in a machine-assisted system, water (and sometimes air) flowing from beneath the sample achieves this separation. In deciding which system to use, it is important to consider the initial cost of equipping the system, the cost of running it, the speed and sediment capacity of the system, and its capacity to recover remains reliably from the sediments of the site. Considering these factors will allow selection of a system that gives good, speedy recovery of macroremains that keeps pace with excavation.

In general, manual flotation systems like those illustrated in Figure 3.4 are inexpensive to build ($100–$125) but are more costly in terms of operating time than machine-assisted

FIGURE 3.4 Manual water flotation: (a) small flotation bucket in an irrigation canal at Panaulauca Cave, Peru; (b) wooden flotation device in Lindberg Bay, U.S. Virgin Islands; (c, d) wooden IDOT (Illinois Department of Transportation) flotation device in caulked garbage can during flotation training exercise, Museum Support Center; in a–c floating materials are removed by hand, as shown in d; (e, f) the washover technique: soil is poured into a bucket filled with water, stirred, and floating material poured off into a sieve-bottomed bucket during flotation training exercise.

systems: flotation rates vary between 0.05 and 0.08 m³ sediment/day for manual systems, and 0.50 and 0.80 m³/day for most water separator or SMAP (Shell Mound Archaelogical Project) systems (see Pearsall 2015 for details). Thus a factor of roughly 10 times separates machine-assisted and manual water systems in terms of how fast samples can be processed. Machine-assisted systems are more expensive to build, however, costing $200 to $650, depending on if a pump is used and whether it is gasoline or electric. The type of sediment to be processed is also a factor in choice of flotation system. All systems can recover a high percentage of seeds if soil is loose and friable, but machine-assisted systems may be better at keeping seed recovery high in heavier, clayey sediments.

In some situations, fine-sieving is a better choice for recovering macroremains than flotation; for example, in waterlogged deposits, in which macroremains are not buoyant (i.e., air spaces in plant tissues are filled with water), and in desiccated or habitually dry deposits, containing materials that may be damaged by wetting, for example, large seeds and fragile plant parts. Although desiccated plant tissues may look sturdy and almost modern, tissue breakdown has begun and wetting may accelerate decomposition. Charcoal that has rarely been wetted may "explode" on contact with water during flotation. In setting up a system for fine-sieving, it is important to remember that recovery efficiency is based solely on mesh size(s) used. See Pearsall (2015) for further details on recovering macroremains from waterlogged and desiccated deposits.

Flotation Example: Using a SMAP-Style System

The following procedure is one I have followed using a SMAP-style flotation system constructed of plastic components and run using either tap water pressure or a 25-cc gasoline pump (Figure 3.5). The system can be operated by one or two people. Sample plans and details on the components of this type of machine-assisted system are in Pearsall (2015), as are guidelines for using other systems. In machine-assisted flotation, upward water flow coming from beneath the sample separates plant remains from the sediment matrix and carries them to the water surface, where they flow out of the machine into a fine sieve. Nonbuoyant materials sink and are caught on another screen inside the body of the machine. These components and the steps in flotation are illustrated in Figure 3.5 and described next.

Pre-Flotation Preparations

To begin, assemble all supplies on a work surface near the flotation station: indelible pen for labeling heavy-fraction newspaper and light-fraction papers or tags; supply of newspaper or clean cloth squares (18" × 18", muslin or similar tightly woven but water-permeable cloth) to hold processed samples; notebook or clipboard of forms for recording flotation data; pens or pencils; rocks or other weights to hold down flotation cloths or papers; measuring scoop or bucket marked in liters; plastic sheet for holding measured soil; and tags with string. If cloth squares are used to hold light or heavy fractions, a clothesline in the shade is handy for drying samples. If newspapers are used, cardboard flats, cafeteria trays, or the like are helpful to hold the wet papers.

Assemble and order sediment samples to be processed during the flotation session: locate all bags belonging to the same sample and place them together; determine flotation order (if ordering by date, flotation number, provenience, etc., has been decided upon); and open

FIGURE 3.5 SMAP-style flotation: (a) the insert and main barrel of the unit illustrated are made from heavy plastic barrels, which last a number of field seasons if protected from sun; (b) the unit uses 5/8" hose and plumbing fixtures so that it can be run either from the tap or using a 25-cc pump; (c) soil is poured slowly into the water in the insert; the light fraction flows through the outflow into a small sieve-bottomed bucket (0.5-mm mesh); (d) water agitation is assisted by stirring; when all buoyant remains have been floated out, nonbuoyant materials are siphoned off the bottom; (e) after flotation is completed, the light fraction is carefully rinsed out of the sieve onto a cloth square; (f) the heavy fraction, caught on the barrel insert screen, will be dumped onto a cloth or newspaper to dry.

bags to check that soil is reasonably friable and dry to slightly damp. Remove wet samples or samples hardened into clay lumps, which require pre-flotation soaking.

Ready the Flotation Machine

Be sure all components of the device are clean and check for broken screens or signs of fatigue (i.e., metal barrels are susceptible to rust at weld joints, plastic barrels to cracking after prolonged sun exposure). Small breaks in screens can be fixed with liquid steel or liquid plastic caulk. Position the barrel insert and sieve bucket in the machine. If using a gasoline pump, fill the pump with gasoline and check oil level. Connect the suction and discharge hoses to the pump, and attach the discharge hose to the barrel intake pipe. The garden hose is also attached to the barrel intake pipe. All connections must be watertight and airtight; otherwise, the pump will not pull water. Apply plumber's putty to threads before attaching hoses and connectors to help produce a good seal. Make sure the sludge valve in flotation barrel is closed.

Flotation

To begin, select a sample and enter provenience data, flotation number, and other information in the flotation record. Note flotation personnel. Measure and record sample weight or volume. Label cloth squares or newspapers to hold the light and heavy fractions with sample provenience or flotation number and position them. If using a pump, submerge the intake (suction) hose in water, open the gate valve to the barrel, and start the pump. Alternatively, connect the intake hose to the tap and turn on the water. Fill the barrel of the flotation device. Once the barrel is filled with water, adjust the gate valve to establish a gentle yet rolling agitation. Check the position of the sieve bucket to make sure that water outflow passes through the sieve without striking the side of the bucket (which may damage remains).

Begin processing by pouring sediments slowly into the center of the barrel insert (i.e., directly above the showerhead outflow). After the sample has been poured in (or during this process, if two operators are used), assist water agitation by slowly stirring water to encourage sediment that sinks and collects around the edges of the screen to move to the center where water flow will break it up. As water flow begins to break up sediments and carry floating material out the sluiceway, adjust water pressure with the gate valve to maintain even water movement; as sediment volume decreases, less pressure is needed.

Once no further botanical material is observed rising to the surface and all floating material has been guided over the sluiceway, shut off water pressure by closing the barrel gate valve. Open the garden hose valve at the same time to reduce back-pressure strain on the pump. With a fine wire cloth hand sieve, scoop below the water surface to capture any semibuoyant botanical materials floating beneath the surface in the barrel insert and clean the water surface of any late-floating materials. Deposit these in the light-fraction sieve. Alternatively, semibuoyant or nonbuoyant botanical materials can be siphoned off the heavy-fraction screen using an aquarium siphon.

When flotation is done, remove the light fraction from the screen bucket by gently washing it out onto a cloth square. Hang to air dry in the *shade*: too rapid drying of wet charcoal can lead to breakage, decreasing identifiability of samples. Rinse out the sieve bucket. Remove the heavy fraction by tapping or rinsing it out of the barrel insert. Tag it with provenience information and air dry. The barrel insert should be rinsed and checked for damage. If the sludge level in the barrel is high and the water dirty, open the barrel sludge valve and drain sludge and water. Thoroughly clean the unit. Otherwise, reposition the barrel insert and the light-fraction sieve bucket for processing the next sample. Note any problems or observations on the processing of the sample in the entry for that sample in the flotation record.

Post-Flotation Cleanup

After the day's flotation is done, all heavy and light fractions should be taken to a secure location for final drying. Dry samples are then transferred to plastic or paper bags, proveniences checked, and samples packed for transfer to the analysis lab. Samples stored in plastic bags must be completely dry, or residual moisture will support growth of bacteria or fungi. Flotation papers or cloths are brushed clean for reuse or new ones prepared. Notes on the day's flotation are made. These might include numbers of samples processed, soil volume floated, time required, problems encountered, changes in procedure to be implemented, sample numbers of recovery efficiency tests, if carried out, and so on. Samples for which the field crew needs immediate feedback are examined, either cursorily for an idea of recovery efficiency or in detail, depending on what information is needed. Finally, all equipment is checked and any repairs made.

Hints for Good Recovery of Macroremains by Machine-Assisted Flotation

Flotation is most effective at recovering macroremains if sediments are friable (i.e., loamy to sandy) and dry to slightly damp. Machine-assisted systems can also effectively process fine-grained, clayey sediments, but a longer running time per sample is necessary, sediment must be added more slowly, and agitation must be monitored carefully so that fine sediments are not carried over the sluiceway, dirtying the light fraction. Because refloating dried light fractions in the lab results in seed and charcoal breakage, it is important to be alert to the nature of the sediments being processed and to adjust processing to produce clean light fractions. If clayey sediments have dried into large lumps, these may not break up entirely, even after a long processing run. Such samples should be deflocculated (chemically dispersed into fine particles), ideally before they dry completely, and fine-sieved instead (see Pearsall 2015 for procedures).

Effective recovery depends on a properly functioning flotation machine. Unlike manual flotation, where equipment breakdown is a rare source of data loss or processing delays, machine-assisted flotation systems can suffer equipment failure. Because the operator provides little agitation and does not remove light fractions from the barrel, any problems with operation of the machine or damage to screens can result in a dramatic reduction in recovery. Recovery efficiency tests (see Pearsall 2015) should be run on a frequent basis, and equipment must be inspected regularly for damage and proper functioning. Systems in which water is recycled should be tested periodically to make sure there is no contamination among samples.

Using a SMAP-style flotation system, sediment samples can be processed rapidly and effectively, giving consistently high rates of seed recovery. To ensure comparability of data, however, operating procedures must be held as constant as possible throughout the course of an excavation. This means providing standard training in how to carry out flotation, periodically monitoring flotation in progress (i.e., to catch errors like hurrying through flotation or not cleaning equipment between samples), and checking recovery tests and notes in a timely way.

One can never have too many notes; these are especially important if changes were made during a project, such as in sample size or sieve mesh size.

Finally, guard against post-flotation sample damage or loss by handling samples gently. Allow them to dry slowly, in the shade, and avoid rewetting them. Be careful transferring remains from drying papers or cloths to bags. Paper or plastic bags containing samples should be folded/rolled up after being closed to hold material steady, packed loosely in a storage box, and padded carefully for transport. Placing samples in individual jars, vials, or boxes allows material to rattle around inside the container during transport; for this reason I recommend using bags. Avoid aluminum foil unless samples are destined for radiocarbon dating, as it can deteriorate over time.

Collecting Artifacts and Residues for Starch (and Other Microfossil) Analysis

Starch has been recovered from artifacts that were washed and displayed or stored for decades in museums and curation facilities. Such artifacts have more complex "histories" than those collected in situ during excavation for residue analysis. Good handling in the field can maximize the quantity and quality of information from an artifact residue study. The following guidelines for selecting and handling artifacts for starch analysis are summarized from Fullagar (2006) and may also be applied to selecting artifacts for pollen and phytolith analysis.

Guidelines for Selecting Artifacts

Criteria for Artifact Selection

Based on the research question(s), determine the kinds of artifacts required for residue analysis; select a sample of each artifact type. Sampling may be based on morphological types, sizes, and raw materials, as well as temporal and spatial contexts. To get a reasonable sample size per excavation unit, Torrence (personal communication, 2013) recommends determining a standard sample size and routinely collecting that number of tools (including a random sample, not just tools suspected to have residues).

Control Samples

Collect at least some artifacts in situ during excavation and place each in a sealed plastic bag with minimal handling (see later). Starch recovered from these artifacts can be compared to that recovered from artifacts subjected to more handling (i.e., washed, recovered during sieving). Collect a sediment sample from each context associated with artifacts. The sediment adhering to artifacts collected in situ ("bag soil") becomes a proxy control sample (Barton et al. 1998).

Handling Artifacts

Avoid damaging starch: wet sieving causes more damage to starch residues than dry sieving. Allow some sediment to remain attached to the artifact. To avoid contamination with modern starch, limit handling of artifacts that may be studied for residues (i.e., use starch-free gloves and plastic implements to retrieve artifacts with their adhering sediments; place artifacts in individual plastic bags). Avoid use of metal tools, which can transfer metallic residues to artifacts. Be aware of likely associations between artifacts and contexts or processes unrelated to artifact use; for example, if possible, avoid selecting artifacts recovered in excavation screens.

Provenience Information

Artifact bags should be individually labeled with full provenience information; contact between artifacts and staples, ink, or paper labels should be avoided.

Archaeologists have long given artifacts with obvious residues special handling. What research over the past two decades has shown, however, is that starch can also be present on artifacts without obvious encrustations. This is especially true of flaked and ground stone tools, but ceramic sherds with no visible residues can also produce starch. Should more artifacts routinely be bagged up, unwashed? Given the potential that artifact residue studies hold for current and future research questions, this is an issue worth serious consideration.

Field-Sampling of Residues for Microfossil Study

There may be situations in which artifacts selected for residue study cannot be sent to the laboratory where the study will take place. There may be restrictions on exporting artifacts, for example, or an artifact may be embedded in architecture or be too large and heavy to transport. In these cases field-sampling of residues can be carried out. The following is a procedure developed by Logan (2006) for field-sampling artifacts for starch and phytoliths; it is a modification of the MU multisediment microfossil sampling approach (Chandler-Ezell and Pearsall 2003; Pearsall et al 2004). A somewhat similar approach is used to sample artifacts for pollen (i.e., the "pollen wash"); see discussion in Pearsall (2015).

Supplies

Distilled water (if not available, send a sample of water used to the analyst), wash bottle, unpowdered latex gloves, new toothbrushes, new plastic zip-top bags (about three per artifact), new or clean plastic bottles in a range of sizes (40–250 mL), duct tape, standard office supplies (permanent markers, labels, etc.), small ultrasonic cleaner (approximately US$200–$300 from scientific suppliers).

Procedure for Unwashed Artifacts

Record contextual information in the sampling log. Label three bags large enough to fit the artifact inside with provenience information, and mark as Sediment 1, Sediment 2, and Sediment 3. Put new gloves on. Place the artifact inside the bag labeled Sediment 1. Using a new, clean toothbrush scrub off dry sediment, keeping the artifact and sediment inside the bag. Remove the artifact from the bag. Seal the bag and put it aside. This is Sediment 1.

Put the artifact in the bag labeled Sediment 2. Add some distilled water and using the same toothbrush scrub the artifact, keeping the artifact and sediment inside the bag as noted earlier. Most of the adhering sediment should be removed in this step. Remove the artifact from the bag. Seal the bag and put it aside. This is Sediment 2.

Put the artifact in the bag labeled Sediment 3, or if it is small enough, place it inside a bottle. Be sure to rinse each bottle with distilled water before use. Add enough distilled water to cover the artifact. Fill the sonicator with water (there is no need to use distilled water, as it never touches the artifact or sample). Place bottle/bag with the artifact in the sonicator. Water levels in the artifact bag/bottle should be the same as the water level in the sonicator. Sonicate for 5 minutes. If visible material remains on the artifact, run the sonicator for an additional 5 minutes. Note how much time the artifact is in the sonicator.

Remove the bottle/bag from the sonicator. Using distilled water, rinse the artifact, catching the water in the bottle/bag, then remove the artifact and allow to dry. If using a bag, cut a corner and drain the liquid into a bottle labeled Sediment 3. Rinse any remaining material into the bottle using distilled water. Similarly, drain the Sediment 2 bag into a bottle labeled Sediment 2.

Three components should result from these steps: Sediment 1, dry, in a bag; Sediment 2, wet, in a bottle; and Sediment 3, wet, in a bottle. All wet sediments are placed in bottles to facilitate transport.

If artifacts have been washed, they do not need to be brushed, only sonicated, following the procedure described earlier. Increase sonication to 10 minutes, and record that the artifact was washed previously.

Increasingly, there are restrictions about the volume of liquids that may be shipped. The following is Logan's (2006) procedure for reducing water volume of samples.

Reducing Water Volume

Decanting without centrifugation (pouring off excess liquid after sediment has settled to the bottom) is not recommended unless absolutely necessary. If excess water must be removed, leave bottles in a secure place for the sediment to settle out of the water to the bottom of the bottles. When water is clear (after several days), you may CAREFULLY decant excess water. Smoothly pour the water out of the bottle into an extra container without agitating the sediment at the bottom. Leave at least 3 centimeters of water remaining on top of the sediment. Remember that phytoliths and starch granules are transparent, so you will not be able to see if you are pouring them off. Note in the log whether you have decanted the bottles. For shipping, make sure each bottle is tightly sealed and clearly labeled. Use duct tape or equivalent to seal each bottle. Pack bottles upright carefully with padding.

As an alternative to decanting, purchase large disposable pipettes before fieldwork, and pipette excess water from samples after they have settled for several days. In addition to using duct tape to seal each bottle, place each in a zip-top bag for further containment.

What if an artifact is too large for sonication, especially as a small sonicator may be taken to the field? One can put large artifacts in a clean basin and wash them using a sonic toothbrush (Perry 2010). Use a wash bottle of distilled water to keep water flowing over the artifact, and clean the surface with a new brush head, or one that has been boiled to destroy starch from prior samples. Allow sediments to settle in the basin, and decant or pipette excess water. Transfer sample into a bottle. Larger artifacts could also be cleaned by sonic toothbrush within a large new zip-top bag, following Logan's (2006) procedure, which might help contain splatter and would eliminate cleaning a basin between samples. Alternatively, one could sonicate a large artifact by holding successive portions of it in the sonicator. A sonicating toothbrush could also be used to collect a sample from an immovable object, if water can be pipetted from the surface.

References

Barton, H., R. Torrence and R. Fullagar 1998 Clues to stone tool function re-examined: Comparing starch grain frequencies on used and unused obsidian artefacts. *Journal of Archaeological Science* 25:1231–1238.

Bryant, Vaughn M., Jr. and Richard G. Holloway 1983 The role of palynology in archaeology. In *Advances in Archaeological Method and Theory*, Vol. 6, edited by M. S. Schiffer, pp. 191–223. Academic Press, New York.

Chandler-Ezell, Karol and Deborah M. Pearsall 2003 "Piggyback" microfossil processing: Joint starch and phytolith sampling from stone tools. *Phytolitharian Newsletter* 15(3):2–8.

Fullagar, Richard 2006 Starch on artifacts. In *Ancient Starch Research*, edited by R. Torrence and H. Barton, pp. 177–203. Left Coast Press, Walnut Creek, CA.

Lennstrom, Heidi A. and Christine A. Hastorf 1992 Testing old wive's tales in palaeoethnobotany: A comparison of bulk and scatter sampling schemes from Pancán, Peru. *Journal of Archaeological Science* 19(2):205–229.

Lentfer, C. J. 2006 Sampling sediments for starch analysis. In *Ancient Starch Research*, edited by R. Torrence and H. Barton, pp. 153–155. Left Coast Press, Walnut Creek, CA.

Logan, Amanda L. 2006 The application of phytolith and starch grain analysis to understanding formative period subsistence, ritual, and trade on the Taraco Peninsula, Highland Bolivia. Masters Thesis, Anthropology, University of Missouri, Columbia.

Pearsall, Deborah M. 2015 *Paleoethnobotany: A Handbook of Procedures*. Third ed. Routledge, New York.

Pearsall, Deborah M., Karol Chandler-Ezell and James A. Zeidler 2004 Maize in ancient Ecuador: Results of residue analysis of stone tools from the Real Alto site. *Journal of Archaeological Science* 31:423–442.

Perry, Linda 2010 Starch extraction protocol, http://fossilfarm.org/Methods/Index.html, accessed 6/17/14.

4

APPROACHES TO PALEOETHNOBOTANICAL INTERPRETATION

Glossary

plant cultivation   human activities involved with caring for a plant, including but not limited to, planting, watering, pruning, and weeding. A *cultivated plant* is a plant that is the object of these activities; it may or may not be domesticated.

plant domestication   the evolutionary process through which a plant becomes dependent on humans for survival. Some genetic changes associated with plant domestication include, but are not limited to, loss of natural dispersal mechanism and increased seed size in seed crops, and loss of sexual reproduction in vegetatively propagated crops (i.e., those grown from cuttings, tuber offsets, and the like).

Introduction

Fieldwork is done; the flotation samples are sorted; the pollen, phytolith, and starch extracts have been mounted and scanned—it's time to interpret the results and address our research questions. This is a good time to review those questions, to think about what we might expect to see in the archaeobotanical record if we answer them one way or another, and to decide how best to examine and transform our data to arrive at answers. It's also a good time to think about the factors that potentially affected the deposition, preservation, and recovery of the remains we've analyzed, any potential biases introduced by sampling, and any limitations arising from the precision or certainty of our identifications. It is a lot to consider. Luckily there are tried-and-true approaches for interpreting paleoethnobotanical data that can guide us to strong inferences about past plant–people interrelationships.

These approaches fall into two broad types: qualitative and quantitative approaches. I will introduce both, then will focus on quantitative approaches, which are essential for addressing many questions, including those illustrated in the case studies. To help illustrate these approaches, I have created tables of archaeobotanical data for the hypothetical house floor illustrated in Figure 3.1. This house floor was divided into eight excavation units (A-H) and five features were identified (Features 1–5). In our hypothetical study, one flotation sample was taken and processed from each of these contexts; macroremains were preserved by char-ring. In addition, six artifacts were recovered and sampled for starch and phytolith residues: two vessels from Feature 2; one vessel and two ground stone tools from Feature 4; and one large sherd from Feature 5. To simplify things, pollen from artifact washes and phytolith data from floor and feature sediments are not included in the illustration, and charred wood was not identified to plant taxon. In the final section of this chapter I'll guide the reader through reading and interpreting stratigraphic pollen and phytolith diagrams.

Qualitative Analysis

The qualitative aspect of archaeobotanical data is the information gained from determining that a given plant was present at a site or context. To trace the spread of a crop outside its hearth area, for example, one is interested in where securely identified remains were found and during which time periods. A report of presence of wheat or barley at an early site in Europe, for instance, and a detailed description of the appearance and size of its grains can help us discover when those crops spread from Southwest Asia. Determining which plants co-occurred in the archaeological record of a region is another important qualitative aspect of data. Plants from different ecological zones found in the same deposits may give insights into patterns of trade or seasonal population movements. To get the most out of rosters of plants recovered at sites, it is necessary to understand the ecology and potential utility of those plants for human populations.

For example, Table 4.1 lists 24 plant taxa that were identified in the floor and feature sedi-ments, and on the artifacts, of the hypothetical house illustrated in Figure 3.1. These plant remains were identified to different taxonomic levels. Three taxa were identified to species *(Psidium guajava, Trianthema portulacastrum, Zea mays)*, ten to genus (for example, *Capsicum, Chusquea, Heliconia)*, three to subfamily (bambusoideae, chloridoid, and panicoid grasses), and eight to family (for example, Poaceae, Marantaceae, Ulmaceae). These taxa represent wild and domesticated plants of the lowland Neotropics. The taxonomic level of identification can affect interpretation of results in significant ways. For instance, knowing the species can give us more precise information on habitat and potential uses than knowing only the genus if there are marked differences in these characteristics among species. In the hypothetical exam-ple, four of the genus-level identifications *(Capsicum, Cucurbita, Manihot, Phaseolus)* were based on remains that resembled domesticated rather than wild representatives of their respective genera. In other words, although the analyst could not determine *which* domesticated chili pepper was represented, she or he knew it was likely to have been a domesticated, rather than a wild, species. Notice how the amount of useful information from family-level identifica-tions can also vary. Considering this hypothetical assemblage of identified plants as a whole, we have learned that a variety of lowland habitats were accessed by the inhabitants of the house; that wild, cultivated/managed, and domesticated plants all played a role in the house-hold economy; that weeds and other open-habitat plants grew around the house and became incorporated into the deposits; that several kinds of plants useful for thatch, flooring, and other utility purposes were available; and that roots, seeds, grain (maize), and a variety of fruits were potentially processed, consumed, and discarded in the house.

In summary, documenting the occurrence (presence) of plants at a site or a context like a house, without quantitative analysis of data, can be an important source of information on seasonality of occupation, past vegetation and ecology, diet, subsistence practices, trade, and

TABLE 4.1 Plants identified in the hypothetical house floor from charred macroremains (excluding wood), starch, and phytoliths. Unknown types are omitted. Plant family names end in *aceae* (e.g., Boragin*aceae*); species-level names are binomial (e.g., *Zea mays*); genus-level names are one-part names (e.g., *Arundinella*). Bambusoideae, chloridoid, and panicoid are subfamily groupings of the Poaceae (grasses)

	Potential Use	Habitat
Arecaceae (palm family)	edible fruit, thatch	forest, cultivated/managed
Arundinella (a grass)	?	moist, open
Asteraceae (daisy family)	?	open, disturbed
bambusoideae grasses	utility	forest
Boraginaceae	?	?
Capsicum (chili pepper)	spice	cultivated
Carex (a sedge)	?	moist, open
chloridoid grasses	?	dry, open
Chrysobalanaceae	edible fruit, wood	forest
Chusquea (a bamboo)	utility	forest
Cucurbita (squash)	edible fruit	cultivated
Eriochloa (a grass)	?	moist, open
Heliconia (bird-of-paradise)	utility	forest edges
Manihot (manioc)	edible roots	cultivated
Marantaceae (arrowroot family)	edible roots, utility	cultivated and wild
panicoid grasses	?	moist, open
Pharus (a bamboo)	utility	forest
Phaseolus (bean)	edible fruit	cultivated
Poaceae (grass family)	?	open
Podostemaceae (water weed family)	?	moist
Psidium guajava (guava)	edible fruit	cultivated
Trianthema portulacastrum	?	open, disturbed
Ulmaceae (elm family)	wood	forest
Zea mays (maize)	edible seeds	cultivated

domestication, among other issues. Seasonality of occupation is difficult to document without use of biological indicators, including botanical remains. Plotting monthly availabilities of plants recovered from sites allows one to pinpoint the most likely season of occupation or to argue for year-round occupation. Insight into diet can be gained by compiling nutritional data on plants considered foods. To infer which plants may have been foods, fuels, accidental weedy inclusions, or medicinal plants, one relies on ethnographic analogy, historical records, and biochemical characteristics of plants. Determining present-day habitats of wild taxa found in archaeobotanical assemblages allows modeling of resource zone use. Similarly, recovery of domesticated plants or agricultural weeds may give insight into agricultural practices such as irrigation and field construction. Careful description and measurement of domesticated plant remains permits comparisons of materials among sites, leading to increased understanding of crop evolution and dispersal.

Whereas the *presence* of a given plant(s) in an archaeobotanical assemblage can be very informative, *absence* is largely uninterpretable. As discussed in Chapter 2, there are a great many reasons why a given plant may be absent from the archaeological record. Even if some factors can be eliminated, there are always unknown ones that cannot be accounted for.

Quantitative Analysis

Quantitative analysis of archaeobotanical remains is based on the premise that abundance of remains may provide additional insights into human behaviors concerning that plant than presence alone. For instance, returning to the example of identifying wheat or barley at an early site in Europe, we would likely draw different inferences about the role of these grains in food systems if charred wheat seeds were found in every analyzed sample but charred barley in only 10 percent of samples, or if wheat seeds were very abundant relative to all other charred seeds recovered. Such quantitative comparisons can be made only if remains were recovered in a consistent way across site contexts and if the plants of interest likely became preserved and deposited in similar ways. These factors being equal, in this example we might conclude that wheat was more commonly used and was more important than barley because of the greater abundance of wheat seeds recovered from the site.

It is impossible to infer how much wheat or barley was actually consumed, however. The raw quantities of macroremains or microfossils recovered from archaeological contexts have little to no relationship with the abundance of plant tissues used. Cooking experiments have shown, for instance, that there is no relationship between the absolute quantity of maize cooked in a pot and abundance of maize starch and phytoliths recovered in residues (Raviele 2011). Similarly, if an orange contains a dozen or so seeds, whether 10 or 100 were recovered archaeologically tells us little about how many actual oranges were eaten: each of 10 seeds could have come from a separate fruit; 100 seeds could have come from 100 fruits, 8 fruits, or anything in between. If it is the case that organic remains are exceptionally well preserved, raw quantities of macroremains can be used to reconstruct the minimum number of plants or edible portions needed to produce the recovered assemblage (see Flannery 1986, discussed in Pearsall 2015, for an example of this approach). In most cases, however, quantitative approaches rely on the relative abundances of archaeobotanical remains to draw inferences about plant–people interrelationships.

In summary, quantitative analysis includes everything from tabulations of counts or weights that describe quantities of remains identified in samples to multivariate approaches that search for patterns in an assemblage of data; many different approaches are in use today. I recommend quantification of archaeobotanical data, but with three qualifications: do not use any statistical technique you do not fully understand; begin with simple tabulations and then apply more complex techniques; and do not use approaches that require more rigor than the data are capable of sustaining. Finally, it is advisable to become familiar with a broad array of traditional statistical and exploratory data analysis approaches in order to determine which might be the most helpful in a specific instance. Among useful texts are Baxter (1994, 2003), Drennan (2010), Grimm and Yarnold (1995), Pielou (1984), Shennan (1997), Thomas (1986), Tukey (1977), VanPool and Leonard (2011), and Velleman and Hoaglin (1981). Multivariate approaches will not be covered in detail here.

Common Measures Used to Interpret Archaeobotanical Data

Raw Data Tabulation

Macroremain analyses usually include counts and/or weights of all identified remains. For example, Table 4.2 presents counts of charred macroremains recovered by flotation and

TABLE 4.2 Macroremain counts from hypothetical house floor samples. Column 1, identified plants; column 2, totals of each plant; columns 3–10, units; columns 11–15, features. The designation cf. (e.g., cf. Arecaceae) indicates that the remains were consistent with that taxon but could not be identified with absolute certainty. The terms *kernel, cupule,* and *cob rachis* refer to parts of the maize fruit. The terms *cotyledon* and *endosperm* refer to seed tissues (see Chapter 1)

House 1 floor	Totals	Unit A	Unit B	Unit C	Unit D	Unit E	Unit F	Unit G	Unit H	Feature 1 stone working	Feature 2 burial pit	Feature 3 hearth	Feature 4 milling area	Feature 5 trash pit
Liters of sediment floated	140	10	10	10	10	10	10	10	10	5	20	10	10	15
cf. Arecaceae	6	0	1	0	0	4	0	0	0	0	0	0	0	0
Maize kernel frags	449	1	2	0	1	48	0	2	2	0	2	0	0	334
Fused maize kernel mass	228	0	0	0	0	1	1	0	0	0	0	0	0	226
Maize cupules >2 mm	375	0	9	0	4	351	1	0	0	0	1	0	0	1
Maize cupules <2 mm	119	1	12	0	0	100	0	0	0	0	3	3	0	0
Cob rachis segment	3	0	0	0	0	1	0	0	0	0	1	1	0	0
Maize total	1174	2	23	0	5	501	2	2	2	1	7	4	0	561
Trianthema portulacastrum	20	3	3	0	0	12	0	0	0	1	1	0	0	0
cf. Poaceae seed	1	0	0	0	0	1	0	0	0	0	0	0	0	0
Psidium guajava seed	1	0	0	0	0	1	0	0	0	0	0	0	0	0
Spherical seed, unknown	4	0	0	0	0	2	0	0	0	0	0	0	0	2
Small seed damaged, unk	2	0	2	0	0	0	0	0	0	0	0	0	0	0
Porous tissue	86	0	3	0	4	16	3	0	0	0	1	15	10	33
Porous endosperm frags	28	0	2	0	0	26	0	0	0	0	0	0	0	0
Porous, possible root/tuber	4	2	0	0	0	2	0	0	0	0	0	0	0	0
Wood	3715	14	298	0	52	581	54	2	36	14	37	1604	35	820
Dense tissue	224	0	21	0	2	31	1	0	0	0	4	56	2	100
Phaseolus bean frag	456	0	12	0	4	137	0	0	0	0	0	1	0	262
Thick fruit/nut rind	118	0	1	0	0	84	0	0	0	0	0	0	0	29
Thin fruit/nut rind	8	0	0	0	0	1	1	0	0	0	0	0	0	2
Dense cotyledon frag	3	0	0	0	0	3	0	0	0	0	0	0	0	0
Total counts	5850	21	366	0	67	1402	60	2	38	15	50	1680	47	1809
Total excluding wood	2135	7	68	0	15	821	6	0	2	1	13	76	12	989

identified, either to plant taxon or tissue morphotype, from the hypothetical house floor and features depicted in Figure 3.1. These remains came from both the light and nonbuoyant fractions of flotation samples (combined as one sample on the table); each sample was split into two size components (<2 mm, >2 mm) and different materials removed from each size split. Notice that a flotation sample of uniform size was taken from each floor unit (see row 1 of Table 4.2, liters of sediment floated), but that different sizes of sediment samples were floated for the features. Starch results are also typically reported by total count of each identified type and distinctive, but unknown, morphotypes. For example, the top of Table 4.3 shows the starch counts for the six artifact residue samples from the hypothetical house. Raw data may be presented in tabular form for every sample analyzed, as shown in Table 4.2 and Table 4.3, or summarized for each taxon, stratigraphic level, or other relevant grouping. Ungrouped data are useful in that they can form the basis for spatial analysis and other measures such as diversity and ubiquity, as discussed later.

Two types of counts are commonly used in pollen and phytolith analysis: counts that yield relative or percentage occurrence data and counts that yield absolute frequency data. Each has its advantages, but relative counts are more commonly used. In a relative count, occurrence of each plant taxon is expressed as a proportion of some specified pollen or phytolith sum; in this approach, the "raw data" are actually ratios. For example, the bottom portion of Table 4.3 presents phytolith counts for the six artifacts from the hypothetical house floor. The target was to tally 200 phytoliths per artifact residue sample. Notice that this goal was achieved for three artifacts: Vessel 2 from the burial pit and the mano and metate from the milling area (see bottom row of Table 4.3). For those samples, counting stopped when 200 phytoliths had been tallied. For each of the other artifacts, the entire slide was scanned without achieving a 200-count; the total number of phytoliths counted was entered in the bottom row of the table. In this example, then, the abundances of individual plant taxa or phytolith morphotypes can be compared directly among Vessel 2, the mano, and the metate (i.e., all the counts are proportions of 200), but not among the other samples.

In palynology, a common approach is to count all pollen encountered in a sample until a predetermined sum is reached and use total pollen (TP) as the basis for the pollen sum. Moore et al. (1991) recommend tailoring the sum to fit the goals of research by making a series of counts, calculating relative occurrence data, and then assessing the results. Some pollen types may be overrepresented (e.g., local water-edge plants). These can then be eliminated from the sum, permitting higher counts of rarer, more ecologically significant taxa. Similarly, if local vegetation is of greatest interest, types transported long distances could be eliminated. Counting is handled similarly for phytoliths: all phytoliths identifiable at the species, genus, subfamily, family, or higher taxonomic level encountered in a sample may be included in the sum (as in the hypothetical phytolith data set presented in Table 4.3), or a subset may be counted for some particular purpose. It is common, for instance, to count grass short cells, because the relative abundance of short cells from different subfamilies of grasses can give data on environmental conditions.

The technique of calculating absolute pollen frequencies was developed as an alternative to relative counting; it was later also applied in phytolith research. Absolute pollen or phytolith frequency estimates the deposition of each microfossil type independently of all other types (concentration) and independently of changing rates of sedimentation (accumulation) (Birks and Gordon 1985). Pollen or phytolith concentration is the number of microfossils deposited per unit volume or unit weight of sediment. Accumulation (or deposition rate, or influx)

TABLE 4.3 Starch and phytolith counts and ubiquity, hypothetical house floor artifacts. Column 1, identified plants, starch (top), phytoliths (bottom); columns 2–7, the six artifacts; column 8, ubiquity

	Feature 2	Feature 2	Feature 4	Feature 4	Feature 4	Feature 5	Ubiquity
	burial pit	burial pit	milling area	milling area	milling area	trash pit	n = 6
	Vessel 1	Vessel 2	mano	metate	Vessel 3	large sherd	
Starch:							
Zea mays	5	4	16	21	10	2	6
cf. Zea mays	1	3	2	2	1	5	6
Capsicum		1		1			2
cf. Capsicum	2			2			2
cf. Manihot	1						1
hemisphere	1	1	1	1	1		4
unknown		3				1	3
gelatinized						1	1
damaged	1	1	1		1	2	5
Total Starch	11	13	20	27	13	11	
Grass Phytoliths:							
Panicoid:							
panicoid (lobed) short cells	36	83	54	57	25	5	6
Zea mays leaf short cells		1		1	3	1	4
Zea mays cob bodies	2	2	2	2	1		5
panicoid complex top				1	3		2
Eriochloa					1		1
Arundinella			1				1
Chloridoid:							
saddle	10	22	16	25	10		5
Bambusoideae:							
Pharus				3			1
Chusquea			2	2			2

saddle/bilobate				18	1	2
cross (Var 3, Var 8)			3			1
Other grass phytoliths:						
redundant short cells	2	13	12	12	2	6
other grass phytoliths	22	27	22	8	8	5
Nongrasses:						
Arecaceae	5	5	5	9	3	4
Asteraceae			1			1
cf. Boraginaceae	1	1				1
Cucurbita, domesticated		1	1			2
Chrysobalanaceae			4		3	2
Cyperaceae, *Carex*	4	4	1	7	1	4
Heliconia	4	4	30	6	3	4
Marantaceae	8	8	21	28	11	5
Ulmaceae	4					1
generalized arboreal	7	7	7	2	1	4
fruit/seed transport element				4	3	2
root/tuber transport element	3	3		1	3	3
woody dicots	6	6		6	1	4
blocky epidermal cells			5		1	3
burnt epidermal cells	7	7	12	11	11	6
Podostemaceae	3	3		4		2
sponge spicules	2	2		1		4
diatoms	2	2	1			2
Total phytoliths (target sum = 200)	88	200	200	200	95	26

is the number of microfossils deposited per unit area of sediment surface per unit of time. See Pearsall (2015) for descriptions of the ways of arriving at absolute pollen and phytolith frequencies.

Ubiquity/Percentage Presence

Ubiquity is the occurrence of a plant taxon expressed by the percentage of the total number of units analyzed that contain that taxon (Hubbard 1980). For example, if peach pits occurred in 6 of 10 samples analyzed, ubiquity/percentage presence would be 60 percent. How many pits occurred in a sample, whether 2 or 200, is immaterial for this calculation. As discussed earlier, stating that a plant was present at a site, whether in the form of macroremains, pollen, phytoliths, or starch, can convey important information. Stating that a plant was ubiquitous at a site, that is, that it occurred widely in site deposits, implies that many households had access to it: the plant was common enough to be frequently charred and preserved, incorporated into numerous food residues, deposited on many grinding stones, and so on. Percentage presence is also useful for considering diverse classes of data together, for example, plant and animal species over the same contexts, or plants represented by different kinds of archaeobotanical remains. Residue studies lend themselves to this approach: each tool or tool sector is a locus; finding starch, phytoliths, or pollen of an economic plant on 100 percent of grinding stones/chipped stone tools/cooking residues/dentitions suggests a different level/context of use than finding it on 10 percent. It is important to remember, however, that interpretations based on percentage presence/ubiquity are constrained by sample size and preservation (Kadane 1988).

In the case of macroremains from the hypothetical house floor depicted in Figure 3.1 (Table 4.4), ubiquity can be calculated on the basis of all the contexts (n = 13) or only the units (n = 8) or the features (n = 5). As shown in column 11 of Table 4.4, ubiquity based on the eight floor units indicated that charred maize remains (row 2) were present in three-quarters of floor sediments (6 of 8) and porous (row 8) and dense (row 11) tissues were present in half of the units; otherwise, different plant taxa and morphotypes were represented in a spotty fashion around the house floor. Considering the floor units and features together (column 17) produced a similar pattern.

In terms of ubiquity of plant taxa in artifact residues (see Table 4.3, column 8), maize starch (rows 1 and 2) was ubiquitous, whereas manioc (cf. *Manihot*, row 5) and chili pepper starch (*Capsicum*, cf. *Capsicum*, rows 3 and 4) were present on one and three artifacts, respectively. Maize phytoliths were not as commonly found in association with artifacts (rows 12 and 13), but a number of other silicified tissues were ubiquitous in artifact residues (i.e., panicoid grass short cells [row 11], redundant grass short cells [row 22], and burnt epidermal cells [row 38]), or nearly so (i.e., saddle-shaped short cells [row 17], other grass phytoliths [row 23], and Marantaceae [row 31]). Based on the potential uses of these plants (Table 4.1), we might argue from these microfossil ubiquity patterns that foods made from maize and root crops (Marantaceae), sometimes flavored with chili pepper, were commonly prepared or served using the artifacts studied, but that manioc was rarely prepared, perhaps only as a burial food/offering. As shown in Table 4.4, maize was regularly charred due to cooking accidents or deliberate disposal and likely spread around the house floor when the hearth was cleaned out (note that there was little but charred wood in the hearth itself; see Table 4.2, results for Feature 3, hearth).

TABLE 4.4 Macroremains percentages and ubiquity, hypothetical house floor samples. Column 1, identified plants; column 2, housewide percentages of each plant based on total count, excluding wood; columns 3–10, percentages for each unit; column 11, ubiquity based on 8 units; columns 12–16, percentages for each feature; column 17, ubiquity based on all contexts

House 1 floor	Entire house	Unit A	Unit B	Unit C	Unit D	Unit E	Unit F	Unit G	Unit H	Ubiquity (house units, n = 8)	Feature 1 (stone working)	Feature 2 (burial pit)	Feature 3 (hearth)	Feature 4 (milling area)	Feature 5 (trash pit)	Ubiquity (all contexts, n = 13)
Percentages, excluding wood																
cf. Arecaceae	0.28		1.47			0.49				2						2
Maize total	54.99	28.57	33.82		33.33	61.02	33.33		100	6		53.85	5.26		56.72	9
Trianthema portulacastrum	0.94	42.86	4.41			1.46				3	100	7.69				5
cf. Poaceae seed	0.05					0.12				1						1
Psidium guajava seed	0.05					0.12				1						1
Spherical seed, unknown	0.19					0.24				1					0.20	2
Small seed damaged, unk	0.09		2.94							1						1
Porous tissue	4.03		4.41		26.67	1.95	50.00			4		7.69	19.74	83.33	3.34	8
Porous endosperm frags	1.31		2.94			3.17				2						2
Porous, possible root/tuber	0.19	28.57				0.24				2						2
Dense tissue	10.49		30.88		13.33	3.78	16.67			4		30.77	73.68	16.67	10.11	8
Phaseolus bean frag	21.36		17.65		26.67	16.69				3			1.32		26.49	5
Thick fruit/nut rind	5.53		1.47			10.23				2					2.93	3
Thin fruit/nut rind	0.37					0.12				1					0.20	2
Dense cotyledon frag	0.14					0.37				1						1
Total counts, excluding wood	2135	7	68	0	15	821	6	0	2		1	13	76	12	989	

Ratios

Patterning in data (e.g., changes in taxon frequency over time, differences in occurrences among features) is often obscured by unevenness in those data. For example, site components may differ in total number of samples analyzed or total amount of sediment floated. Such unevenness may obscure significant differences in wood or seed assemblages. Or assemblages may be so complex, with so many plants represented, that differences among samples cannot be easily recognized from raw data. The simplest measure used by paleoethnobotanists to standardize macroremain data (i.e., to "even out" unevenness in data) is the ratio (Miller 1988). There are two types: those in which material in the numerator is included in material in the denominator (e.g., percentage of seeds that are *Chenopodium*), and those in which materials quantified in the numerator and in the denominator are mutually exclusive (e.g., seed:wood ratio).

Density ratios are a common example of the first type. In a density ratio, the denominator is the total volume of sediment floated or fine-sieved to obtain the count or weight of botanical material of interest. In flotation analysis, it is not uncommon to express seed, nut, or wood occurrence by count or weight per liter of sediment processed. In Table 4.5, a density ratio of wood (by count)/liter sediment (row 2) is presented for each flotation sample from the hypothetical house floor and its features. Recall that for each floor unit a standard-sized flotation sample was taken, but that sample sizes varied considerably among the features (see Table 4.2, row 1). Calculating wood density ratios permits direct comparisons among all samples, floor units, and features. Notice, for example, that Feature 3, the hearth, had the highest density of charred wood for the house, followed by unit E (the unit in which the hearth was located), Feature 5 (the trash pit), and unit B (unit adjacent to the hearth). From this we might infer that burning activity and spread of ash and char were centered on the hearth and the area immediately around it and that ash was also disposed in the trash pit. Otherwise, the house floor was comparatively clean of charred debris.

Percentages are another commonly used ratio of the first type (i.e., numerator is included in the denominator) that permit comparisons in the relative abundances of plant taxa among samples with different quantities of materials. For example, Table 4.4 presents the identified macroremains in the hypothetical house floor as percentages of total count per flotation sample, excluding wood (see the last row of the table for total counts used in the percentage calculations). As the wood density ratios indicated, there were wide variations in the quantities of remains recovered from the different floor units and features in this example. Not unexpectedly, this resulted in half the percentage calculations being based on very low counts (i.e., on 20 or fewer nonwood macroremains). In an actual study, samples with such low counts would likely be discussed in terms of presence, rather than percentage. Focusing on the more robust data (i.e., Unit B, Unit E, Feature 3, Feature 5), notice that in three contexts maize (row 2) made up the highest proportion of nonwood plant material recovered, followed by dense tissue (row 11) or *Phaseolus* (bean) fragments (row 12). In one context dense tissue made up the highest proportion of plant material. From these observations we might infer that maize, beans, and some kind of fruit or seed with dense tissues were commonly used by the household and/or commonly preserved through charring. Notice how plants rarely represented in the house deposits usually occurred in Unit E. In other words, this was the richest sample (i.e., it had greatest variety of identified items) in terms of plants represented by macroremains (see Table 4.5, row 3, for macroremain richness values). Interestingly, Unit E did not have the

TABLE 4.5 Transformations of macroremain, starch, and phytolith data from the hypothetical house floor samples and artifacts: ratios, richness, and indices. For the phytolith richness calculation, maize was totaled, and redundant, other grasses, sponge spicules, and diatoms were excluded

Transformations of Macroremain Data:

	Totals	Unit A	Unit B	Unit C	Unit D	Unit E	Unit F	Unit G	Unit H	Feature 1	Feature 2	Feature 3	Feature 4	Feature 5
										stone working	burial pit	hearth	milling area	trash pit
kernel:cupule ratio	1.36	1.00	0.10	no maize	0.25	0.11	1.00	no maize	2 kernels	no maize	0.40	3 cupules	no maize	560.00
wood density/liter sediment	26.54	1.40	29.80	0.00	5.20	58.10	5.40	0.20	3.60	2.80	1.85	160.40	3.50	54.67
richness (n = 16, maize totaled)		4	10	0	5	15	4	1	2	2	5	5	2	8

Transformations of Starch Data:

	Feature 2	Feature 2	Feature 4	Feature 4	Feature 4	Feature 5
	burial pit	burial pit	milling area	milling area	milling area	trash pit
	Vessel 1	Vessel 2	mano	metate	Vessel 3	large sherd
richness (n = 5, maize, chili totaled; gelatinized, damaged excluded)	4	4	2	3	2	2

Transformations of Phytolith Data:

aridity index	0.21	0.20	0.22	0.29	0.23	no chloridoid
richness (n = 26)	8	13	16	17	17	2

highest nonwood counts, suggesting that plant richness was not simply a function of larger sample size. As discussed earlier, pollen and phytolith data are usually presented as proportions of a fixed sum, and comparisons among samples are made in similar ways.

The second type of ratio described by Miller, that in which numerator and denominator are mutually exclusive, compares quantities of two different items (individual taxa or material categories). Comparison ratios can be used to demonstrate that one taxon replaced another over time or differed in their spatial distribution. In other words, one can test an idea that one fuel type replaced another, or that one food plant increased in use at the expense of another, by comparing the occurrence of one to the other through time or over space. I calculated one comparison ratio from the macroremains recovered from the hypothetical house floor: maize kernel:cupule ratio (Table 4.5, row 1). Notice that the ratio was calculated for only seven contexts; the other six lacked maize or had only kernels or cupules, as noted on the table. The ratio was calculated from the raw data in Table 4.2 (rows 3–7). In two contexts the same numbers of kernels and cupules occurred (Unit A, Unit F), in four contexts cupules dominated (i.e., kernel:cupule ratios were very low; Unit B, Unit D, Unit E, Feature 2), and in one context virtually all the maize was kernels (Feature 5). Given that the contexts were all contemporaneous in this hypothetical example, these results indicate distinctive spatial patterning in the deposition of cupules (a waste produce) versus kernels (edible portion).

Several phytolith ratios, or indices, have been found useful for interpreting phytolith patterning in terms of past vegetation when grasses form a significant component of the flora. Twiss (1992) first proposed that the proportion of grasses following the C_3 and C_4 photosynthetic pathways could be approximated by the ratio of pooid phytoliths to the sum of pooid, chloridoid, and panicoid phytoliths. This ratio was eventually named the Ic, or climatic index. In fossil assemblages, high values suggested a cool climate (i.e., high latitudes or high elevation, dominated by C_3 grasses), and low values a warm and humid to warm and dry climate (i.e., low latitudes and elevations, dominated by C_4 grasses). A related index is the aridity index, the ratio of short cells from chloridoid grasses (those favoring drier conditions) to the sum of short cells of chloridoid and panicoid grasses (those favoring moister conditions) (Twiss 2001). In Table 4.5, the second to last row shows aridity index values for five of the six artifact residue samples from the hypothetical house floor. Notice how consistent the index values are: the ratios of grass short phytoliths in the residue samples indicated moist background conditions (i.e., very low aridity index values) in all contexts sampled. Other ratios have been developed to serve as proxy measures of tree cover and water stress; see Pearsall (2015) for details.

Diversity

Species diversity is a measure that takes into account both total number of species or taxa present in a population and abundance of each species (Pielou 1984). High diversity results when a large number of species are evenly distributed, that is, when it is difficult to predict what a randomly selected item would be. Low diversity results when the number of species present is low, or when one or a few species account for most of the population. Because archaeobotanical data deal in both numbers of taxa and counts of each, combining these into one index, diversity, is useful in some situations. Absolute diversity values are dependent on quantity of remains preserved; thus, differences in preservation conditions among sites or components of a site can affect the measure.

It can also be informative to compare simple richness (the numbers of kinds of taxa present) among contexts. In the hypothetical house floor example, recall how Unit E stood out from the other contexts in terms of the richness of its macroremain assemblage: 15 of a possible 16 taxa/morphotypes occurred in this context (Table 4.5, row 3). In terms of richness of starch and phytolith assemblages in artifact residues (Table 4.5, row 4 and last row, respectively), Vessel 1 and Vessel 2 from the burial recorded the highest richness in terms of plants identified by starch (4 of 5 possible), but the richest contexts in terms of plants identified by phytoliths were the artifacts from the milling area: Vessel 3, the metate, and the mano (16 or 17 of 26 possible). From these results we might infer differences in how plants were utilized and/or disposed of in the different contexts of the hypothetical house floor.

Application of Multivariate Techniques

It is beyond the scope of this summary to describe the many multivariate approaches that have been used in paleoethnobotany. Those used in research described in the case studies will be briefly explained in context. Simply stated, multivariate statistical approaches aid the researcher in identifying significant patterning in data when the units of analysis are characterized by several variables. In Marquardt's (1974) quantitative analysis of botanical material in coprolites from Mammoth Cave, for example, coprolites (preserved feces) were units of analysis and the variables were the plant taxa (i.e., the kinds of seeds and nuts identified) within the coprolites. Each unit (coprolite) was characterized by the values (counts or weights) of its variables (plant taxa). There are three main reasons for using multivariate approaches in paleoethnobotanical interpretation: to group or classify previously ungrouped data, to determine the best way to distinguish among known groups of data, and to reduce the number of variables needed to account for differences among ungrouped data.

Reading a Stratigraphic Diagram

Stratigraphic pollen and phytolith diagrams can be intimidating. In large part this is because they present a large amount of information in a very compact format. Unpacking a complex diagram is well worth the effort, as we will see in several of the case studies.

The construction of diagrams to present stratigraphic pollen data is described in most palynology texts; the discussion presented here was taken largely from Moore et al. (1991) and Faegri et al. (1989). Phytolith diagrams are organized in a similar fashion. Figure 4.1, a simplified percentage diagram from a lake in Alabama studied by Fearn and Liu (1995), illustrates most of the following points about stratigraphic diagrams.

1. The vertical axis of the diagram depicts depth or time; the horizontal axis depicts relative (and/or absolute) pollen abundance. Figure 4.1 illustrates relative abundance. Pollen sums may be shown in a column at the right of the diagram or discussed in the text.
2. The stratigraphic sequence, or lithology, is shown in a column on the right or left vertical axis. Sediment types may be depicted with symbols or described, as in Figure 4.1. Horizontal lines may be used to separate sediment types to increase clarity in complex diagrams. Radiocarbon dates, accumulation rates, or pollen concentration data may also be shown on the vertical axis. In Figure 4.1, dates are on the left axis.

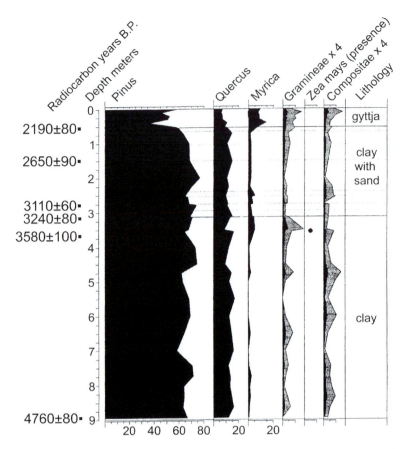

FIGURE 4.1 Simplified pollen percentage diagram for core S3E2 from Lake Shelby, Alabama. Sand layers are indicated by dotted lines. Patterned Gramineae and Compositae curves are exaggerated by 4 (Figure 2 from Fearn, M. L. and Kam-biu Liu. 1995. Maize pollen of 3500 B.P. from southern Alabama. *American Antiquity* 60(1):109–117.)

Reproduced with permission of Cambridge University Press and the Society for American Archaeology.

3. For each deposit sampled, abundance of pollen types (e.g., *Pinus, Quercus*) is depicted by a bar histogram or by a point on a continuous curve (as in Figure 4.1). Major types or types of particular interest are given individual curves. Curves may be superimposed using standardized symbols for major taxa, but this can reduce clarity in a complex diagram. The pollen sum for each sample can be included on the diagram or, if standardized, mentioned in the text. Ruled vertical lines between pollen types may enhance clarity.

4. The scale used for relative or absolute frequency data should be consistent throughout the diagram and clearly indicated. In Figure 4.1, the scale is at the bottom of the diagram. If it is necessary to use an exaggerated scale for minor types, this should be clearly indicated, as shown for the Gramineae and Compositae curves in Figure 4.1.

5. The conventional order for types along the top horizontal axis is arboreal taxa, shrubs, herbs, and spores. Alternative orderings include ecological groupings or distance groupings (local, regional, long distance).

Summary or composite curves indicating how the sum is divided into arboreal, shrub, and herbaceous components, or into other subunits, are often included on complex stratigraphic diagrams.

How are the patterns displayed on a stratigraphic phytolith or pollen diagram interpreted in terms of research questions? The first step is typically to divide up the sequence into biozones. Biozones are not determined by stratigraphy or radiocarbon dates, but by changes in the contained pollen or phytolith data. There are two approaches to establishing biozones: the "subjective" approach and the "objective," or numerical, approach (Moore et al. 1991). In the subjective approach, zone lines are placed in the sequence where the analyst sees several concurrent changes in microfossil types that have significance, for example, as ecological indicators. Although pollen or phytolith assemblages—the taxa present and their abundances—are key to establishing biozones, other factors may be taken into account, such as concentration values, patterning of particulate charcoal, and the lithology of the sequence. For a discussion of numerical approaches to biozonation, see Birks and Gordon's *Numerical Methods in Quaternary Pollen Analysis* (1985).

Division of a stratigraphic sequence into biozones highlights changes in pollen or phytolith assemblages that are interpretable in terms of vegetation. There is no one-to-one correspondence in representation of species in the fossil record and in vegetation cover, however. Differences among plant taxa in productivity, transport, and preservation of pollen and phytoliths makes it important to study the relationship between vegetation cover and microfossil deposition. This can be accomplished, for example, by collecting samples of modern pollen rain from known vegetation formations and modeling the relationship between the composition of the vegetation and the pollen assemblages. Similarly, phytoliths can be extracted from surface soil samples and assemblages compared to vegetation growing in the sampled area. Past vegetation around a coring locality can then be reconstructed from microfossil assemblages by direct reference to corresponding patterns between present-day vegetation and contemporary pollen or phytolith assemblages. Alternatively, or in addition to this approach, the presence of one or more key pollen or phytolith types can be used to infer occurrence of a certain plant community in the past.

How are human impacts on the landscape identified in stratigraphic pollen and phytolith records? Because different kinds of human activities change vegetation in different ways, there is no single indicator that denotes human influence in all environments. However, plant cultivation and animal husbandry do have certain common features that result in recognizable traces in microfossil records (Faegri et al. 1989). To create fields, for example, trees and shrubs are removed to allow light to penetrate to the crops. This often involves burning of vegetation, which sends particulate charcoal into the air. Open soil permits the growth of weeds that otherwise would not become established. Reduced soil fertility leads to fields being taken out of production, or fallowed, and regrowth of natural vegetation. Grazing of domesticated animals on fallowed fields alters natural succession. To interpret sedimentary sequences, then, the analyst models these processes for particular environmental and cultural settings using the approaches discussed earlier. It can be challenging, however, to distinguish between "natural" influences on vegetation—changes in rainfall patterns, volcanic eruptions, forest fires, and the like—and the impact of humans on the landscape. Blanketing by volcanic ash, use of fire to clear fields, or a drying trend can all reduce tree cover in lowland tropical forests, for example. To sort out the contributions of nature and humans to reducing levels of arboreal pollen in a sequence, one has to consider both the magnitude of observed changes and the association or lack of association of multiple indicators.

Finally, a word on dating sedimentary pollen or phytolith sequences. Radiocarbon, or ^{14}C, dating is widely used to establish chronologies in sediment cores. Accurate, closely spaced radiocarbon ages are essential for establishing the chronology of short-duration events, as well as for determining sedimentation rates necessary for influx calculations. Dating of total organic carbon from bulk sediment samples was once common in palynology, but problems have long been recognized with this approach (Faegri et al. 1989). Younger carbon from roots may penetrate deposits, for example, and although rootlets can be removed mechanically from recent samples, they may become indistinguishable from the matrix in older deposits, yielding ages that are too young. Another problem encountered in dating freshwater sediments is "old-carbon error," that is, incorporation of carbon that is ^{14}C deficient into lake deposits (MacDonald et al. 1991). This can yield radiocarbon ages that are too old. Accelerator mass spectrometry (AMS) dating, which requires much smaller samples, has largely mitigated these problems, because individual terrestrial plant tissues, concentrations of terrestrial plant pollen, or organic material extracted from phytoliths can now be dated directly.

In summary, stratigraphic pollen and phytolith records are invaluable sources of data on past vegetation, making it well worth the effort for nonspecialists to seek out such studies, unpack their complex diagrams, and learn to evaluate their results. In recent decades studying sedimentary sequences for the purpose of investigating human–environment interrelationships has become an increasingly common part of paleoethnobotany; this will be illustrated in the case studies that follow.

References

Baxter, Michael J. 1994 *Exploratory Multivariate Analysis in Archaeology*. Edinburgh University Press, Edinburgh.
———— 2003 *Statistics in Archaeology*. Arnold, London.
Birks, H. J. B. and A. D. Gordon 1985 *Numerical Methods in Quaternary Pollen Analysis*. Academic Press, London.
Drennan, Robert D. 2010 *Statistics for Archaeologists: A Commonsense Approach*. Second ed. Springer, New York.
Faegri, Knut, Peter Emil Kaland and Knut Krzywinski 1989 *Textbook of Pollen Analysis by Knut Faegri and Johs Iversen*. Fourth ed. John Wiley and Sons, Chichester, England.
Fearn, M. L. and Kam-biu Liu 1995 Maize pollen of 3500 B.P. from southern Alabama. *American Antiquity* 60(1):109–117.
Flannery, Kent V. 1986 Food procurement area and preceramic diet at Guilá Naquitz. In *Guilá Naquitz: Archaic Foraging and Early Agriculture in Oaxaca, Mexico*, edited by K. V. Flannery, pp. 303–317. Academic Press, Orlando.
Grimm, L. G. and P. R. Yarnold (editors) 1995 *Reading and Understanding Multivariate Statistics*. American Psychological Association, Washington, DC.
Hubbard, R. N. L. B. 1980 Development of agriculture in Europe and the Near East: Evidence from quantitative studies. *Economic Botany* 34:51–67.
Kadane, Joseph B. 1988 Possible statistical contributions to paleoethnobotany. In *Current Paleoethnobotany: Analytical Methods and Cultural Interpretations of Archaeological Plant Remains*, edited by C. A. Hastorf and V. S. Popper, pp. 206–214. University of Chicago Press, Chicago.
MacDonald, G. M., R. P. Beukens and W. E. Kieser 1991 Radiocarbon dating of limnic sediments: A comparative analysis and discussion. *Ecology* 72(3):1150–1155.
Marquardt, William H. 1974 A statistical analysis of constituents in human paleofecal specimens from Mammoth Cave. In *Archeology of the Mammoth Cave Area*, edited by P. J. Watson, pp. 193–202. Academic Press, New York.

Miller, Naomi F. 1988 Ratios in paleoethnobotanical analysis. In *Current Paleoethnobotany: Analytical Methods and Cultural Interpretations of Archaeological Plant Remains*, edited by C. A. Hastorf and V. S. Popper, pp. 72–85. University of Chicago Press, Chicago.

Moore, P. D., J. A. Webb and M. E. Collinson 1991 *Pollen Analysis*. Second ed. (reprinted in 1999) Blackwell Scientific Publications, Oxford.

Pearsall, Deborah M. 2015 *Paleoethnobotany: A Handbook of Procedures*. Third ed. Routledge, New York.

Pielou, E. C. 1984 *The Interpretation of Ecological Data: A Primer on Classification and Ordination*. John Wiley & Sons, New York.

Raviele, Maria E. 2011 Experimental assessment of maize phytolith and starch taphonomy in carbonized cooking residues. *Journal of Archaeological Science* 38:2708–2713.

Shennan, Stephen 1997 *Quantifying Archaeology*. Second ed. Edinburgh University Press, Edinburgh.

Thomas, David Hurst 1986 *Refiguring Anthropology: First Principles of Probability and Statistics*. Waveland Press, Prospect Heights.

Tukey, John W. 1977 *Exploratory Data Analysis*. Addison-Wesley Publishing Company, Reading.

Twiss, Page 1992 Predicted world distribution of C_3 and C_4 grass phytoliths. In *Phytolith Systematics: Emerging Issues*, edited by G. Rapp, Jr. and S. C. Mulholland, pp. 113–128. Plenum Press, New York.

——— 2001 A curmudgeon's view of grass phytolithology. In *Phytoliths: Applications in Earth Sciences and Human History*, edited by J. D. Meunier and F. Colin, pp. 7–25. A.A. Balkema, Lisse.

VanPool, Todd L. and Robert D. Leonard 2011 *Quantitative Analysis in Archaeology*. Wiley-Blackwell, Chichester, West Sussex, UK.

Velleman, Paul F. and David C. Hoaglin 1981 *Applications, Basics, and Computing of Exploratory Data Analysis*. Duxbury Press, Boston.

PART II

Interpreting Paleoethnobotanical Data

Case Studies

5

INVESTIGATING NEANDERTHAL LIFEWAYS THROUGH PALEOETHNOBOTANY

Glossary

Holocene   geological epoch that began after the Pleistocene, approximately 11,700 years ago, characterized by warmer temperatures following the last glacial period.

hominin   humans and their closest fossil ancestors.

humans, archaic   in paleoanthropology, members of the genus *Homo* who had brain sizes that overlapped with modern humans, but distinctive anatomical features, such as prominent brow ridges and the lack of a prominent chin. Neanderthals (*Homo neanderthalensis* or *H. sapiens neanderthalensis*) are a well-known example.

humans, (anatomically) modern   in paleoanthropology, large-brained members of the genus *Homo* with appearances consistent with the range of variation of living human populations. Referred to as *modern humans* in this chapter.

Mousterian   an archaeological flaked stone tool industry associated primarily with Neanderthal populations of the Middle Paleolithic.

Neolithic   the cultural period (literally, New Stone Age) associated with the beginning of farming.

Paleolithic, middle   a subdivision of the Paleolithic, or Old Stone Age, cultural period, dated approximately 300,000 to 40,000 years ago.

Pleistocene   geological epoch spanning the most recent period of repeated continental glaciations, dating approximately 2.5 million to 11,700 years ago.

Introduction

Direct data on plant–people interrelationships drop off as one goes back through time in the archaeological record. There are fewer early Holocene campsites than Neolithic villages, and even fewer sites of Pleistocene age, but smaller site numbers are not the whole story. Plant macroremains, traditionally an important source of data on foodways, are preserved and recovered much more rarely in Pleistocene than in later contexts. The discovery that microfossils, especially starch and phytoliths, can be well preserved in sediments of Pleistocene age, as well as on stone tools and in dental calculus (hardened dental plaque), has provided a new window into the most ancient patterns of plant use by humans and human ancestors. In this case study we will explore how paleoethnobotany has contributed to investigating one of the major debates in human evolution: the nature of Neanderthal lifeways and how they differed from those of early modern human populations who overlapped with, and eventually replaced, Neanderthals and other archaic humans.

Background to the Case Study

The prevailing view of human evolution is that modern humans spread out of Africa sometime after 200,000 BP and that the adaptive advantages held by these populations in terms of cognition and behavior allowed them to outcompete and ultimately replace archaic humans (including Neanderthals) throughout the Old World (Henry 2003b). In the cognitive domain, it has been argued that Neanderthals had inferior language, planning, artistic, motor, and symbolling abilities compared to modern humans. Studies of stone tools have indicated a high degree of Neanderthal competence in a domain involving complex production procedures, however.

In the absence of compelling evidence for cognitive inferiority, differences in behavioral organization may have helped modern humans outcompete Neanderthals. For example, Neanderthals may have engaged in less efficient subsistence strategies than early modern humans, such as relying on scavenging of big game and opportunistic encounters of animals rather than preplanned hunting (Henry 2003b).

Gathering a diverse array of plant foods characterizes the foodways of many living hunter-gatherers (Crittenan and Schnorr 2017). There is no one pan-forager diet, but rather a wide variation based on ecology, seasonality, and resource availability. Traditional food processing (cooking, pounding, winnowing, cutting, peeling) significantly increases nutritional accessibility of both meats and plant foods (Crittenan and Schnorr 2017). Cooking, especially, had substantial evolutionary significance due to the net rise in energy value of cooked foods: even small improvements in energy balance can confer significant advantages in reduced costs of digesting meats and detoxifying and defending against pathogens and increased digestibility of starch and protein (Carmody and Wrangham 2009). Did Neanderthals follow practices similar to those of living foragers, or were modern foraging and food preparation practices limited to early modern humans? Paleoethnobotanical data can help address these issues of diet and subsistence practices.

It should also be possible to test archaeologically several proposed differences in archaic and modern human social organization, for example, to investigate whether Neanderthals lived in family units, with male/female division of labor (Henry 2003b). Based on observations of living foragers, this family structure should be reflected in campsites, with a hearth and sleeping area for a single family. Studying intrasite activity patterns can provide insights into social organization; botanical data can play a vital role here as well.

After modern humans emerged in Africa and began to disperse across Eurasia, they encountered late archaic humans at different times and places. The degree to which these older populations were absorbed varied by region (Trinkaus 2007). Morphological analysis of modern human remains dating to ca. 33,000 BP indicated modest levels of assimilation of Neanderthals into early modern populations in Europe, for example. Reanalysis of teeth from Grotta del Cavallo, Italy, dated 45,000 to 43,000 BP, identified those specimens as modern humans, not Neanderthal as previously thought (Benazzi et al. 2011). The associated Uluzzian tool complex, which included personal ornaments, worked bone, and colorants, was not a Neanderthal industry. Modern humans spread to northwestern Europe by 44,200 to 41,500 BP (Higham et al. 2011, Kent's Cavern, UK). AMS dating of 40 key Mousterian and Neanderthal sites, from Russia to Spain, established that the Mousterian ended by 41,030 to 39,260 cal. BP and that Neanderthals disappeared at different times in different regions (Higham et al. 2014). There was thus 2,600 to 5,400 years of overlap between Neanderthals and modern humans. Rather than a rapid model of replacement, Higham et al. (2014) argued for a more complex biological and cultural mosaic of several thousand years.

As we will see, paleoethnobotany has contributed in no small way to an emerging viewpoint that Neanderthal behavior was more varied and more complex, and in some aspects, more similar to that of modern humans, than would have been thought possible 20 years ago. In reviewing literature for this case, it seemed that virtually everything I read demanded "unlearning" some aspect of perceived wisdom on Neanderthals. The case will focus on three major areas of research on Neanderthal lifeways: diet (and its similarity/difference to that of early modern humans), plant–people interrelationships beyond diet (medicinal plant use, fuel selection, environmental management), and social organization. With each new analytical approach and study, it becomes increasingly difficult to argue that many significant behavioral differences existed between Neanderthals and early modern humans in terms of their plant–people interrelationships. Table 5.1 lists the scientific names of plants mentioned in the text.

TABLE 5.1 Scientific names of plants mentioned in the text (does not include plants referred to by scientific name in the text)

acorn	*Quercus*
African false banana	*Ensete ventricosum*
African potato	*Hypoxis*
African wine palm	*Hyphaene petersiana*
annual mercury	*Mercurialis annua*
Atlantic pistachio	*Pistacia atlantica*
birch	*Betula*
chamomile	*Matricaria chamomilla*
cycad	Zamiaceae
date palm	*Phoenix dactylifera*
fig-tree family	Moraceae
forest moss	*Physcomitrella patens*
grape	*Vitis vinifera*
grass	Poaceae or Gramineae
grey shag mushroom	*Coprinopsis cinerea*
gymnosperm	Gymnospermae
horse–tail rush	*Equisetum*
legume	Fabaceae or Leguminosae
nettle-leaved goosefoot	*Chenopodium murale*
nut–grass	*Cyperus*
palm	Arecaceae or Palmae
pistachio	*Pistacia*
pine nut	*Pinus koraiensis*

(Continued)

TABLE 5.1 (Continued)

poplar	*Populus trichocarpa*
reed	*Phragmites*
sedge	Cyperaceae
sorghum	*Sorghum*
split gill mushroom	*Schizophyllum commune*
waterlily family	Nympheae
wild barley	*Hordeum*
wild/bulbous barley	*Hordeum spontaneum/bulbosum*
wild radish	*Raphanus raphanistrum*
yarrow	*Achillea millefolium*

Neanderthal Diet(s): The Contribution of Plant and Animal Foods

Neanderthals as Top Predators: Faunal and Isotope Evidence

An abundance of faunal remains, especially those of large, extinct herbivores, in many Neanderthal sites has long supported the view that Neanderthals ate quantities of meat. A measure of lifelong diet—stable isotope analysis of skeletal remains—supports this view: overall, nitrogen isotope ($\partial^{15}N$) studies have indicated that Neanderthals were highly carnivorous (Schoeninger 2014) (Box 5.1). Interestingly, complete carnivory exists in only one living primate; the highest rate among living human foragers is 60 percent animal products, including fat-rich meats. Isotope studies of living foragers show that, like Neanderthals, they can have high $\partial^{15}N$ values that overlap with other predators in their ecosystems (for example, Great Basin foragers overlap extensively with Great Basin canids) (Schoeninger 2014). There was similar overlap in $\partial^{15}N$ values between Neanderthal individuals and European hyenas contemporary to them.

BOX 5.1   RECONSTRUCTING DIET USING STABLE ISOTOPE ANALYSIS

Analyzing skeletal remains for carbon (C) and nitrogen (N) stable isotopes—variants of the same element that differ in the number of neutrons—provides a measure of the relative contributions to lifelong diet of marine and terrestrial foods, or of plants of different photosynthetic pathways. The stable isotopes of a given element, such as ^{12}C and ^{13}C of carbon and ^{14}N and ^{15}N of nitrogen, react chemically in the same way, but at different rates, due to this difference in atomic weight. For example, during the process of photosynthesis, plants incorporate ^{12}C, the most abundant carbon isotope, preferentially into their tissues over ^{13}C, giving plant tissue a lower ratio of ^{13}C to ^{12}C than the ratio in air. Nitrogen-fixing plants, other terrestrial plants, and marine plants differ in absorption of ^{14}N and ^{15}N. This process of isotope ratio change is called fractionation (Hoefs 1987). The ratio of two isotopes (i.e., $^{15}N/^{14}N$) is expressed in delta (∂) values in parts per thousand (‰), relative to a standard.

Stable carbon and nitrogen isotopes can be used for reconstructing ancient diets because differences in isotope ratios in plant tissues are passed from one trophic level to the next (i.e., up the food chain) to the consumers of those plants, with additional fractionation factors. For instance, $\partial^{15}N$ values increase up the food chain, from plants, to herbivores, to carnivores. Fractionation between trophic levels for nitrogen is around +3‰ (Minagawa and Wada 1984; Schoeninger and DeNiro 1984). Within a given food-web, differences in $\partial^{15}N$ values among omnivores like humans will reflect the relative consumption of meat (degree of carnivory) by those individuals.

Terrestrial plants follow one of three photosynthetic pathways, referred to as the C3, C4, and CAM pathways, which produce different $\partial^{13}C$ values in plant tissues (van der Merwe 1982). For instance, $\partial^{13}C$ values for C4 plants (tropical and warm-season grasses and a few other plants) are higher (less negative, −7 to −16‰) than those for C3 plants (trees, most shrubs and herbs, and temperate cool-season grasses; −20 to −35‰)(O'Leary 1981). Differences in $\partial^{13}C$ values among individuals will reflect their relative consumption of C4 and C3 plants; in the Americas this is a useful indicator for the consumption of maize, a C4 plant. Although researchers can use mean $\partial^{13}C$ and $\partial^{15}N$ values for classes of plants and animals (C3 plants, C4 plants, legumes, etc.) to calculate the percentage of those foods in diet, a better approach is to use actual $\partial^{13}C$ and $\partial^{15}N$ values for plant and animal foods in the foodweb of the human population being studied. See Pearsall (2015) for further details and discussion of preservation issues.

Although the core meat source for Neanderthals in all regions appears to have been ungulates (hoofed mammals), systematically recovered faunal data have indicated flexibility in foraging systems, with adaptations to different environments and variation in species hunted. A wide variety of fauna was utilized in the Mediterranean region, for example, including small prey and marine resources (Fiorenza et al. 2015). In the mammoth steppe ecosystem of northern Europe, dietary diversity was lower. For example, isotope analysis of Neanderthals and their potential prey from the Troisième cavern of Goyet, Scladina, and Spy Cave sites, Belgium, indicated that all Neanderthals studied grouped with animal carnivores and showed low dietary diversity: most dietary protein came from megaherbivores such as mammoths (Wißing et al. 2016). $^{15}\partial N$ studies based on collagen, which reflects the isotopic signals of main dietary protein sources rather than whole diet, have likely underestimated the contribution of plants to the Neanderthal diet, however (Fiorenza et al. 2015). This is because plants have much lower protein densities than meat: moderate quantities of meat consumption can mask significant plant consumption.

A promising way around this problem is nitrogen isotope analysis of individual amino acids, the building blocks of protein (Naito et al. 2016). This approach can be used to determine the trophic positions (i.e., T1, primary producer; T2, primary consumer; T3, secondary consumer) of different animal species. $\partial^{15}N$ of the amino acid phenylalanine reflects $\partial^{15}N$ of the nitrogen source of the ecosystem, that is, the primary producers, or plants in the case of terrestrial systems. The isotopic spacing between this amino acid and that of glutamic acid, which shows a large prey–predator shift, estimates the trophic position of animals. Samples from two Neanderthal individuals from Spy Cave were analyzed, as well as faunal specimens from a nearby contemporary site. Using the new approach, there was larger interindividual variation between the Neanderthals than shown in the earlier bulk collagen study. Terrestrial herbivores also showed a wider range of values. Furthermore, Neanderthals were not the top predators in the ecosystem: hyenas had the highest tropic position estimate, followed by wolves and then Neanderthals. The authors estimated that up to 20 percent of dietary protein in the diet of Spy Neanderthals could have originated from plant foods. Given that wild plants generally have low levels of protein, this level indicated potential for a high contribution of carbohydrates to diet.

In summary, there are biases in $^{15}\partial$N studies based on collagen and in the zooarchaeological and paleoethnobotanical records of Neanderthal sites that have presented challenges for determining the importance of different animal species, and of the relative contribution of plants and animals, in the Neanderthal diet. Available data have indicated that Neanderthals were not vegetarians, but neither were they living on meat alone. Amino acid isotope analysis confirmed that plant foods contributed to Neanderthal diet even in the mammoth steppes of Europe. What plants were on the menu, and what does plant use tell us about Neanderthal lifeways?

Neanderthals as Foragers: Botanical Evidence

Near East and Mediterranean

Flotation-recovered charred seeds and other potential vegetal foods were among the remains found in Kebara Cave, Israel (Lev et al. 2005). The Mousterian (Neanderthal) levels of Kebara date to ca. 65,000 to 48,000 BP. A total of 3,956 seeds or fruit fragments were identified; 3,313 of these were legume seeds (Papilionaceae) of three sizes (small, medium, and large seeded) (Table 5.2). Other taxa represented by more than several seeds/fruit fragments include Atlantic pistachio, acorn, annual mercury, grasses, and nettle-leaved goosefoot. Seasonality of remains indicated gathering in the spring, early summer, and fall, with spring being the main gathering season. Although legume plants could have been used as fire starters, most charred seeds were mature or almost mature, suggesting consumption by the cave's users. Almost-ripe legume pods were perhaps gathered and parched before consumption, which resulted in deposition of material lost to charring. Pistachio nuts are good oil sources, and also commonly parched before consumption. Of taxa with edible underground storage organs (USOs) available today in the vicinity of the cave, seeds of wild radish, nut-grass, and wild/bulbous barley were present in the deposits (no actual USOs were recovered). High-caloric resources included acorns, legumes, and cereals. The only evidence of use of fresh fruits was one grape seed. Twelve of the identified plants had potential medicinal uses. In summary, the Neanderthals of Kebara Cave apparently relied heavily on plant foods from a variety of environments, they cooked their vegetal food, and they used the cave for multiple seasons (Lev et al. 2005).

Phytolith analysis of sediments from Amud Cave, Israel, occupied from ca. 70,000 to 55,000 BP, indicated use of a broad spectrum of plants by Neanderthals from at least the end of the Middle Paleolithic (Madella et al. 2002). Samples were analyzed from intact hearths and general cave sediments. Mineralogical analyses revealed evidence for wood fires. Phytoliths were abundant and well preserved from all Middle Paleolithic cave strata, but assemblages were not homogeneous. Hearth sediments had higher concentrations of phytoliths from dicot wood and leaves, for example. Herbaceous monocots, including grasses, also contributed substantially to assemblages. Well-developed phytoliths characteristic of mature grass seed heads made up between 10 and 50 percent of grass phytoliths present in strata. Palm and fig family phytoliths were also recovered. In summary, the Neanderthals of Amud Cave burned wood as

TABLE 5.2 Mousterian plant remains from Kebara Cave (after Lev 1992, Latin names after Danin 1998, common names after Fragman et al. 1999). (Table 2 from Lev, Efraim, Mordechai Kislev and Ofer Bar-Yosef. 2005. Mousterian vegetal food in Kebara Cave, Mt. Carmel. *Journal of Archaeological Science* 32:475–484. Reproduced with permission of Elsevier.) Notice that although richness of the botanical assemblage was high, a few resources dominated in terms of numbers of seeds recovered

Latin name	Family	No. of seeds	Common name/figure no. ()/Stratigraphic level or unit []/optional medicinal uses *
Aegilops geniculata/peregrina	Gramineae	2	Ovate goat-grass [VII, X]
Astragalus echinus	Papilionaceae	1	Milk-vetch [IX–X]
Avena barbata/wiestii	Gramineae	1	Slender oat (Fig. 3) [VII] *
Bellevalia sp.	Liliaceae	2	Roman squill [VII]
cf. *Brachypodium distachyon*	Gramineae	2	Purple false-brome [X]
cf. *Bromus*	Gramineae	1	Brome cf. [IX–X]
Carthamus sp.	Compositae	1	Safflower [IX–X] *
Carthamus tenuis	Compositae	1	Slender safflower [IX–X] *
Chenopodium murale	Chenopodiaceae	19	Nettle-leaved goosefoot [VII, IX–X]
Cicer pinnatifidum	Papilionaceae	1	Judean chickpea [IX–X] *
cf. *Cynodon dactylon*	Gramineae	1	Bermuda grass cf. [X]
cf. *Cyperus*	Cyperaceae	2	Nut-grass cf. [VIII] *
Echium angustifolium/judaeum	Boraginaceae	1	Hispid/judean viper's bugloss [IX–X]
cf. *Euphorbia aleppica*	Euphorbiaceae	1	Pine spurge cf. [VII] *
Galium sect. *Kolgyda*	Rubiaceae	6	Bedstraw [VII, VIII, IX–X, X]
Hordeum spontaneum	Gramineae	2	Wild barley [IX–X] *
Hordeum spotaneum/bulbosum	Gramineae	1	Wild/bulbous barley [VII]
Hymenocarpos circinnatus	Papilionaceae	1	Disk trefoil [VII]
Lathyrus hierosolymitanus	Papilionaceae	1	Jerusalem vetchling (Fig. 4) [VII]
Lathyrus inconspicuous	Papilionaceae	1	Small-flowered vetchling [IX–X]
Lathyrus sect. *Cicercula*	Papilionaceae	16	Vetchling [VII]
cf. *Lathyrus* sect. *Cicercula*	Papilionaceae	56	Vetchling cf. [VII, VIII, IX–X, X]
Lens sp.	Papilionaceae	247	Lentil [VII, VIII, IX, X]
Malva sp.	Malvaceae	1	Mallow [IX–X] *
Mercurialis annua	Euphorbiaceae	43	Annual mercury [VII, VIII, IX–X, X]
Onosma gigantea	Boraginaceae	1	Giant golden-drop [X]
Onosma orientalis	Boraginaceae	5	Syrian golden-drop [VII, IX–X]
Pistacia atlantica (nutlet fragments)	Anacardiaceae	503	Atlantic pistachio (Fig. 5) [VII, VIII, IX–X, X] *
Pisum fulvum/Vicia palaestina	Papilionaceae	2	Yellow wild pea/Palestine vetch [VII]
Pisum fulvum/Vicia narbonensis/peregrina	Papilionaceae	1	Yellow wild pea/purple broad-bean/rambling vetch [IX–X]
Quercus sp. (shell fragments)	Fagaceae	43	Oak [VII, VIII, IX–X, X] *
Raphanus raphanistrum	Cruciferae	1	Wild radish [VII] *
cf. *Raphanus raphanistrum*	Cruciferae	1	Wild radish cf. [VII] *
Scorpiurus muricatus	Papilionaceae	1	Two-flowered caterpillar (prickly scorpiontail) [VII]
cf. *Scorpiurus muricatus*	Papilionaceae	1	Two-flowered caterpillar cf. (prickly scorpiontail) [VII]
cf. *Silene aegyptiaca*	Caryophullaceae	1	Egyptian campion cf. [VIII]
Trifolium sp.	Papilionaceae	1	Clover (trefoil) [VII]
Vicia cuspidata/lathyroides	Papilionaceae	8	Spring vetch [VII, VIII, IX–X, X]
Vicia ervilia	Papilionaceae	8	Bitter vetch (Fig. 6) [VII, IX–X, X] *
Vicia laxiflora/tetrasperma	Papilionaceae	1	Slender/smooth tare [IX–X]
Vicia lutea/sativa/sericocarpa	Papilionaceae	1	Yellow/common (true) vetch [VII]
cf. *Vicia narbonensis*	Papilionaceae	1	Purple broad-bean cf. [VII]
Vicia palaestina	Papilionaceae	1	Palestine vetch [IX–X]
Vicia palaestina/sativa	Papilionaceae	1	Palestine/common (true) vetch [IX–X]
Vicia palaestina/villosa	Papilionaceae	1	Palestine/winter (hairy) vetch [VII]
Vicia peregrina	Papilionaceae	1	Rambling vetch [VIII]
Vicia pubescens	Papilionaceae	2	Vetch [VIII]
Vitis vinifera ssp. *sylvestris*	Vitaceae	1	Wild grape-vine [IX–X] *
Large-seed legumes	Papilionaceae	712	[VII, VIII, IX, IX–X, X]
Medium-seed legumes	Papilionaceae	1369	[VII, VIII, IX, IX–X, X]
Small-seed legumes	Papilionaceae	877	[VII, VIII, IX, IX–X, X]
Unidentified		249	All units
Total		4205	

fuel, used palm and fig leaves and/or fruits, brought grass vegetative tissues into the cave for fuel or bedding, and gathered mature grass fruiting heads as food. Gathering of grass seeds at Amud and legumes at Kebara Cave (discussed earlier), together with the faunal evidence for use of small mammals and nonmammals, demonstrated that broad-spectrum foraging (i.e., use of an increasingly diverse array of resources) was part of Paleolithic lifeways long before its proposed foundation for the appearance of agriculture (Madella et al. 2002).

Direct evidence for consumption of plant foods by Neanderthals in the Near East was first revealed by starch and phytoliths recovered from dental calculus of an individual from Shanidar Cave, Iraq (Mousterian levels dated 50,000–44,000 BP) (Henry et al. 2011a; see results for Spy Cave, later). Three teeth from the Shanidar III skeleton were studied; a total of 93 microfossils were recovered (Table 5.3). Most were starch grains: Triticeae (cf. *Hordeum*, barley, on all teeth), cooked Triticeae, probable legume (Fabaceae), a possible underground storage organ, and several other kinds of unidentified and damaged types of starch (some damage was characteristic of cooking). Date palm *(Phoenix* spp.) phytoliths were also recovered from all teeth. The overall pattern of damage suggests Triticeae grains were cooked by heating in the presence of water (boiling, baking) rather than a dryer form of cooking like parching or popping. Results indicated that Neanderthals in both environments (Mediterranean, northern Europe [see later]) included a spectrum of plant foods in their diets, that some were cooked, and that several required moderate to high levels of preparation (i.e., husking grass seeds, digging USOs). In response to Collins and Copeland (2011), who argued that the damage observed on some starch grains was due to spontaneous gelatinization over time rather than cooking, Henry et al. (2011b) argued this was unlikely in the dry archaeological contexts of the sites. Furthermore, starch recovered from equally ancient stone tools from Shanidar Cave showed no evidence for gelatinization.

Direct evidence for consumption of plant foods and potential medicinal compounds was recovered from dental calculus of Neanderthals from El Sidrón, Spain, dated to 50,600 to 47,300 BP (K. Hardy et al. 2012). Mass spectrometry (a technique for identifying organic compounds) was combined with morphological analysis of plant microfossils in a study of 10 calculus samples from five individuals. Starch was recovered from 9 of the 10 samples; 2 of these included granules that showed evidence of cooking with dry heat. Starches of different sizes and shapes were recovered, suggesting that more than one plant genus was consumed. Mass spectrometry results also indicated a diversity of carbohydrate sources. The presence of the compounds azulene and coumarin in one individual was consistent with consumption of bitter-tasting plants such as yarrow and chamomile. These have no nutritional value, suggesting self-medication. Two individuals inhaled woody smoke; one had contact with oil shale/ bitumen. Exposure to smoke is consistent with cooking, a key technological advance that improved carbohydrate digestibility (K. Hardy et al. 2012, K. Hardy et al. 2015).

DNA was also extracted from the dental calculus of El Sidrón Neanderthals (Weyrich et al. 2017; see results from Spy, later). DNA from El Sidrón individuals was a combination of bacterial, archaeal (single-celled organisms), eukaryotic (plants, animals, fungi), and viral DNA. The bacteria taxa that dominate in the modern human mouth also characterized these Neanderthals. DNA from edible split gill mushroom, pine nuts, forest moss, and poplar was identified in the El Sidrón calculus samples; no DNA sequences matching large herbivores or suggesting high meat consumption were found. Presence of DNA from plant fungal pathogens suggested that moldy herbaceous material, which contains the natural antibiotic penicillin, was consumed. Consumption of poplar, which contains the active ingredient in aspirin, and moldy herbaceous material both support self-medication by this individual, as inferred by K. Hardy et al. (2012). Overall, the DNA profile of microorganisms from dental calculus of El Sidrón Neanderthals resembled that of modern foragers who consumed limited quantities of meat.

TABLE 5.3 Counts and descriptions of plant microfossils recovered from the dental calculus from Shanidar III. (Table 1 from Henry, Amanda G., Alison S. Brooks and Dolores R. Piperno. 2011a. Microfossils in calculus demonstrate consumption of plants and cooked foods in Neanderthal diets (Shanidar III, Iraq; Spy I and II, Belgium). *Proceedings of the National Academy of Sciences of the United States of America* 108(2):486–491. Reproduced with permission of the National Academy of Sciences of the United States.)

Tooth no.	Type 1 Triticeae (cf. *Hordeum*)	Type 1 cooked	Type 2	Type 3	Type 4	Other	Other cooked	Dmg/Enc	*Phoenix* spp. (date palm) phytolith	Other phytolith	Total
Shanidar III tooth 3 LuC	4	0	2	4	1	2	0	4	7	3	27
Shanidar III tooth 4 RM[3]	4	3	0	2	0	7	2	5	7	1	31
Shanidar III tooth 5 LI$_2$	2	12	0	1	1	0	14	3	2	0	35
Totals per type	10	15	2	7	2	9	16	12	16	4	93

Type 1: Medium, circular to oval to D shaped, lenticular when turned, center usually dimpled/marked hilum, usually with clear lamellae visible under normal light but always visible at least under polarized light, cross arms are occasionally faded, line down center of grain when turned, sometimes dimpled. Type 2: Small, decorated oval with distinct projections, center hilum, clean cross. Type 3: Small, oval to circular, mostly central dimpled hilum occasionally with a fissure that crosses the grain entirely, too small for other features. Type 4: Small, subangular/rectangular, center dimpled hilum, clean cross. Other: A variety of unique/unusual forms that do not fit into the other types. Dmg/Enc: A variety of starches that may belong to one of the named types but are too damaged (cracked, broken) or encrusted (covered in calculus material) to be confidently identified.

An alternative explanation for the presence of nonedible, potentially medicinal plants, such as yarrow and chamomile, in dental calculus has been proposed: that Neanderthals ate herbivore stomach contents, or chyme (Buck and Stringer 2014; Buck et al. 2016). There is ethnographic evidence for consumption of chyme, also referred to as gastrophagy, for its taste and health benefits (i.e., vitamins, minerals, and carbohydrates, which may be lacking in a diet low in plant foods). Some foragers, like the Hadza of Tanzania, frequently practice gastrophagy, especially at kill sites. Consuming semidigested chyme would have allowed Neanderthals to gain calories from plant sources without the cost of digesting them.

In response, K. Hardy et al. (2016), while acknowledging that chyme can be an important food source among hunter-gatherers, consider this an unlikely pathway for introducing plant microfossils and organic compounds into the dental calculus of El Sidrón individuals. Ethnographic observations have documented two ways to eat chyme: removed from the stomach or eaten with the stomach tissues. The latter would result in minimal contact between stomach contents and teeth, and would be the most likely mode of consumption for Neanderthals, for whom there is no evidence for liquid-food containers. Furthermore, neither yarrow nor chamomile is sought out by herbivores. There should also be abundant grass phytoliths in dental calculus if herbivore chyme was the source of calculus microfossils, and this was not the case at El Sidrón or at other sites (e.g., Henry et al. 2011a; Henry et al. 2014). K. Hardy et al. (2016) concluded that self-medication using medicinal plants, a well-documented behavior among living higher primates, was the most likely explanation for nonfood plant residues in dental calculus of El Sidrón Neanderthals.

In an overview of evidence from faunal and stable isotope studies of Neanderthal diets from sites in central and southeastern Iberia, Salazar-García et al. (2013) concluded that although some dietary variation existed due to environmental differences within the region, there was an overall pattern of reliance by Neanderthals on large terrestrial game, supplemented by plant foods. Paleoenvironmental studies characterized the landscape of late Iberian Neanderthals as a mosaic of habitats that were warmer, wetter, and more diverse than today. Conditions supported abundant plant foods in denser concentrations than would have been found in northern Europe. A wide variety of terrestrial game was consumed by Neanderthals in the Iberian region; according to $\partial^{15}N$ levels, almost all protein came from animal sources. Residue analysis of stone tools and dental calculus from Neanderthal individuals from the Sima de las Palomas site in southeastern Iberia (dated ca. 50,000 BP, Walker et al. 2012) provided direct evidence of the plant component of diet in this region. Eleven teeth, seven Mousterian tools, and several control samples were analyzed. Nine kinds of microfossils, including phytoliths and starch grains, were recovered from Neanderthal calculus samples. These indicated consumption of dicot leafy matter (polyhedral phytoliths), hard endosperm of seeds or nuts, grass seeds (Triticeae), and possible USOs. Starch grains in calculus largely overlapped with types on tools. No starch was present in carnivore calculus or in control samples. Finding evidence for consumption of a variety of plants on Neanderthal teeth suggested that populations were using the environment in ways comparable to later, modern human foragers. Plant consumption may have been seasonal.

Direct evidence of diet of Neanderthals living at El Salt, a Middle Paleolithic site in Spain dating to ca. 50,000 BP, was found from fecal biomarkers in site sediments (Sistiaga et al. 2014). Sterols and stanols were the focus of the study; these are lipids that are relatively stable through food chains. Specifically, the relative proportions of 5β-stanols, formed during metabolic reduction by bacteria in the gut of cholesterol (from animal foods) and phytosterols (plant-derived compounds), indicate dietary preferences. Five sediment samples were analyzed. There was a predominance of coprostanol in samples and a near absence of 5β-stigmastanol, which indicated the Neanderthals had a meat-dominated diet. These results must be tempered by the fact that animal tissues have much higher abundances of the precursor sterols than do plant tissues. Higher plant intake would be indicated by the presence of 5β-stigmastanol; this compound occurred in one sample. Taken together, the result indicated that both meat and vegetables were eaten (Sistiaga et al. 2014).

In summary, flotation-recovered macroremains; phytoliths and organic compounds from site sediments; and phytoliths, starch, organic compounds, and DNA from dental calculus or stone tools have provided evidence for Neanderthal gathering and consumption of plant foods in the Near East and Iberian Peninsula from 70,000 BP to 44,000 BP. There was evidence that some foods were prepared using wet and dry cooking techniques; that food processing techniques such as husking and pounding were utilized; and that USOs were dug. Some plants were likely consumed for their medicinal effects. Among the foods that have been documented we see legumes, other small-seeded dicots, grasses (including Triticeae, cf. *Hordeum)*, nuts (including acorn, pistachio, pine nut), palm, fig, grape, mushrooms, and unknown USOs.

Central and Northern Europe

Functional studies (combined use-wear and residue analysis) of Middle Paleolithic stone tools have demonstrated that tools were used for a variety of purposes, suggesting that European Neanderthals were broad-based foragers. For example, tools from two sites in Ukraine, Starosele (80,000–40,000 BP) and Buran Kaya III (37,000–32,000 BP), were studied by B. Hardy et al. (2001) to investigate Middle and Early Upper Paleolithic tool function and late Neanderthal subsistence. Plant residues (starch grains, wood fragments, raphids [needle-shaped crystals], cellular plant tissues) were present on artifacts from both sites. At both sites in some cases starch and wood fragments were associated with striations produced by hafting, that is, from the binding or mastic (gum or resin) of a haft. Residues from use surfaces indicated animal, bird, and woody and nonwoody plants were cut or scraped by the inhabitants of both sites. Starch representing food residues was observed on working areas of tools. In one case gymnosperm wood was identified. Evidence from both sites showed exploitation of a wide range of resources and use of tools for multiple functions (B. Hardy et al. 2001).

Functional study of 300 tools from the Middle Paleolithic site of La Quina, France, dated ca. 48,000 to 40,000 BP, also supported broad-based foraging by Neanderthals (B. Hardy 2004). Residues on tools were compared to those recovered from site sediments, and only those found exclusively on tools, and not in sediments, were considered to be related to tool use. About half the tools showed some type of functional evidence; 106 had residues. Eight different categories of plant residues were found: five defined by cell wall structures, raphids, pollen, and wood fiber. The most specific identification of wood fiber was gymnosperm tissue on four tools. Many tools had recognizable polishes, most resulting from contact with hard/high silica material, such as wood, bone/antler, or grass. A few showed the polish characteristic of soft material (hide, herbaceous plants). Animal residues were present, but less often. Neanderthals at La Quina exploited a wide range of resources, including soft and hard plants, wood, mammals, birds, and bone or antler (B. Hardy 2004). Cold-adapted Neanderthals would have needed energy sources other than meat (i.e., digestible carbohydrates), especially when animals were lean (fat depleted) (B. Hardy 2010). Starchy USOs, a concentrated source of carbohydrates, would have been available throughout the Neanderthal range, even during the coldest periods.

Lithic residue and use-wear analysis was carried out on artifacts from Payre, Ardèche, France, occupied 250,000 to 125,000 BP (B. Hardy and Mocel 2011). Zooarchaeological remains indicated that three kinds of large herbivores were hunted and other very large animals scavenged. Of 182 artifacts examined, 125 preserved some kind of functional evidence. Tools were used for a wide range of purposes, including woodworking activities, which were identified on 23 artifacts by presence of woody tissues and associated hard/high silica polish and striations. Gymnosperm and birch tissues were found. Starchy plant processing was identified on 18 artifacts by presence of starch grains, ranging in size from 3 to 16 microns, and other plant tissues. Tool morphology and use-wear patterns suggested that starchy tissues were scraped or cut, for example, removal of outer tissues from USOs. Residues of mammals, fish, and in one case bird were also identified. These results demonstrated that early Neanderthals had a varied subsistence base and had the capability to exploit small game and plant resources (B. Hardy and Moncel 2011).

Evidence for a wide range of resource use, behavioral variability, and complexity among Neanderthals was also found at Abri du Maras Cave, France (B. Hardy et al. 2013). Lithic residue and use-wear analysis was carried out on 129 stone tools from level 4, dated just after 90,000 BP. Plant residues observed included wood, bark, fibers, starch grains, calcium oxalate crystals, plant tissue, and resin. Fish remains were also found on tools. Twelve tools were used for processing fibrous plants, 2 for starchy plants, 22 for wood, and 2 for mushrooms. Some of the fibers observed were twisted, suggesting that string or cordage was being made. Multicellular monocot fibers were among those observed twisted. Construction of snares, nets, and other traps for small game and fish would have been possible with string/cordage. When the spatial distribution of artifacts by use-material was examined for the two sublevels of layer 4 (Figure 5.1), it was clear that processing of individual materials was not highly localized. Exceptions included that both artifacts with mushroom spores were in the same location (square M6), as were six of the artifacts with fiber residues (squares E6 and F6); artifacts with fish residues were found with fish remains. Faunal remains included both large herbivores, such as reindeer and horse, and small fast prey, including rabbits.

Recovery of microfossils and DNA from dental calculus of individuals from Spy Cave, Belgium (dated ca. 36,000 BP), has confirmed consumption of USOs, grasses, and mushrooms by northern European Neanderthals in the context of a meat-rich diet (Henry et al. 2011a; Weyrich et al. 2017). A total of 136 microfossils were recovered from dental calculus of two Spy individuals (Henry et al. 2011a). The most common starch type, found on three teeth, was a large ovoid form most likely from an underground storage organ. Another type resembled starch of grass seeds in the Andropogoneae tribe. Other unidentified starches occurred, but no phytoliths were present. DNA was extracted from dental calculus of the same individuals by Weyrich and colleagues. One sample had suffered environmental contamination (i.e., evidence of modern DNA), but the other (Spy II) had robust ancient bacterial, archaeal, eukaryotic, and viral DNA. The bacteria taxa that dominate in the modern human mouth also characterized Spy II. Eukaryotic DNA indicated that rhinoceros, sheep, and edible grey shag mushrooms were eaten. The DNA results agreed with the highly carnivorous lifestyle inferred from stable isotope and dental microwear studies of Spy individuals. As discussed by O'Regan et al. (2016), however, mushrooms, which have high protein values, have a wide

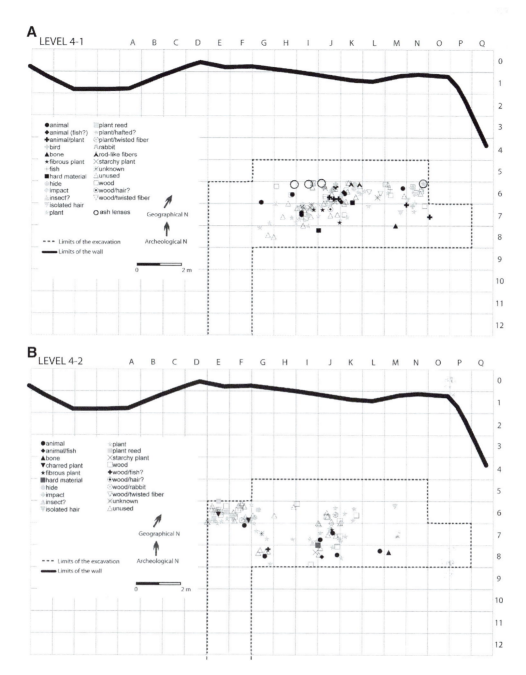

FIGURE 5.1 **A:** Spatial distribution of analyzed artifacts by use-material, from Level 4–1; **B:** Spatial distribution of analyzed artifacts by use-material, from Level 4–2. (Figures 15 and 16 from Hardy, Bruce L., Marie-Hélène Moncel, Camille Daujeard, Paul Fernandes, Philippe Béarez, Emmanuel Desclaux, Maria Gema Chacon Nararro, Simon Puaud and Rosalia Gallotti. 2013. Impossible Neanderthals? Making string, throwing projectiles and catching small game during Marine Isotope Stage 4 (Abri du Maras, France). *Quaternary Science Reviews* 82:23–40.)

Reproduced with permission of Elsevier. Notice that for the most part tools used for different purposes at Abri du Maras Cave were scattered throughout the deposits rather than clustered into discrete activity areas.

range of $\partial^{15}N$ isotope values and if consumed frequently, could potentially affect skeletal $\partial^{15}N$ values, leading to a trophic level effect (i.e., mimicking higher carnivory). The DNA from microorganisms from Spy II dental calculus (i.e., the individual's microbiota) did resemble that of hunter-gatherers and pastoralists with a frequent meat diet, however.

In summary, the record of plant use by Neanderthals of central and northern Europe extends from 250,000 to 36,000 BP. Plant residues were observed on artifacts from multiple sites in association with use-wear patterning, and starch and DNA were recovered from dental calculus of the Spy Cave Neanderthals. From the earliest times, northern European Neanderthals processed soft plant tissues with stone tools, resulting in the deposition of unidentified starch grains, raphids, and plant cellular tissues, as well as mushroom spores and monocot fibers. Processing included scraping and cutting, perhaps to remove outer tissues from USOs, and production of twisted string or cord. Tools were used for working the wood of gymnosperms, birch, and likely other species, as well as for processing game and fish. The Spy individuals consumed USOs, grass seeds, and mushrooms, but their overall diet was meat-rich.

Foraging Practices of Early Modern Humans

Near East, Europe, and Africa

A comparative study of plant residues from dental calculus and stone tools of Neanderthals and early modern humans has shed new light on the question of whether Neanderthals had a narrower diet, and were therefore at a competitive disadvantage compared to early modern humans in terms of calories, nutrition, and population that could be supported (Henry et al. 2014). As discussed earlier, this inference is largely based on faunal and stable nitrogen isotope data. Henry and colleagues sampled 30 populations from 20 sites in the Near East, Europe, and Africa. Recovered starch grains and phytoliths were assigned to types, which were defined by shared unique, diagnostic morphology and probably represented single plant taxa. Unique and damaged microfossils were counted singly as unique types. Numbers of types should thus roughly correlate with the number of plant species consumed, or richness. Richness values were calculated using a technique (Menhinick's index) that accounted for differences in sample sizes. The study revealed a wide range in the richness of plant resources used by both Neanderthal and early modern human populations (Table 5.4). Among the highest richness values for Neanderthal populations were Spy dental calculus, Shanidar dental calculus, Shanidar Mousterian tools and for early modern humans, Shanidar Upper Paleolithic tools, Klasies River Cave tools, and Skhul tools. Plant taxa and parts identified included USO of the waterlily family, grass seeds in the Andropogoneae or Paniceae tribes (AP grasses on table), grass seeds in the Triticeae tribe (two different kinds of starches), wild barley seeds, possible legume seed (subfamily Faboideae), and date palm, as well as other unknown USOs, tree fruits, and unknown types. Phytoliths were rare with a few exceptions; this suggested no contamination from burial sediments and that starch came from direct consumption of starchy foods, not chyme, because most large herbivores consume phytolith-rich grasses. Some starch grains showed evidence of cooking or grinding.

When Neanderthal and early modern human populations from the same sites were compared, overlap of microfossil types was observed. This suggested that many of the same plant foods were being consumed (Henry et al. 2014). An evaluation of richness values in terms of whether microfossil richness was a function of hominin species, stone tool technology, and/

TABLE 5.4 Populations included in this study. (Table 1 from Henry, Amanda G., Alison S. Brooks and Dolores R. Piperno. 2014. Plant foods and the dietary ecology of Neanderthals and early modern humans. *Journal of Human Evolution* 69:44–54. Reproduced with permission of Elsevier.) These are the results of a comparative study of plant residues from dental calculus and stone tools. Richness values for each site/site component (Menhinick's index, fourth column from right) take into account sample sizes (numbers of microremains) and numbers of types (identified and unique unknowns). Notice the wide range of values for both populations

	Population	Max age (ka)	Min age (ka)	Samples within pop.	Number of microremains	Number of types	Identified types	Menhinick's index	Species	Tech.	Area.
Neanderthal only	Arcy-sur-Cure (Grotte des Fées) calculus	?	?	1	0	0		0.00	N	MP/MSA	E
	Goyet 8 calculus	41	40	1	1	1		1.00	N	MP/MSA	E
	Kůlna calculus	50	40	4	19	7	Triticeae	1.61	N	MP/MSA	E
	La Chapelle-aux-Saints isolated molar calculus	68	60	1	0	0		0.00	N	MP/MSA	E
	La Ferrassie I and II calculus	74	68	8	2	2		1.41	N	MP/MSA	E
	La Quina tools	71	48	8	41	14	Triticeae, AP grass	2.19	N	MP/MSA	E
	La Quina V calculus	71	57	3	3	3	?USO, ? Triticeae	1.73	N	MP/MSA	E
	Malarnaud calculus	100	50	1	0	0		0.00	N	MP/MSA	E
	Spy I and II calculus	37	36	4	136	48	Nymphaeae (USO), AP grass	4.22	N	MP/MSA	E
Sites with both species	Abri des Merveilles Mousterian tools	49	39	7	15	10	Triticeae, AP grass	1.44	N	MP/MSA	E
	Abri des Merveilles Gravettian tools	27	25	8	10	7	Triticeae, AP grass	2.21	H	UP/LSA	E
	Gorham's Cave Mousterian tools	47	33	16	17	12	Triticeae, AP grass	2.91	N	MP/MSA	E
	Gorham's Cave Upper Paleolithic tools	18	11	7	15	10	Triticeae, AP grass, USO	2.43	H	UP/LSA	E
	Shanidar III calculus	50	46	3	96	46	Palm, *Hordeum* (Triticeae), USO, ?Fabeae	4.77	N	MP/MSA	NE
	Shanidar Mousterian tools	100	44	32	35	21	Triticeae, AP grass, USO, ? Fabeae	3.55	N	MP/MSA	NE
	Shanidar Upper Paleolithic tools	33	27	21	84	48	Triticeae, USO	5.24	H	UP/LSA	NE

(*Continued*)

TABLE 5.4 (Continued)

	Population	Max age (ka)	Min age (ka)	Samples within pop.	Number of microremains	Number of types	Identified types	Menhinick's index	Species	Tech.	Area.
Modern human only	Abri Pataud N°2 calculus	22	20	5	6	4	USO	1.63	H	UP/LSA	E
	Blombos layer BBC1 calculus	99	70	2	3	3	AP grass	1.73	H	MP/MSA	A
	Blombos layer BBC2 calculus	99	70	3	41	14	AP grass	2.19	H	MP/MSA	A
	Cro Magnon 2 calculus	28	22	1	1	1		1.00	H	UP/LSA	E
	Ishango 15, 16, 24 calculus	20	20	6	16	8	Triticeae, AP grass, USO	2.24	H	UP/LSA	A
	Ishango 17 and 23A calculus	10	8	2	5	5	Triticeae, AP grass	2.00	H	UP/LSA	A
	Klasies River Shelter 1B layer 10 calculus	102	98	1	6	5	Triticeae, ?USO	2.04	H	MP/MSA	A
	Klasies River Shelter 1B layer 10 tools	102	98	9	14	10	AP grass	2.27	H	MP/MSA	A
	Klasies River Cave 1 layer 14 calculus	102	98	9	14	10	Triticeae, AP grass, ?USO	2.67	H	MP/MSA	A
	Klasies River Cave 1 layer 14 tools	102	98	14	34	20	Triticeae, AP grass, ?USO	3.43	H	MP/MSA	A
	La Madeleine (Lartet and Christy) calculus	13	13	2	1	1		1.00	H	UP/LSA	E
	Piedmosti 21 and 26 calculus	27	26	4	0	0		0.00	H	UP/LSA	E
	Skhul II, V, VI and VII calculus	130	100	6	15	7	Palm, ?Triticeae	1.81	H	MP/MSA	NE
	Skhul tools	130	100	26	100	51	Palm, Triticeae, AP grass, USO	5.10	H	MP/MSA	NE

Key: A question mark indicates reduced confidence in the identification. H = early modern human; N = Neanderthal; MP/MSA = Middle Paleolithic or Middle Stone Age; UP/LSA = Upper Paleolithic or Later Stone Age; E = Europe; NE = Near East; A = Africa. Dates, technology, and taxonomy were collected from the literature and are presented, along with details on exact samples, in the supplementary information. AP grass indicates a starch that may be from the seeds of grass in the Andropogoneae or Paniceae tribes.

or geographic region indicated that none of those predictors strongly influenced the number of microfossils recovered. On the basis of these findings, Henry and colleagues concluded that both Neanderthals and early modern humans consumed grass seeds and/or USOs, both potentially "costly" plant foods, and there was no evidence for a dietary shift, at least in plant diet. In combination with pursuit of big game, Neanderthals routinely used a variety of plant foods, which reflected an investment in technology and division of labor. Modern humans had a more sophisticated toolkit, which potentially gave them a competitive advantage in terms of big game. Perhaps Neanderthals responded to competition by consuming more (and lower ranked) plant foods, which was of limited success in meeting their high-energy needs (Henry et al. 2014).

Study of starch from stone tools from the Mikuyu site, Mozambique, has provided evidence that early modern humans in Africa engaged in foraging practices often associated with later Stone Age populations (Mercader et al. 2008). Based on the artifact assemblage, the Mikuyu site was occupied during the Middle Stone Age (no dates provided). Thirty-three scrapers, cores and core tools, points, flakes, and other tools were studied, as were control samples. In all, 208 individual starch granules were recovered from tools and 10 morphotypes defined (Table 5.5), representing use of seeds, fruits, pith, and USOs of a diverse group of some dozen botanical families. Starch from control samples was typologically different from that recovered from tools. Among the likely taxa used were sorghum grains, African wine palm pith and sap, *Amaryllis belladonna* bulbs, cycad trunk starch, and legume seeds. Although it is not certain that all starch represented direct tool function, all starch-bearing tools were exposed to starch-rich materials by use in processing foods, ancient transfer of starch from hands to tool, or accidental contact with plant parts. Cycads produce high-quality trunk starch that has to be detoxified. Punching of palm trunks to access pith demonstrates ancient manipulation of sap (used to make wine in later times). Both practices have parallels in later Stone Age food practices (Mercader et al. 2008).

Residue analysis of stone tools from Ngalue Cave in Mozambique also revealed evidence for broad-based foraging, including of grass seeds, by early modern humans in the Middle Stone Age, beginning at least 105,000 BP (Mercader 2009). A total of 70 tools of all types in the assemblage were selected for study. Most tools (80 percent) had starch residues, with a total of 2,369 granules recovered. Scrapers and core/grinding tools were especially productive. Most granules recovered (89 percent by count, on 55 of 70 tools, or 79 percent ubiquity) were sorghum, which grows naturally in the region. Ancient granules displayed morphologies like those seen in modern sorghum specimens. Other taxa present on tools included lenticular granules observed in fruits of Fabaceae, Malvaceae, and Apocynaceae; African wine palm pith; African false banana mesocarp or corm; and African potato. Large numbers of altered granules were observed on 15 tools, including granules that were flattened with an enlarged centric hole and bulging edges and granules with fissures and surface roughening. These changes could be due to aging, cooking, fermentation, and/or grinding. Overall the results indicated that early modern humans from southern Africa consumed both underground plant foods and above-ground plant resources, including sorghum (Mercader 2009).

South and Southeast Asia

Insights into the antiquity and nature of early modern human foraging activities in rainforest environments have been provided by research at Niah Cave on the island of Borneo, occupied

TABLE 5.5 Starch morphometrics and estimated plant parts and families present in the archaeological sample. (Table 6 from Mercader, Julio, Tim Bennett and Mussa Raja. 2008. Middle Stone Age starch acquisition in the Niassa Rift, Mozambique. *Quaternary Research* 70:283–300. Reproduced with permission of Cambridge University Press.) Notice that in some cases more than one botanical family could have been the source of a starch morphotype recovered from Mikuyu samples

Type	3-D descriptor	2-D descriptor	Surface texture	Surface features	Arm morphology	Arm centricity	Mean max. length	Size range	N	Plant part	Producing families
1	Lenticular planoconvexe, biconvexe	Ellipsoid to orbicular	Lamellae, psilate	Slit, depression, Y, X, pocking, slit along edge	Diffuse, straight	Centric	23.52 ± 6	8–36.6	73	**Seed**, legume, mesocarp	**Fabaceae**, Malvaceae, Apocynaceae
2	Subrounded parallelepiped	Suborbicular	Psilate, irregular	Slit, Y,V,T, stellated fissures	Sharp, straight, bent	Centric, slightly eccentric	17.2 ± 3.5	11.5–28.7	57	**Caryopsis, legume**, mesocarp, pith, USO	**Fabaceae, Poaceae,** Strychnaceae, Apocynaceae, Cyperaceae
3a	Pear-shaped; one taper end	Ellipsoid	Lamellae, Psilate	Eccentric cuneiform slit	Sharp, Curved	Eccentric	41.1 ± 10.3	30.2–42.4	3	**Pith**	Arecaceae
3b	Pear-shaped	Ovate	Lamellae	Eccentric slit ><	Sharp, straight, curved	Eccentric	60.7 ± 14.1	51.2–77	3	USO	**Amaryllidaceae**
3c	Oblong sphere	Ellipsoid	Lamellae, psilate	Fissures, slit V	Sharp, curved	Eccentric	63.4 ± 12.4	52.3–80	4	**Pith**	Arecaceae
4	Sphere; hemisphere	Orbicular, ellipsoid	Lamellae, psilate	Centric vacuole, fissure, pressure facets	Sharp, straight, curved	Centric, slightly eccentric	9.7 ± 2.3	6.2–14	35	Mesocarp, pith, USO	**Bombacaceae,** Annonaceae, Cucurbitaceae,
5	Oblong sphere	Orbicular, ellipsoid	Lamellae, psilate	Centric fissuring ~, pressure facets	Sharp, straight, bent	Centric	21.1 ± 4.2	15.7–26.3	6	USO, legume	**Polygonaceae, Fabaceae**
6	Tear drop	Subtriangular	Psilate	Featureless, centric vacuole	Sharp, curved, bent	Eccentric	9.5 ± 1.5	7.0–12.0	9	USO	**Araceae**
7	Hemisphere, hyperhemisphere	Plano-ovoid	Psilate	Vacuole, pressure facets	Sharp, straight, curved, bent	Eccentric, centric	11.6 ± 2.9	8.7–15.8	13	USO, legume, nut, **mesocarp**	**Fabaceae**, Lamiaceae, Arecaceae, **Annonaceae**
8	Pear-shaped	Ovate	Psilate	Featureless	Sharp, straight	Eccentric	18.5 ± 3.1	16.3–20.8	2	USO, seed, pith	**Asphodelaceae, Nymphaeaceae,** Strychnaceae, Zamiaceae
9	Oblong sphere	Ellipsoid	Psilate, irregular	Centric fissuring ~	Diffuse, straight	Centric	22.3 ± 6.7	17.6–27.1	2	Legume	**Fabaceae**
10	Bell-shaped	Subtriangular	Psilate	Centric vacuole, fissure, pressure facets	Sharp, curved, bent	Eccentric	28	28	1	**Pith**, USO	**Arecaceae,** Apocynaceae, Taccaceae, **Zamiaceae**

Bold captions indicate the plant part and family considered by the authors to be the most likely or abundant source of starch found in this study.

46,000 to 34,000 BP (Barton 2005; Barker et al. 2007). Renewed fieldwork in the west mouth of the cave confirmed the antiquity of the "Deep Skull," which is anatomically modern. Botanical macroremains (charred parenchyma, fruit and nut fragments, and seeds) were recovered by water flotation or during excavation. In addition, 94 sediment samples from the cave were analyzed for starch, including 57 samples from Hell Trench, the location of the Deep Skull and the focus of the new fieldwork (the other contexts were later and are not discussed here). Thirteen samples from Hell Trench contained starch that could be assigned to types or groups with distinctive morphologies. Richness was high (seven starch types, including unknowns), indicating that a wide range of starchy plants was deposited. Among the key findings of the botanical studies were roots and tubers (*Alocacia longiloba* complex, cf. *Colocasia*, Araceae, cf. *Dioscorea hispida, Dioscorea*, unidentified tuber), fruit (Moraceae, *Pangium edule*), unidentified nuts, and sago palm pith (*Eugeissona utilis* or *Cartyota* spp.) gathered from nearby rainforest habitats. All botanical remains came from deposits yielding evidence for human activity, and in the case of palm starch, from a flaked tool surface. Palm starch was present from the earliest excavated levels in Hell Trench, below the Deep Skull levels dated to ca. 40,000 BP. Study of flaked stone tools suggested many were used to work hard or siliceous materials such as bamboo or rattan. Others were used to process soft plant tissues. Palm wood fibers were recovered from one flake. Presence of *Dioscorea hispida* and *Pangium edule* remains implied that early modern human foragers had knowledge and technology for neutralizing plant toxins. Pollen from a sediment column inside the cave mouth suggested habitat modification in the area of the cave. Very high frequencies of pollen of *Justicia* (Acanthaceae), which colonizes the landscape after fires, occurred. Deliberate burning would have enhanced open habitats favored by tubers and other foods. Overall, paleoethnobotanical research at Niah Cave documented direct association of early anatomically modern humans and complex foraging behaviors, including tuber digging, plant detoxification, and forest burning (Barton 2005; Barker et al. 2007).

Excavations at Batadomba-lena rock shelter in the rainforest of Sri Lanka, used by early modern humans beginning ca. 36,000 BP, have offered insights into the ecological context and nature of early human settlement in South Asia (Perera et al. 2011). Faunal remains, macroremains, phytoliths, and other microremains were analyzed. The earliest occupation level at the site, layer 7, was characterized by a very wet phytolith assemblage, with grasses, shrubs, and trees, including palm (Arecaceae), banana *(Musa)*, and breadfruit *(Artocarpus)*. Wood charcoal and charred vegetable tissues were also present. There was evidence for hearth building, food processing (including roasting), and formation of habitation floors from burning, trampling, and deposition of organic materials. Overall, the faunal remains indicated broad-spectrum foraging. The Batadomba-lena site preserved evidence for use of South Asian rainforests by early human foragers from ca. 36,000 BP and after (Perera et al. 2011).

In summary, when plant food dietary richness of Neanderthals and early modern humans was compared by Henry et al. (2014) using data from Europe, the Near East, and Africa recovered from the same kinds of contexts (phytolith and starch residues from dental calculus and stone tools) and classified following the same protocols, results were broadly similar. A wide range of richness values characterized both Neanderthal and early modern human populations; there were examples of high richness for both, and both used relatively "high-cost" plant resources, such as grass seeds and USOs. These patterns characterized the earliest sites included for each population, as well as some of the latest. Paleoethnobotanical data from other early modern human sites in Africa, as well as sites in southeast and south Asia, have demonstrated the diverse array of resources and environments utilized by early modern human foragers and confirmed the early emergence of complex food processing behaviors such as plant detoxification.

Discussion: Plant Foods in the Neanderthal Diet

Where do the contributions of paleoethnobotany leave us in terms of the debate about the nature of Neanderthal diet(s) and the role of diet in the eventual extinction of Neanderthal populations? Systematic recovery of macroremains; study of phytoliths and organic compounds from site sediments; and analysis of microfossils, organic compounds, and DNA from dental calculus or stone tools have started to provide us with the missing plant food "menus" necessary for a complete picture of Neanderthal subsistence. Plants potentially contributed 20 percent of protein to the diet of individuals at Spy Cave in the mammoth steppes of northern and central Europe; foraging of grass seeds and USOs would have provided abundant carbohydrates to these populations. Mushrooms were potentially important vegetable protein sources. The plant menu appears to have been longer outside northern and central Europe and included legumes, other small-seeded dicots, grasses (including Triticeae, cf. *Hordeum*), nuts (including acorn, pistachio, pine nut), palm, fig, grape, mushrooms, and unknown USOs. Many of these potential foods were identified only at Kebara Cave in Israel, however, where macroremains were preserved and systematically recovered; comparable data are largely lacking from other sites. When only dental calculus results are considered (for example, for Spy [Belgium], Shanidar [Iraq], and El Sidrón [Spain]), plant food menus appear to have been somewhat longer outside northern and central Europe, but not strikingly so, suggesting that a comparably wide range of plant species was likely used by Neanderthals throughout Eurasia. Faunal and isotope studies have provided similar results: the meat component of Neanderthal diets varied regionally, but had core similarities in the major taxa utilized and the overall large contribution of meat to the diet.

Paleoethnobotanical data have confirmed that plant gathering and consumption were part of Neanderthal lifeways and that foraging practices included harvesting of small seeds, picking of fruits of annual plants and trees, and digging plant underground storage organs. These were activities that required advance planning and detailed environmental knowledge, for example, in scheduling of foraging by season of ripening and locations of resources, in picking legume fruits slightly green (i.e., before seeds dispersed), and in finding USOs when fully mature (i.e., after vegetation may have died back). Food preparation practices included cutting, peeling, pounding, and cooking by wet and dry heat. Evidence for food storage was lacking. Plants were also used as raw materials for cordage and in woodworking, as well as for fuel, bedding, and medicinal purposes (discussed further later in the text).

In terms of the debate about the nature of Neanderthal diet(s), paleoethnobotany has contributed, with other lines of research, to establishing that plant foods were part of the diet throughout the temporal and geographic ranges of Neanderthals, both before and after the arrival of early modern humans. Neanderthals were hunter-gatherers with meat-rich diets, but were not carnivores. The kinds of plant taxa and foraging practices used by Neanderthals in many cases had parallels to utilized taxa and practices of early modern humans. Explanations for the eventual extinction of Neanderthals must take into account the fact that in terms of subsistence, they interacted with the plant world, at least, in ways similar to those of early modern populations with whom they competed.

Neanderthal–Plant Interrelationships Beyond Diet

Medicinal Plant Use

During the study of pollen from sediment samples from Shanidar Cave in Iraq, two samples stood out (Leroi-Gourhan 1975). These samples, among those taken from the burial area of the Shanidar IV skeleton, contained clusters of seven pollen taxa, including some that retained the form of the flower anther (pollen-producing organ). The Shanidar IV individual was apparently placed on a bed of flowers from at least seven species (Leroi-Gourhan 1975). All the plants in question that could be identified, *Achillea* type, *Centaurea solstitialis*, *Senetio* type, *Muscari* type, *Ephedra altissima*, and *Althea* type, contained compounds with healing properties (Lietava 1992). Species of *Achillea*, for example, contain azulenes, which possess important anti-inflammatory effects, and *Centaurea solstitialis* has strong diuretic effects and antiseptic properties. Lietava (1992) concluded that the presence of pollen from plants with demonstrated therapeutic potential indicated Neanderthals had knowledge of the curative properties of plants. As discussed earlier, a similar conclusion can be drawn from the presence of the compounds azulene and coumarin in the dental calculus of an individual from El Sidrón Cave, Spain (K. Hardy et al. 2012) and recovery of 12 species of plants with potential medicinal uses from Kebara Cave, Israel (Lev et al. 2005).

Fuel Selection

Phytolith analysis of hearths from Kebara Cave, which was occupied ca. 60,000 to 44,000 BP, has provided insight into use of fire by Mousterian populations (Albert et al. 2000). The central area of the cave contained many superimposed hearths, the most common type being a flat lens, but bowl-shaped hearths also occurred. More widely spread ash deposits were also identified, including thick accumulations in the rear of the cave, likely the result of dumping ash there. Prior study of hearth samples documented grass phytoliths and charcoal of Tabor oak *(Quercus ithaburensis)*, Kermes oak *(Q. calliprinos)*, *Pistacia, Crataegus, Salix*, and *Ulmus*. Phytolith analysis of 20 additional samples was undertaken to learn more about fuel used for fires and to understand phytolith preservation (Albert et al. 2000). A reference collection of modern plants was studied that focused on woody taxa, but also included herbaceous dicots and grasses. Two kinds of phytoliths were recognized in hearth and ash samples: highly variable forms impossible to classify ("v") and forms of consistent morphology ("c"). Modern wood and bark samples studied had v/c ratios that ranged from 1.3 to 17.4; bark samples included variable numbers of grass phytoliths, presumably deposited in bark through wind action. For cave samples, v/c ratios fell between 0.5 and 1.9. The authors concluded that wood ash made up a major component of cave samples and that the contribution of grasses in most cases was due to their association with bark burned in fires. Phytolith concentrations and assemblages in samples within the cave were very different from samples taken from the exterior, showing that phytolith deposition in the cave was due to human activities. Phytolith compositions varied significantly in different sedimentary layers and in samples located between hearths, demonstrating differential input of plant materials, including for purposes unrelated to fuel for fires.

Micromorphological analysis of combustion features was later undertaken in combination with phytolith analysis to investigate further Neanderthal use of plants at Kebara Cave (Albert et al. 2012). Samples came from large ash layers from the earliest occupation phases at the site (e.g., Units XIII and XI). Figure 5.2 shows one such area sampled in Unit XI. Phytoliths were abundant in most of the 30 samples studied; in general, assemblages were dominated by grasses, with phytoliths from dicot leaves and wood/bark present in variable amounts. Palm and sedge phytoliths were present in low numbers. Overall, samples showed considerable

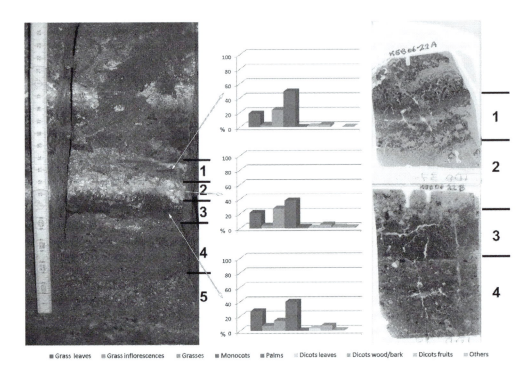

■ Grass leaves   ■ Grass inflorescences   ■ Grasses   ■ Monocots   ■ Palms   ▨ Dicots leaves   ■ Dicots wood/bark   ▨ Dicots fruits   ▨ Others

FIGURE 5.2   **At left:** Photograph of combustion feature from archaeological Unit XI sampled in Square N18 at 7.70 m below datum (Sample KEB06–22). Ruler is 25 cm long. Numbers refer to layers described in the field and corresponding collected loose samples: 1) Brown at top with charcoal, and gray brown and white particles; 2) Orange/yellow white and orangey particles; 3) Black, soft organic-rich material with yellow particles; 4) Reddish zone under block; 5) Massive, soft brown with orangey particles, charcoal and some white particles. **Center:** Histograms showing the phytolith morphological distribution of combustion feature KEB06–22. **At right:** Macroscans of thin sections processed from undisturbed block sampled in the same area. All thin sections measure 50 × 75 mm. From the top thin sections KEB-22A, and KEB-22B. (Figure 5 from Albert, Rosa M., Francesco Berna and Paul Goldberg. 2012. Insights on Neanderthal fire use at Kebara Cave (Israel) through high resolution study of prehistoric combustion features: Evidence from phytoliths and thin sections. *Quaternary International* 247:278–293.)

Reproduced with permission of Elsevier. Note that the histograms are in the same order as the list of phytolith types in the legend. The first three correspond to grass phytoliths of different origins in tissue; "Grasses" are short cells; "Monocots" refer to phytoliths from herbaceous monocots, grasses, and sedges that cannot be distinguished; all Dicots types include woody herbs, shrubs, and trees.

variability. For example, among samples from the earliest phase, some had elevated levels of dicot leaf phytoliths, others low levels of grasses, and some abundant Boraginaceae seed coat phytoliths. Analysis of a culturally sterile control sample indicated that grasses and Boraginaceae fruits accumulated in the cave naturally. Grasses also likely adhered to bark, as discussed earlier, representing up to 30 percent of counts. Albert and colleagues concluded that phytolith morphotypes most directly related to human activities were from the wood and leaves of trees used as fuel for fires. In many contexts grasses most likely represented contamination from wood bark burning, but other potential sources included natural deposition or use of grass as a fire starter.

Similar results were found in the phytolith analysis of ash from hearths and associated Mousterian (250,000–100,000 BP) deposits in Hayonim Cave, Israel (Albert et al. 2003). Grasses were common in all Mousterian samples, but dicot leaf and wood/bark phytoliths were relatively abundant (Figure 5.3, A). There were differences in phytolith assemblages among samples, implying use of different sources of vegetation at different times. The amounts of vegetal matter contributed to the deposits by grasses, dicot leaves, and wood/bark were estimated based on comparative data on phytolith concentrations per unit weight of dry organic material (Figure 5.3, B). Based on these estimates, it appeared that small, leafy branches from dicot trees or bushes were the major source of fuel during the Mousterian, and grasses a minor component. Interestingly, comparisons to later Natufian levels indicated use of more grasses and fewer dicot leaves as fuel then.

Phytolith analysis at Abrigo de la Quebrada, Spain, has provided evidence for deliberate introduction and burning of grasses by Neanderthals utilizing the cave ca. 82,000 to 40,000 BP (Esteban et al. 2017). Deposits were characterized by a large number of overlapping hearths, indicating repeated, short-term occupations. Identification of wood charcoal showed dominance of *Pinus, Juniperus*, and other gymnosperms. *Quercus, Rhamnus*, and other dicot woods were present in low quantities. The phytolith study included hearths, hearth–related sediments, non–hearth-related sediments, and culturally sterile areas; 12 samples produced enough phytoliths for reliable morphological analysis. Mineral components of sediments were also identified. As determined by refractive index, more than 60 percent of the phytoliths in the 12 samples had been burnt, regardless of their provenience. This, along with presence of wood-ash calcite, suggested that hearth ashes were dispersed throughout the occupation floor by trampling and cleaning activities. Grass phytoliths, including leaf and inflorescence forms, dominated all samples (above 77 percent in all productive samples) and were slightly more abundant in non–hearth sediments. Grass dominance was associated with elongate phytoliths not classifiable to family level. Phytoliths from dicot leaves and wood/bark were present in all samples in lower numbers, with most recovered from hearth samples. Two samples contained dicot fruit phytoliths. Esteban and colleagues concluded that the near absence of phytoliths in samples from the sterile level, contrasting with the high concentrations in the cultural levels, demonstrated the anthropogenic origin of the plant remains represented by phytoliths. Use of wood as fuel was documented by the charcoal studies; the scarcity of woody phytoliths was likely due to partial dissolution and low phytolith production in woody taxa (i.e., as discussed earlier). The high levels of grass phytoliths suggested grasses were intentionally introduced, not just present as contamination in bark. There was not enough evidence to support grass seed processing, although slightly more husk phytoliths were recovered from hearth and hearth–related sediments.

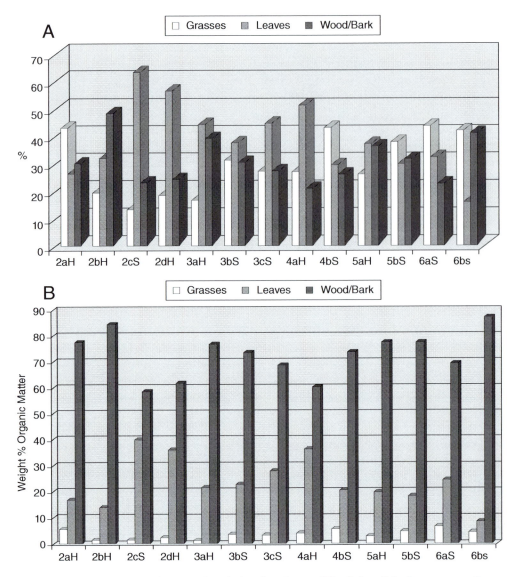

FIGURE 5.3 **A:** Histogram showing the relative abundances (%) of phytoliths from grasses, dicot-yledonous leaves, and dicotyledonous wood/bark obtained from sediments from the Mousterian levels E and F. See Table 1 for the identification of the samples; **B:** Histogram showing the weight % volume of vegetal material derived from grasses, dicotyledonous leaves, and dicotyledonous wood/bark in the Mousterian levels E and F. (Figure 8 and Figure 11 from Albert, Rosa M., Ofer Bar-Yosef, Liliane Meignen and Steve Weiner. 2003. Quantitative phytolith study of hearths from the Natufian and Middle Palaeolithic levels of Hayonim Cave (Galilee, Israel). *Journal of Archaeological Science* 30:461–480.)

Reproduced with permission of Elsevier. Refer to Table 1 in the article for identifications of samples. Notice how taking into account differences in phytolith production between grasses and woody dicots alters the interpretation of their relative contributions to the deposits of Hayonim Cave.

Ecosystem Management

Daniau et al. (2010) examined microcharcoal from two deep-sea cores located off Iberia and France to evaluate whether there were changes in natural fire regimens associated with use of fire for ecosystem management by Neanderthals or early modern human populations. Fire became a widespread technology at the beginning of the Middle Paleolithic. If early modern humans had greater control of fire than Neanderthals and used it to manage ecosystems, it might have given them a competitive advantage. For purposes of this study, Neanderthal extinction was considered to occur at ca. 34,000 to 35,000 BP in western Europe and ca. 30,000 BP in southern Iberia. This period falls into MIS 3 (Marine Isotope Stage 3) and MIS 2 (marine isotope stages are alternating warm and cool periods determined from oxygen isotope data).

Microfossil concentrations in the core located off Iberia revealed a fire regimen that was in phase with vegetation shifts during MIS 3 and MIS 2: high fire was associated with relatively warm and wet climate (i.e., with higher plant biomass), whereas low fire was observed during cold and dry climatic phases (i.e., lower plant biomass). The core located off France broadly showed the same pattern, but vegetation shifts and fire were not as strongly correlated after 40,000 BP, perhaps due to the expansion of fire-prone ecosystems. Both Neanderthals and modern humans were associated with both high and low fire regimens, which were correlated with climate change. Unlike findings from Southeast Asia (discussed earlier), Daniau et al. (2010) found no evidence for an increase in fire in Europe associated with modern human populations, or any association of fire change with Neanderthals. Caveat: either or both populations may have used fire in ways that did not affect natural fire trends.

Spatial Organization of Sites as a Reflection of Modern Behavior

Research at Tor Faraj, a rock shelter site in Jordan dated ca. 69,000 to 49,000 BP, has provided insights concerning the extent to which Neanderthal behavior resembled that of modern humans (Henry 2003a). Rosen (2003) conducted a study of plant microfossils focused on reconstructing local vegetation, paleoclimate, and pattern of plant use by the shelter's inhabitants. Samples were taken horizontally across a living floor (Floor II). Abundant phytoliths were recovered, as well as some spores, starch granules, and calcium oxalate crystals. Among the plants identified were pooid (festucoid) grasses, horse-tail rush, reed, sedge (*Cyperus* type), date palm, and abundant phytoliths from dicot trees or shrubs, suggesting that moister conditions existed in the area at the time of site occupation than at present. Date palm fruits and/or leaves were likely used. Several kinds of starch granules were found, likely indicative of nuts, such as pistachio, roots, and tubers brought into the shelter. The distribution of microfossil remains across the living floor indicated that grasses were spread on the floor near the back wall and in between the hearths, perhaps indicating prepared sleeping areas (Figure 5.4, A). Phytoliths from grass seeds and palm were concentrated near a central hearth, suggesting a food preparation area (Figure 5.4, B), and high concentrations of dicot phytoliths beyond the dripline of the shelter suggested a brush windbreak (Figure 5.4, C). These microfossil results contributed significantly to the overall finding that the Neanderthals of Tor Faraj organized their activities and living space essentially along the lines of modern hunter-gatherers, habitually and formally segregating their behaviors during the three major occupational episodes of the shelter (Henry 2003a).

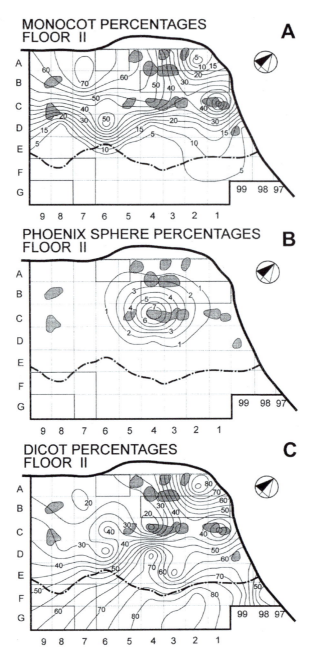

FIGURE 5.4   **A:** Distribution of phytoliths from monocotyledons across Floor II (hearth data not included) at Tor Faraj; **B:** Distribution of phytoliths from date palms *(P. dactylifera)* across Floor II at Tor Faraj; **C:** Distribution of dicotyledon phytoliths across Floor II (high dicot percentages from hearths not included) at Tor Faraj. (Figure 7.5, Figure 7.9, and Figure 7.6 from Rosen, Arlene Miller. 2003. Middle Paleolithic plant exploitation: The microbotanical evidence. In *Neanderthals in the Levant. Behavioral Organization and the Beginnings of Human Modernity*, edited by D. O. Henry, pp. 156–171. Continuum, London.)

Reproduced with permission of Bloomsbury Publishing Plc. Samples were collected from the centers of 24 excavation squares and six hearths of Floor II at Tor Faraj; results were tabulated as percentages and occurrence of selected taxa depicted as topographic lines on the maps of the floor.

Phytolith, Fourier-transform infrared spectroscopy (FTIR, a technique used to identify chemical compounds), and soil micromorphological studies conducted at Esquilleu Cave, Spain, have provided further evidence for use of grass as bedding during the Late Mousterian occupation of this shelter (ca. 60,000–37,000 BP) (Cabanes et al. 2010; Mallol et al. 2010). FTIR and soil micromorphological analyses indicated that anthropogenic-rich layers of unit C, which showed intensive combustion activity, had been altered by an unknown source of dissolved phosphate, leading to partial dissolution of bone and ash. But both were still present and documented a trampled succession of accumulation of remains related to fire activity (Mallol et al. 2010). Thin laminae of phytoliths in anatomical position were observed in some layers of the unit. Phytolith concentrations were especially high in unit C, but not uniformly so (Cabanes et al. 2010). The majority of phytoliths in most samples were long cells produced by palms, sedges, and grasses. No diagnostic palm or sedge phytoliths were observed, making it likely these epidermal phytoliths represented grass leaves. Grass inflorescence phytoliths were also recovered. Several layers contained concentrations of wood and bark phytoliths; a few phytoliths from dicotyledonous leaves occurred. Cabanes and colleagues concluded that phytolith accumulations in unit C represented human activities related to hearths and bedding. Very high concentrations of wood and bark phytoliths were recovered from a central hearth area, indicating that wood was the main type of fuel used. Abundant grass phytoliths in the lowermost hearth sample suggested that wood ash was mixed with previously deposited grass remains lying on the cave's ancient surface. This inference was supported by the presence of semicontinuous laminae of phytoliths in anatomical position (Mallol et al. 2010). Research at Esquilleu Cave identified repetitive behaviors by Neanderthals involving the preparation of grass bedding on a floor made up of reworked hearth remains. There was no clear evidence that the beds were intentionally burnt after use.

Early Modern Human Example: Sibudu Cave, South Africa

Micromorphological analysis of sediments at Sibudu Cave, a Middle Stone Age site located in KwaNulu-Natal, South Africa, and dated 64,000 to 36,000 BP, has provided insights into early human activities, including construction of hearths and bedding and maintenance of occupation surfaces (Goldberg et al. 2009). Site deposits were composed of numerous lenses of ashy and charcoal-rich deposits that appeared to represent intact hearths. Many were lenticular in shape; others were circular; many burning episodes were superimposed. It appeared that ash had been spread and trampled; hearths and sediments between them were almost indistinguishable based on phytolith content. For this study undisturbed blocks of sediment were taken for micromorphological analysis. Among the results, bone was found in all samples, sometimes forming distinctive layers, and charcoal was abundant. Evidence for human trampling of deposits was seen. Charred fibrous plant material (from herbaceous plants, likely sedges and/or grasses) was commonly found within layers of phytoliths, which were sometimes the sole component of a layer. Some phytolith layers were laminated. A variety of phytolith types were present; sedge was tentatively identified. Two types of combustion features were defined, hearths and burning of bedding (i.e., plant material on the use surface), with the latter identified by laminated fibrous material. Goldberg and colleagues concluded that routine burning of bedding that included sedge plants was used to maintain hygienic conditions.

Another mechanism for the charring of bedding material at Sibudu Cave was proposed by Sievers and Wadley (2008): fires built on top of buried plant material formerly used for sleeping or sitting areas. These authors conducted experiments that demonstrated that hearth fires could char plant material buried beneath the hearth. In this scenario, sedge bedding at Sibudu could have been burnt unintentionally. Subsequently, Miller and Sievers (2012) conducted experiments to address the source of laminated carbonized material and phytoliths in Sibudu Cave to determine whether layers of bedding were deliberately burned or not. They set up experiments to determine whether indirect charring of buried bedding layers by an overlying fire would produce the same micromorphological signature as direct ignition of bedding. They found that an overlying fire produced charred plant material, as seen in Sievers and Wadley's (2008) experiments, but original cellulose remained in the material and no layer of phytoliths was produced. All experimental fires with direct burning produced laminated fibrous charcoal and phytolith layers that resembled the Sibudu sediments. Miller and Sievers concluded that complete ashing from direct burning was needed to produce laminated phytoliths and that a very large amount of bedding material would have been needed to produce the observed archaeological deposits at Sibudu Cave.

Summary and Discussion: Neanderthals and Modern Behaviors Beyond Diet

Studies of Neanderthal medicinal plant use, fuel selection, and spatial organization reviewed here suggest that Neanderthal behaviors in these realms had many parallels to behaviors of modern humans. There was indirect evidence for medicinal plant use at Shanidar and Kebara Caves—the presence of plant taxa with medicinal properties associated with a burial in the former case, and in occupational debris in the latter. Direct evidence of self-medication came from recovery of active organic compounds in dental calculus from an individual at El Sidrón Cave. As will be discussed further in Chapter 9, these lines of evidence constitute relatively strong archaeological evidence for medicinal plant use. Data from Neanderthals have provided further evidence that use of plants for healing was an ancient hominin practice.

In cases in which macroremains of wood charcoal were preserved and identified, it appears that Neanderthal groups selected fuel for domestic fires from woody plants available near occupation sites. In general wood cannot be identified to taxon by phytoliths, but phytolith studies have documented that in some cases fuel included leaves, that is, that smaller branches or bushes were targeted. Grass phytoliths were also commonly incorporated into sediments of combustion features; in many cases abundances matched what might be expected from grass phytolith contamination in wood bark, but at Abrigo de la Quebrada abundances indicated use of grasses as fuel or fire starter. Based on available data, there appears to have been little pressure on wood resources around Neanderthal occupation sites.

Evidence is lacking that Neanderthal (or early modern human) populations used fire for large-scale modification of landscapes in Europe. It was possible, but not documented, that either or both populations used fire in ways that did not affect natural fire trends, for example, to encourage certain plant or animal species in a favored foraging area.

Studies of site spatial organization have shown that Neanderthal groups organized their activities—at least those that left records in cave sites—along much the same lines as human hunter-gatherers. Hearths were not permanent features in shelters, but were usually built and rebuilt in a central area with easy access, light, and headroom. Food was prepared near the hearth. Sleeping areas with grass and/or sedge bedding were created near hearths and in low-traffic areas like the back or sides of the shelter. Ash was dumped out of the way. Heat was retained by construction of brush windbreaks at the shelter entrance/dripline. Occupation "floors" were created by trampling. There was no clear evidence that old bedding was burned when shelters were reoccupied, a practice inferred for early modern humans at Sibudu Cave. Overall, Neanderthal groups appear to have used caves as shelters for short-term or seasonal occupations, using the space in ways that fit the characteristics of the shelter and the diverse needs and activities of the occupants. Conditions were perhaps less hygienic, and features less permanent, than similar occupations of early modern humans.

Conclusion: Investigating Neanderthal Lifeways Through Paleoethnobotany

In this case study we explored how paleoethnobotany has contributed to investigating a major debate in human evolution: the nature of Neanderthal lifeways and how they differed from those of the early modern human populations who replaced them. The case focused on three areas of research: diet, plant–people interrelationships beyond diet, and social organization. In these realms, at least, it becomes increasingly difficult to argue that there were many significant behavioral differences in the plant–people interrelationships of Neanderthals and those of early modern humans.

A striking aspect of the body of research reviewed here is the great diversity of approaches and kinds of data that have been brought to bear on investigating Neanderthal lifeways. This is largely by necessity. The age and scarcity of sites, the varied histories of their excavations, the complex stratigraphies and preservation environments of cave deposits—all these circumstances and more have created challenging conditions for investigating complex behaviors involving plants. Different data and approaches, generating multiple lines of evidence, have been essential for filling in gaps in evidence provided from any single source. Some examples include the following: Studies of microfossils, organic molecules, and DNA in dental calculus have provided direct data on Neanderthal plant consumption even when organic remains were poorly preserved in sites or excavations were carried out prior to systematic recovery of such materials. Phytoliths have contributed to the identification of activity areas in the absence of preserved macroremains. Micromorphological analyses of intact sediments have confirmed stratigraphic relationships among complex depositional events, for instance, in identifying in situ combustion features or trampled surfaces.

Multiple lines of evidence have done more than fill in gaps in data, however; they have documented Neanderthal plant–people interrelationships at different scales of analysis. For example, dental calculus data have provided insights into diet or health status of Neanderthal individuals— what foods or medicinal preparations were consumed and how these were prepared. Comparing results from multiple individuals has provided some insights, albeit based on limited numbers of samples, into how diet varied within populations at the scale of the site/group or region. Artifact residue and functional studies have generated a second type of individual-scale data. The use histories of individual tools have provided considerable insights into Neanderthal plant use, as have comparisons of tool assemblages at the level of the site/group or region.

Macroremains and microremains recovered from site sediments have also provided essential data on Neanderthal plant–people interrelationships, but at the level of the group/site rather than individual. Because site-level data represent the accumulation of remains from multiple kinds of behaviors by multiple individuals, richness (numbers of plant taxa identified) is often correspondingly high. Macroremains preserved at Kebara Cave, for example, have provided a long list of potentially utilized plants, including foods and medicines not identified to date in individual Neanderthal dental calculus samples or on artifacts. Analysis of control samples and comparative specimens, as well as experimental studies, have provided essential insights for investigating which archaeobotanical remains may have become deposited through pathways other than Neanderthal behavior.

Finally, incorporation of multiple lines of evidence and approaches into the study of Neanderthal lifeways has helped ameliorate some of the challenges inherent in identifying different plant species and tissues. For example, if a number of families of USOs available to Neanderthals in a region produce similar starch grains, a shorter "menu" can be inferred from incidentally deposited seeds or phytoliths identified at a lower taxonomic level. Similarly, charred wood from combustion features identifiable at the genus level can help narrow the probable sources of less diagnostic phytoliths of wood and bark in generalized ash deposits. Experimental approaches have been used to great effect to enhance "identifiability" and to facilitate interpretation, for example, in documenting the effects of wet or dry cooking or pounding on starch, in reconstructing the quantities of wood and grasses needed to produce observed concentrations of phytoliths, or in modeling whether deliberate or accidental burning produced combustion features.

References

Albert, Rosa M., Ofer Bar-Yosef, Liliane Meignen and Steve Weiner 2003 Quantitative phytolith study of hearths from the Natufian and Middle Palaeolithic levels of Hayonim Cave (Galilee, Israel). *Journal of Archaeological Science* 30:461–480.

Albert, Rosa M., Francesco Berna and Paul Goldberg 2012 Insights on Neanderthal fire use at Kebara Cave (Israel) through high resolution study of prehistoric combustion features: Evidence from phytoliths and thin sections. *Quaternary International* 247:278–293.

Albert, Rosa M., Steve Weiner, Ofer Bar-Yosef and Liliane Meignen 2000 Phytoliths in the Middle Palaeolithic deposits of Kebara Cave, Mt Carmel, Israel: Study of the plant materials used for fuel and other purposes. *Journal of Archaeological Science* 27:931–947.

Barker, Graeme, Huw Barton, Michael Bird, Patrick Daly, Ipoi Datan, Alan Dykes, Lucy Farr, David Gilbertson, Barbara Harrisson, Chris Hunt, Tom Higham, Lisa Kealhofer, John Krigbaum, Helen Lewis, Sue McLaren, Victor Paz, Alistair Pike, PPhil Piper, Brian Pyatt, Ryan Rabett, Tim Reynolds, Jim Rose, Garry Rushworth, Mark Stephens, Chris Stringer, Jill Thompson and Chris Turney 2007 The 'human revolution' in lowland tropical Southeast Asia: The antiquity and behavior of anatomically modern humans at Niah Cave (Sarawak, Borneo). *Journal of Human Evolution* 52(3):243–261.

Barton, Huw 2005 The case for rainforest foragers: The starch record at Niah Cave, Sarawak. *Asian Perspectives* 44(1):56–72.

Benazzi, Stefano, Katerina Douka, Cinzia Fornai, Catherine C. Bauer, Ottmar Kullmer, Jiří Svoboda, Ildikó Pap, Francesco Mallegni, Priscilla Bayle, Michael Coquerelle, Silvana Condemi, Annamaria Ronchitelli, Katerina Harvati and Gerhard W. Weber 2011 Early dispersal of modern humans in Europe and implications for Neanderthal behaviour. *Nature* 479:525–529.

Buck, Laura T., J. Colette Berbesque, Brian M. Wood and Chris B. Stringer 2016 Tropcial forager gastrophagy and its implications for extinct hominin diets. *Journal of Archaeological Science: Reports* 5:672–679.

Buck, Laura T. and Chris B. Stringer 2014 Having the stomach for it: A contribution to Neanderthal diets? *Quaternary Science Reviews* 96:161–167.

Cabanes, Dan, Carolina Mallol, Isabel Expósito and Javier Baena 2010 Phytolith evidence for hearths and beds in the late Mousterian occupations of Esquilleu cave (Cantabria, Spain). *Journal of Archaeological Science* 37:2947–2957.

Carmody, Rachel N. and Richard W. Wrangham 2009 The energetic significance of cooking. *Journal of Human Evolution* 57:379–391

Collins, Matthew J. and Les Copeland 2011 Ancient starch: Cooked or just old? *Proceedings of the National Academy of Sciences* 108(2):145.

Crittenan, Alyssa N. and Stephanie L. Schnorr 2017 Current views on hunter-gatherer nutrition and the evolution of the human diet. *American Journal of Physical Anthropology* 162:84–109.

Daniau, Anne-Laure, Francesco d'Errico and Maria Fernanda Sánchez Goñi 2010 Testing the hypothesis of fire use for ecosystem management by Neanderthal and Upper Palaeolithic Modern Human populations. *PLoS ONE* 5(2):e9157. doi:9110.1371/journal.pone.0009157.

Danin, A. 1998 Wild Plants of Eretz Israel and their Distribution. Carta, Jerusalem.

Esteban, I., Rosa M. Albert, A. Eixea, J. Zilhão and V. Villaverde 2017 Neanderthal use of plants and past vegetation reconstruction at the Middle Paleolithic site of Abrigo de la Quebrada (Chelva, Valencia, Spain). *Archaeological and Anthropological Science* 9:265–278.

Fiorenza, Luca, Stefano Benazzi, Amanda G. Henry, Domingo C. Salazar-García, Ruth Blasco, Andrea Picin, Stephen Wroe and Ottmar Kullmer 2015 To meat or not to meat? New perspectives on Neanderthal ecology. *Yearbook of Physical Anthropology* 156:43–71.

Fragman, O., U. Plitmann, D. Heller and A. Shmida 1999 *Checklist and Ecological Data-Base on the Flora of Israel and its Surroundings*. The Hebrew University, Jerusalem.

Goldberg, Paul, Christopher E. Miller, Solveig Schiegl, Bertrand Ligouis, Francesco Berna, Nicholas J. Conard and Lyn Wadley 2009 Bedding, hearths, and site maintenance in the Middle Stone Age of Sibudu Cave, KwaZulu-Natal, South Africa. *Archaeological and Anthropological Science* 1:95–122.

Hardy, Bruce L. 2004 Neanderthal behaviour and stone tool function at the Middle Palaeolithic site of La Quina, France. *Antiquity* 78(301):547–565.

——— 2010 Climatic variability and plant food distribution in Pleistocene Europe: Implications for Neanderthal diet and subsistence. *Quaternary Science Reviews* 29:662–679.

Hardy, Bruce L., Marvin Kay, Anthony E. Marks and Katherine Monigal 2001 Stone tool function at Paleolithic sites of Starosele and Buran Kaya III, Crimea: Behavioral implications. *Proceedings of the National Academy of Sciences* 98(19):10972–10977.

Hardy, Bruce L. and Marie-Hélène Moncel 2011 Neanderthal use of fish, mammals, birds, starchy plants and wood 125–250,000 years ago. *PLoS ONE* 6(8):e23768. doi:23710.21371/journal.pone.0023768.

Hardy, Bruce L., Marie-Hélène Moncel, Camille Daujeard, Paul Fernandes, Philippe Béarez, Emmanuel Desclaux, Maria Gema Chacon Nararro, Simon Puaud and Rosalia Gallotti 2013 Impossible Neanderthals? Making string, throwing projectiles and catching small game during Marine Isotope Stage 4 (Abri du Maras, France). *Quaternary Science Reviews* 82:23–40.

Hardy, Karen, Jennie Brand-Miller, Katherine D. Brown, Mark G. Thomas and Les Copeland 2015 The importance of dietary carbohydrate in human evolution. *The Quarterly Review of Biology* 90(3): 251–268.

Hardy, Karen, Stephen Buckley, Matthew J. Collins, Almudena Estalrrich, Don Brothwell, Les Copeland, Antonio García-Tabernero, Samuel García-Vargas, Marco de la Rasilla, Carles Lalueza-Fox, Rosa Huguet, Markus Bastir, David Santamaría, Marco Madella, Julie Wilson, Ángel Fernández Cortés and Antonio Rosas 2012 Neanderthal medics? Evidence for food, cooking, and medicinal plants entrapped in dental calculus. *Naturwissenschaften* 99:617–626.

Hardy, Karen, Stephen Buckley and Michael Huffman 2016 Doctors, chefs or hominin animals? Non-edible plants and Neanderthals. *Antiquity* 90(353):1373–1379.

Henry, Amanda G., Alison S. Brooks and Dolores R. Piperno 2011a Microfossils in calculus demonstrate consumption of plants and cooked foods in Neanderthal diets (Shanidar III, Iraq; Spy I and II, Belgium). *Proceedings of the National Academy of Sciences of the United States of America* 108(2):486–491.

——— 2011b Reply to Collins and Copeland: Spontaneous gelatinization not supported by evidence. *Proceedings of the National Academy of Sciences of the United States of America* 108(22).

——— 2014 Plant foods and the dietary ecology of Neanderthals and early modern humans. *Journal of Human Evolution* 69:44–54.

Henry, David O. 2003a Behavioral organization at Tor Faraj. In *Neanderthals in the Levant: Behavioral Organization and the Beginnings of Human Modernity*, edited by D. O. Henry, pp. 237–269. Continuum, London.

——— 2003b The emergence of modern humans: Issues and debates. In *Neanderthals in the Levant: Behavioral Organization and the Beginnings of Human Modernity*, edited by D. O. Henry, pp. 3–11. Continuum, London.

Higham, Tom, Tim Compton, Chris Stringer, Roger Jacobi, Beth Shapiro, Erik Trinkaus, Barry Chandler, Flora Gröning, Chris Collins, Simon Hillson, Paul O'Higgins, Charles FitzGerald and Michael Fagan 2011 The earliest evidence for anatomically modern humans in northwestern Europe. *Nature* 479:521–524.

Higham, Tom, Katerina Douka, Rachel Wood, Christopher Bronk Ramsey, Fiona Brock, Laura Basell, Marta Camps, Alvaro Arrizabalaga, Javier Baena, Cecillio Barroso-Ruíz, Christopher Bergman, Coralie Boitard, Paolo Bascato, Miguel Caparrós, Nicholas J. Conard, Christelle Draily et al. 2014 The timing and spatiotemporal patterning of Neanderthal disappearance. *Nature* 512:306–309.

Hoefs, J. 1987 *Stable Isotope Geochemistry*. Springer-Verlag, New York.

Leroi-Gourhan, Arlette 1975 The flowers found with Shanidar IV, a Neanderthal burial in Iraq. *Science* 190(4214):562–564.

Lev, Efraim 1992 The vegetal food of the "Neanderthal" man in Kebara cave, Mt. Carmel in the Middle Paleolithic period. M.Sc. thesis, Department of Life Sciences, Bar-Ilan University, Israel (in Hebrew with English summary).

Lev, Efraim, Mordechai Kislev and Ofer Bar-Yosef 2005 Mousterian vegetal food in Kebara Cave, Mt. Carmel. *Journal of Archaeological Science* 32:475–484.

Lietava, Jan 1992 Medicinal plants in a Middle Paleolithic grave Shanidar IV? *Journal of Ethnopharmacology* 35(3):263–266.

Madella, Marco, Martin K. Jones, Paul Goldberg, Yuval Goren and Erella Hovers 2002 The exploitation of plant resources by Neanderthals in Amud Cave (Israel): The evidence from phytolith studies. *Journal of Archaeological Science* 29:703–719.

Mallol, Carolina, Dan Cabanes and Javier Baena 2010 Microstratigraphy and diagenesis at the upper Pleistocene site of Esquilleu Cave (Cantabria, Spain). *Quaternary International* 214:70–81.

Mercader, Julio 2009 Mozambican grass seed consumption during the Middle Stone Age. *Science* 326(5960):1680–1683.

Mercader, Julio, Tim Bennett and Mussa Raja 2008 Middle Stone Age starch acquisition in the Niassa Rift, Mozambique. *Quaternary Research* 70:283–300.

Miller, Christopher E. and Christine Sievers 2012 An experimental micromorphological investigation of bedding construction in the Middle Stone Age of Sibudu, South Africa. *Journal of Archaeological Science* 39:3039–3051.

Minagawa, M. and E. Wada 1984 Stepwise enrichment of ^{15}N along food chains: Further evidence and the relation between $\partial15$ and animal age. *Geochimica and Cosmochimica Acta* 48:1135–1140.

Naito, Yuichi I., Yoshito Chikaraishi, Dorothée G. Drucker, Naohiko Ohkouchi, Patrick Semal, Christoph Wißing and Hervé Bocherens 2016 Ecological niche of Neanderthals from Spy Cave revealed by nitrogen isotopes of individual amino acids in collagen. *Journal of Human Evolution* 93:82–90.

O'Leary, M. H. 1981 Carbon isotope fractionation in plants. *Phytochemistry* 20:553–567.

O'Regan, Hannah J., Angela L. Lamb and David M. Wilkinson 2016 The missing mushrooms: Searching for fungi in ancient human dietary analysis. *Journal of Archaeological Science* 75:139–143.

Pearsall, Deborah M. 2015 *Paleoethnobotany: A Handbook of Procedures*. Third ed. Routledge, New York.

Perera, Nimal, Nikos Kourampas, Ian A. Simpson, Siran U. Deraniyagala, David Bulbeck, Johan Kamminga, Jude Perera, Dorian Q. Fuller, Katherine Szabó and Nuno V. Oliveira 2011 People of the ancient rainforest: Late Pleistocene foragers at the Batadomba-lena rockshelter, Sri Lanka. *Journal of Human Evolution* 61:254–269.

Rosen, Arlene Miller 2003 Middle Paleolithic plant exploitation: The microbotanical evidence. In *Neanderthals in the Levant: Behavioral Organization and the Beginnings of Human Modernity*, edited by D. O. Henry, pp. 156–171. Continuum, London.

Salazar-García, Domingo C., Robert C. Power, Alfred Sanchis Serra, Valentín Villaverde, Michael J. Walker and Amanda G. Henry 2013 Neanderthal diets in central and southeastern Mediterranean Iberia. *Quaternary International* 318:3–18.

Schoeninger, Margaret J. 2014 Stable isotope analyses and the evolution of human diets. *Annual Review of Anthropology* 43:413–430.

Schoeninger, Margaret J. and Michael J. DeNiro 1984 Nitrogen and carbon isotopic composition of bone collagen from marine and terrestrial animals. *Geochimica et Cosmochimica Acta* 48:625–639.

Sievers, Christine and Lyn Wadley 2008 Going underground: Experimental carbonization of fruiting structures under hearths. *Journal of Archaeological Science* 35:2909–2917.

Sistiaga, Ainara, Carolina Mallol, Bertila Galván and Roger Everett Summons 2014 The Neanderthal meal: A new perspective using faecal biomarkers. *PLoS ONE* 9(6):e101045. doi:101010.101371/journal.pone.0101045.

Trinkaus, Erik 2007 European early modern humans and the fate of the Neandertals. *Proceedings of the National Academy of Sciences* 104(18):7367–7372.

van der Merwe, Nikolaas J. 1982 Carbon isotopes, photosynthesis, and archaeology. *American Scientist* 70:596–606.

Walker, Michael J., Mariano V. López-Martínez, Jon Ortega-Rodrigáñez, María Haber-Uriarte, Antonio López-Jiménez, Azucena Avilés-Fernández, Juan Luis Polo-Camacho, Matías Campillo-Boj, Jesús García-Torres, José S. Carrión García, Miguel San Nicolás-del Toro and Tomás Rodríguez-Estrella 2012 The excavation of buried articulated Neanderthal skeletons at Sima del las Palomas (Murcia, SE Spain). *Quaternary International* 259:7–21.

Weyrich, Laura S., Sebastian Duchene, Julien Soubrier, Luis Arriola, Bastien Llamas, James Breen, Alan G. Morris, Kurt W. Alt, David Caramelli, Veit Dresely, Milly Farrell, Andrew G. Farrer, Michael Francken, Neville Gully et al. 2017 Neanderthal behaviour, diet, and disease inferred from ancient DNA in dental calculus. *Nature* 544:357–362.

Wißing, Christoph, Hélène Rougier, Isabelle Crevecoeur, Mietje Germonpré, Yuichi I. Naito, Patrick Semal and Hervé Boucherens 2016 Isotopic evidence for dietary ecology of late Neandertals in north-western Europe. *Quaternary International* 411:327–345.

6

THE PALEOETHNOBOTANY OF MAIZE

Understanding Domestication and Agriculture

Glossary

agriculture   food system based primarily, but not exclusively, on the cultivation of domesticated plants; may include rearing of domesticated animals.

alluvium   unconsolidated sediments that have been eroded and redeposited by water.

anthropogenic soils/black earths   very dark, fertile soils of pre-Columbian human origin, mixtures of soil and occupation debris (charcoal, bone, human and animal feces, pottery sherds, plant matter, and the like).

Classic period   a chronological division of prehistory (for example, of Mesoamerica) characterized by large-scale political entities, sophisticated art and architecture, and intensive agriculture.

cluster analysis   a multivariate statistical approach that groups together previously ungrouped data according to defined criteria (e.g., measured values of variables), producing a classification in which members of each resulting group are more similar to each other than to members of other groups.

discriminant function analysis   a multivariate statistical approach designed to discover and emphasize those variables that best discriminate between two groups, thus allowing ungrouped units to be assigned to them. A related approach, canonical variate analysis, is used for discriminating among three or more groups.

Formative period   a stage of prehistoric cultural development, often used as a chronological division of prehistory (for example, of Ecuador), characterized by the first appearance of public/ceremonial structures, the growth of agricultural villages, and the appearance, or increasing sophistication, of pottery making.

genetic drift   the change in the frequency of genetic variants in a small population due to random sampling.

Preceramic period   a chronological division of prehistory (for example, of Peru), characterized by the absence of pottery making, and during which plant and animal species were domesticated and the first villages appeared.

raised fields   artificial earthen planting surfaces (circular to elongated mounds) built above the level of flood waters and separated by shallow, water-filled canals (dug out to create the raised surfaces).

squared–chord distance analysis   a multivariate statistical approach for assessing how different (or similar) the compositions of entities (e.g., proportions of phytolith morphotypes) within samples are from each other.

Introduction

Plant domestication and the origins of agriculture are topics of long-standing interest in archaeology, anthropology, and the plant sciences, among other disciplines. These are topics that can be approached in many ways, from genetic studies of crops and their ancestors, to analyses of crop names in diverse languages, to modeling productivity under different environmental conditions. Having said this, the study of actual ancient crop remains is central to understanding when, where, and the cultural context for emergence of food systems incorporating domesticated plants. These understandings, in turn, are essential for understanding/ modeling why people turned to agriculture.

I have selected maize for this case study of how paleoethnobotany contributes to our understanding of plant domestication and agriculture because it's a crop I have been interested in since I was a student and it can be identified using all the major kinds of archaeobotanical data. Its importance and archaeological visibility mean there is a large literature on the crop, only a small sample of which can be discussed here. The case is organized around two broad topics: identifying and characterizing maize (i.e., how do we know that a charred bit, starch grain, etc., is maize?) and inferring how important maize was in foodways (i.e., is it maize agriculture?). This case study illustrates what can be learned about the archaeology of a single important plant species if multiple kinds of evidence are brought to bear on investigating it. Table 6.1 provides the scientific names for plants mentioned in the text.

Is It Maize? Identifying and Characterizing Maize Remains

Introduction

Maize is a domesticated plant that can be identified and characterized by the morphology and starch of its edible seeds (called kernels), the morphology and phytoliths of the inedible part of the fruit (the cupules and glumes of the cob), its pollen (produced in the male inflorescence, the tassel), and some kinds of leaf and stem phytoliths (Figure 6.1). Some maize tissues other than the fruit are also distinctive, but are rarely preserved and will not be our focus. In some ways maize is easy to distinguish from its wild ancestor, the grass Balsas teosinte, related members of *Zea*, its genus, and other wild grasses; in others it is a more daunting task that has required considerable research efforts. The importance of maize to cultural developments throughout the New World has driven research into ways of identifying and characterizing it reliably in all kinds of archaeological settings and in environmental records.

In this section I review how maize is identified by macroremains, pollen, phytoliths, and starch and present examples to illustrate how methods are applied, especially for documenting when maize was domesticated and the route and timing of its spread. Maize is a very diverse

TABLE 6.1 Scientific names of plant taxa mentioned in the text

algarrobo	*Prosopis*
arrowhead	*Sagittaria*
arrowroot	*Maranta arundinacea*
arrowroot family	Marantaceae
Balsas teosinte/wild maize	*Zea mays* ssp. *parviglumis*
bean	*Phaseolus*
black algarrobo	*Prosopis nigra*
Cheno-Am	Chenopodiaceae and *Amaranthus*
chili pepper	*Capsicum*
cocoyam	*Xanthosoma*
legume family	Fabaceae
leren/lleren	*Calathea*
maize (corn)	*Zea mays*
manioc (yuca, cassava)	*Manihot esculenta*
marunguey	*Zamia*
mint family	Lamiaceae
palm family	Arecaceae
ragweed	*Ambrosia*
red mangrove	*Rhizophora*
squash	*Cucurbita*
sweet potato	*Ipomoea batatas*
teosinte	wild *Zea*
wild rice	*Zizania*
yam family	Dioscoreaceae

crop, and identification often includes characterization of the kind of maize (referred to as variety or race) present from archaeological remains. I'll end with comments on the potential and limitations of identifying and characterizing maize from archaeobotanical remains and the implications of this for understanding New World agriculture.

Macroremains

Once consensus was reached that Balsas teosinte was the ancestor of maize (a fascinating story, but too complex to summarize here), identifying maize macroremains became straightforward— maize ears (made up of the cob and kernels, covered by a husk) are very different from teosinte fruits. There are hundreds of traditional varieties of maize, however, so archaeobotanists have long been interested in characterizing the *kinds* of maize present in sites. The ear is a complex structure for which there are dozens of possible measurements (Bird 1994). Some 60 were used to characterize traditional maize races in Andean Peru, for example. Based on his experience, as well as the research of others, Bird (1994) recommended seven measurements that could be taken on fragmented archaeological cobs and that incorporated useful variables for distinguishing modern maize races. These were (1) cupule width, (2) cupule length, (3) cupule depth, (4) cupule wing width, (5) rachis segment length, (6) rachis diameter, and (7) row number (Figure 6.2). Each cupule supports the tips of two kernels; if a complete cob circumference is preserved, row number is twice the number of ranks of cupules making up

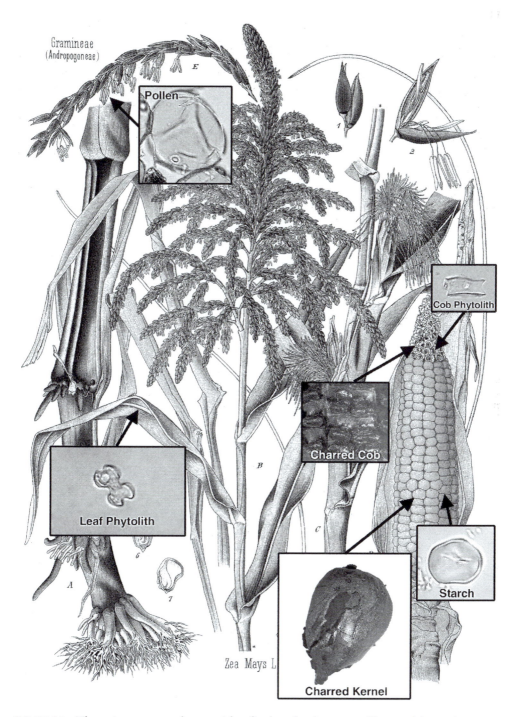

FIGURE 6.1 The primary research materials of paleoethnobotany, as illustrated by maize: macroremains (charred kernel, cob fragment), pollen, phytoliths (cob and leaf), and starch (from kernels). Although rarely preserved by charring, macroremains of leaves, stalks, and other plant parts can be preserved by desiccation or waterlogging. Phytoliths are also present in other plant tissues, including roots (background image from *Köhler's Medizinal-Pflanzen in naturgetreuen Abbildungen*. 1887; accessed at www.botanicus.org/).

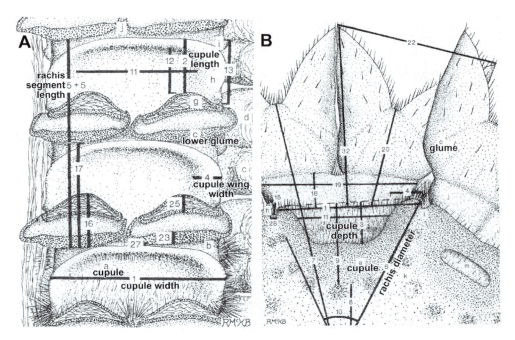

FIGURE 6.2 **A:** View of a segment of an Ioway Blue Flour maize cob with four ranks (eight rows). The chaff is cut away from the near side. Indicated are (a) cupule, (b) interali-cole rachis tissue, (c) lower glumes, (d) upper glumes, (g) rachillas, (h) cupule wings, and (i) sulcus (longitudinal furrow between ranks). Numbers refer to measurements discussed in the text. Hairs have not been removed from the lowest alicole. Three silks lie between ranks on the left. Seen for the first time in this specimen are fragile protrusions at the lower edges of the cupule wings. Sessile and pedicellate spikelets are very similar. Cupule wide is ca. 9.8 mm; **B:** Cross-section of an Andean flint maize cob, basal aspect. Two alicoles side by side are shown with the cupules cut and lower glumes visible. The cupule wing line is drawn in dashes. The letters and numbers are as in Figures 1.1 and 1.2. Adapted from Bird (1970). (Figure 1.1 and Figure 1.3 from Bird, Robert Mck. 1994. Manual for the measurement of maize cobs. In *Corn and Culture in the Prehistoric New World*, edited by S. Johannessen and C. A. Hastorf, pp. 5–22. Westview Press, Boulder, CO.)

Reproduced and modified with the permission of Westview Press, an imprint of Hachette Book Group. Numbers refer to measurements discussed in Bird (1994); labels for the seven essential measurements for distinguishing maize races have been added.

that circumference. Row number can also be estimated from the angle formed by the planes on each side of the cupule (Bird 1994). For kernels, length, width, and thickness are usually measured, and row number can be estimated from the angles of the kernel sides (King 1994). Using cob and kernel measurements for a population of maize remains, one can characterize the general kind of the maize—for example, as a low row number variety with broad, flat kernels—explore diversity within the assemblage, compare populations in a region, investigate changes over time, and so on.

Maize cobs shrink when charred, and shrinkage varies somewhat among measurements and races (Benz 1994). This creates challenges if one wants to compare a population of charred maize cobs directly to modern maize races to investigate whether they are related. The analyst needs to have an idea of the general racial affiliation of the archaeological maize to determine which modern races to use to develop shrinkage correction factors. Maize kernels also change shape when charred, tending to increase substantially in thickness, with lesser increases in width and length (King 1994). King and others have found that many combinations of heat and time produce highly distorted kernels, unlike those recovered archaeologically. Well-preserved archaeological kernels may have been boiled or treated with lye (for hominy) prior to charring. There is considerable variation in row numbers estimated from kernel angles; basing row number on a few kernels may give inaccurate results (King 1994).

The shapes and sizes of maize cobs and kernels reflect their genetic relationships, but are also influenced by environment. Field trials using a traditional race from the American Southwest showed that many archaeobotanically relevant characters were affected in some way by differences in moisture (amount and/or timing) (Adams et al. 1999). Among the least variable characters are row number, kernel volume, kernel width/length ratio, and ear diameter/length ratio. More variable characters include kernel width, kernel length, rachis segment length, ear length, cob diameter, and cupule width. The research of Adams and colleagues suggested that row number (little affected by moisture), cupule width (moderately affected), and certain ratios were among the better indicators of different maize varieties.

Maize macroremains have been identified and characterized at many sites in the New World. An example from early in my career was a study of a cache of charred kernels from a pot from Manabí Province, Ecuador (Pearsall 1980). The study explored what could be learned by measuring the kernels and comparing the results to living races, or varieties, of maize from Ecuador and surrounding countries. I measured a sample of 100 kernels as described earlier and estimated the row numbers. I experimented with measuring kernel side angles from cobs of known row numbers and learned that kernels from 8- and 10-row cobs could not be separated by kernel angle, but that any kernel giving an angle of 12 or 14 rows was from a higher row number cob. There appeared to be two different groups of kernels in the cache, an 8- to 10-row group and a 12-row group, but whether these represented two races or one race with varying row number was unclear. Interestingly, both groups had kernels that were shaped differently from most modern races of the region with kernels of similar sizes (i.e. they were very broad: w/l ratios 1 or greater). I concluded that the cache was related to a group of races with low row numbers and broad kernels. In hindsight, perhaps these undistorted kernels represented charred hominy.

The next two studies illustrate how changes in maize can be documented over time in a region by study of macroremains. A well-known population of archaeological maize is that recovered from sites in the Tehuacan Valley in central Mexico. Morphological analysis of directly dated dried maize remains from this population revealed variable rates of change in the crop over time (Benz and Long 2000). The authors measured four traits with high heritability (rachis diameter, row number, cupule width, rachis length) and calculated one ratio (cupule width/rachis length), then calculated rates of change in these traits over the 5,505 years represented by the population. Rachis diameter showed the greatest overall change and most continuous size increase through time. Row number and rachis length also increased early (between 3400 and 2700 cal. BC), while cupule width decreased. The changes observed prior to 2700 cal. BC were attributed to human selection for increased yield, although environmental changes and genetic drift may also have contributed. Rates of change slowed from 2700 cal. BC to AD 150 (late Preceramic and Formative periods), but continued toward increased grain size or number. This result appeared counterintuitive, because this was the time period when agriculture was believed to become dominant, but could have been due to population isolation or changes in growing conditions. Rates of change increased after AD 150, probably associated with the intensification of maize agriculture during the Classic period and after.

A study by Diehl (2005) of charred maize from three sites in the Tucson Basin, Arizona, spanning the San Pedro (1200–800 BC), Early Cienega (800–400 BC), and Late Cienega (400 BC–AD 50) phases of the Early Agricultural Period, also explored potential changes in maize productivity. Cob and cupule morphology—specifically cupule size, pith diameter, and row number—was used to model potential yield. If cupule size limits kernel size, then variation in cupule size should reflect relative yields. Larger piths are required to feed larger developing seeds, making pith diameter another proxy for productivity. The study found that pith diameters and row numbers for the study population, shown in Table 6.2, A, were consistent with maize from other Early Agricultural Period sites, shown in Table 6.2, B. Mean cupule width increased significantly from the Early to Late Cienega phases of the Early Agricultural Period in the study population (i.e., from 3.1 mm to 3.8 mm), signaling an early increase in potential maize yields. There was an overall trend in the region of increasing cupule width from the Early Agricultural Period (mean widths from 2.56 to 2.93 mm) through the Hohokam Classic Period (mean widths from 2.8 to 8.2 mm).

Ethnographic studies have shown that specific morphological attributes of maize ears may be selected for ceremonial purposes or to demonstrate social identity and status. Being able to distinguish maize varieties archaeologically might provide insight into such practices in prehistoric societies. For example, Turkon (2006) used maize cupule size to infer preferred access to distinctive maize varieties by elite households in the Malpaso Valley, Mexico. People would not have selected for cupule characteristics directly, but cupule morphology is closely related to kernel size and shape. Maize was studied from household midden deposits from three sites inferred to have different statuses. Cupules were measured and ratios used to quantify their general shapes. These data were then analyzed statistically by cluster analysis, and a three-cluster solution was determined. Variables most responsible for differences among clusters were cupule width and overall shape (elongated or cube shaped). Only the highest-ranked households had access to ears from Cluster 3, the most morphologically distinctive cluster, suggesting that a specific maize variety had been used as a status marker. Cluster 2, characterized by larger cupules, was also found more frequently in high-ranking households, leading Turkon to conclude that those households had preferred access to maize grown under better conditions.

Pollen

Maize is a grass, and like other grasses, produces simple pollen grains that are roughly spheroidal in shape, with a single pore bordered by an annulus (a raised ring) and an essentially smooth surface (Sluyter 1997; see photo in Figure 6.1). What is most distinctive is the size of maize pollen: typically 58 to 99 μ, significantly larger than pollen of unrelated wild grasses. There are subtle differences in surface sculpturing between maize and some other grasses, but major diameter remains the primary characteristic used to identify maize pollen (Sluyter 1997).

Identifying maize pollen is more complex in Mesoamerica, where wild grasses related to maize are native. Recent research has found more overlap in pollen size between maize and wild *Zea* taxa than previously documented (Holst et al. 2007). Holst and colleagues studied

TABLE 6.2 A: Mean maize cupule dimensions, row numbers, and pith diameters from the Clearwater, Las Capas, and Los Pozos sites; **B:** Cupule measurements and row numbers from other studies of Arizona maize. (Table 2 and Table 3 from Diehl, Michael W. 2005. Morphological observations on recently recovered Early Agricultural Period maize cob fragments from southern Arizona. *American Antiquity* 70(2):361–375

A

Site	Phase	Mean Cupule Dimension (mm)							Cob Row Number and Pith Diameter (mm)					
		Thickness	n	Width	n	Overall Length	n	Range	Mean	Mode/ Median	n	Pith Diameter	n
Los Pozos	L. Cienega	2.3	95	3.8	88	1.9	98	-	-	-	-	-	-
Clearwater	E. Cienega	1.8	8	3.1	8	1.5	8	-	-	-	-	-	-
Las Capas	San Pedro	2.3	210	3.2	272	2.2	266	8-14	11.58	10/12	29	2.08	23

B

Site	Cupule Dimensions (means in mm.)			Cob Row Numbers	Source
	Width	Length	Depth		
Early Agricultural Period					
Donaldson Site	2.56; n = 102	-	1.72; n = 101	8-20 rows; mode 12-14; n = 10	L. Huckell (1995)
Los Ojitos Site	2.93; n = 338	-	1.67; n = 336	8-22 rows; mode 12-14; n = 46 cobs	L. Huckell (1995)
Milagro	2.86; n = 28	-	1.73; n = 28	8-14rows: mean 10.8; n = 5 cobs	L. Huckell (1995)
Ceramic Period					
Tumamoc Hill[a]	3.8; n= 13	-	2.6; n=13	estimated 10-14rows	Fish et al. (1986:567)
Hohokam					
Gatlin Site	5.0	-	-	mode = 12 rows; mean = 11.7; n = 18	Miksicek (1979:137)
West Branch Site	2.8-7.6; n = 25	1.9-5.6	-	-	Miksicek (1986:302)
AZ T:14:12	6.4	-	-	10-12 rows; mean = 11.7; mode = 12; n = 13	Miksicek (1979)
Reeve Ruin	6.1	-	-	8-12 rows; mean = 12: mode = 12; n = 6	Miksicek (1979)
Alder Wash	8.2	-	-	10-16 rows; mean = 12.7; mode = 12; n = 85	Miksicek (1979)
Historic Papago Varieties[b]					
White Flour	6.9	-	-	10-16 rows; mean = 13.1; mode =12, 16; n = 14	Miksicek (1979)
Pink Flour	9.4	-	-	8 rows; n = 1	Miksicek (1979)
Red Flour	7.0	-	-	10 rows; n = 1	Miksicek (1979)
Yellow Flint	6.9	-	-	12 rows; n = 2	Miksicek (1979)
Blue Flint	9.4	-	-	12 rows; n = 1	Miksicek (1979)

[a]In association with AMS samples but not directly dated. Fish et al. (1986) linked them with "pre-Ceramic" contexts but the AMS dates are consistent with the Early Ceramic Period occupations at this multiple-component site.
[b]Miksicek (1979) reduced measurements on uncarbonized modern Papago specimens by 20 percent to correct for shrinkage in carbonized prehistoric specimens.

Reproduced with permission of Cambridge University Press and the Society for American Archaeology. Notice that much larger (wider) cupules characterized maize of the later time periods (Ceramic Period, Hohokam Period) in the Tucson Basin, as well as historic Papago varieties of maize.

multiple examples of five teosinte taxa and five species of *Tripsacum*, a genus related to *Zea*. Whereas prior research indicated that fossil grains >90 μ could be identified as maize rather than wild *Zea*, the new research found overlap in larger grains between maize and some teosintes, leading the authors to conclude that maize and teosinte could not be differentiated reliably by pollen size. Like other researchers, they found no discernable differences between teosinte and maize pollen surfaces. In terms of *Tripsacum*, four of the five species studied produced pollen smaller than that of teosinte and maize; there was size overlap with *Tripsacum pilosum*. However, *Zea* and *Tripsacum* pollen differed distinctly in the nature of surface sculpturing, effectively separating pollen of the two genera.

Pollen size can be affected by the medium used to make slide mounts, an important consideration for identifications based on size. Sluyter (1997) compared diameter measurements 1 day after mounting and 30 days later for maize pollen mounted in silicone oil (considered to preserve true dimensions), glycerin jelly (thought to distend grains progressively over time), and acrylic resin (not previously studied). The study confirmed that maize pollen measurements were stable in silicone oil mounts and increased progressively in glycerin and that acrylic resin distended grains 10 percent and then the size stabilized. Sluyter recommended that if glycerin was used, measurements be made immediately after mounting; a correction factor could be used for acrylic resin mounts.

Grasses are wind-pollinated plants, but the large pollen of maize does not travel far, basically falling from the tassel onto the silks of nearby ears. Maize pollen is also relatively flimsy and easily torn. These characteristics, among others, are thought to account for the low concentrations of maize pollen (i.e., low counts per unit volume or weight of sediment) typically deposited in a lake's sediments from maize fields in its watershed. To investigate more fully what influenced maize pollen concentrations in lakes, Lane et al. (2010) studied maize pollen deposition along transects of surface sediment samples from four lakes in Wisconsin that differed in size and land use. The lakes were all near each other; the amount of land under recent maize cultivation within 200 m of each lake varied from 30 to 67 percent. The study found that maize pollen concentrations were highly variable within and between lakes. Nonetheless, there was a significant positive relationship between maize pollen concentrations and percentage area under cultivation. Not all samples showed this pattern; several samples close to fields contained no pollen, whereas some distant samples contained high concentrations. Smaller lakes had higher maize pollen concentrations, being more sensitive to local watershed conditions. Maize concentrations often peaked on the shore nearest the largest fields, but this was not observed if there was thick vegetation along the shore. The authors concluded that although maize pollen concentrations in lakes were subject to many landscape variables, concentration values were significantly positively correlated with amount of land under maize cultivation. We'll look at an example of using maize pollen concentrations to evaluate the importance of the crop later.

Given the tendency of maize pollen to occur in low quantities in samples, methods have been developed to maximize its recovery. The analyst may scan additional slide mounts solely for maize after completing a standard 200-count of all pollen, with or without sieving residues to concentrate larger grains. Whitney et al. (2012) recommended incorporating a sieving step into standard processing of tropical lake sediments to enhance recovery of all large cultigen pollen. Tests of the new methodology successfully isolated maize pollen from lake sediments for which no maize had been found using standard methods.

As discussed in Chapter 2, pollen is often not well preserved in archaeological sediments and soils in the absence of waterlogging or desiccation. However, pollen has contributed significantly to documenting maize use at sites in drier regions, for example, in the American Southwest. One interesting example was Hall's (2010) investigation of early maize use in Chaco Canyon by study of pollen in prehistoric woodrat middens. Multiple pollen samples were taken from two woodrat middens; pollen extracts were dated by accelerator mass spectrometry (AMS) to 2567 to 409 cal. BC, demonstrating that the middens accumulated over a long period of time. Pollen was abundant (12,000–111,0000 grains/gr) and included maize, but in relatively low concentrations (0.47–60 grains/gr). This nonetheless represented significant quantities of maize pollen, given its poor dispersal. Hall argued that maize fields were likely located nearby, in the alluvial floor of Chaco Canyon, close to the cliff where the woodrat middens were located. Maize pollen from the middens was measured and compared to modern and Pueblo II Period maize (Figure 6.3). The size–frequency distribution of the oldest three samples (E, D, C) showed great variability and were likely each from more than one population of maize (i.e., the diameters were not normally distributed [not a bell-shaped graph]). The younger Archaic Period samples (B, A) and the later Pueblo II sample were normally distributed. Hall concluded that more than one variety of maize was grown in the earlier fields and that the maize grown during the Archaic Period produced pollen that was significantly larger than that of later varieties.

There are examples from throughout the New World of identifying maize in lake and swamp sediments by pollen. Along with phytoliths, pollen from environmental records has allowed us to date and track the spread of maize and to evaluate the impact of its cultivation on the landscape. We'll look at two examples of tracking maize through environmental records in the next section.

Phytoliths

Like all grasses, maize is a heavy silica accumulator. It produces a variety of distinctive phytoliths, and this diversity has led to the development of different approaches to identifying maize by phytoliths, beginning in the mid-1970s.

The first approach, developed by myself, Dolores Piperno, and colleagues for application in the lowland Neotropics outside the range of wild *Zea* (teosintes), was based on cross-shaped phytoliths produced in maize leaves and other vegetative tissues (see Ball et al. 2016, Pearsall 2015, and Piperno 2006b for details and citations for original studies). Comparisons to wild grasses revealed that maize typically produced more crosses, and larger crosses (>16 μ on the shortest side), than most wild grasses. Many maize crosses had a distinctive three-dimensional morphology (Variant 1, cross-shaped on both flat faces) that was rarer in wild grasses, which produced other cross variants. Using discriminant function formulae developed from studies of wild grasses and maize races, we demonstrated that an assemblage of crosses could reliably be classified as maize or wild grass based on cross size and three-dimensional morphology. Wild *Zea* species were found to produce crosses that overlapped in size and morphology with maize. However, the discriminant function formulae could be applied to sites within the range of teosinte if archaeological assemblages lacked the distinctive fruitcase phytoliths produced by wild *Zea*. Subsequently the cross identification method was expanded to other regions; Iriarte (2003), for example, demonstrated that the discriminant function formulae successfully separated wild grasses and maize in the grasslands of southeastern South America. Overall, phytolith assemblages from lowland Neotropical settings in which maize vegetative tissues were deposited have these traits: abundant panicoid phytoliths, high ratios of crosses to bilobates, abundant large crosses, extra-large crosses, high proportions of Variant 1 crosses, low proportions of Variant 5/6 crosses, and large and extra-large Variant 1 crosses.

Further study of maize and teosinte culms (stalks) by Piperno et al. (2009, supplemental information) revealed that distinctive phytoliths were produced by these tissues. In maize, culm phytoliths were predominantly bilobate or irregularly cross-shaped, often thick and

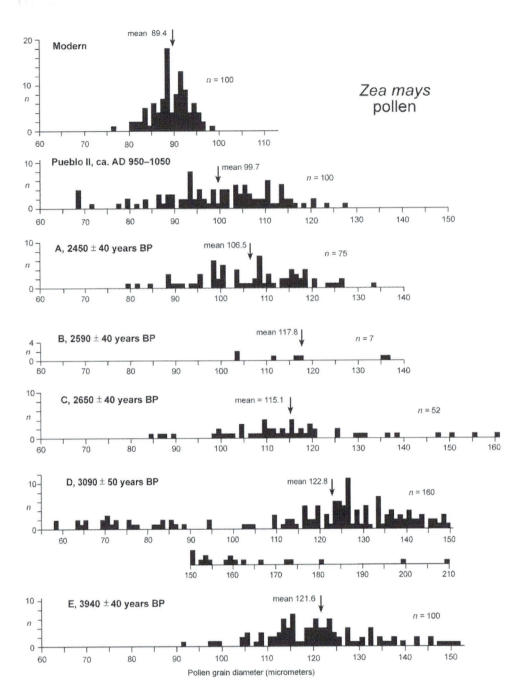

FIGURE 6.3 Size–frequency diameters of *Zea mays* pollen grains: modern, Pueblo II, and fossil midden samples A through E from Chaco Canyon, New Mexico; the Pueblo II *Zea* pollen is from the Spadefoot Toad site at Chaco Canyon dated AD 950 to 1050; the modern pollen is from Greer Laboratories. (Figure 6 from Hall, Stephen A. 2010. Early maize pollen from Chaco Canyon, New Mexico, USA. *Palynology* 34(1):125–137.)

Reproduced with permission of Taylor & Francis. Notice the changes in mean diameters (indicated by an arrow) of maize pollen through time (i.e., from the bottom to the top graphs).

with unusual, deeply notched bases. These forms were distinctive from maize leaf and cob phytoliths (see later). Balsas teosinte culms produced forms similar to those seen in maize, as well as distinctive forms.

The other two approaches to identifying maize by phytoliths are based on cob forms, most of which are kinds of rondels (short cells that are circular to oval or square in planar view). Several researchers described the distinctive phytoliths produced in maize cobs and wild *Zea* fruitcases (Bozarth 1993; Mulholland 1993; Piperno and Pearsall 1993). These types were subsequently formalized and compared to complex rondels produced in wild grasses common in the lowland Neotropics (Pearsall et al. 2003). It was found that maize, wild *Zea*, and non-*Zea* panicoid grasses could be distinguished on the basis of several cob types. Study of grasses native to higher elevations in the South American Andes found considerable overlap in inflorescence phytoliths of maize and high-elevation grasses, but established that two rondel forms were diagnostic of maize there (Logan et al. 2012). It has been determined that formation of teosinte fruitcase and maize cob phytoliths is controlled by a gene known as *teosinte glume architecture 1 (tga1)* (Piperno 2006b). Hart et al. (2011) demonstrated that rondel assemblages from fruitcases of different teosinte taxa reflected teosinte taxonomy and could be statistically discriminated on the basis of rondel types.

A third approach for identifying maize by phytoliths was developed to identify maize in cooking residues using rondel assemblages (Hart et al. 2003; Thompson 2006). Charred cooking residues were assumed to be dominated by phytoliths from foods cooked in the pots. In this approach assemblages of rondels recovered from residue samples were compared to rondel assemblages from modern maize and other edible grasses (e.g., wild rice in Hart et al. 2003). Residue and comparative assemblages were compared statistically using squared-chord distance, and residue samples interpreted as maize or wild grass based on the distance values. In an Andean application, applying cluster analysis to the squared-chord distance data revealed groupings in the data, which were interpreted as genetically related maize varieties (Thompson 2006).

This approach was subsequently streamlined by Hart and Matson (2009), who identified maize in charred cooking residues from sites in central New York by multiple discriminant analysis using 7 variables, a considerably reduced number from earlier studies (e.g., Hart et al. 2003, 2007), which used 209 variables. In the revised method, dimensional variables were reduced to 3 and rare rondel types were eliminated, resulting in 60 variables. Stepwise selection of these resulted in a seven-variable discriminant function, which included one size variable and six morphotypes. Applying the revised method to previously analyzed data produced the same results. The most important variable for discriminating maize rondels from those of wild grasses was found to be size.

Phytolith analysis has contributed greatly to documenting the prehistory of maize in the Americas, most notably by identifying maize at archaeological sites with poor organic preservation and by providing another line of evidence to complement pollen in environmental cores. The first application of the cross-body method for identifying maize was at the Real Alto site, Santa Elena Province, Ecuador (Early Formative, 3500–1500 BC, uncal.). Maize crosses were initially identified by size in site sediments, and subsequently by discriminant function, which incorporated cross size and variant (Pearsall 1978; Pearsall and Piperno 1990). Flotation had recovered no recognizable maize macroremains, but maize phytoliths occurred throughout the sequence. The antiquity of maize in this region was pushed back to 6000 BC (uncal.) by identification of maize crosses in sediments at Las Vegas, a Preceramic site also characterized by poor organic preservation (Piperno 1988; Pearsall and Piperno 1990). The earliest records of maize are phytoliths in many regions, for example, in northeastern North America (i.e., the work of Hart and colleagues discussed earlier) and widely in the lowland tropics (Piperno and Pearsall 1998; Piperno 2009).

One early and significant study that incorporated phytolith analysis into environmental coring was research at Lake Ayauchi in the Ecuadorian Amazon (Bush et al. 1989; Piperno 1990). Maize pollen and phytoliths were both absent in the lowest part of the core and appeared together at 6000 cal. BP. The appearance of maize was associated with increases in pollen of herbs and trees characteristic of disturbance and reduced mature forest indicators. Maize pollen and phytoliths occurred sporadically thereafter, consistent with shifting agriculture. This was the first indication that maize cultivation had spread into the Amazon lowlands soon after maize arrived in South America. Beginning at 2400 BP, frequencies of maize pollen and phytoliths increased in the Lake Ayauchi sequence, suggesting intensification of agriculture and perhaps cultivation on a somewhat lowered lake edge.

Recent research at Lake San Pablo in northern Andean Ecuador has revealed that maize was grown equally early in this region, despite lack of early archaeological sites, which are likely buried by volcanic ash (Athens et al. 2016). Phytoliths, analyzed only in the lower section of the core, identified maize beginning ca. 6200 or 6600 cal. BP and after (Table 6.3). Both cob and leaf phytoliths were found. Maize pollen appeared at ca. 4900 cal. BP and increased in frequency significantly in the upper part of the core. Pollen size increased after 2435 cal. BP, perhaps representing the development or introduction of new, more productive, maize varieties. The presence of maize phytoliths, which are fluvially deposited, but the absence of maize pollen in the earliest levels indicated that cultivation took place initially at some distance from the lakeshore.

Ancient agricultural fields can also be productively studied using phytoliths. Iriarte et al. (2010), for example, investigated Late Holocene raised field agriculture in French Guiana through phytolith and stable carbon isotope analysis. This is one of several regions in South America where raised fields were constructed in seasonally flooded savannas, in this case, at two sites dated 670 to 700 cal. BP and 920 to 950 cal. BP. Four raised fields were studied by analysis of phytoliths from soil cores or profiles. The stratigraphy for all fields was similar; results from Piliwa Ridged Field 2 were representative (Figure 6.4): a basal level of clayey marine sediments dominated by globular granulate and globular psilate phytoliths, a middle stratum (next four levels) representing the establishment of freshwater marshes (*Cyperus*, Cyperaceae, and Panicoideae grasses), and an upper stratum (top two levels) representing the raised fields with phytolith assemblages of crops and regrowing vegetation. Maize cob and leaf phytoliths were identified in all fields, indicating that maize represented a major crop. Stable carbon isotope analysis of sediments from one field showed the transformation from mixed C3/C4 wetland vegetation to fields dominated by C4 plants. As mentioned earlier (see Box 5.1), maize follows the C4 pathway.

Starch

Maize starch has a long history of use in the food industry; it was described and illustrated over a century ago by Reichert (1913). Maize kernels produce predominantly simple starch grains that are spheroidal to polyhedral in shape, depending on the hardness of the kernel endosperm; that is, the hard endosperm of flint and popcorn varieties produces more starch

TABLE 6.3 Recovery of *Zea mays* pollen and phytoliths, Core 4, Lake San Pablo. (Table 2 from Athens, J. Stephen, Jerome V. Ward, Deborah M. Pearsall, Karol Chandler-Ezell, Dean W. Blinn and Alex E. Morrison. 2016. Early prehistoric maize in northern highland Ecuador. *Latin American Antiquity* 27(1):3–21. Reproduced with permission of Cambridge University Press and the Society for American Archaeology.) Notice the higher maize pollen counts in the upper section of the core. Maize phytoliths were not abundant in any level, but were present in all analyzed samples

Core, depth interval, cm	Zea pollen[a] grains, no.	Zea phytoliths;[a, b] P = present	Regression date, cal. B.P., 2s (median)	Interpolated date cal. B.P., median
SP-4,surface	1	NA	-	0
SP-4,338-346	2	NA	1804-1883 (1845)	1665
SP-4,388-396	18	NA	2071-2160 (2116)	1771
SP-4,490-498	13	NA	2370-2471 (2421)	2435
SP-4,550-558	25	NA	2691-2804 (2748)	2721
SP-4,590-598	14	NA	2903-3024 (2964)	2911
SP-4,641-649	24	NA	3180-3313 (3246)	3159
SP-4,700-711	30	NA	3430-3572 (3501	3388
SP-4,746-753	19	NA	3663-3815 (3740)	3733
SP-4,792-796	NA	P (df, 2c, 6b, 1V1)	3902-4064 (3983)	4071
SP-4,796-805	19	NA	3940-4103 (4022)	4093
SP-4,811-815	NA	P (1b)	4005-4171 (4089)	4126
SP-4,819-825	7	NA	4059-4228 (4144)	4155
SP-4,823-825	NA	P (df, 2c, 1b, 4V1)	4065-4233 (4149)	4158
SP-4,835-837	3	NA	4135-4307 (4221	4196
SP-4,846-848	NA	P (df, 1V1)	4168-4341 (4255)	4213
SP-4,848-853.5	10	NA	4173-4346 (4260)	4218
SP-4,862.5-867	6	NA	4227-4403 (4316)	4247
SP-4,867-869	NA	P (df)	4260-4437 (4349)	4263
SP-4,886-890	NA	P (df)	4352-4533 (4443)	4312
SP-4,890-895	2	NA	4363-4544 (4454)	4319
SP-4,961-965	NA	P (1b, 3V1)	4635-4827 (4731)	4734
SP-4,965-971	2	NA	4651-4844 (4748)	4760
SP-4,973-977	2	NA	4689-4883 (4787)	4822
SP-4,987-995	1	NA	4776-4974 (4875)	4963
SP-4,1102-1104	NA	P (1V1)	5394-5618 (5507)	5327
SP-4,1311-1315	NA	P (2c, 1V1)	5752-5991 (5872)	5863
SP-4,1331-1332	NA	P (1b, 2V1)	5844-6087 (5967)	6075
SP-4,1348-1350	NA	P (2c, 2b)	5937-6183 (6061)	6300
SP-4,1362-1366	NA	P (df, 1V1)	6018-6268 (6144)	6493
SP-4,1372-1374	NA	P (df, 1V1)	6067-6319 (6194)	6609

[a]NA = not analyzed (each interval was analyzed for either pollen or phytoliths, but not both). Twelve pollen samples were analyzed below the 987-995 cm interval, but no maize pollen was found.
[b]Basis of maize phytolith identification: df, discriminant function; c, cob bodies; b, large bilobates; V1, large or extra-large Variant 1 crosses. Counts given for c, b, V1.

grains with compression facets, the soft endosperm of flour varieties more grains with smooth outlines (Piperno and Holst 1998; Pearsall et al. 2004). Surfaces sometimes have irregular depressions or raised areas. Hemispherical and vase-shaped grains also occur. Other starch characteristics include a distinct and continuous double border; a central to slightly eccentric (off–center), open hilum; radiating fissures (linear, Y, and X shaped) that can be pronounced; and absence of distinctive lamellae (rings). Typical size range is 4 to 24 μ.

Maize starch does not resemble starches produced by other New World crops, and can be distinguished from starch of non–*Zea* wild grasses on the basis of its larger size, or in the case of non–*Zea* taxa that produce large grains, on the basis of grain morphology. For instance,

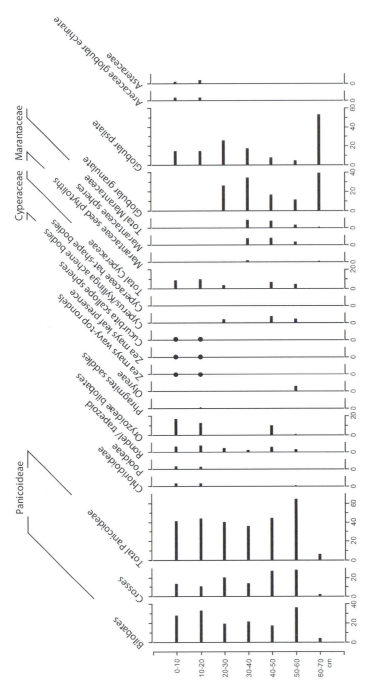

FIGURE 6.4 Percentage phytolith diagram from Piliwa Ridged Field 2. (Figure 4 from Iriarte, José, Bruno Glaser, Jennifer Watling, Adam Wainwright, Jago Jonathan Birk, Delphine Renard, Stéphen Rostain and Doyle McKey. 2010. Late Holocene Neotropical agricultural landscapes: Phytolith and stable carbon isotope analysis of raised fields from French Guianan coastal savannahs. *Journal of Archaeological Science* 37:2984–2994.)

Reproduced with permission of Elsevier. Notice that both maize cob (wavy top rondel) and leaf phytoliths were identified in the two uppermost samples, suggesting that initial crop processing (i.e., shelling, removing kernels from the cob, and discarding it) may have taken place in fields.

Piperno and Holst (1998) studied four genera of panicoid grasses and found size and/or morphological separation with maize; Zarrillo and Kooyman (2006) tested four genera of grasses common in their study region (Canadian Plains) with the same result; Musaubach et al. (2013) compared starch grain morphology of maize and 23 native wild grasses in four subfamilies from the central pampas of Argentina and found potential overlap only with *Sorghastrum pellitum*, a grass that could be eliminated by the presence of distinctive starch masses. As part of his research into the potential of starch grain research in the Eastern Woodlands of North America, Messner (2011, supplemental materials) tested 46 grasses from five subfamilies and described and illustrated all starch types. He found that maize starch could be distinguished from all other grasses native to the Eastern Woodlands on the basis of size and the morphological attributes described earlier.

To investigate whether maize starch could be distinguished from that of wild *Zea*, starch from most teosinte taxa and 12 races of Latin American maize were compared (Holst et al. 2007). Starch content of teosintes was typically poor, with far more oil observed in slide mounts than starch. Except for one specimen of *Zea luxurians*, maize and teosinte mean starch sizes did not overlap (maize starch means were larger), but there was overlap in maximum length ranges (all teosintes, 4–18 μ; all maize races, 4–26 μ). Given these patterns, the authors concluded that larger starch size (greater than or equal to 12.5 μ mean length and 18 μ maximum length) was useful for identifying maize in regions where teosinte was present. Morphological attributes also helped separate maize from wild *Zea*, including whether irregular grains dominated assemblages, oval and bell-shaped grains were absent or rare, grains with transverse fissures were common, and grains with defined compression facets were common; these traits characterized maize starch grain assemblages rather than those of teosinte (Holst et al. 2007).

As discussed in Chapter 2, factors that influence starch survival in archaeological contexts are incompletely understood, but include degree of protection from starch-degrading enzymes and sheer numbers of granules deposited. The discovery that starch deposited in and on artifacts during food processing often survived in identifiable form has resulted in significant new findings concerning the antiquity, spread, and uses of maize.

Among the first applications of starch analysis to investigating New World agriculture was a study by Piperno and Holst (1998) of stone tools from the Aguadulce, Monogrillo, La Mula, and Cerro Juan Diaz sites in Panama. The main focus of their study was demonstrating the potential of starch grains recovered from stone tools to document early tuber use, given that underground storage organs (USOs) were very poorly represented at sites. In terms of maize, maize starch was recovered from tools from each site, providing further evidence for use of maize during the Late Preceramic and after, and demonstrating its association with USOs and other economic plants.

Another significant early application was Perry's (2004) study of ground stone and flaked artifacts from a late prehistoric site, Los Mangos del Parguaza (AD 1000–1500), in the middle Orinoco River region, Venezuela. Her research investigated the relationship between tool form and starch residues, specifically, whether ground stone was used to grind maize kernels and flaked "grater teeth" to shred manioc roots. The surprising results were that no tools had manioc starch on them, although other USOs were represented, and that maize occurred on every tool tested, regardless of form (Table 6.4). Besides charred wood, macroremains were dominated by seed/palm nutshell, with relatively little maize and no evidence of USOs. These results illustrated what starch analysis could add to the picture of subsistence in this region and the potential pitfalls of drawing inferences about plant use from artifact form.

TABLE 6.4 **A:** Starch remains recovered from Los Mangos del Parguaza, noted as numbers of granules; **B:** Macrobotanical remains recovered from Los Mangos del Parguaza. (Table 1 and Table 3 from Perry, Linda. 2004. Starch analyses reveal the relationship between tool type and function: An example from the Orinoco valley of Venezuela. *Journal of Archaeological Science* 31:1069–1081. Reproduced with permission of Elsevier). On A: Artifact 3: groundstone tool fragment; Artifacts 5, 6, 8, 9, 7, 10: flaked artifacts; Artifacts 1, 2: mano fragments; Artifact 4: polished stone. Notice that *Zea mays* starch was ubiquitous on tools (last column) and very abundant. On B: In contrast to starch, notice how rare *Zea mays* macroremains were at the site, by count or ubiquity

A

Taxon	Artifact number and level (see Figs. 2–5)										Total	Ubiquity
	3, 1	5, 2	6, 3	8, 3	9, 4	1, 5	7, 5	10, 5	4, 6	2, 7		
Maranta sp.				3		1	1		1		6	4 of 10
cf. *Maranta* sp.		1				1					2	2 of 10
Myrosma sp.		1		1		1					3	3 of 10
Unidentified grass					1ᵃ						1	1 of 10
Zea mays hard, flint-type	8	8	22	44	40	20	2	12	9	26	191	10 of 10
Zea mays soft, flour-type	10		6	3	10	1		5	3	25	63	8 of 10
cf. *Zea mays*	7	2	6	6	5	3	2	3	3		37	9 of 10
Zingiberaceae					1						1	1 of 10
Unidentified	5	2	16	16	5	17	3	24	2	13	103	10 of 10
Total	30	14	50	73	62	44	8	44	18	64	407	

ᵃ The single notation of the unidentified grass starch represents a large cluster of granules.

B

Taxon or description	Level 3 (0.2–0.3 m)	Level 5 (0.4–0.5 m)	Level 7 (0.6–0.7 m)
Sample size	4.5 l	5.4 l	6 l
Cucurbit squash rind	1 fragment	2 fragments	1 fragment (cf.)
Grass (Poaceae) seed	1, smaller than Lev. 7	1, smaller than Lev. 7	5 fragments
Seed/palm nutshell	61 fragments	40 fragments	1 seed fragment
cf. Euphorbiaceae	14 seed fragments	1 entire seed	
Zea mays kernels		1 entire, 1 fragment	
Zea mays cob frags.		6 cupules, glumes	
Fruit pedicel		1 unknown taxon	
Unidentified fruits		3 fragments exocarp	
Unidentified seeds	1 fragment	6, weedy looking	2 fragmentary
Unidentified tissue		3 fragments, starchy	
Wood charcoal	17.54 g, 1130 frags.	17.95 g, 1526 frags.	8.59 g, 626 frags.
Fungal parathecium		1 entire fruit body	
Fungal basidiocarp		1 fragment	

Zarrillo et al. (2008) employed a new technique to recover starch from charred cooking-pot residues to investigate plant use at the Early Formative Period Loma Alta site in coastal Ecuador. Eight sherds were processed for starch; three residues were directly dated. All sherd residues contained maize starch, including granules that showed evidence of milling (grinding) and heating in water. In addition to maize, *Canavalia* beans, chili peppers, manioc, and arrowroot were prepared in the cooking pots. Maize starch was also recovered from grinding stones and sediment samples from the site. Recovery of maize and other starches from directly dated cooking pot residues provided a firm chronology for its presence and consumption.

Recovering evidence of maize from artifact use surfaces establishes a direct link between the plant and the people using it. This linkage has contributed significantly to dating early maize and documenting its spread. For example, Piperno et al. (2009) recovered starch and phytolith evidence for maize dating to 8700 cal. BP at Xihuatoxtla shelter in the Central Balsas river valley, Mexico. Starch and phytoliths were extracted from 26 ground and chipped stone tools, and 21 sediment samples were analyzed for phytoliths. Most tools (22) preserved starch residues; maize starch was present and dominant on every tool, accounting for 90 percent of all starch recovered. Average grain size was commonly 12 to 17 μ, which is characteristic of maize and outside the mean for teosinte, and the largest granules (20–26 μ) exceeded that of teosinte starch. Starch grain morphologies also matched maize and were of the hard-endosperm type. Phytoliths diagnostic of the glumes and cupules of maize cobs (wavy-top and ruffle-top rondels) were present in sediments associated with the tools. Teosinte fruitcase phytoliths were not present in any sample, nor were *Zea*-type culm phytoliths. The authors concluded that maize, not teosinte, was exploited at Xihuatoxtla shelter and that the focus of use was the kernels. Starch analysis has helped document the early spread of maize into South America: Pagán-Jiménez et al. (2016) recently identified maize starch on 10 stone tools from the Cubilán 2 site in Azuay Province in the southern Ecuadorian Andes, dating 8078 to 7959 cal. BP. These results demonstrated that the Andean highlands were an important pathway of maize dispersal.

Summary and Discussion: Identifying Maize

Maize provides a good example of how paleoethnobotany contributes to our understanding of plant domestication and agriculture, in part because maize can be identified and characterized through recovery and analysis of its macroremains, pollen, phytoliths, and starch grains. Identifying maize macroremains is straightforward—maize ears, even when fragmented, are very different from the fruits of wild grasses and other crops—but characterizing what *kind* of maize is present from macroremains is more complex. Exploring the diversity of an assemblage of maize remains requires the measurement and analysis of multiple characteristics of cob tissues and kernels. Like other grasses, maize produces simple pollen grains that are roughly spheroidal in shape, with a single pore bordered by an annulus, and an essentially smooth surface. Maize pollen is significantly larger than pollen of unrelated wild grasses, but does overlap with teosinte pollen. Maize is a heavy silica accumulator that produces a variety of distinctive phytoliths. Maize can be identified by diagnostic cross-shaped phytoliths, produced in the leaves and other vegetative tissues, and distinctive cob forms, many of which are complex rondels. Maize, teosinte, and non-*Zea* wild grasses can be distinguished on the basis of several diagnostic cob phytoliths. Rondel assemblages can also be used to identify maize in cooking residues and to characterize its diversity. Maize kernels produce predominantly simple starch grains that are spheroidal to polyhedral in shape, with a distinct and continuous double border and radiating fissures that can be pronounced. Maize starch does not resemble starches produced by other New World crops and can be distinguished from starch of teosinte and non-*Zea* wild grasses on the basis of its larger size and morphology.

I hope that this necessarily brief overview of identifying and characterizing maize from archaeobotanical remains has illustrated the great potential that exists for tracking this important New World crop in archaeological sites of different types and ages, and on the landscape. This kind of direct data contributes greatly to our understanding of the age, cultural context, and environmental setting of early plant domestication and the emergence of agriculture. As the examples have shown, maize cultivation and use can leave different kinds of traces, which require different approaches to recovery, identification, and analysis. Searching for maize—or any other crop—using multiple indicators greatly increases our chances of finding it.

All methods discussed here require precision and care in their applications, which often include measurements and statistical analyses of multiple characteristics/variables of ancient and comparative specimens. This is often the case when domesticated plants are the focus of research, because it is essential to distinguish crops from related wild or weedy forms or other "confusers." The development, testing, and refinement of identification methods are important aspects of archaeobotanical research on domesticated plants.

We have focused to this point on how the presence of maize is demonstrated in various contexts through archaeobotanical remains. In what form maize will be present depends on how people interacted with the crop and how likely those interactions led to the deposition and preservation of identifiable remains. Focusing on the ways a crop is present—that is, what kind(s) of archaeobotanical remains—can provide insights in human behaviors surrounding the crop. It is essential to acknowledge, however, that even with multiple ways of identifying a plant archaeologically, we may fail to find it and that there are potentially multiple explanations for why a targeted plant is absent.

Let's now turn to the question of how paleoethnobotany has contributed to understanding the role of maize in subsistence systems in the New World.

Assessing the Importance of Maize in Prehistoric Foodways

Introduction

Inferring the importance of a crop like maize from its archaeobotanical remains has been a central focus of the paleoethnobotany of domesticated plants. There are two common approaches: demonstrating increasing quantities of maize in archaeological contexts, and demonstrating the increasing impact of maize cultivation on the environment. There are many examples of arguments for the importance of maize based on its ubiquity, or percentage presence (i.e., its occurrence in a large number of samples or contexts), and relative frequency (i.e., its large proportion of a total count or other ratio) in archaeological contexts. Less commonly arguments are made based on absolute concentration of remains, for example, of pollen grains, or by demonstrating increased productivity of the crop. The increasing impact of maize on the environment has primarily been addressed through study of changes in pollen, phytolith, and particulate charcoal profiles in lake and swamp records. Only a limited number of examples of each approach can be given here. Changes in the role of maize in the sociopolitical realm are explored as part of the Cahokia case (Chapter 7) and will not be discussed here.

Assessing the Abundance of Maize

Given its limited dispersal, maize pollen is unlikely to become deposited in habitation sites through pollen rain. Pollen is generally absent on kernels or shucked ears (i.e., those with the husks, the outer covering of the ear, removed). For this reason, storing or processing maize in these forms is unlikely to lead to pollen deposition. Deposition of husks or direct use of maize pollen—for example, in ritual—has been found to result in abundant pollen deposition. Geib and Heitman (2015) used these inferences from pollen ecology and experimental washes to assess the extent of maize production in Chaco Canyon using maize pollen data from 78 samples from four Chacoan sites. Overall, 87 percent of samples contained maize pollen, with ubiquities ranging from 40 to 93 percent at sites. Maize was also relatively abundant (>10 percent) in 35 to 42 percent of samples; this was a much higher frequency than typically found in maize fields or at sites outside Chaco Canyon. The authors concluded that these quantities of pollen indicated that maize was grown locally, not received via trade.

Two measures of agricultural dependence, mano (handheld grinding stone) grinding surface area and ubiquity of maize macroremains, were found to be correlated in six regions of the American Southwest (Hard et al. 1996). Size of a grinding surface is a critical variable affecting the amount of grain that can be ground: other factors being equal, a larger grinding surface permits increased output per unit of time. Based on ethnographic examples, a strong correlation was found between mano area and agricultural dependence. A review of archaeological data on mano size and maize ubiquity revealed a strong correlation and differences in the timing of the transition to maize as a staple crop. Figure 6.5 illustrates one pattern: at Black Mesa there was early, substantial use of maize (i.e., notice how high ubiquity and mano area values are in the first time period) followed by gradual increases in dependence. This contrasted with other regions, such as Southern Jornada, where maize use increased over time but never to the levels observed at Black Mesa, implying a later transition to a maize-based economy (Hard et al. 1996).

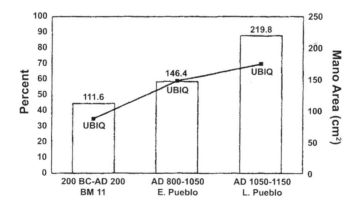

FIGURE 6.5   Black Mesa data. The maize ubiquity points are plotted against the left *Y* axis and mano area bars refer to the right *Y* axis. (Figure 7 from Hard, Robert J., Raymond P. Mauldin and Gerry R. Raymond. 1996. Mano size, stable isotope ratios, and macrobotanical remains as multiple lines of evidence of maize dependence in the American Southwest. *Journal of Archaeological Method and Theory* 3(3):253–318.)

Starch grains preserved in human dental calculus have provided insights into foodways in the Caribbean from ca. 350 BC to AD 1600 (Mickleburgh and Pagán-Jiménez 2012). One central issue is the antiquity of maize and its role—was it a staple food or restricted to ritual or high-status contexts? The authors studied residues from 30 teeth from 14 sites; many teeth showed evidence from dental wear and pathology for consumption of large amounts of starchy foods. Starch was recovered from all but three samples, but overall quantities were low. Five root-tuber resources were identified—marunguey, sweet potato, cocoyam, arrowhead, and manioc—as was starch of Cannaceae and Marantaceae. Legumes and palm were also eaten. These results confirmed that a great variety of starchy plant foods were consumed in the region. In terms of maize, maize starch was present in the dental calculus of 13 individuals from 11 sites. The pattern of damage on granules and the association of maize starch with particulate charcoal indicated consumption of dried maize, probably ground and baked in or over an open fire. There was no difference in the occurrence of maize by sex and no indication of social status differences. The data gave no reliable indication of whether substantial quantities of maize were consumed, but the crop was a component of diet during the Archaic, Early Ceramic, and Late Ceramic Periods.

Plant use at the Middle Formative Los Naranjos site, Honduras, was investigated through analysis of starch, phytoliths, and macroremains and compared to results from a pollen core in adjacent Lake Yojoa (Morell-Hart et al. 2014; Rue 1987). Ubiquity values for identified taxa from the site were calculated based on combined microbotanical and macrobotanical data sets from selected samples. These samples showed high overall richness (36–70 taxa, taking into account possible redundancies), but relatively low ubiquity. Maize and mint family were the most frequently recovered taxa, in 4 of 17 loci, followed by palm family and *Manihot* (manioc genus). Maize was present in the form of phytoliths, starch grains, and one charred kernel, and root crop use was revealed by starch grains of leren, manioc, and sweet potato on obsidian tools. The authors concluded that inhabitants of Los Naranjos exploited a wide range of plants between 1000 BC and 700 BC, making use of seed and root crops and resources from managed forests. Maize agriculture did not seem to be well established by 1000 BC.

This finding contrasted with the pollen record from Lake Yojoa, which provided evidence for maize cultivation beginning ca. 2500 BC (before Los Naranjos was occupied) and intensifying around 1000 BC (Rue 1987). Pollen diversity was relatively low; the arboreal component was dominated by *Pinus* and *Quercus* (upland trees), as many local lowland trees were insect-pollinated (i.e., did not contribute to pollen rain). A biozone of early maize occurrence was characterized by decreases in arboreal pollen and increases in Cheno-Ams, but with few other indications of environmental disturbance. This pattern was interpreted as long fallow agriculture (i.e., fields were cultivated for a short time, then allowed to grow back to forest). At ca. 1000 BC, Ambrosiae and other Compositae field weeds increased, suggesting agricultural intensification (i.e., fields were cultivated longer, with shorter regrow periods) (Rue 1987). Maize pollen was not abundant (usually 1 percent or less of sum) but occurred in most levels after ca. 1000 BC. My thought on reconciling the evidence from these two studies is that perhaps the patterning of maize as seen after 1000 BC in the pollen diagram corresponded to a mixed agricultural system of the kind inferred from the Los Naranjos data, with maize being the crop most visible in the lake pollen record (i.e., given lower pollen production by root crops, legumes, and insect-pollinated arboreal resources).

Multiple lines of evidence were also essential in investigating the role of maize in subsistence at Real Alto, a Valdivia period (4400–1800 cal. BC, Marcos and Michczynski 1996) site in coastal Ecuador. Although the 1974–1975 Real Alto excavations yielded over 900 flotation samples, organic preservation was poor and no maize macroremains were found. As discussed earlier, maize phytoliths were recovered beginning with the initial occupation of the site (Pearsall 1978; Pearsall and Piperno 1990). During the Valdivia 3 period, Real Alto grew to a 12.4-ha town with a central ceremonial precinct. This was the period of maximum settlement size and residential population (Lathrap et al. 1977). Did maize play a central role in the growth of the site from village to town by Valdivia 3?

To assess how common maize was, I reanalyzed 14 phytolith samples taken from six different Valdivia 3 house floors using a discriminant function to classify cross-shaped phytoliths as maize or wild grass. If maize was commonly used at the site, evidence for it should appear routinely in the compacted refuse that made up house floors. As shown in Table 6.5, A, this was the case: crosses were classified as maize in each house (Pearsall 2015). The maize cob

TABLE 6.5 Microfossil indicators for maize and other crops during the Valdivia 3 period, Real Alto site. From Pearsall et al. 2004, Chandler-Ezell et al. 2006, Pearsall 2015

A. Discriminant function test for maize in sediment samples from 6 structures. See Pearsall 2015 for discriminant function formulae.

	No. Crosses	Mean Size Var 1 (mm)	Mean Size Var 5/6	% Var 1	Maize Prediction	Wild Prediction	Outcome
Structure 1, #61	9	14	15	0.56	37.99	35.80	maize
Structure 1, #53–96	23	14.72	15.56	0.39	37.62	35.87	maize
Structure 1, #51–96	19	14.5	15	0.53	39.34	37.04	maize
Structure 2, #3–96	4	17.5	15	0.75	55.87	50.54	maize
Structure 2, #80–96	56	15	15.7	0.48	40.71	38.23	maize
Structure 7, #83–96	52	14.08	16.08	0.31	33.72	32.68	maize
Structure 7, #87–96	30	13.88	15.35	0.37	33.73	32.65	maize
Structure 10, #90	61	13.6	15.3	0.41	33.43	32.28	maize
Structure 10, #81–96	61	16.15	15.88	0.43	44.33	41.44	maize
Structure 10, #77–96	32	13.45	15.13	0.25	29.36	29.30	wild
Structure 20, #1–96	6	14.18	12.5	0.5	35.84	34.62	maize
Structure 20, #2–96	16	15.33	11.88	0.5	40.00	38.30	maize
Structure 22, #82–96	62	15.48	16.6	0.44	42.35	39.58	maize
Structure 22, #84–96	10	12.5	13.3	0.3	25.48	26.18	wild

B. Crop residues from stone tools from Structure 20. Maize starch was present on 17 tools (100%); maize cob phytoliths on seven (41%)

	Ubiquity (n = 17)
maize	100
manioc	29
arrowroot	47
Calathea	12
arrowroot family	35
Canna	35
rooty transport	53
rooty parenchyma	71
fruity transport	47

body approach was also applied to samples from Real Alto (Pearsall et al. 2004). Phytolith and starch residues were studied from 17 stone tools from Structure 20, a Valdivia 3 domestic house. Maize starch was recovered from all tools, for a total of 91 granules (Table 6.5, B). In addition, maize cob phytoliths were found on tools and in floor sediments from Structure 20. This residue study also helped place maize use at Real Alto in context of the whole food system of the site: in addition to maize, manioc, arrowroot, *Calathea (lleren)*, arrowroot family, *Canna*, and silicified transport or parenchyma tissues of roots and fruits were identified on many tools (Chandler-Ezell et al. 2006). Later, an unknown disk-shaped starch morphotype was identified as chili pepper starch (Perry et al. 2007). The Structure 20 starch and phytolith residue study demonstrated that maize was commonly prepared by grinding or pounding as a component of a diet that included roots and tubers, fruits, and other plant foods.

Environmental coring in the former mangrove swamp of the Chanduy estuary, located 4 km downstream from Real Alto, provided further evidence for the importance of maize (Pearsall et al. 2016). Pollen was well preserved from strata dated 3236 to 502 cal. BC in core Ch-045 and documented that the locality was a freshwater habitat, such as a slough inland from the mangrove swamp, at that time. Pollen of herbs and cultigens dominated the record; maize pollen was abundant in the basal level of the core (6 percent by count) and present throughout the sequence in quantities, suggesting that fields were located nearby. Other cultigen pollen was recovered—*Canna* type, *Manihot* (manioc genus), and Malvaceae (cf. *Gossypium*, cotton genus)—and high percentages of weeds indicated intensive human activity. These results provided direct evidence that Valdivia people grew maize and other crops in alluvial settings by at least 3236 cal. BC, the base of the Ch-045 core. The Chanduy area was farmed throughout most of the Formative Period, attesting to the long-term stability of alluvium-based agriculture. In summary, maize was ubiquitous at Real Alto by Valdivia 3; coring data confirmed an agricultural system of maize cultivation oriented to alluvial lands. Both site-based and core results indicated a mixed agricultural system that included root crops and arboreal resources, as well as maize and other annuals.

As a final example of investigating the importance of maize through archaeobotanical remains, let's look at two recent studies from desert coastal Peru that documented early maize cultivation there, but came to different conclusions concerning its importance and subsequent role in cultural developments. New excavations were conducted by Grobman et al. (2012) at the Huaca Prieta and Paredones sites on the north coast. Maize macroremains, phytoliths, and starch were present in Preceramic (Archaic) contexts dated 6700 to 3000 cal. BP. There were 293 maize macroremains recovered during excavation or by screening (cobs and cob fragments; pieces of husk, stalk, tassel; one kernel), most from Middle to Late Preceramic contexts (6700–4000 cal. BP). These macroremains occurred intermittently through time and space at the sites, leading the authors to conclude that maize was not a primary part of the diet. The earliest cob, directly dated to 6775 to 6504 cal. BP, was eight-rowed, short, slender, and cylindrical in shape and identified as belonging to the Proto-Confite Morocho race, a primitive popcorn. The cobs from Middle Preceramic contexts were predominantly this type, but Confite Chavinense, a fasciated race, was also present. Fasciation (in this case, a mutation leading to thickened or flattened growth) of the cob allowed for a larger number of rows and was likely an early mechanism for increasing grain yields. Microfossils were extracted from 54 sediment samples and one tool. Maize phytoliths and starch grains occurred, but not in many contexts (three to four were mentioned); overall starch grains were infrequent in sediments.

Maize starch was consistent with grains found in hard-endosperm varieties of maize, including grains extracted from the archaeological kernel.

Hass et al. (2013) recovered evidence for more extensive maize use during the Late Archaic (5000–3800 cal. BC) in the Norte Chico region of the central coast. This inference was based on botanical evidence from 13 sites, including larger excavations at 2, Caballete and Huaricanga. Over 400 fine sieve– or flotation-recovered macroremain samples were analyzed, and only 9 examples of maize were found (stalks, leaves, cob fragments, kernels). Maize pollen, by contrast, was present in 48 percent of 126 site sediment samples analyzed, and was the second most common pollen type found, after *Typha* (cattail). This abundance was considered consistent with use of maize as a major cultigen. Maize starch was recovered from 79 percent of tools analyzed from Caballete (n = 14), and 68 percent of human coprolites (n = 34) and 75 percent of dog coprolites (n = 16) from Caballete and Huaricanga. Sweet potato and bean starch was also present on some tools, and sweet potato starch in some coprolites. Other roots and tubers, seeds, and fruits were consumed. The authors concluded that the combined microfossil evidence from soil samples, stone tools, and coprolites established that maize was actively grown, processed, and eaten at sites in the valley. Its prevalence in multiple contexts and at multiple sites indicated it was widely grown and significant in diet.

My thoughts on the evidence from these two studies is that perhaps differences in how maize was *represented* at these sites have obscured underlying similarities in its role: the habitual processing and consumption of maize and other crops (i.e., Norte Chico tool- and coprolite-based starch results) resulted in deposition in sediments of relatively few maize macroremains (i.e., results from all sites), starch grains, or phytoliths (i.e., Huaca Prieta and Paredones results), whereas growing maize close by resulted in abundant pollen deposition (i.e., Norte Chico pollen results from sediments; the lack of husks and other pollen-bearing tissues).

Assessing the Impact of Maize on the Landscape

Many examples illustrate how maize cultivation can be identified, and its extent and impact evaluated, through the study of environmental records, that is, by assessing changes in pollen, phytolith, and charcoal abundances in lake and swamp cores. A number of studies have already been discussed in the context of identifying the spread of maize or in association with site-based data on maize abundance. To explore the landscape approach to identifying agriculture and its impacts more thoroughly, I discuss several studies that focus on investigating prehistoric human impacts in Amazonia. There is ongoing debate about the nature and diversity of plant–people interrelationships in this vast region during prehistory, with agricultural practices forming a key component of the discussion.

For example, Bush et al. (2007) investigated the extent to which two regions of terra firma forest (i.e., forest located away from major rivers, in interfluvial settings) had been managed by Native peoples prior to European conquest. Because humans often transform landscapes through burning, and evidence of burning is well preserved in paleoecological records, fire activity is a useful proxy of human activity in Amazonia. Natural fires are rare in many parts of the Amazon; in the wettest parts it is difficult to burn forest at all. Bush and colleagues studied cores from lakes in less seasonal (i.e., wetter) forests in two areas: the western Amazon (four lakes near Puerto Maldonado, Peru) and the eastern (three lakes near Prainha, Brazil). Only one of the lakes in the western Amazon (Gentry Lake) showed evidence of agriculture, with maize pollen occurring from 3700 to 500 BP, in association with *Manihot* pollen at 2400 BP. Abundant charcoal was present in Gentry samples, beginning several thousand years prior to direct evidence of cultivation. Taking the charcoal and crop data together, the authors concluded that although the western region was occupied for more than 8,000 years, landscape alteration was quite localized: only one lake recorded evidence of crop cultivation, whereas other nearby lakes did not. A similar pattern was found for the eastern Amazonian lakes. Maize was found in only one of the three lakes cored (Geral Lake), from ca. 4030 to 850 BP, in association with a consistent occurrence of relatively high charcoal concentrations. There was much lower fire frequency at the other two lakes, even though they were nearby. The authors concluded that, for less seasonal forests, a long history of use and human impact at a central location (i.e., a terra firma lake) had relatively small impacts on nearby areas. In forests with higher seasonality, impacts would likely be more pronounced.

A similar argument was made from a study of phytoliths from soils sampled under present-day forests in western and central Amazonia, including both interfluvial and riverine settings (McMichael et al. 2012; Piperno et al. 2015). At issue: whether large-scale landscape alterations documented along major rivers, in seasonally flooded savannas, and highly seasonal forests also characterized terra firma forests. Interfluvial samples analyzed included samples from 13 sites along a 450-km-long transect from Porto Velho to Manaus in the central Amazon. ^{14}C dates indicated that the phytolith records from these soils spanned several thousand years. The study found little to no evidence for human occupation and vegetation disturbance in the terra firma locales sampled; some riverine areas also showed this pattern. Phytoliths from taxa characteristic of closed, mature forest dominated many samples (>90 percent by count). Maize phytoliths were recovered from a single sample in the Porto Velho to Manaus transect; this sample also showed a higher proportion of phytoliths from early successional herbaceous plants (ESH) and burned grass and *Heliconia* phytoliths. Burned tree phytoliths, another indicator of burning to clear forest for agriculture, were absent at most sites. Although many useful fruit trees do not produce diagnostic phytoliths, palms do, but were not abundant in samples. Overall, it appeared that human impacts on interfluvial forests in the central and western Amazon were infrequent and highly localized, and did not include cultivation or selective management of palms at the sites tested.

Clement et al. (2015a) took issue with the conclusions drawn in the studies just summarized (and others not discussed here), arguing that microfossil and charcoal records did not tell the whole story. There is a consensus among historical ecologists that prehistoric Amazonia was a complex mosaic of coupled human–natural systems, occupied by societies with different levels of complexity that had different impacts on their landscapes. Although population densities varied among major rivers, minor rivers, and interfluvial areas of the Amazon, few pristine landscapes remained by the European conquest. Clement and colleagues argued that these conclusions are supported when a broader array of data is considered, not just microfossil and charcoal records: botanical and ecological data—such as the current distributions of useful plant taxa, including forests dominated by single species, like Brazil nut stands—as well as distributions of anthropogenic soils (black earths), earthworks, and other landscape features. Considering all these sources, they concluded that significant anthropogenic influences occurred throughout the Holocene in portions of all major Amazonian subregions and that landscape domestication accelerated with the transition to food production, ca. 4000 BP and after.

The details of the ensuing comments and responses by McMichael et al. (2015) and Clement et al. (2015b) are very interesting, but beyond the scope of this discussion. In my view there is more agreement than disagreement among researchers: the Amazon is, and was, a highly heterogeneous environment that supported dense populations in some areas, such as along major waterways, and less dense settlement in others. More data of all kinds are needed to understand the history of human occupation in the different parts of the basin; ethnobotany and paleoethnobotany both have important roles to play.

A final example from the western Amazon returns us to maize and evaluating its role in subsistence. Coring in Lake Sauce in the seasonal forest of the Peruvian Amazon has provided a 6,900-year record of climate, vegetation change, and agriculture (Bush et al. 2016). A diverse array of taxa from the lowland seasonal forest was recovered from the core (Figure 6.6). Maize

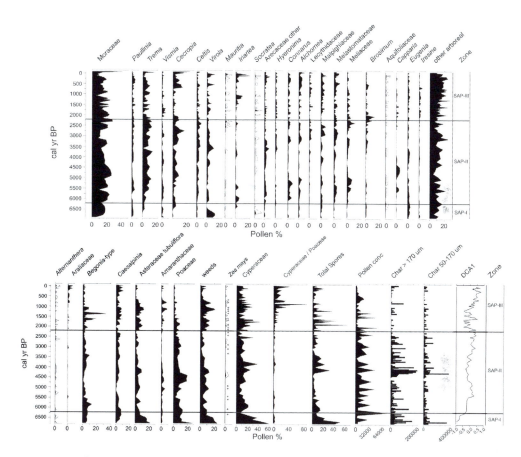

FIGURE 6.6   Percentage occurrence of the most abundant fossil pollen taxa recovered from the sediments of Lake Sauce, Peru, plotted against time. Upper panel shows arboreal taxa, whereas lower panel shows herbaceous taxa, spores, concentration values, and two charcoal size fractions. The values of the DCA Axis 1 sample scores are also plotted against time. (Figure 4 from Bush, M. B., A. Correa-Metrio, C. H. McMichael, S. Sully, C. R. Shadik, B. G. Valencia, T. Guilderson, Steinitz-Kannan M. and J. T. Overpeck. 2016. A 6900-year history of landscape modification by humans in lowland Amazonia. *Quaternary Science Reviews* 141:52–64.)

Reproduced with permission of Elsevier. Notice that *Zea mays* pollen (middle of the lower panel) occurred more consistently in the upper levels of the core.

pollen was present beginning at 6320 cal. BP, about 400 years after first indicators of disturbance (i.e., note the frequencies of Asteraceae, Poaceae, and weeds in the first pollen biozone, SAP-I) and a fire event (i.e., note charcoal peaks in that biozone). These data indicated human presence and were consistent with dates of human disturbance from other lakes in the western Amazon. Maize pollen occurred at low frequencies in core samples, but a relative measure of the intensity of maize agriculture can be gained by considering the proportion of samples that contained maize pollen. In the Lake Sauce sequence, from 3380 to 700 cal BP, maize occurred in 60 percent of samples (N = 54), compared with 30 percent of earlier samples (N = 31). This shift at 3380 BP corresponded with a shift in diatoms indicative of more nutrient-rich conditions and evidence of increased erosion. Taken together, the authors concluded that these were strong indications of intensification of land use after 3380 cal BP. Maize agriculture was either abandoned after 700 cal BP, or cultivation practices changed such that its pollen was no longer carried into the lake.

To end this discussion of landscape approaches to assessing the role of maize in subsistence, I return to the use of maize pollen concentrations as a proxy for scale of maize cultivation within a watershed. Lane et al. (2008a, 2008b) explored this approach in combination with measures of $\partial^{13}C$ of total organic carbon and mineral influx in core sediments. As discussed in Box 5.1, $\partial^{13}C$ values provide a proxy measure of maize cultivation because maize and some field weeds are C4 plants, whereas Neotropical forest ecosystems are dominated by C3 plants. Mineral influx serves as a proxy measure of erosion and sediment transport, which increase as land is cleared for agriculture. Because maize pollen generally disperses only short distances, it reflects cultivation on the lakeshore and locally within the watershed. Cores were taken from Laguna Castilla and Laguna de Salvador, two small lakes in the interior of the Dominican Republic. Maize pollen was present in 20 samples in the premodern interval of Laguna Castilla, dating 1062 to 1271 cal AD. Fewer samples were analyzed from Laguna de Salvador, but the timing of maize deposition was similar. Maize pollen concentrations were relatively low and variable in Zone E, marking the first appearance of maize in the watershed (Figure 6.7). This likely represented initial human occupation of the watershed. This interval was followed by decreased maize (Zone D), then a significant increase in Zone C to the highest concentration in the record between 765 and 730 cal BP, likely the period of greatest prehistoric human impacts in the watershed. Maize concentration then gradually dropped until the crop disappeared from the record in Zone A. As the figure shows, there was close correspondence between $\partial^{13}C$ values, mineral influx, and maize pollen concentrations in Laguna Castilla sediments.

Interestingly, Taylor et al. (2012) found no relationship among maize pollen concentrations, $\partial^{13}C$ values, and abundance of organic matter (increased mineral influx results in lower organic matter values) in cores from Laguna Zoncho, in Costa Rica. In this case there was considerable intrabasin heterogeneity in maize pollen concentrations, with one core having much more maize pollen. The other measures were more uniform among the cores and showed the expected pattern of low organic matter and less negative $\partial^{13}C$ values during the agricultural period, and higher organic matter and more negative $\partial^{13}C$ values after forest recovery. Maize presence was correlated with both agricultural indicators.

Summary and Discussion: Identifying the Importance and Impact of Maize

This case study has focused on two common paleoethnobotanical approaches for assessing the importance of maize and other domesticated plants: by quantifying the abundance of crop

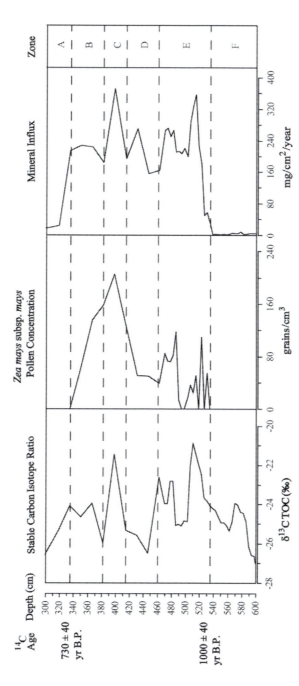

FIGURE 6.7 Summary diagram of Laguna Castilla sedimentary $\partial^{13}C_{TOC}$ values, maize pollen concentrations, and mineral influx variation. Radiocarbon dates (^{14}C yr B.P.) at left are uncalibrated. (Figure 4 from Lane, Chad S., Claudia I. Mora, Sally P. Horn and Kenneth H. Orvis. 2008b. Sensitivity of bulk sedimentary stable carbon isotopes to prehistoric forest clearance and maize agriculture. *Journal of Archaeological Science* 35:2119–2132.)

Reproduced with permission of Elsevier. Biozones A–F are depicted on the right. TOC: total organic carbon.

remains recovered from sites and by assessing the impacts of growing the crop on the environment, as revealed in changes in proxy indicators in sediment cores. In the first approach, the analyst assesses the abundance of the crop relative to other resources, including wild plants and other crops, or considers how commonly it was eaten, processed, or disposed of. As discussed in Part I, abundance measures, including ubiquity, can be significantly affected by differential deposition, preservation, and recovery of archaeobotanical remains. The better these factors can be controlled or modeled, the easier it is to make a convincing argument that changes in abundance represented changes in human behavior regarding resources. As the examples have illustrated, ubiquity is a versatile measure for assessing the importance of a crop like maize that can be applied using any type of archaeobotanical remains or a combination of them. Further, comparing the patterning of different kinds of remains in terms of their ubiquity may reveal changes in how a crop was stored, processed, cooked, consumed, or disposed of, thus providing additional insights into its role in subsistence. That being said, it remains challenging to assess the relative importance of resources that differ markedly in their representation in the archaeobotanical record.

In the second approach, the analyst models the impact of crop cultivation on the environment by identifying burning activity and deforestation and tracking increases in abundances of weeds, early succession plants, and crops. Representation of these indicators may be significantly affected by the pollination biology and phytolith production patterns of key species (including crops) and landscape and other factors affecting phytolith, pollen, and particulate charcoal deposition. There are no absolute indicators of agricultural intensification; as the examples have shown, one looks for changes in proxy indicators that are consistent with the creation and maintenance of an agricultural landscape.

In terms of maize, this review has attempted to illustrate the diversity of ways this productive, nutritious resource was incorporated into foodways in the prehistoric New World. It is difficult to understate the importance and impact of maize agriculture late in prehistory, but the more we have learned about the history of maize, the more complex the picture of its development as a staple crop has become.

Conclusion: Contributions of Paleoethnobotany to Studying Domestication and Agriculture

Paleoethnobotany has been central to our understanding of the origins and evolution of agriculture. Recovering, identifying, and characterizing the actual remains of ancient crops are central to understanding when, where, and the cultural and environmental contexts for emergence of food systems incorporating domesticated plants. These understandings, in turn, are essential for investigating the processes through which plants became domesticated and why people came to rely increasingly on agriculture. Any agricultural origins hypothesis we might want to evaluate must be grounded in the evidence of ancient crops.

I selected maize as our example not only because it is an important crop, but because it is relatively visible archaeologically. The visibility of maize comes from our ability to identify and characterize it using macroremains, pollen, phytoliths, and starch. The means of doing so were developed or formalized primarily by paleoethnobotanists and formed an important component of research into the domestication and evolution of maize. Identifying maize involved delineating the differences between maize and its closest relatives, the teosintes (wild *Zea*), and related genera in its subfamily, as well as the systematic search for "confusers" in unrelated grasses. Another important aspect of basic research was investigating the extent to which races or varieties of maize could be determined from different kinds of archaeobotanical remains. Although some other crops, most notably other grains, have been studied as intensely as maize utilizing similar approaches, untapped potential exists for tracking the domestication of many others, including important root/tuber crops (USOs).

As discussed at some length in the conclusion of the Neanderthal case study, bringing multiple lines of evidence to bear on questions of subsistence fills in gaps in the archaeobotanical record resulting from differential deposition, preservation, and recovery. This feature of using multiple indicators is highly relevant for documenting domestication and agriculture. For example, there are relatively few early Holocene sites at which remains of early crops would be expected in contrast to the greater numbers of mid-Holocene agricultural villages. Evidence for domestication and early, small-scale plant cultivation will be rarer than evidence for established agriculture, making each find a critical one. Early sites are often quite ephemeral, being occupied by small groups who lacked elaborate material culture (including pottery, in the New World). In many cases early domesticated plants are found in settings that suggest seasonal, rather than full-time, occupation. These characteristics do not create conditions ideal for preservation of organic remains, which survive better when buried deep in middens or protected in/on artifacts. The earliest site-based evidence for crops is likely to be phytoliths and microfossils embedded in stone tool surfaces. Or early farming may only leave its mark on the landscape, in the form of particulate charcoal spikes or pollen or phytoliths of crops found in lake cores.

Beyond identifying and characterizing domesticated plants, paleoethnobotany provides a set of tools for assessing the importance of a crop like maize relative to other plant food resources. Although all the abundance measures described in Chapter 4 and illustrated in the case study examples are subject to potential biases and provide relative, rather than absolute, measures of maize's contribution to foodways, their systematic application in sites of different ages and locations has the potential to generate data sets large enough to permit strong inferences about the importance of the crop. Such inferences will be especially strong for comparisons among plants that have similar pathways into the archaeological record: maize in comparison to other crops that have robust inedible portions and distinctive starch and phytoliths, for instance. Comparing the abundance or ubiquity of a plant that is a phytolith producer to one that is not, or one represented in the trash by cobs to one with thin peels (maize and manioc, for instance), is especially challenging; one's success will hinge on independent lines of evidence, such as diagnostic starch or pollen, or distinctive stable isotope signatures. Similarities in likelihood of representation of different crop remains in sites will also make measures of richness or diversity more meaningful indicators of changes in diet breadth, useful indicators for investigating the origins and evolution of agriculture (e.g., Piperno 2006a).

Similarly, intensification of agriculture—clearing more land and shortening fallow cycles to increase production—can be identified at the local and regional scale through systematic study of environmental cores (in addition to other landscape indicators, such as building of raised fields, creation of black earths, and the like). Microfossils of crops may be a minor component of assemblages relative to weeds and other open-habitat plants, however. As illustrated in the examples discussed here, interpreting changes in proxy indicators in sedimentary records in terms of agriculture is grounded in an understanding of the pollination biology (i.e., which plants [crops and wild taxa] are overrepresented and underrepresented in the record), phytolith production patterns (i.e., which plants are producers or nonproducers), and response to fire of the regional flora. In the case of maize, for instance, maize phytoliths may be present but pollen lacking or sparse in a core until fields are planted quite close to the lakeshore.

Finally, recovering the remains of a crop like maize in secure, well-dated archaeological contexts—in situ in occupation floors or garbage middens; in cooking residues, dental calculus, or coprolites; on grinding and pounding stones—provides direct links between the crop and the context of its use, processing, or discard. This provides data essential for understanding its role in foodways, as well as identifying potential differences in access among members of a society.

References

Adams, Karen R., Deborah A. Muenchrath and Dylan M. Schwindt 1999 Moisture effects on the morphology of ears, cobs, and kernels of a South-western U.S. maize (*Zea mays* L.) cultivar, and implications for the interpretation of archaeological maize. *Journal of Archaeological Science* 26:483–496.

Athens, J. Stephen, Jerome V. Ward, Deborah M. Pearsall, Karol Chandler-Ezell, Dean W. Blinn and Alex E. Morrison 2016 Early prehistoric maize in northern highland Ecuador. *Latin American Antiquity* 27(1):3–21.

Ball, Terry B., Karol Chandler-Ezell, Ruth Dickau, Neil Duncan, Thomas C. Hart, José Iriarte, Carol Lentfer, Amanda Logan, Houyuan Lu, Marco Madella, Deborah M. Pearsall, Dolores R. Piperno, Arlene M. Rosen, Luc Vrydaghs, Alison Weisskopf and Jianping Zhang 2016 Phytoliths as a tool for investigations of agricultural origins and dispersals around the world. *Journal of Archaeological Science* 68:32–45.

Benz, Bruce F. 1994 Can prehistoric racial diversification be deciphered from burned corn cobs? In *Corn and Culture in the Prehistoric New World*, edited by S. Johannessen and C. A. Hastorf, pp. 23–33. Westview Press, Boulder, CO.

Benz, Bruce F. and Austin Long 2000 Prehistoric maize evolution in the Tehuacan Valley. *Current Anthropology* 41(3):459–465.

Bird, Robert Mck. 1970 *Maize and its Cultural and Natural Environment in the Sierra of Huánuco, Peru*. Ph. D. Dissertation, University of California, Berkeley.

——— 1994 Manual for the measurement of maize cobs. In *Corn and Culture in the Prehistoric New World*, edited by S. Johannessen and C. A. Hastorf, pp. 5–22. Westview Press, Boulder, CO.

Bozarth, Steven R. 1993 Maize (*Zea mays*) cob phytoliths from a Central Kansas Great Bend aspect archaeological site. *Plains Anthropologist* 38(146):279–286.

Bush, Mark B., A. Correa-Metrio, C. H. McMichael, S. Sully, C. R. Shadik, B. G. Valencia, T. Guilderson, M. Steinitz-Kannan and J. T. Overpeck 2016 A 6900-year history of landscape modification by humans in lowland Amazonia. *Quaternary Science Reviews* 141:52–64.

Bush, Mark B., Dolores R. Piperno and Paul A. Colinvaux 1989 A 6000 year history of Amazonian maize cultivation. *Nature* 340:303–305.

Bush, Mark B., Miles R. Silman, Mauro B. de Toledo, Claudia Listopad, William D. Gosling, Christopher Williams, Paulo E. de Oliveira and Carolyn Krisel 2007 Holocene fire and occupation in Amazonia: Records from two lake districts. *Philosophical Transactions of the Royal Society, B* 362:209–218.

Chandler-Ezell, Karol, Deborah M. Pearsall and James A. Zeidler 2006 Root and tuber phytoliths and starch grains document manioc (*Manihot esculenta*), arrowroot (*Maranta arundinacea*), and llerén (*Calathea* sp.) at the Real Alto site, Ecuador. *Economic Botany* 60(2):103–120.

Clement, Charles R., William M. Denevan, Michael J. Heckenberger, André Braga Junqueira, Eduardo G. Neves, Wenceslau G. Teixeira and William I. Woods 2015a The domestication of Amazonia before European conquest. *Proceedings of the Royal Society, B* 282(1812): http://dx.doi.org/10.1098/rspb.2015.0813.

——— 2015b Response to comment by McMichael, Piperno and Bush. *Proceedings of the Royal Society, B* 282(1821): http://dx.doi.org/10.1098/rspb.2015.2459.

Diehl, Michael W. 2005 Morphological observations on recently recovered Early Agricultural Period maize cob fragments from southern Arizona. *American Antiquity* 70(2):361–375.

Fish, Paul R., Suzanne K. Fish, Austin Long and Charles H. Miksicek 1986 Early corn remains from Tumamoc Hill, southern Arizona. *American Antiquity* 51:563–572.

Geib, Phil R. and Carrie C. Heitman 2015 The relevance of maize pollen for assessing the extent of maize production in Chaco Canyon. In *Chaco Revisited: New Research on the Prehistory of Chaco Canyon, New Mexico*, edited by C. C. Heitman and S. Plog, pp. 66–95. The University of Arizona Press, Tucson.

Grobman, Alexander, Duccio Bonavia, Tom D. Dillehay, Dolores R. Piperno, José Iriarte and Irene Holst 2012 Preceramic maize from Paredones and Huaca Prieta, Peru. *Proceedings of the National Academy of Sciences of the United States of America* 109(5):1755–1759.

Haas, Jonathan, Winifred Creamer, Luis Huamán Mesía, David Goldstein, Karl Reinhard and Cindy Vergel Rodríguez 2013 Evidence for maize (*Zea mays*) in the Late Archaic (3000–1800 B.C.) in the Norte Chico region of Peru. *Proceedings of the National Academy of Sciences of the United States of America* 110(13):4945–4949.

Hall, Stephen A. 2010 Early maize pollen from Chaco Canyon, New Mexico, USA. *Palynology* 34(1):125–137.

Hard, Robert J., Raymond P. Mauldin and Gerry R. Raymond 1996 Mano size, stable isotope ratios, and macrobotanical remains as multiple lines of evidence of maize dependence in the American Southwest. *Journal of Archaeological Method and Theory* 3(3):253–318.

Hart, J. P., H. J. Brumbach and R. Lusteck 2007 Extending the phytolith evidence for early maize (*Zea mays* ssp. *mays*) and squash (*Cucurbita* sp.) in central New York. *American Antiquity* 72(3):563–583.

Hart, J. P. and R. G. Matson 2009 The use of multiple discriminant analysis in classifying prehistoric phytolith assemblages recovered from cooking residues. *Journal of Archaeological Science* 36:74–83.

Hart, J. P., R. G. Matson, R. G. Thompson and M. Blake 2011 Teosinte inflorescence phytolith assemblages mirror *Zea* taxonomy. *PLoS ONE* 6(3): e18349. doi:10.1371/journal.pone.0018349.

Hart, J. P., R. G. Thompson and H. J. Brumbach 2003 Phytolith evidence for early maize (*Zea mays*) in the northern Finger Lakes region of New York. *American Antiquity* 68(4):619–640.

Holst, Irene, J. Enrique Moreno and Dolores R. Piperno 2007 Identification of teosinte, maize, and *Tripsacum* in Mesoamerica by using pollen, starch grains, and phytoliths. *Proceedings of the National Academy of Sciences of the United States of America* 104(45):17608–17613.

Huckell, Lisa W. 1995 Farming and foraging in the Cienega Valley: Early Agricultural Period paleoethnobotany. In *Of Marshes and Maize: Preceramic Agricultural Settlements in the Cienega Valley, Southeastern Arizona*, edited by B. Huckell, pp. 74–97. Anthropological Papers No. 59, University of Arizona Press, Tucson.

Iriarte, José 2003 Assessing the feasibility of identifying maize through the analysis of cross-shaped size and three-dimensional morphology of phytoliths in the grasslands of southeastern South America. *Journal of Archaeological Science* 30(9):1085–1094.

Iriarte, José, Bruno Glaser, Jennifer Watling, Adam Wainwright, Jago Jonathan Birk, Delphine Renard, Stéphen Rostain and Doyle McKey 2010 Late Holocene Neotropical agricultural landscapes: Phytolith and stable carbon isotope analysis of raised fields from French Guianan coastal savannahs. *Journal of Archaeological Science* 37:2984–2994.

King, Frances B. 1994 Variability in cob and kernel characteristics of North American maize cultivars. In *Corn and Culture in the Prehistoric New World*, edited by S. Johannessen and C. A. Hastorf, pp. 35–54. Westview Press, Boulder, CO.

Lane, Chad S., Katherine E. Cummings and Jeffrey J. Clark 2010 Maize pollen deposition in modern lake sediments: A case study from northeastern Wisconsin. *Review of Palaeobotany and Palynology* 159:177–187.

Lane, Chad S., Sally P. Horn and Kenneth H. Orvis 2008a The earliest evidence of Ostionoid maize agriculture from the interior of Hispaniola. *Caribbean Journal of Science* 44(1):43–52.

Lane, Chad S., Claudia I. Mora, Sally P. Horn and Kenneth H. Orvis 2008b Sensitivity of bulk sedimentary stable carbon isotopes to prehistoric forest clearance and maize agriculture. *Journal of Archaeological Science* 35:2119–2132.

Lathrap, Donald W., Jorge G. Marcos and James A. Zeidler 1977 Real Alto: An ancient ceremonial center. *Archaeology* 30(1):2–13.

Logan, Amanda L., Christine A. Hastorf and Deborah M. Pearsall 2012 "Let's drink together": Early ceremonial use of maize in the Titicaca Basin. *Latin American Antiquity* 23(3):235–258.

Marcos, J. G. and A. Michczynski 1996 Good dates and bad dates in Ecuador—Radiocarbon samples and archaeological excavations: A commentary based on the "Valdivia Absolute Chronology". *Andes: Boletín de la Misión Arqueológica Andina (Warsaw)* 1:93–114.

McMichael, C. H., D. R. Piperno and M. B. Bush 2015 Comment on Clement et al. 2015 The domestication of Amazonia before European conquest. *Proceedings of the Royal Society, B* 282(1821): http://dx.doi.org/10.1098/rspb.2015.1837.

McMichael, C. H., D. R. Piperno, M. B. Bush, M. R. Silman, A. R. Zimmerman, M. F. Raczka and L. C. Lobato 2012 Sparse Pre-Columbian human habitation in western Amazonia. *Science* 336(6087):1429–1431.

Messner, Timothy C. 2011 *Acorns and Bitter Roots. Starch Grain Research in the Prehistoric Eastern Woodlands.* University of Alabama Press, Tuscaloosa.

Mickleburgh, H. L. and J. R. Pagán-Jiménez 2012 New insights into the consumption of maize and other food plants in the pre-Columbian Caribbean from starch grains trapped in human dental calculus. *Journal of Archaeological Science* 39(7):2468–2478.

Miksicek, Charles H. 1979 From parking lots to museum basements: The archaeobotany of the St. Mary's site. *Kiva* 45:131–140.

———— 1986 Plant remains. In *Archaeological Investigations at the West Branch Site Early and Middle Rincon Occupation in the Southern Tucson Basin*, edited by F. W. Huntington, pp. 289–313. Anthropological Papers No. 5, Institute for American Research, Tucson.

Morell-Hart, Shanti, Rosemary J. Joyce and John S. Henderson 2014 Multi-proxy analysis of plant use at Formative Period Los Naranjos, Honduras. *Latin American Antiquity* 25(1):65–81.

Mulholland, Susan C. 1993 A test of phytolith analysis at Big Hidatsa, North Dakota. In *Current Research in Phytolith Analysis: Applications in Archaeology and Paleoecology*, edited by D. M. Pearsall and D. R. Piperno, pp. 131–145. MASCA, The University Museum of Archaeology and Anthropology, University of Pennsylvania, Philadelphia.

Musaubach, María Gabriela, Anabela Plos and María del Pilar Babot 2013 Differentiation of archaeological maize (*Zea mays* L.) from native wild grasses based on starch grain morphology: Cases from the Central Pampas of Argentina. *Journal of Archaeological Science* 40:1186–1193.

Pagán-Jiménez, Jaime R., Ana M. Guachamín-Tello, Martha E. Romero-Bastidas and Angelo R. Constantine-Castro 2016 Late ninth millennium B.P. use of *Zea mays* L. at Cubilán area, highland Ecuador, revealed by ancient starches. *Quaternary International* 404:137–155.

Pearsall, Deborah M. 1978 Phytolith analysis of archeological soils: Evidence for maize cultivation in Formative Ecuador. *Science* 199:177–178.

———— 1980 Analysis of an archaeological maize kernel cache from Manabí province, Ecuador. *Economic Botany* 34(4):344–351.

Pearsall, Deborah M. 2015 *Paleoethnobotany: A Handbook of Procedures.* Third ed. Routledge, New York.

Pearsall, Deborah M., Karol Chandler-Ezell and Alex Chandler-Ezell 2003 Identifying maize in Neotropical sediments and soils using cob phytoliths. *Journal of Archaeological Science* 30(5):611–627.

Pearsall, Deborah M., Karol Chandler-Ezell and James A. Zeidler 2004 Maize in ancient Ecuador: Results of residue analysis of stone tools from the Real Alto site. *Journal of Archaeological Science* 31:423–442.

Pearsall, Deborah M., Neil A. Duncan, John G. Jones, Dorothy E. Freidel, Cesar I. Veintimilla and Hector Neff 2016 Human-environment interactions during the early mid-Holocene in coastal Ecuador as revealed by mangrove coring in Santa Elena Province. *The Holocene* 26(8):1262–1289.

Pearsall, Deborah M. and Dolores R. Piperno 1990 Antiquity of maize cultivation in Ecuador: Summary and reevaluation of the evidence. *American Antiquity* 55(2):324–337.

Perry, L., R. Dickau, S. Zarrillo, I. Holst, D. M. Pearsall, D. R. Piperno, M. J. Berman, R. G. Cooke, K. Rademaker, A. J. Ranere, J. S. Raymond, D. H. Sandweiss, F. Scaramelli, K. Tarble and J. A. Zeidler

2007 Starch fossils and the domestication and dispersal of chili peppers (*Capsicum* spp. L.) in the Americas. *Science* 315(5814):986–988.

Perry, Linda 2004 Starch analyses reveal the relationship between tool type and function: An example from the Orinoco valley of Venezuela. *Journal of Archaeological Science* 31:1069–1081.

Piperno, D. R., A. J. Ranere, I. Holst, J. Iriarte and R. Dickau 2009 Starch grain and phytolith evidence for early ninth millennium B.P. maize from the Central Balsas River Valley, Mexico. *Proceedings of the National Academy of Sciences of the United States of America* 106(13):5019–5024.

Piperno, Dolores R. 1988 *Phytolith Analysis: An Archaeological and Geological Perspective*. Academic Press, San Diego.

——— 1990 Aboriginal agriculture and land usage in the Amazon basin, Ecuador. *Journal of Archaeological Science* 17:665–677.

——— 2006a The origins of plant cultivation and domestication in the Neotropics. In *Behavioral Ecology and the Transition to Agriculture*, edited by D. J. Kennett and B. Winterhalder, pp. 137–166. University of California Press, Berkeley.

——— 2006b *Phytoliths: A Comprehensive Guide for Archaeologists and Paleoecologists*. AltaMira Press, Lanham, MD.

——— 2009 Identifying crop plants with phytoliths (and starch grains) in Central and South America: A review and an update of the evidence. *Quaternary International* 193(1–2):146–159.

Piperno, Dolores R. and Irene Holst 1998 The presence of starch grains on prehistoric stone tools from the humid Neotropics: Indications of early tuber use and agriculture in Panama. *Journal of Archaeological Science* 25(8):765–776.

Piperno, Dolores R., Crystal McMichael and Mark B. Bush 2015 Amazonia and the Anthropocene: What was the spatial extent and intensity of human landscape modification in the Amazon Basin at the end of prehistory? *The Holocene* 25(10):1588–1597.

Piperno, Dolores R. and Deborah M. Pearsall 1993 Phytoliths in the reproductive structures of maize and teosinte: Implications for the study of maize evolution. *Journal of Archaeological Science* 20:337–362.

——— 1998 *The Origins of Agriculture in the Lowland Neotropics*. Academic Press, San Diego.

Reichert, E. T. 1913 *The Differentiation and Specificity of Starches in Relation to Genera, Species, etc.* Chapman, London.

Rue, David J. 1987 Early agriculture and early Postclassic Maya occupation in western Honduras. *Nature* 326:285–286.

Sluyter, Andrew 1997 Analysis of maize (*Zea mays* subsp. *mays*) pollen: Normalizing the effects of microscope-slide mounting media on diameter determinations. *Palynology* 21:35–39.

Taylor, Z. P., S. P. Horn and D. B. Finkelstein 2012 Maize pollen concentrations in Neotropical lake sediments as an indicator of the scale of prehistoric agriculture. *The Holocene* 23(1):78–84.

Thompson, Robert G. 2006 Documenting the presence of maize in Central and South America through phytolith analysis of food residues. In *Documenting Domestication: New Genetic and Archaeological Paradigms*, edited by M. A. Zeder, D. G. Bradley, E. Emshwiller and B. D. Smith, pp. 82–95. University of California Press, Berkeley.

Turkon, Paula 2006 Morphological variation of maize cupules and access to high quality maize in the prehispanic Malpaso Valley, Zacatecas, Mexico. *Journal of Ethnobiology* 26(1):139–164.

Whitney, Bronwen S., Elizabeth A. C. Rushton, John F. Carson, José Iriarte and Francis E. Mayle 2012 An improved methodology for the recovery of *Zea mays* and other large crop pollen, with implications for environmental archaeology in the Neotropics. *The Holocene* 22(10):1087–1096.

Zarrillo, S. and B. Kooyman 2006 Evidence for berry and maize processing on the Canadian plains from starch grain analysis. *American Antiquity* 71(3):473–499.

Zarrillo, Sonia, D. M. Pearsall, J. S. Raymond, Mary Ann Tisdale and J. Quon Dugane 2008 Directly dated starch residues document early Formative maize (*Zea mays* L.) in tropical Ecuador. *Proceedings of the National Academy of Sciences of the United States of America* 105(13):5006–5011.

7

ARCHAEOBOTANY AND INSIGHTS INTO SOCIAL RELATIONSHIPS AT CAHOKIA

Glossary

chiefdom a kind of complex society in which status is based on kinship (i.e., is inherited); authority is centralized in an elite kin group or individual (chief).

complex society in anthropology and archaeology, a social formation characterized by hierarchy in the form of a ruling elite (individuals of higher status), commoners, and sometimes other groups (for example, slaves, warriors).

decoction the liquid resulting from boiling down plant material steeped in water, typically for producing an herbal tea.

Introduction

Many examples could be given of the centrality of food in social relationships: feasting as display of social status; differential access to foods by different members of a society; control of the food supply as a way to exercise power; the different contributions of men and women to family meals. We can understand much about social relationships from investigating foodways, "the fuller context of [food] production, storage, distribution, preparation, and presentation in a social and cultural setting" (Johannessen 1993:182). Where and how foods were prepared, served, and disposed of can reveal relationships among groups. "Special" kinds of ingredients may distinguish foods for ritual or ceremony; the same ingredients may be prepared in different ways, the actors may change, and the places may change.

There are diverse ways in which archaeobotanical data can be used to reveal social relationships, including providing insight into the emergence and maintenance of inequality. Some approaches are 1) studying differences in diet and access to resources among segments of a society; 2) documenting production of food and drink for feasting; 3) providing evidence for support of specialists; and 4) investigating changes in how resources were used and stored.

In this chapter we will explore how paleoethnobotany contributes to understanding relationships among people in ancient societies by considering the case of Cahokia, the mound site at the heart of the Mississippian chiefdom. There is a long history of research at the site and the surrounding region, the American Bottom. Extensive excavations were conducted in the corridors of planned interstate highways (the FAI-270 and related projects) or improvements at the Cahokia site (visitor center excavation). Systematic recovery of botanical and faunal data was conducted during all mitigation projects. An ideal case would allow us to investigate social relationships at different levels within diverse segments of the society. The Cahokia case provides robust macroremain and faunal data relevant to the emergence of elites, and relationships among elites and nonelites, at the scale of the community (site), subcommunity, and household. It is possible, for example, to compare elite households, ceremonial contexts, and nonelite/rural households. Intrahousehold data are available, but are often represented by too few samples to explore relationships at the domestic scale. Stable isotope analyses of human skeletal remains provide insight into individual lifelong dietary patterns; studies of pottery residues provide insight into food preparation.

Our focus will be on Cahokia during the emergence and florescence of Mississippian culture in the American Bottom (rather than its decline) and on how understanding foodways contributes to our understanding of relationships among members of Mississippian society and how these changed over time. As we will see, there was virtually no change in the *kinds* of plants used over the occupation of Cahokia; rather there were differences in the social settings in which certain foods were produced and consumed and in the abundance and form in which foods were eaten among different members of the society. Foods and other plants played a role in ritual practices that marked important transitions in the personal and social lives of Mississippians. Maize was not the only food or plant that marked social identity, but it was among the more visible. Table 7.1 lists the scientific names of plants mentioned in the text.

Overview of Cahokia: The Site, Chiefdom, and Subsistence Base

Cahokia: Site and Cultural Sequence

A chiefdom developed late in prehistory in Eastern North America in a stretch of the Mississippi river valley known as the American Bottom, a broad floodplain and adjoining bluffs extending from the mouth of the Illinois River in the north to the Kaskaskia to the south (Figure 7.1). The Cahokia site, dominated by the enormous earthen Monk's Mound, grew and declined over the course of 600 years (Table 7.2). The Lohmann and Stirling phases represented cultural florescence, growth, and internal differentiation at the site; the Moorehead and Sand Prairie phases decline. The Emergent Mississippian occupation at Cahokia was part of an expansion of settlements in the American Bottom (Dalan et al. 2003). Construction of Monk's Mound and the adjoining Grand Plaza subsumed large parts of the Emergent Mississippian village, which became sacred space. It appears that the plaza was laid down as one massive fill during the Lohmann phase (Alt et al. 2010). Mound building began at other sites as well, but Cahokia quickly eclipsed them. Mounds were also built on the edges of the Cahokia community, and internal subdivisions developed. At its height, the entire American Bottom may have been controlled from Cahokia (Dalan et al. 2003).

Cahokia is located in the widest part of the American Bottom; there was high ground for habitation, well-drained agricultural soils, waterways that connected mound centers and the uplands, and a diversity of habitats. Agriculture was likely an infield–outfield system (i.e., communal fields around the settlements, plots associated with houses within the settlement) (Dalan et al. 2003).

TABLE 7.1 Scientific names of plants mentioned in the text

American lotus	*Nelumbo lutea*
Arrow arum	*Peltandra virginica*
Bald cypress	*Taxodium distichum*
Barnyard grass	*Echinochloa muricata*
Bean	*Phaseolus vulgaris*
Chenopod/goosefoot★	*Chenopodium berlandieri*
Duck potato	*Sagittaria*
Gourd	*Lagenaria siceraria*
Grass	Poaceae
Holly	*Ilex*
Jimsonweed	*Datura stramonium*
Knotweed★	*Polygonum erectum*
Lily	Liliaceae
Little barley★	*Hordeum pusillum*
Maize	*Zea mays*
Maygrass★	*Phalaris caroliniana*
Morning glories	Convolvulaceae
Nightshade	*Solanum ptycanthum*
Panic grass	*Panicum*
Persimmon	*Diospyros virginiana*
Pine	*Pinus*
Ragweed	*Ambrosia trifida*
Red cedar	*Juniperus virginiana*
Squash★	*Cucurbita pepo, C. argyrosperma*
Sunflower★	*Helianthus annuus*
Sumpweed★	*Iva annua*
Tobacco	*Nicotiana*
Water knotweed	*Polygonum amphibium*
Waterlily	*Nymphaea odorata*
Wild potato	*Dioscorea villosa*

★ Native cultigens of the Eastern Agricultural Complex.

The center of Cahokia was the 200-ha Grand Plaza fronting Monk's Mound and ringed by smaller mounds (Figure 7.2). Monk's Mound, topped by chiefly buildings, was the site center for the entire length of the occupation of Cahokia, but the boundaries of the community core changed over time. Other tall mounds were built 1 to 2 km from the plaza; these represented centers of residential subcommunities within the site and the emergence of midlevel controls (Dalan et al. 2003). The size of Cahokia, the other large mound complexes (i.e., St. Louis, East St. Louis, both largely destroyed), and the cultural debris scattered over the bottomland ridges indicate that the American Bottom once supported one of the most socially complex cultural systems in North America (Milner et al. 1993).

Many of the remains of this cultural system were excavated during the FAI-270 highway mitigation project. All but one Mississippian site investigated during the project, the Lohmann site, were sparsely settled occupations, lacking mounds, which surrounded the mound complexes of the region (Milner et al. 1993). Structures, pits, postmolds (outlines of decayed wooden posts), and postpits (excavations to hold the bases of larger posts) were the most frequently encountered Mississippian features in American Bottom sites. Lohmann-phase

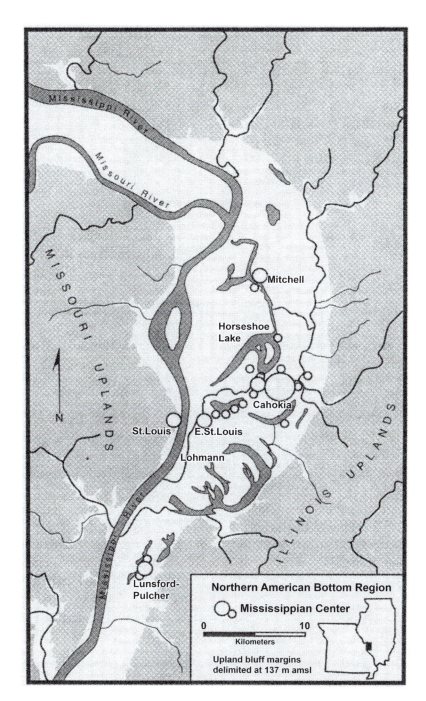

FIGURE 7.1 Mississippian centers in the northern American Bottom. (Figure 1.2 from Pauketat, Timothy R. and Thomas E. Emerson. 1997. Introduction: Domination and ideology in the Mississippian world. In *Cahokia: Domination and Ideology in the Mississippian World*, edited by T. R. Pauketat and T. E. Emerson, pp. 1–29. University of Nebraska Press, Lincoln.)

Reproduced with permission of the University of Nebraska Press. Notice the broad river floodplain with its numerous lakes (cutoff river channels, or meanders).

TABLE 7.2 Cultural sequence and dating of Cahokia. Data from Dalan et al. (2003)

Emergent Mississippian	AD 800–1000 (cal. AD 925–1050)		
Mississippian	AD 1000–1400 (cal. AD 1050–1350)		
		Lohmann phase	AD 1000–1050 (cal. AD 1050–1100)
		Stirling phase	AD 1050–1150 (cal. AD 1100–1200)
		Moorehead phase	AD 1150–1250 (cal. AD 1200–1275)
		Sand Prairie phase	AD 1250–1400 (cal. AD 1275–1350)

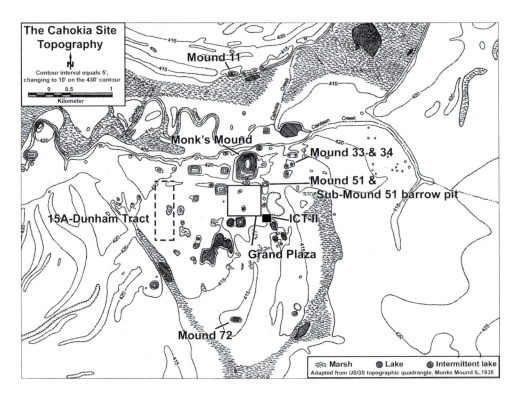

FIGURE 7.2 A topographic map of the Cahokia Mounds site reveals meanders, creeks, borrows, and mounds. The area covered by the map corresponds roughly to the boundaries of the site and park.

Adapted from Figure 29, drawn by Harold W. Watters, Jr., from Dalan, Rinita A., George R. Holley, William I. Woods, Harold W. Watters, Jr. and John A. Koepke. 2003. *Envisioning Cahokia: A Landscape Perspective*. Northern Illinois University Press, DeKalb, IL. Reproduced and modified with permission of the authors. Locations mentioned in the case study are labeled.

structures were rectangular with semisubterranean basins. Most had walls constructed using closely set posts in wall trenches. Lohmann–phase structures were smaller than those seen in later phases; an increase in house size over the Mississippian period was also seen at Cahokia itself. Very few Lohmann–phase houses had large internal storage pits, which were common later. Structures were often associated with external pits, forming household units. Clusters of features were thought to be farmsteads or homesteads.

Stirling-phase materials were the most commonly recovered of any Mississippian phase in the American Bottom (Milner et al. 1993). Most Stirling-phase structures were rectangular, semisubterranean buildings with walls of wall-trench construction. Smaller, more ephemeral structures were interpreted as sweat lodges. An above-ground storage facility was identified at one site. More than half of the rectangular structures had one or more large internal storage pits, an increase from the previous phase. Like during the Lohmann phase, Stirling features were scattered along ridges in spatially discrete groups, and structures were usually at some distance from each other. Overall, American Bottom sites without mounds showed remarkable similarities in organization over the Mississippian period, for example, in the internal organization of households, location on well-drained, higher-ridge areas, and subsistence (see later). Small households occupied by nuclear or extended families appear to have been the minimum economic unit. There were some functional differences in households, however. For example, some had sweat lodges associated with them or above-ground, communal storage facilities. These different-looking households were in topographically prominent positions on ridges and were likely the focal points of communities (Milner et al. 1993).

In broad terms, there are two positions on the nature of Mississippian society (Milner 2006, and sources therein). In one, Cahokia is considered to be a powerful place, the urban center of a highly elaborated, four-tiered sociopolitical system. From this perspective, three levels of densely populated mound centers were supported by outlying farming communities; trade in nonlocal items buttressed the elites. Milner (2006) argues for an alternative view, that Cahokia was less populated and Mississippian society less centralized, a series of locally important centers that were self-sufficient and linked by political arrangements that changed over time. Population estimates based on different assumptions of the length of time of structure occupations and numbers of occupants puts the population of Cahokia at 3,000 to 8,000 at its peak, and of the American Bottom as a whole at 18,000 to 50,000 (Milner 2006). It is likely that enough crops could have been produced in the American Bottom to support this population, and fish and other aquatic resources were abundant, but for deer, hunters likely ranged into the adjoining uplands.

Subsistence and Land Use

Excavation of sites in the American Bottom affected by FAI-270 highway construction and subsequent projects produced a large database of systematically recovered archaeobotanical data (sources used for this review: Johannessen 1984, 1993; Lopinot 1992, 1997; Simon and Parker 2006). The currently recognized suite of native crop plants (also known as the Eastern Agricultural Complex) included four that provided starchy seeds—chenopod, erect knotweed, maygrass, little barley—and three that produced oily seeds—sunflower, sumpweed, squash (Table 7.1). Maize was the most important introduced crop, with bean appearing late in the sequence. Tobacco was also present. Occupation of the American Bottom began in the Archaic Period (7900–900 BC), but relatively few sites have been excavated. By the Late

Archaic, plant assemblages indicated the harvest of a number of seed plants from disturbed habitats, including sumpweed, chenopod, little barley, ragweed, and barnyard grass, along with continued reliance on nuts. During the Woodland Period (800 BC—AD 1050) subsistence changed from low-level cultivation of native crops to fully agricultural economies incorporating native crops and maize. There was an irregular pattern of maize occurrence at Late Woodland sites, but by the Terminal Late Woodland Period (AD 900–1050), maize and native starchy and oily crops appeared to have formed a relatively balanced agricultural strategy. Among the native crops, maygrass and chenopod typically dominated; most chenopod assemblages contained both wild- and domestic-type seeds.

As of Simon and Parker's (2006) overview, the Mississippian Period botanical database represented more than 50 components from 43 sites. There were no striking differences in overall subsistence patterns between Terminal Late Woodland and Mississippian sites. Maize occurred in virtually every Mississippian assemblage; variability among maize cob row numbers indicated several varieties were being grown, but a race with 10 to 12 rows tended to dominate.

Pollen, sediment, and isotope records from Horseshoe Lake, an abandoned river channel adjacent to Cahokia, have documented the onset, intensification, and cessation of prehistoric human impacts in the American Bottom (Munoz et al. 2014) (Figure 7.3). Six biozones were defined in the core, interpreted as pre-agricultural (HORM-1), early agriculture (HORM-2), agricultural intensification (HORM-3), agricultural contraction (HORM-4), regional abandonment (HORM-5), and Anglo-American land use (HORM-6). The pre-agricultural biozone was characterized by high abundances of upland and floodplain trees and increasing ragweed levels. Beginning at ca. AD 450, most arboreal taxa declined rapidly and nonarboreal pollen increased, including pollen taxa that incorporate cultigens of the Eastern Agricultural Complex: Amaranthaceae/Chenopodiaceae, Poaceae, *Helianthus* type, *Iva* type, and *Polygonum*. From ca. AD 600 to AD 1200, pollen of floodplain and upland trees was at the lowest levels, replaced by pollen taxa associated with native crops (most notably grass). Maize appeared. It was during this time period that carbon isotope levels increased (i.e., became less negative)—this was interpreted as intensification of maize agriculture and/or the expansion of aquatic plants stimulated by increased nutrients washed into the lake. The core documented that an open landscape, dominated by native crops and including maize, predated maize intensification (ca. AD 900), as well as the emergence of Cahokia around AD 1050. These patterns began to reverse beginning at AD 1200, when a large flood event was documented (Munoz et al. 2015). Cahokia grew and agriculture intensified during an absence of large floods from AD 600 to AD 1200. The return of large floods, which would have inundated fields, food caches, and settlements across the American Bottom, was correlated with site reorganization and depopulation.

Changing Social Relationships and Foodways: An Overview

Data generated by the FAI-270 project have allowed food to be viewed in its social and cultural setting in the American Bottom over 600 years (AD 500–1100) (Johannessen 1993). Some assumptions that must be made: plant remains (flotation-recovered macroremains) reflected the agricultural system; there was cultural continuity in the region; ceramic vessels were used to cook and serve foods; and certain types of vessels were likely used for cooking, others for serving foods. Through comparisons of pottery assemblages, plant assemblages, and settlement

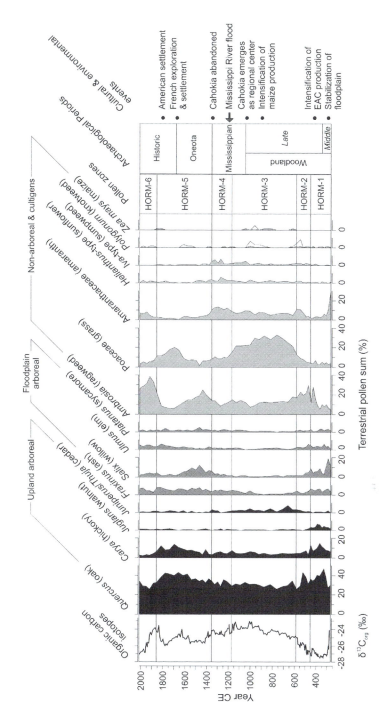

FIGURE 7.3 Organic carbon isotope ratios ($\delta^{13}C_{org}$) and relative abundances of selected pollen taxa (expressed as percentage of terrestrial pollen sum) and archaeological periods and cultural and environmental events of the Cahokia region (Illinois, USA), after Fortier et al. (2006) and Simon and Parker (2006). EAC—Eastern Agricultural Complex. (Figure 4 from Munoz, Samuel E., Sissel Schroeder, David A. Fike and John W. Williams. 2014. A record of sustained prehistoric and historic land use from the Cahokia region, Illinois, USA. *Geology* 42(6):499–502.)

Reproduced with permission of the Geological Society of America. Notice that disturbance indicators and native cultigens are documented before maize in the core and correlated with very negative carbon isotope values (i.e., indicating C3 plants).

types and patterning over time, changes in how people stored, distributed, and presented food can be seen (Figure 7.4). These changes occurred in the context of changing forms of local communities and inferred shifts in how people related to one another. For example, during the early Mississippian Lohmann Phase, the same basic foods as earlier were used, but there were drastic changes in social settings in which these were consumed. From nucleated villages, people now lived either in scattered hamlets or in growing mound centers. In the centers there was evidence of the growing power and prestige of an elite class (i.e., Mound 72 burial data, sub-Mound 51 feasting context, discussed later). There was increased elaboration in cooking pots and dishes. Johannessen (1993) argued that to understand how and why changes in food production came about, one needed to look beyond strictly dietary considerations to foodways more broadly and the relationships among people that these reflected.

Changes in social structure can also be seen within Cahokia itself, for example, through the Interpretive Center II (ICT-II) excavations, during which machine blading of topsoil exposed house plans and related features. In this half-hectare tract southeast of the Grand Plaza were 70 domestic structures, grouped into 18 households (Collins 1997). Lohmann-, Stirling-, and Moorehead-phase communities were identified. Lohmann-phase households were arranged in a linear fashion, whereas during the Stirling phase households were arranged around a small central plaza. A mound developed late in the phase to the south of the plaza. Lohmann-phase households were larger and consisted of more separate features than Stirling-phase households, which were smaller and more numerous. Assuming that size of household reflected size of the domestic group, Collins (1997) argued there was a change from suprafamily domestic units to smaller units, likely nuclear families. There was also a reduction in the variety of activities carried out by households. Data suggested that storage was communal during the Lohmann phase and more private during Stirling. Exterior fire pits were more common during Lohmann, suggesting that cooking was also communal and became more private over the Stirling occupation. Thus although the Lohmann-phase population carried over communal patterns from Emergent Mississippian times, over time status distinctions, subgroup solidarity, and household autonomy became increasingly important at the local level (Collins 1997). Essentially, the ICT-II excavations revealed that local elites developed from what was an egalitarian residential population and related in changing ways to the paramount Cahokia elites.

As will be discussed further later, there were no differences in the *kinds* of food plants associated with communal feasts, other elite contexts, and typical domestic refuse at Mississippian sites. The *quantities* of maize and native crops that were consumed by different members of the society showed some interesting differences, however. Tobacco seeds occurred regularly at sites in ceremonial and domestic refuse, in the latter perhaps reflecting processing or storage of the crop. More rarely recovered nightshade, morning glory, and jimsonweed, all plants with psychoactive properties, mostly occurred in ritual contexts (Simon and Parker 2006).

Maize, Elites, and Ritual at Cahokia

There is long-running debate about the role(s) maize played in the rise of complex societies in the Eastern Woodlands (e.g., Lopinot 1992, 1997; Reber 2006; VanDerwarker et al. 2013, among others). Among the issues: Was early use of maize ceremonial? If so, when did this change, how, and why? How did maize compare to native crops in terms of its cultivation, productivity, environmental impact, storage, and food preparation? Was maize consumed equally by all members of society? Because these issues are too numerous, and too complex,

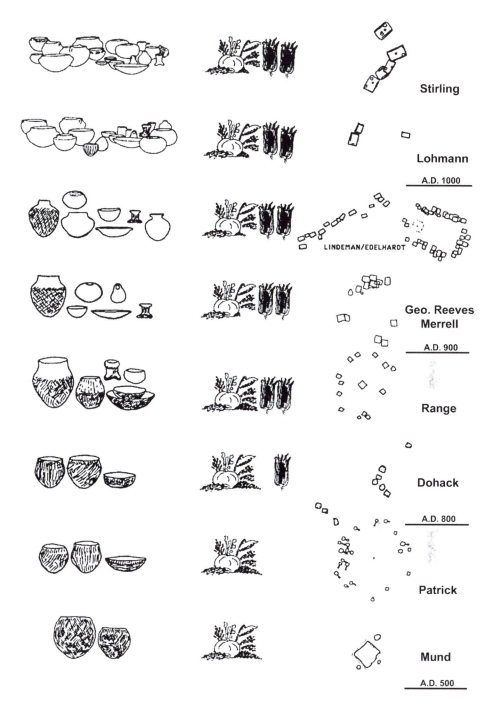

FIGURE 7.4 A summary of changes in food, dishes, and community patterns over 600 years in the American Bottom. (Figure 12.11 from Johannessen, Sissel. 1993. Food, dishes, and society in the Mississippi valley. In *Foraging and Farming in the Eastern Foodlands*, edited by C. M. Scarry, pp. 182–205. University Press of Florida, Gainesville.)

to consider all of them in depth, the focus here will be on how data on maize use has contributed to an understanding of relationships among members of Mississippian society.

Insights From Macroremains, Cooking Pots, and Residues

One approach to understanding how maize was used in the past is to examine the *kinds* of remains recovered archaeologically. Quantities of charred maize cob parts (inedible portion) can be compared to kernels, for instance. Lopinot (1992, 1997) argued that an increase in abundance of maize cob parts relative to kernels in refuse reflected an increase in use of shellable maize relative to consumption of green maize. In other words, more cob parts meant that more maize was grown to maturity and could be stored and used in dry form. Looking at maize data grouped by site and phase, there was a decrease in the kernel/cob ratio over time in American Bottom sites. As illustrated in Figure 7.5, the major change occurred in the late Emergent Mississippian (Lindeman, Edelhardt phases) and continued into the Mississippian (Pauketat 1994). Preservation may have accentuated this pattern: mature maize cobs were a robust byproduct that could have been used as fuel, and thus potentially overrepresented relative to other remains (Lopinot 1992). Interestingly, maize from the ICT-II tract excavations, mentioned earlier, was dominated by small fragments from kernel tops, which were often shriveled or distorted (i.e., they were not dry when charred). Roasting of green corn, rather than processing of mature kernels, may have characterized those contexts (Lopinot 1992).

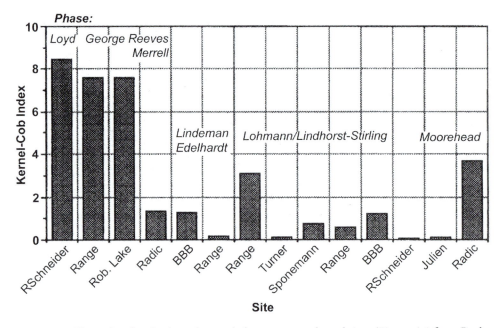

FIGURE 7.5 The ratio of maize kernels to cob fragments at selected sites. (Figure 4.4 from Pauketat, Timothy R. 1994. *The Ascent of Chiefs: Cahokia and Mississippian Politics in Native North America.* The University of Alabama Press, Tuscaloosa.)

Reproduced with permission of the University of Alabama Press. Notice that the most striking change occurred between the Merrell and Lindeman phases, before the growth of the Cahokia center.

Insights into how maize was used have also come from the study of pottery. Briggs (2016) proposed that a standard jar form, found in large numbers throughout the region during the Mississippian, was used to nixtamalize maize (i.e., to produce hominy). The form, a globular jar with a broad rounded base, was an effective shape for boiling (i.e., suspended above or propped on hot coals). Ethnographic accounts indicate that hominy—maize kernels soaked in an alkaline solution and boiled—was the most widely practiced maize foodway in the Eastern Woodlands. Nixtamalization makes the hard kernels of flint maize easier to grind, and maize products easier to digest, preventing the nutrient-deficiency disease pellagra. Briggs (2016) proposed that nixtamalizing practices were spread during the Late Woodland and Early Mississippian Periods along with flint maize and represented a shift in diet and identity. Declining numbers of slab metates (inferred to be associated with small seed grinding), increased numbers of bell-shaped storage pits, and increased caries may also be associated with hominy production and a shift from use of green to mature shelled maize (Myers 2006).

Whether maize was cooked in a ceramic pot can be investigated through study of food residues. Reber and colleagues (Reber and Evershed 2004; Reber et al. 2004), for example, applied a new technique—compound-specific stable isotope analysis—to identify maize in absorbed (i.e., not visible) organic residues. During cooking unglazed pottery absorbs organic residues, which are primarily composed of lipids. By determining the $\partial^{13}C$ value of lipids in absorbed residues, it can be determined whether C4 plants (i.e., maize) were cooked. The compound n-dotriacontanol, abundant in maize but rare in most other plants, was analyzed. Reber and colleagues studied residues from 134 sherds from 17 sites. Stable isotope analysis detected a maize signature in seven sherds from three sites, including two from the American Bottom: Mees-Nochta, an Emergent Mississippian hamlet, and Halliday, a Lohmann-phase village. Eleven sherds from Cahokia showed no maize, but had homogeneous residues, suggesting that a variety of foods had been cooked in the pots, which over time produced similar residues. Reber and colleagues concluded that because maize was cooked/consumed more at outlying sites than at Cahokia, it was not a high-prestige food. This paralleled human skeletal stable isotope results (see later), but indicated less maize use overall than those results. This difference could have resulted from sampling bias in sherds selected for study from Cahokia or differences in how maize was processed there (i.e., not using pottery).

Stable isotope analysis has also been conducted on visible charred residues from Mississippian pottery (Beehr and Ambrose 2007a, 2007b). Like study of absorbed residues, isotopic analysis of charred residues allows consumption of C3 and C4 (i.e., maize) foods at the household level—of meals—to be investigated. Beehr and Ambrose compared charred pottery residue samples from the sub-Mound 51 feasting pit at Cahokia to sites of the contemporary Richland complex, located in the uplands to the east of Cahokia (including Halliday, part of Reber's study). The mean percentages of C4 foods (i.e., maize) cooked in pots from the sites, calculated from the $\partial^{13}C$ values, varied from 7.3 to 42 percent for Richland sites, and 36 percent for sub-Mound 51. Individual sherds varied from 0 to 95 percent maize. The authors argued that these should be considered minimum estimates, as maize might have been prepared in ways that left no burned residues. The pattern of variation among Richland sites indicated higher maize consumption by nonelites: consumption at the single-mound Pfeffer site was lower than at the farming villages sites (Grossmann, Halliday). The sub-Mound 51 results—relatively high maize levels—contrasted with the rarity of maize macroremains in this feasting context, as discussed later. Perhaps ceramic vessels used to prepare maize were discarded by individuals/households of lower status who were participating in the feast, or vessels usually used to cook maize were used to prepare high-status foods at the feast (Beehr and Ambrose 2007a, 2007b). Either hypothesis supports the idea that feasts served to integrate members of the society. A sample of residues was pretreated to remove soil organic contaminants; this did not significantly alter the isotopic composition of the residues or the resulting conclusions.

To summarize, several lines of evidence indicate changes in how maize was consumed in the Emergent and Early Mississippian Periods and after in the American Bottom. Fragmented remains of cobs of mature maize became more common relative to charred kernels, and pottery vessels suited for long boiling became ubiquitous at sites, suggesting that foods made from hominy or other mature maize products came to dominate Mississippian cuisine. Green maize use continued and may have been underrepresented in the macroremain record, because immature cobs were likely consumed with roasted green ears or burned up completely in trash. Stable carbon isotope data that demonstrated maize was cooked in pottery vessels could not discriminate between mature and green products. Were there differences in maize consumption—over the lifetime or in kinds and contexts of meals—among members of the society? Comparing macroremains from elite and nonelite contexts and considering human isotope data in a cultural context can help address this question.

Fill to level the Grand Plaza of Cahokia and create platform mound bases was "borrowed" from a series of large pits, some of which were ritually refilled and buried; one such was found under Mound 51 (Pauketat et al. 2002). Dating to the Lohmann phase, the sub-Mound 51 pit was 3 m deep, 56+ m long, and 19 m wide. Ten units were excavated into the pit, each showing seven clearly defined strata. Macroremains of more than 30 kinds of edible plants were recovered; the assemblage was as diverse as an ordinary domestic assemblage (Fritz and Lopinot 2003–2004). Tobacco seeds, charred and uncharred, were found in large numbers. Charred and uncharred wood was present, including abundant uncharred red cedar, bald cypress, and pine. Some was in the form of thin split pieces, probably representing woodworking byproducts. Pauketat et al. (2002) have argued that the deposits represented debris from a series of individual gatherings in which huge quantities of pottery vessels were used and broken, ritual and sumptuary goods were deposited, hundreds of deer were consumed along with select items not usually eaten (swans, prairie chickens, large fish), sufficient tobacco was used to leave hundreds of thousands of seeds, native starchy plant foods were consumed, and ritual woods were used (for purification and in construction). These events were likely large-scale public feasts, perhaps held in the Grand Plaza.

Comparing macroremains of maize and native crops from the sub-Mound 51 feasting context to contemporary domestic contexts in Cahokia's center (ICT-II tract excavations) has provided insight into the role(s) of maize in Early Mississippian society (Fritz and Lopinot 2003–2004). The ICT-II sample was 149 flotation samples, including 38 from the Lohmann phase. Samples represented fill from basins of domestic structures and pits. Most sub-Mound 51 samples were not from flotation, but did include a number of fine-sieved bulk matrix samples. The two areas were compared using relative frequencies (based on counts) of key plant types: nutshell, fruit seeds, squash and gourd, native starchy crops, oily seeds, maize, tobacco, and other economic items (Figure 7.6). Among the findings were the following: Food plants represented in the two areas were quite similar in terms of taxa present, although the assemblage was more diverse in the domestic context, as might be expected from longer-term household activities (also recall that the domestic context samples were recovered by flotation). Starchy seeds dominated both contexts, with maygrass the most abundant in each.

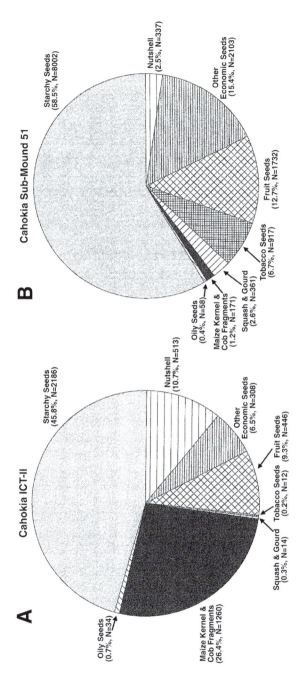

FIGURE 7.6 **A:** Frequencies of selected plant types from the ICT-II Tract, Cahokia; **B:** Frequencies of selected plant types from the sub-Mound 51 Pit, Cahokia. (Figure 2 and Figure 3 from Fritz, Gayle J. and Neal H. Lopinot. 2003–2004). Native crops at Early Cahokia: Comparing domestic and ceremonial contexts. *Illinois Archaeology* 15 & 16:90–111.)

Reproduced with permission of the Illinois Archaeological Survey. Notice the similarity in the relative abundance of starchy seeds in the assemblages between domestic (A) and ceremonial (B) contexts, but the distinctive difference in representation of maize macroremains.

As the figure shows, there were distinctive differences in the abundance of maize (ICT-II, 26.4 percent; sub-Mound 51, 1.2 percent) and tobacco (ICT-II, 0.2 percent; sub-Mound 51, 6.7 percent), among other resources. Large numbers of native starchy seeds were found in the sub-Mound 51 feasting refuse, with no indication that maize held special social or ceremonial significance, unless it was prepared in a way that left little trace as macroremains. Fritz and Lopinot (2003–2004) concluded that dishes prepared and served at communal gatherings called for maygrass, chenopod, and knotweed—traditional staples with long histories of use in the region—with maize being a less essential ingredient.

As mentioned earlier, excavations at the ICT-II tract revealed 70 domestic structures, grouped into 18 households (Collins 1997). For each occupation phase, flotation-recovered macroremains could be compared among feature types, for example, for structure basins and internal and external pits (Lopinot 1991). Differences in densities of materials indicated spatial differences in plant processing activities. For example, in the Lohmann, Early Stirling, and Late Stirling phases, processing and disposal of nuts mostly occurred within structures, whereas maize and starchy seeds were processed outside structures (i.e., charred remains were disposed of in external pits). Over these three phases, there was increasing emphasis on producing maize for storage (Lopinot 1991). Internal storage pits were more common in the Late Stirling phase, which suggested an emphasis on producing surplus for storage (and hiding it). As discussed by Collins (1997), these shifts in foodways in one of the subcommunities of Cahokia occurred in the context of the emergence of local elites.

Similar changes in crop storage occurred in dispersed Mississippian households in the rural areas of the American Bottom, outside the Central Political-Administrative Complex (i.e., outside Cahokia and the East St. Louis and St. Louis mound sites) (Pauketat 1994). Over time rural households showed increased reliance on intrahouse subterranean storage, perhaps to hide crops from appropriating forces. Based on recovered botanical and faunal data, these households and household groups appeared capable of satisfying their subsistence requirements and had a diverse diet. As shown in Figure 7.5, kernel/cob ratios were low at American Bottom sites beginning in the last phase of the Emergent Mississippian and after. Although this trend has been interpreted as a change in maize consumption and production (i.e., from green to mature maize, Lopinot 1992, 1997), Pauketat (1994) has argued that the paucity of shelled maize kernels at rural homesteads could also reflect its appropriation by elites living at centers. For example, at the Olszewski site, which had higher densities of domestic features than a typical rural site, there was also a high kernel to cob ratio (17.91), suggesting it was a local center (i.e., was being provisioned with shelled maize). Only kernels, and no cobs, were recovered from the Horseshoe Lake mound site, and the Lohmann mound site had a kernel to cob ratio that was higher (3.5) than nearby homestead sites. These three examples may show that elites were provisioned with maize (Pauketat 1994).

Lohmann was an 11-ha site located southeast of East St. Louis on a point bar ridge (Esarey and Pauketat 1992). Dating to the Lohmann and Stirling phases, it consisted of a single platform mound and a large aggregate of households. Lohmann has been interpreted as a subsidiary center, serving to link the local population to Cahokia's elites (Esarey and Pauketat 1992). Maize, maygrass, knotweed, and goosefoot were all highly ranked by ubiquity; by count, small starchy seeds made up 92 percent of the seed macroremain assemblage (Johannessen 1992). One Lohmann-phase structure, Structure 1, was larger than other structures of this phase, including those in the Cahokia ICT-II tract (Esarey and Pauketat 1992). It was the only structure at Lohmann that was rebuilt, and probably had an extra-domestic function, or was a high-ranking household. There was only one flotation sample from this structure, but it had the highest density of seeds + Mesoamerican crops (144 count/liter) at the site, mostly representing maize remains (130 count/liter) (Johannessen 1992). This unique Lohmann–phase structure combined an uncommon pattern of maize dominance, with a very low kernel/cob ratio (0.08); perhaps preparation of food from mature maize was among its functions. Most of the other structures and features at the site had high numbers of small seeds and variable kernel/cob ratios.

Systematically recovered macroremain data are also available from the East St. Louis Mound Center of Greater Cahokia. Cahokia and its two contiguous civic-ceremonial precincts, East St. Louis and St. Louis, formed the central administrative core of Greater Cahokia (Pauketat et al. 2013) (see Figure 7.1). There were 45 mounds in East St. Louis, all thought to have been destroyed, until intact deposits were found under nineteenth- and twentieth-century fills. Excavations exposed 25 small post and wall-trench structures (huts) dating to the Late Stirling phase and located immediately inside a palisade wall. Of these, 22 were destroyed by fire; the remains appeared to be in situ and deliberately burned. Pauketat and colleagues have argued these were not typical domestic structures: the ceramic artifacts were in unusual proportions; there were more whole stone tools; other unusual objects like crystals were present. The presence of charred masses of maize was also unusual: eight huts had 1 to 3 L of maize on their floors, mostly shelled kernels, heaped on the floor or in a container. Figure 7.7 shows two such huts. No huts were full of maize, that is, these were not granaries but special domestic stores or ritual offerings. Most of the maize kernels were large (8- to 10-row type) and appeared mature (Simon 2007). Flotation-recovered macroremains from the intentionally burned structures were dominated by wood (including abundant red cedar), followed by maize; other food remains, including seeds of the native starchy grain complex, were poorly represented. Grass seeds from burned thatch occurred, however. Maize kernels, rather than native starchy seeds, appeared to have been the food product placed for burning in these structures. The buildings were apparently built, offerings and special objects placed there, then they were incinerated and abandoned (Pauketat et al. 2013). Other examples of incinerated buildings and burned maize caches exist from the late Sterling phase, when there was significant transformation of Cahokian society, including at East St. Louis, which lost most of its resident population.

In most cases, multiple flotation samples were taken from the different sediment zones and sectors (e.g., north, south) within the burned structures discovered during the East St. Louis Mound center excavations (see data in Simon 2007). Five samples were taken from F656, for example, one of the huts illustrated in Figure 7.7. Virtually all the maize (6,685 fragments, kernel/cob: 397) recovered from this structure came from one sample taken from the southern sector, the location of a visible charcoal and maize concentration. The other areas of the floor, including oxidized soil on the north side, contained very little maize. Similarly, in F536, most of the maize (2,428 fragments, kernel/cob: 0.46) came from a sample from the southwest sector, with relatively little in the other three samples. These results support the inference that maize was placed prior to deliberate burning of structures in a particular sector, with other items in other locations.

Similar to the macroremains results, faunal assemblages from the East St. Louis Mound center huts did not resemble household subsistence refuse (Scott 2007). Numbers and weights of refuse were lower than would be expected in a domestic setting, and species composition was unlike that found at habitation sites, at which fish, waterfowl, and deer were common.

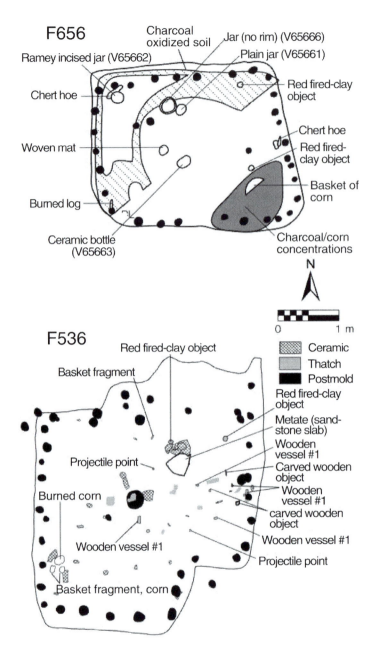

FIGURE 7.7 Plan maps showing the distributions of materials found on the floors of catastrophi‐
cally burned huts F536 and F656. (Figure 6 from Pauketat, Timothy R., Andrew C.
Fortier, Susan M. Alt and Thomas E. Emerson. 2013. A Mississippian conflagration
at East St. Louis and its political‐historical implications. *Journal of Field Archaeology*
38(3):210–226, copyright Trustees of Boston University.)

Reproduced with permission of Taylor & Francis Ltd., on behalf of Trustees of Boston University. Notice the basket
of corn (maize) and charcoal/corn concentration in the southeast sector of F656 (top image) and the burned corn
and basket fragments in the southwest sector of F536 (bottom image).

There were relatively high numbers of turkey bones in East St. Louis Mound samples, and a dog burial was found; both these are results associated elsewhere with elite contexts. Scott (2007) argued that overall the assemblage represented limited subsistence activity in a ritual precinct and lacked evidence for on-site preparation of meat for large-scale feasting.

In summary, comparisons of macroremains of maize and other foods from elite and nonelite contexts, both within Cahokia and between mound sites and nonmound, rural sites, have indicated that the maize played different roles through time for different members of Cahokian society. Foods for early large-scale feasting events, represented by refuse from the Lohmann phase sub–Mound 51 pit, were prepared mostly using traditional native crops such as maygrass and chenopod, rather than maize. This contrasted with domestic food refuse of both emerging elites (i.e., ICT-II results) and nonelites (i.e., most FAI-270 sites), which were characterized by a more balanced mixture of maize and native crops. A further contrast was seen in the late Stirling-phase burned huts at the East St. Louis Mound center, where maize, not native crops, was included in ritual offerings.

Stable Isotope and Skeletal Studies of Human Remains

As discussed earlier, stable isotopic analysis of absorbed and visible cooking residues has provided insights into proportions of C3 and C4 plants in meals prepared at Mississippian sites, from which can be drawn inferences about the roles different foods played in various social settings. Similarly, isotope studies of human skeletal remains, which provide data on consumption patterns over individuals' lifetimes, potentially provide insights into dietary differences among and within American Bottom populations. Pauketat (2010) has argued that mortuary practices transformed personal and corporate identities at Cahokia. There were group mortuaries—ridgetop mounds—associated with the florescence of Cahokia; between 8 and 17 existed at the site and its environs, with a number destroyed in St. Louis and East St. Louis. Based on excavation of one ridgetop mound, Mound 72, located south of Monk's Mound, and accounts of the destruction of others, each mound was thought to have an associated ancestral temple, principal burials, and mass graves. Studies of the remains of individuals interred at Mound 72 and several other sites have documented dietary and health differences related to sex, social standing, and home location within the Cahokia polity (Box 7.1).

BOX 7.1 SKELETAL INDICATORS OF DIET AND HEALTH

A number of skeletal indicators can provide information on the nutritional status and overall health of individuals and populations, in particular, health issues associated with dietary sufficiency. Most skeletal indicators of nutrition and health are nonspecific; that is, they cannot be associated with a particular plant, nutritional stressor, or disease state (Larsen 1995). Despite this limitation, skeletal indicators have proven useful for evaluating the health and nutritional status of individuals living within different subsistence regimes, for example, hunter-gatherers contrasted to agriculturalists, or among individuals of different social status in a society. As summarized by Larsen (1995), interpretation of the indicators is supported by studies of living populations and by archaeological cases for which diet can be strongly inferred from independent data.

One of the most striking contrasts between agricultural populations and most foragers, for example, is the poorer dental health of agriculturalists. In many cases high rates of dental caries (cavities) and tooth loss accompanied the shift in prehistory to increased carbohydrates provided by agricultural staples, including maize, other grains, and root-tuber foods. Declining diet quality and the nutritional stress this produces also have an impact on skeletal development, affecting growth rate, ultimate stature, bone thickness and remodeling, and tooth size (Larsen 1995). Defects—lines or grooves—in dental enamel are an indicator of stress often seen in prehistoric dentitions (Skinner and Goodman 1992). Stress from disease and nutritional deficiencies can also result in arrested growth of the long bones. Arrest and resumption of growth produces features known as Harris, or transverse, lines. Insufficient iron intake and/or absorption, or anemia, stimulates increased red blood cell production in the thin bones of the skeleton, such as the cranium. This produces sieve-like lesions in the eye orbits, referred to as cribra orbitalia (Martin et al. 1985). The relationship between diet and skeletal indicators of anemia is complex, but there is a correlation, noted by many researchers, between increased rates of cribra orbitalia and dependence on agriculture (Larsen 1995). In general, interpretation of nonspecific indicators of stress in terms of dietary differences among individuals is strengthened when made in the context of what was eaten (i.e., the floral and faunal remains) and how foods were processed (i.e., the artifacts and features) and what disease load the population faced, given the region (i.e., types of endemic diseases and parasites) and living conditions (i.e., settlement type, population density, sanitation).

Mound 72 was constructed during the Early Mississippian Lohmann phase (Fowler 1991). It was a marker mound, with a deep postpit and a number of arcs of posts, or woodhenges, thought to have been used for solar observations. More than 260 individuals were buried in Mound 72, in three submounds and the final mound stage. The central personage in 72Sub1 was buried on a platform of shell beads. Final Mound 72 was built over an offertory burial pit containing over 50 young women. The principal burials were near large postpits and were likely buried sequentially. Skeletal and stable isotope analyses of 25 individuals from high status (i.e., from principal burials) and mass grave interments at Mound 72 revealed significant differences among individuals (Ambrose et al. 2003). Individuals with special burial treatment had low frequencies of skeletal indicators of poor health and nutrition; the females from mass graves had higher frequencies of these indicators and dental traits that suggested they were not from the same population as the elite individuals. Only 9 of 25 samples produced enough collagen for reliable isotope analysis; 4 individuals were high status, 5 were sacrificed females. In all but one case, higher-status individuals had higher $\partial^{15}N$ values than sacrificed women and less enriched $\partial^{13}C$ values, indicating that these elites ate less maize (about half as much) and more meat than lower-status individuals. Maize can be considered a low-quality dietary staple in comparison to animal foods and most C3 plant foods. Ambrose and colleagues concluded that the sacrificed women came from a population that was more maize dependent, and less healthy, whereas Mound 72 elites ate a more diverse diet.

Applying a new carbon isotope model for reconstructing protein and energy sources in diet, Kellner and Schoeninger (2007) found that all individuals from Mound 72, elites and sacrificed women, had a diet that was predominantly C3 protein (i.e., from deer, nuts), with C4 energy (i.e., from maize, in varying amounts as discussed earlier). They also studied individuals from Late Mississippian contexts (from East St. Louis Stone Quarry, Florence St., Range, Corbin Mounds, and Hill Prairie sites); only five individuals from upland sites had a similar diet (i.e., C3 protein, C4 energy), which was what had been expected based on plant and animal remains at sites. The majority of the other Late Mississippian individuals ingested maize as their main energy source, but also obtained their protein mostly from C4 foods: carnivorous fish, anadromous fish (taxa that migrate from saltwater to spawn in freshwater), and maize. Kellner and Schoeninger (2007) documented a large range of stable carbon isotope values in the Late Mississippian American Bottom populations and a striking difference in protein sources for the Early Mississippian Mound 72 sample from Cahokia, who consumed deer, and most Late Mississippian individuals, who probably ate freshwater fish.

A study of individuals from the Corbin Mounds and East St. Louis Stone Quarry (ESLSQ) sites provides a late Mississippian (terminal Moorehead phase, AD 1275) comparison of status, diet, and health (Hedman 2006). This was the period when there was evidence for reorganization at Cahokia and population decline in the American Bottom. ESLSQ was a large rural "stone box" floodplain cemetery, probably of moderately ranked individuals. Corbin Mounds was a bluff-top ossuary, a new kind of mortuary pattern dating to this period. Both contexts contrast to the large elite mortuaries of central Cahokia. Among the major findings were the following: The amount of maize and protein consumed by individuals in both samples was comparable, but Corbin-mounds individuals had slightly higher caries rates and relied more on C3 sources (native plants, animals). Corbin-Mounds males and females had about the same diet. By contrast, ESLSQ males had more C4 protein in their diets than ESLSQ females, or anyone buried at Corbin Mounds. They also had more caries. All ESLSQ individuals had higher indicators of chronic nutritional and disease stress during childhood. Hedman (2006) concluded that there was considerable variation in diet and health within and between contemporaneous populations that related in some cases to sex or status, ethnic/social differences in food preference, and/or local availability of food (i.e., floodplain versus uplands). There were differences in the amount of maize consumed and the amounts and sources of protein. Cahokia was a multiethnic society composed of diverse groups; to see this complexity required a focus on individuals, not data grouped by site (Hedman 2006).

In summary, stable isotope and skeletal studies of human remains have demonstrated that diet over the lifetime varied considerably for individuals living in the American Bottom. One's sex, social standing, and home location all contributed to the relative contribution to diet of maize and native foods as sources of energy and deer, fish, and plant sources of protein. Based on Mound 72 results, during the florescence of Cahokia elites enjoyed better health and ate less maize than nonelites. Venison or other C3 meats provided protein to the diet of elites and nonelites alike. Later, when Cahokian society was undergoing reorganization and population decline, fish was an important source of protein for most individuals, along with maize, which was also the primary energy source.

Summary: Maize and Social Status at Cahokia

How have archaeobotanical and other data on maize use contributed to understanding the nature of relationships among members of Mississippian society? The kinds of maize macroremains recovered from sites have been used to draw inferences on how maize preparation changed during the Late Emergent Mississippian and after. In conjunction with studies of pottery forms, a sharp drop in kernel/cob ratios has been interpreted as an early and sustained shift from green corn roasting to boiling mature maize, likely in the form of hominy. This inferred change in how maize was eaten—and its emergence as a dietary staple—was supported by evidence from nonelite populations of the American Bottom. It has been more challenging to draw inferences about maize foodways of Early Mississippian elites: sub-Mound 51 feasting refuse contained very low proportions of charred maize macroremains relative to other foods, but there was evidence of maize-based foods in 36 percent of charred pottery residues tested; elite individuals buried in Mound 72 ate less maize over their lifetimes than did sacrificed women; low kernel/cob ratios in assemblages from hamlets and farming villages might indicate that maize harvests (i.e., kernels) were diverted to elites. Taken together, the glimpses into maize foodways provided by these few data from early elite contexts has suggested the hypothesis that production of mature maize (i.e., harvest and shelling of dried cobs) was not associated with early elite households and that maize-based foods were prepared and consumed less by elites. Given the abundance of charred green corn remains from the ICT-II excavations, perhaps production of green corn products (for use in ritual?) was one factor distinguishing emerging elites from nonelites.

Stable isotope evidence from human remains indicated that over time maize was consumed in greater quantities by both elites and nonelites in Mississippian society, but that considerable variation existed among individuals, in some cases between men and women, in others between upland and floodplain populations. Later Mississippian households, both rural and within Cahokia, had more crop storage capacity, in many cases more inside the house than outside it. Did greater demands for maize provisioning by elites lead to increasingly unequal access to this staple and to attempts to hide crops stores of all kinds? Maize kernel caches were ritually burned, reinforcing the importance of the crop to late Mississippian life and identity, but increasing reliance on it had negative health consequences. Recall that ESLSQ males had more C4 protein (i.e., from carnivorous or anadromous fish and maize) in their diets than ESLSQ females, and also more caries; all these elite individuals showed high indicators of chronic nutritional and disease stress during childhood.

In a diachronic overview of the evidence relevant to maize use in the American Bottom, Reber (2006) proposed that maize was adopted differentially over time in the region based on socioeconomic status, gender, geographic location, and ritual-political factors. Macroremains indicated that maize was important in the nonelite farming communities of the American Bottom from the Emergent Mississippian and after. By the Stirling phase maize was nearly ubiquitous at most sites, including mound centers (for 10 sites: range, 14 to 100 percent ubiquity; eight sites 86 percent or higher, including three ceremonial sites [BBB Motor, Sponemann, Lohmann]). Maize was depicted on the Keller figurine from BBB Motor and the Sponemann and Willoughby figurines from the Sponemann site. Reber (2006) concluded that maize was not viewed as an elite crop by early Cahokians, or more would have been recovered from the sub-Mound 51 feasting refuse pit, and maize would have formed a higher proportion of the diet of elites buried in Mound 72. Rather, it became symbolically important later, during the Stirling phase, when both elite and commoner contexts show maize in abundance. See also Vanderwarker et al. (2016), who concluded that maize was not a key element in Mississippian ritual, based in part on the sub-Mound 51 evidence.

These inferences must be tempered, however, by potential biases in the data. As Reber (2006) noted, only macroremain data were available for all relevant time periods; other lines of evidence for the role(s) of maize (i.e., maize iconography and stable isotope data from human remains, absorbed pottery residues, and charred pottery residues) were spotty. The macrore-main record was also subject to potential bias: there were different numbers of sites and site components from different parts of the American Bottom (i.e., uplands versus floodplain; north versus south) as well as differences in the numbers of hamlets, villages, and mound centers that could be compared. Significantly for investigating status differences through foodways, relatively few elite contexts with systematically recovered macroremains exist. For example, all flotation-recovered data sets from the Emergent Mississippian phase came from hamlets and villages, not the emerging mound centers.

Food, Status, and Social Relationships: Beyond Maize

Animals in Ritual and Diet of Elites and Nonelites at Cahokia

To what extent do changes in faunal exploitation reflect changing social, political, and economic conditions within the Cahokia chiefdom? Kelly (1997) explored this question by examining the kinds of body parts (i.e., cuts of meat) recovered and the diversity of animals present in six areas of Cahokia. She found differences in access of elites and nonelites to certain foods. Deer dominated assemblages beginning in the Lohmann phase and in both elite and nonelite Stirling-phase contexts. Remains of birds were more common in elite settings. In terms of deer body-part representation, there were very low percentages of low-utility cuts (i.e., cuts of lower food value) in elite and nonelite contexts during Emergent Mississippian and Mississippian phases. However, nonelites had mostly mid-utility cuts, whereas elites had mid-utility and high-utility (hindquarters) cuts. It appears that low-utility parts were consistently left off-site by hunters and that once meat was brought to the community, it was divided up differentially by status. A similar pattern was found at the Moundville site, a Mississippian center in Alabama, where elite households received mostly high-utility deer cuts, in this case forelimbs (Jackson and Scott 2010). Turkey was also abundant, and in general Moundville elite contexts contained diverse bird assemblages and some carnivore taxa. Comparing faunal assemblages from two mounds, Jackson and Scott (2003) found variation between Moundville elite households in terms of differences in the distribution of rare species—one household had all the unusual taxa (bison, shark, falcon) and the other more fur-bearing species, perhaps related to craft production there.

"Downtown" Cahokia, the core cluster of mounds and habitation areas clustered around Monk's Mound and the Grand Plaza, included residential areas likely occupied by elites. The areas known as Tract 15A and the Dunham tract, located about 1 km west of the Grand Plaza, represent such an elite subcommunity (Pauketat 1998). The tracts were excavated during salvage projects in the early 1960s, late 1970s, and 1985. Faunal samples were hand-picked during excavation, so there was bias against smaller bones (Miracle 1998). White-tailed deer predominated, and deer assemblages were all very similar in there being very few feet/lower legs and heads. This pattern likely indicated initial butchery elsewhere and transport of only high-utility elements into the community. One context indicated marrow processing; another grease processing. These elite assemblages were not as diverse as those from other sites, in which fish and birds were much more common. While acknowledging bias in recovery based on size, Miracle (1998) proposed that these differences indicated greater and more regular access to deer meat by downtown residents: privileged access extracted as tribute or through kin-based obligations. Botanical remains were also hand-picked; maize was most abundant by weight and occurred in about half the samples; no small seeds were recovered (Dunavan 1998).

Feasting debris from Mound 34 further illustrated the relationship of certain animals to ceremony and ritual. Mound 34 was constructed during the Late Mississippian (ca. AD 1200) about 400 m east of Monk's Mound on the edge of the Moorehead-phase Ramey Plaza (Kelly et al. 2007). Feature 3, a refuse trench probably originally dug as a borrow pit for the mound platform, was filled with large quantities of animal remains: mostly deer bones, but also remains of birds, including swans, hawks, and eagles. The feasting refuse assemblage included twice as many bird species as most assemblages from Cahokia. Bird bones, bills, feathers, wings, and "scalps" were present and likely used for ornamentation or in ritual. Maize was recovered, along with a diverse mix of cultivated and wild seeds, intact thatching, and wood remains, in association with elaborate serving plates, platters, and bowls. Kelly and colleagues concluded that the feature likely represented debris from communal feasting, perhaps performance rituals as part of the Southeastern Ceremonial Complex. Other ritual deposits at the site included large linear charcoal deposits likely representing the remains of a deliberately burned mound-top building that incorporated significant quantities of red cedar and bald cypress, two woods of ceremonial significance.

Black Drink and Cacao

Black Drink, a decoction made from holly leaves, was used historically in the Southeast for ritual purification. Crown et al. (2012) investigated whether Black Drink was used prehistorically in the Cahokia area by analyzing absorbed organic residues from eight beakers (inferred to be drinking cups) from four sites. Holly contains the biomarkers theobromine, caffeine, and ursolic acid. Based on the combined presence of these markers, Black Drink was identified in all residue samples, including four from Cahokia itself: beakers from sub-Mound 51, the Dunham Tract, Mound 11, and Mound 33. Because *Ilex vomitoria* is the only native plant in the Southeast with high enough caffeine levels to serve as a stimulant, caffeine is an especially useful biomarker for Black Drink (Reber and Kerr 2012). Caffeine was present in six of the eight samples studied by Crown et al. (2012).

Washburn et al. (2014) analyzed absorbed residues from five vessels from Cahokia. Two Stirling-phase vessels, a jar from Monk's Mound, and a bowl from a structure in the East Stockade had theobromine levels higher than potential background contamination. Comparison to caffeine levels indicated the bowl was used for Black Drink and the jar for cacao. Vessels were also tested from long-destroyed Moorehead-phase mound complexes located in Madison and St. Clair counties surrounding Cahokia. Three contained theobromine levels higher than potential background contamination; two of these had more theobromine than caffeine, suggesting cacao consumption; the other had equal amounts.

There is also indirect evidence that ritual drink preparation was carried out in ceremonial contexts during the Mississippian period. Miller (2015) studied carbonization patterns on two morphologically similar vessel forms, Powell Plain and Ramey Incised jars, as part of a functional analysis to identify cooking mode. These forms often occurred in Mississippian mortuary contexts. Vessels from a variety of site types were studied. Miller compared patterning in exterior and interior carbonization with ethnographic examples of cooking behaviors, such as wet-mode (i.e., stewing, boiling) and dry-mode (i.e., roasting) cooking. Not all vessels with carbonization had patterned zones; 23 had patterning consistent with cooking. Of these, both wet mode and dry mode were found, but more than half did not match those patterns, but rather had oxidation at the shoulder and base of the interior and a thick band of carbonization between these zones. This pattern matched decoction, boiling of lightweight materials in water until the liquid is reduced in volume to prepare a tea or medicinal drink. All decoction-mode examples came from ceremonial contexts. Miller (2015) proposed that the vessels were used to make Black Drink from holly, an inference that could be confirmed through chemical analysis.

Conclusion: Contributions of Paleoethnobotany to Understanding Social Relationships at Cahokia

This case has focused on how paleoethnobotany contributes to understanding social relationships, specifically in the context of emerging social and political complexity. As shown by the research reviewed here, there were apparently few changes in the kinds of plants (and animals) used over time at Cahokia or among contemporary populations; rather there were differences in the social settings in which certain foods were produced and consumed, and in the abundance and form in which foods were eaten by different members of the society. Foods and other plants also played roles in ritual practices that marked important transitions in the personal and social lives of Mississippians. In essence, our focus as paleoethnobotanists interested in understanding social relationships cannot just be on foods and other plants, but must be on foodways—food and plant use in its social and cultural setting. The archaeological contexts of our samples are always important to paleoethnobotanical inference, but here context takes center stage. Not just in understanding contexts after the fact in order to make informed comparisons among data sets, but, if possible, also in contributing to the creation of robust data sets by participating in the design and execution of research.

Our windows into foodways in the Cahokia chiefdom were primarily data sets of charred macroremains—most collected by systematic programs of flotation, some hand-picked during older excavations—and stable isotope analyses of vessel residues (absorbed and charred) and human skeletal remains. Considered in cultural context, and in conjunction with robust faunal data and artifact studies, these data were especially effective for drawing comparisons among sites, site components (subcommunities), and in some cases households or other contexts that differed in status. Finds such as the burned huts in East St. Louis provided insights into the spatial patterning of ritually deposited objects and foods. Compelling inferences about the abundance and form of foods consumed by Cahokian populations were made using many of the quantitative approaches discussed in Chapter 4.

Taking the American Bottom region as a whole, paleoethnobotanical research has shown that people living in the greater Cahokia mound centers, subsidiary centers, and rural hamlets and farmsteads, elites and nonelites alike, subsisted on a mixture of crops and wild foods that included native starchy and oily seeds, maize, squash, nuts, and some other wild seeds and fruits. Venison and fish provided the bulk of the animal protein; beans were introduced late in the sequence. Traces of agricultural fields have not been identified, but the spacing of household clusters within Cahokia, as well as the spacing of rural farmsteads, suggested there was sufficient open, well-drained land to grow crops to support the population. The floodplain forests of the American Bottom were cleared long before Monk's Mound was built; growing of native crops and maize predated both maize intensification and the emergence of the Cahokia chiefdom. Over time there were changes in how people stored, distributed, and presented food, in the context of changes in the size and structure of both households and communities. Larger, extended family households gave way to smaller homes; communal cooking and storage areas to more private ones; some households became centers for their communities.

Comparisons among sites have revealed differences in foodways among members of the Cahokian population. Although maize was common (as measured by percentage frequency or ubiquity) in most sites and site components, stable isotope analyses of absorbed and charred pottery residues revealed that it was cooked more often at rural sites than at Cahokia and less at outlying mound sites than at farmsteads. But there were also fewer burned maize kernels in comparison to burned cobs (as measured by the comparison ratio, kernel:cob) in the refuse of rural households, suggesting that nonelites were providing shelled maize that was consumed by elites, likely in the form of hominy. Although most elite contexts had relatively high kernel:cob ratios, the emerging elites of ICT-II in Cahokia were apparently involved with green corn roasting. The Cahokia population in general had access to mid- to high-utility cuts of deer. By the Late Mississippian, differences in access to meat were indicated between floodplain and upland sites: individuals buried in a mortuary in the uplands consumed more deer and nuts than contemporaries in the floodplain, whose protein came from fish and maize. Stable isotope studies of human skeletal remains indicated that diet over the lifetime varied considerably among individuals, more so than might be expected from broad similarities in sitewide macroremain and faunal data sets.

Comparisons between contemporary elite and nonelite contexts within communities have provided a closer look at how foods and other plants and animals marked social relationships. For example, in comparison to domestic refuse from ICT-II, feasting refuse deposited in sub-Mound 51 indicated selection of native crops over maize (as measured by percentage frequencies) for preparation of foods for ceremonies associated with Early Mississippian mound construction. Such feasts also included remains of rarely used animals and large quantities of high-food-value cuts of deer. Tobacco, psychoactive plants, and red cedar were also associated with ritual. Elite individuals buried in Mound 72 consumed less maize and more meat over their lifetimes than did women sacrificed and interred with them.

Late Mississippian feasting contexts, such as Mound 34, documented the continued role of deer and rare fauna in community ceremonies. Interestingly, maize, rather than native crops, was used to prepare feasting foods for rituals held at Mound 34. Similarly, it was maize that was present in huts burned in association with ritual at the East St. Louis mound site in the late Stirling phase.

To conclude, the research reviewed here from the greater Cahokia center and rural sites of the American Bottom has shown that native crops, several wild plants, and maize were important components of Mississippian foodways. Although not the only plant that marked social identity among Cahokians, maize was among the more visible. Because it is a C4 plant in a largely C3-dominated subsistence system, maize consumption can be inferred from stable isotope study of residues and human remains; other individual foods cannot be identified this way. When grown to maturity, maize produces a robust, inedible cob useful as a fuel; native seed crops do not produce such remains. Maize may thus be overrepresented. Be that as it may, understanding how different foods were prepared from maize and native crops, by whom and for whom, and how their consumption differed among individuals and communities has enhanced our understanding of relationships among people during the emergence of social complexity at Cahokia. These insights would not have been possible without the contribution of systematically recovered archaeobotanical remains.

References

Alt, Susan M., Jeffery D. Kruchten and Timothy R. Pauketat 2010 The construction and use of Cahokia's Grand Plaza. *Journal of Field Archaeology* 35(2):131–146.

Ambrose, Stanley H., Jane Buikstra and Harold W. Krueger 2003 Status and gender differences in diet at Mound 72, Cahokia, revealed by isotopic analysis of bone. *Journal of Anthropological Archaeology* 22:217–226.

Beehr, Dana E. and Stanley H. Ambrose 2007a Reconstructing Mississippian diet in the American Bottom with stable isotope ratios of pot sherd residues. In *Theory and Practice of Archaeological Residue Analysis*, edited by H. Barnard and J. W. Eerkens, pp. 189–199. British Archaeological Reports S1650, Archaeopress, Oxford.

———— 2007b Were they what they cooked? Stable isotopic analysis of Mississippian pottery residues. In *The Archaeology of Food and Identity*, edited by K. C. Twiss, pp. 171–191. Southern Illinois University Carbondale, Center for Archaeological Investigations, Occasional Paper No. 34, Carbondale, IL.

Briggs, Rachel V. 2016 The civil cook pot: Hominy and the Mississippian standard jar in the Black Warrior Valley, Alabama. *American Antiquity* 81(2):316–332.

Collins, James M. 1997 Cahokia settlement and social structure as viewed from the ICT-II. In *Cahokia: Domination and Ideology in the Mississippian World*, edited by T. R. Pauketat and T. E. Emerson, pp. 124–140. University of Nebraska Press, Lincoln.

Crown, Patricia L., Thomas E. Emerson, Jiyan Gu, W. Jeffrey Hurst, Timothy R. Pauketat and Timothy Ward 2012 Ritual black drink consumption at Cahokia. *Proceedings of the National Academy of Sciences of the United States of America* 109(35):13944–13949.

Dalan, Rinita A., George R. Holley, William I. Woods, Harold W. Watters, Jr. and John A. Koepke 2003 *Envisioning Cahokia: A Landscape Perspective*. Northern Illinois University Press, DeKalb, IL.

Dunavan, Sandra L. 1998 Botanical remains. In *The Archaeology of Downtown Cahokia: The Tract 15A and Dunham Tract Excavations*, edited by Timothy R. Pauketat, pp. 333–338. Illinois Transportation Archaeological Research Program, Studies in Archaeology No. 1, University of Illinois, Urbana.

Esarey, Duane and Timothy R. Pauketat 1992 *The Lohmann Site: An Early Mississippian Center in the American Bottom (11-S-49)*. University of Illinois Press, Urbana.

Fortier, A. D., Thomas E. Emerson and D. L. McElrath 2006 Calibrating and reassessing American Bottom culture history. *Southeastern Archaeology* 25:170–211.

Fowler, Melvin L. 1991 Mound 72 and Early Mississippian at Cahokia. In *New Perspectives on Cahokia*, edited by J. B. Stoltman, pp. 1–28. Prehistory Press, Madison, WI.

Fritz, Gayle J. and Neal H. Lopinot 2003–2004 Native crops at Early Cahokia: Comparing domestic and ceremonial contexts. *Illlinois Archaeology* 15 & 16:90–111.

Hedman, Kristin M. 2006 Late Cahokian subsistence and health: Stable isotope and dental evidence. *Southeastern Archaeology* 25(2):258–274.

Jackson, H. Edwin and Susan L. Scott 2003 Patterns of elite faunal utilization at Moundville, Alabama. *American Antiquity* 68(3):552–572.

———— 2010 Zooarchaeology of the Moundville elite. In *Mound Excavations at Moundville: Architecture, Elites, and Social Order*, edited by Vernon James Knight, Jr., pp. 326–347. University of Alabama Press, Tuscaloosa.

Johannessen, Sissel 1984 Paleoethnobotany. In *American Bottom Archaeology*, edited by C. J. Bareis and J. W. Porter, pp. 197–214. University of Illinois Press, Urbana.

———— 1992 Plant remains. In *The Lohmann Site: An Early Mississippian Center in the American Bottom (11-S-49)*, edited by Duane Esarey and Timothy R. Pauketat, pp. 139–144. University of Illinois Press, Urbana.

———— 1993 Food, dishes, and society in the Mississippi valley. In *Foraging and Farming in the Eastern Woodlands*, edited by C. M. Scarry, pp. 182–205. University Press of Florida, Gainesville.

Kellner, Corina M. and Margaret J. Schoeninger 2007 A simple carbon isotope model for reconstructing prehistoric diet. *American Journal of Physical Anthropology* 133:1112–1127.

Kelly, John E., James A. Brown, Jenna M. Hamlin, Lucretia S. Kelly, Laura Kozuch, Kathryn E. Parker and Julieann Van Nest 2007 Mound 34: The context for the early evidence of the Southeastern Ceremonial Complex at Cahokia. In *Southeastern Ceremonial Complex: Chronology, Content, Context*, edited by A. King, pp. 60–85. University of Alabama Press, Tuscaloosa.

Kelly, Lucretia S. 1997 Patterns of faunal exploitation at Cahokia. In *Cahokia: Domination and Ideology in the Mississippian World*, edited by T. R. Pauketat and T. E. Emerson, pp. 69–88. University of Nebraska Press, Lincoln.

Larsen, Clark Spencer 1995 Biological change in human populations with agriculture. *Annual Review of Anthropology* 24:185–213.

Lopinot, Neal H. 1991 Part I: Archaeobotanical remains. In *The Archaeology of the Cahokia Mounds ICT-II: Biological Remains*, edited by Neal H. Lopinot, Lucretia S. Kelly, George R. Milner, and Richard Paine, pp. 1–268. Illinois Historical Preservation Agency, Illinois Cultural Resources Study No. 13, Springfield.

——— 1992 Spatial and temporal variability in Mississippian subsistence: The Archaeobotanical record. In *Late Prehistoric Agriculture: Observations from the Midwest*, edited by W. I. Woods, pp. 44–94. Illinois Historic Preservation Society, Springfield.

——— 1997 Cahokian food production reconsidered. In *Cahokia: Domination and Ideology in the Mississippian World*, edited by T. R. Pauketat and T. E. Emerson, pp. 52–68. University of Nebraska Press, Lincoln.

Martin, Debra L., Alan H. Goodman and George J. Armelagos 1985 Skeletal pathologies as indicators of quality and quantity of diet. In *Analysis of Prehistoric Diets*, edited by Robert I. Gilbert, Jr. and J. H. Mielke, pp. 227–279. Academic Press, Orlando.

Miller, Jessica R. 2015 Interior carbonization patterns as evidence of ritual drink preparation in Powell Plain and Ramey Incised vessels. *American Antiquity* 80(1):170–183.

Milner, George R. 2006 *The Cahokia Chiefdom: The Archaeology of a Mississippian Society*. University Press of Florida, Gainesville.

Milner, George R., Thomas E. Emerson, Mark W. Mehrer, Joyce A. Williams and Duane Esarey 1993 Mississippian and Oneota periods. In *American Bottom Archaeology: A Summary of the FAI-270 Project Contribution to the Culture History of the Mississippi River Valley*, edited by C. J. Bareis and J. W. Porter, pp. 158–186. University of Illinois Press, Urbana.

Miracle, Preston 1998 Faunal remains. In *The Archaeology of Downtown Cahokia: The Tract 15A and Dunham Tract Excavations*, edited by Timothy R. Pauketat, pp. 309–331. Illinois Transportation Archaeological Research Program, Studies in Archaeology No. 1, University of Illinois, Urbana.

Munoz, Samuel E., Kristine E. Gruley, Ashtin Massie, David A. Fike, Sissel Schroeder and John W. Williams 2015 Cahokia's emergence and decline coincided with shifts of flood frequency on the Mississippi River. *Proceedings of the National Academy of Sciences of the United States of America* 112(20):6319–6324.

Munoz, Samuel E., Sissel Schroeder, David A. Fike and John W. Williams 2014 A record of sustained prehistoric and historic land use from the Cahokia region, Illinois, USA. *Geology* 42(6):499–502.

Myers, Thomas P. 2006 Hominy technology and the emergence of Mississippian societies. In *Histories of Maize: Multidiscipinary Approaches to the Prehistory, Linguistics, Biogeography, Domestication, and Evolution of Maize*, edited by J. E. Staller, R. H. Tykot and B. F. Benz, pp. 511–520. Academic Press, Amsterdam.

Pauketat, Timothy R. 1994 *The Ascent of Chiefs: Cahokia and Mississippian Politics in Native North America*. The University of Alabama Press, Tuscaloosa.

——— 1998 *The Archaeology of Downtown Cahokia: The Tract 15A and Dunham Tract Excavations*. Illinois Transportation Archaeological Research Program, Studies in Archaeology No. 1, University of Illinois, Urbana.

——— 2010 The missing persons in Mississippian mortuaries. In *Mississippian Mortuary Practices: Beyond Hierarchy and Representationist Perspective*, edited by L. P. Sullivan and Robert C. Mainfort, Jr., pp. 14–29. University Press of Florida, Gainesville.

Pauketat, Timothy R. and Thomas E. Emerson 1997 Introduction: Domination and ideology in the Mississippian world. In *Cahokia: Domination and Ideology in the Mississippian World*, edited by T. R. Pauketat and T. E. Emerson, pp. 1–29. University of Nebraska Press, Lincoln.

Pauketat, Timothy R., Andrew C. Fortier, Susan M. Alt and Thomas E. Emerson 2013 A Mississippian conflagration at East St. Louis and its political-historical implications. *Journal of Field Archaeology* 38(3):210–226.

Pauketat, Timothy R., Lucretia S. Kelly, Gayle J. Fritz, Neal H. Lopinot, Scott Elias and Eve Hargrave 2002 The residues of feasting and public ritual at Early Cahokia. *American Antiquity* 67(2):257–279.

Reber, Eleanora A. 2006 A hard row to hoe: Changing maize use in the American Bottom and surrounding areas. In *Histories of Maize: Multidisciplinary Approaches to the Prehistory, Linguistics, Biogeography, Domestication, and Evolution of Maize*, edited by J. E. Staller, R. H. Tykot and B. F. Benz, pp. 235–248. Academic Press, Amsterdam.

Reber, Eleanora A., Stephanie N. Dudd, Nikolaas J. van der Merwe and Richard P. Evershed 2004 Direct detection of maize in pottery residues via compound specific stable carbon isotope analysis. *Antiquity* 78(301):682–691.

Reber, Eleanora A. and Richard P. Evershed 2004 How did Mississippians prepare maize? The application of compound-specific carbon isotope analysis to absorbed pottery residues from several Mississippi Valley sites. *Archaeometry* 46(1):19–33.

Reber, Eleanora A. and Matthew T. Kerr 2012 The persistence of caffeine in experimentally produced black drink residues. *Journal of Archaeological Science* 39:2312–2319.

Scott, Elizabeth M. 2007 Faunal remains. In *The Archaeology of the East St. Louis Mound Center, Part II: The Northside Excavations*, edited by A. C. Fortier, pp. 769–776. Illinois Transportation Archaeological Research Program, Transportation Archaeological Research Reports No. 22, University of Illinois, Urbana.

Simon, Mary 2007 Floral remains. In *The Archaeology of the East St. Louis Mound Center, Part II: The Northside Excavations*, edited by A. C. Fortier, pp. 747–768. Illinois Transportation Archaeological Research Program, Transportation Archaeological Research Reports No. 22, University of Illinois, Urbana.

Simon, Mary L. and Kathryn E. Parker 2006 Prehistoric plant use in the American Bottom: New thoughts and interpretations. *Southeastern Archaeology* 25(2):212–257.

Skinner, Mark and Alan H. Goodman 1992 Anthropological uses of developmental defects of enamel. In *Skeletal Biology of Past Peoples: Research Methods*, edited by S. R. Saunders and M. A. Katzenberg, pp. 153–174. Wiley-Liss, New York.

VanDerwarker, Amber M., Dana N. Bardolph, Kristin M. Hoppa, Heather B. Thakar, Lana S. Martin, Allison L. Jaqua, Matthew E. Biwar and Kristina M. Gill 2016 New World paleoethnobotany in the new millennium (2000–2013). *Journal of Archaeological Research* 24:125–177.

VanDerwarker, Amber M., Gregory D. Wilson and Dana N. Bardolph 2013 Maize adoption and intensification in the Central Illinois River valley: An analysis of archaeobotanical data from the Late Woodland to Early Mississippian periods (AD 600–1200). *Southeastern Archaeology* 32(2):147–168.

Washburn, Dorothy K., William N. Washburn, Petia A. Shipkova and Mary Ann Pelleymounter 2014 Chemical analysis of cacao residues in archaeological ceramics from North America: Considerations of contamination, sample size, and systematic controls. *Journal of Archaeological Science* 50:191–207.

8

AN INDIVIDUAL'S RELATIONSHIP TO THE NATURAL WORLD

Ötzi, the Tyrolean Iceman

Glossary

Copper Age (Chalcolithic)   the final phase of the Neolithic archaeological period, characterized by the use of copper for the manufacture of some tools and weapons.

mitochondrial DNA: DNA located in mitochondria, the part of a cell that converts energy from food into a form that the cell can use. mtDNA is passed from mother to offspring in most multicellular organisms, which allows tracing of maternal lineages.

trace elements   elements present in very low concentrations in tissues; includes a number essential for life. Because foods at different trophic levels and from different environments may contain different concentrations of trace elements, dietary patterns influence the concentrations of trace elements in human tissue.

Z-score (standard score)   the number of standard deviations of a data point above or below the mean value of what is being measured.

Introduction

The archaeological record is largely a record of communities of different sizes and complexity: groups of people living in houses, villages, towns, cities, regions. Often our data come from secondary contexts—garbage middens of various sorts—in which objects used by many individuals were intermixed. It can be very challenging to associate a given object or location with identifiable groups (for instance, as defined by gender or status) or to individuals. Burials are an obvious exception: study of human remains can reveal direct data on diet and health; objects discovered in association with human remains may be attributable to that individual(s) in life. Otherwise, a situation of extraordinary preservation may provide a window into the past life and relationships of an individual. This is the situation with Ötzi, a late Neolithic man preserved by glacier ice in the Alps.

Studying the individual—human remains and associated objects—can raise questions concerning appropriate treatment of the dead by archaeologists and other researchers. Should human skeletal remains be disturbed? What kinds of studies and how invasive/destructive are acceptable? Is reburial necessary or appropriate? How are the stakeholders in these decisions identified and brought into decision making? These issues are complex and important, but beyond the scope of this case study discussion.

Ötzi, the Tyrolean Iceman, captured the imagination of scholars and the public alike—the drama of the discovery, the remoteness of the site and difficult conditions of excavation, the unique finds, the wide-ranging research opportunities. After more than 25 years results are still being published; many recent sources were used here. Spindler (1994) is still an excellent resource; Fleckinger (2011) and the website for the permanent Iceman exhibit at the South Tyrol Museum of Archaeology (www.iceman.it) incorporate recent results and interpretations, as well as images of the setting and the Iceman's equipment and clothing (these sources are all in English). Many important results were published in the *Man in the Ice* series (in German, English, Italian): Höpfel, Platzer and Spindler 1992 [Vol. 1]; Spindler, Rastbichler-Zissernig, Wilfing, zur Nedden, Nothdurfter 1995 [Vol. 2]; Spindler, Wilfing, Rastbichler-Zissernig, zur Nedden, Nothdurfter 1996 [Vol. 3] Bortenschlager and Oeggl 2000 [Vol. 4]; Egg and Spindler 2009 [Vol. 6].

The following questions will be our focus: What plant materials were associated with Ötzi, and what do they tell us about the circumstances of his daily life, his journey—where he lived and the areas he traveled through—his cultural affiliation, and his death? What do studies of the site and region tell us about the environment and human relationships to it in the Late Neolithic? What is unique, what is universal about Ötzi's story? As we will see, this extraordinary find has given us extraordinary insights into the life and death of a man who lived 5,000 years ago, informed in no small part by archaeobotanical studies. Table 8.1 lists the scientific names of plants mentioned in the text.

TABLE 8.1 Scientific names of plants mentioned in the text

acorn	*Quercus* sp.
alder	*Alnus* sp.
alpine daisy	*Leucanthemopsis alpina*
ash	*Fraxinus* cf. *excelsior*
barley	*Hordeum vulgare*
bearberry	*Arctostaphylos uva-ursi*
birch	*Betula* sp.
birch fungus	*Piptoporus betulinus*
bracken	*Pteridium aquilinum*
broomcorn millet	*Panicum miliaceum*
cereals	*Cerealia*
cornelian cherry	*Cornus mas*
dock	*Rumex* sp.
dogwood	*Cornus* sp.
dwarf willow	*Salix reticulata*
einkorn	*Triticum monococcum*
elder	*Sambucus* sp.
elm	*Ulmus* sp.
emmer wheat	*Triticum dicoccum*
flax	*Linum usitatissimum*
foxtail millet	*Setaria italica*

(Continued)

TABLE 8.1 (Continued)

gentian	*Gentiana* sp.
glacier buttercup	*Ranunculus glacialis*
goosefoot or chenopod	Chenopodiaceae
grass	Poaceae
green alder	*Alnus viridis*
hazel	*Corylus avellana*
hop hornbeam	*Ostrya* sp.
hulled barley	*Hordeum vulgare*
juneberry	*Amelanchier ovalis*
juniper	*Juniperus* sp.
kingcup	*Caltha* sp.
larch	*Larix decidua*
lentil	*Lens culinaris*
lime tree	*Tilia* sp.
naked barley	*Hordeum vulgare* var. *nudum*
naked wheat (tetraploid)	*Triticum durum/turgidum*
naked wheat (hexaploid)	*Triticum aestivum*
nettle	Urticaceae
Norway maple	*Acer platanoides*
opium poppy	*Papaver somniferum*
pea	*Pisum sativum*
pine	*Pinus* sp.
plantain	*Plantago* sp.
primrose family	Primulaceae
pulse or legume	Papilionaceae
purple saxifrage	*Saxifraga oppositifolia*
rye	*Secale* sp.
sedge	Cyperaceae
sheep's sorrel	*Rumex acetosella*
sloeberry	*Prunus spinosa*
spelt	*Triticum spelta*
spruce	*Picea abies*
true tinder	*Fomes fomentarius*
water chestnut	*Trapa natans*
wayfaring tree	*Viburnum lantana*
wheat	*Triticum* sp.
wild grape	*Vitis vinifera* ssp. *sylvestris*
willow	*Salix* sp.
yew	*Taxus baccata*

Discovery and Excavation

In September 1991, two climbers discovered a body emerging from a glacier in a rocky gully at 3,200 ft. in the Tyrolean Alps near the Austrian–Italian border (Spindler 1994) (Figure 8.1; also see images at www.iceman.it). The remains were removed from the ice by pneumatic chisel and other tools by the local air rescue service; it was thought initially that the corpse was the relatively recent victim of a climbing accident. The remains were first examined by forensic scientists; only later were archaeologists brought in. Numerous people visited the

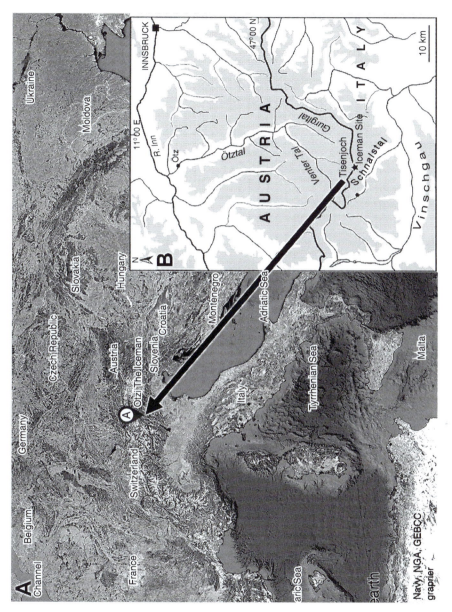

FIGURE 8.1 **A:** open-access map of the region; the location of the Iceman site is indicated; **B:** The location of the Iceman site south of the Ötztal. (Image B: Figure 1 from Heiss, Andreas G. and Klaus Oeggl. 2009. The plant macro-remains from the Iceman site (Tisenjoch, Italian–Austrian border, eastern Alps): New results on the glacier mummy's environment. *Vegetation History and Archaeobotany* 18:23–35.

Reproduced with permission of Springer. The Iceman site is located in the Tyrolean Alps, just south of the Austrian–Italian border (dark line on image B). Valley areas are shown in white on image B.

Hauslabjoch, the location of the find, during the time it took to remove the body; some objects were picked up and dug out. When it became clear from the presence of a copper axe, flint scraper, and wooden bow that the individual was ancient, a media frenzy broke out, as well as debate over whether Austria or Italy had jurisdiction over the find (the location was eventually established as South Tyrol, Italy). A research institute was established, and joint study of the site and the mummified remains and associated artifacts began, with the entire find, now known as Ötzi or the Iceman, protected as an ancient monument. Radiocarbon dates on the remains place Ötzi at 3300 to 3200 cal. BC, during the Late Neolithic period or Copper Age (Table 8.2).

The site was examined briefly by archaeologists in October 1991 before winter snows set in, with the exact position of the body defined and more materials collected, including fragments of a birch-bark container and its contents, scraps of fur and leather, cords of twisted grasses, and ibex bones (Spindler 1994). The following summer, following manual removal of 2 m of snow, excavation of the site was undertaken. Glacial ice was removed by pick or a jet of steam. The end of the bow was found, as was a fur object. Meltwater from the depression in which the body was found was diverted into a channel and passed through a series of sieves of different mesh sizes (Oeggl and Schoch 2000). A large quantity of small botanical and zoological remains (grasses, moss, leaves, charcoal, hair, insects, and additional body tissue fragments) was collected this way. Water used for washing finds was also sieved. At the end of the excavation, the sediment from the gully was sampled (Acs et al. 2005). The gully was surveyed and divided into squares, from which sediment samples were taken. The site was then left to revert to nature.

The Iceman's Equipment and Clothing

Ötzi's equipment and clothing were distributed among three spots in the find area (Spindler 1994). First was in association with the body, which lay extended, face down, in the gully, with head and shoulders raised above the rest of the body by a rock. The man was fully clothed, but the clothing was not completely preserved, especially on the head, shoulders, and back, which emerged first from the ice. A birch-bark container was found about 2 m southwest of his head. A second group of finds was located 4 to 5 m southwest of the head of the corpse on a raised rocky shelf that bounded the site on the valley side. Among these were an axe; bow stave; a second birch-bark container; parts of the wooden frame of a backpack; and remains of fur, cords, and some other small items. An arrow quiver was found at a third location about equidistant from the other two. One question that arises is whether this distribution represented in situ deposition or whether some or all of the finds may have moved. We'll return to this question after reviewing the data.

The largest object found was a 182-cm-long, slender piece of wood interpreted as a bow-stave (Spindler 1994; Oeggl and Schoch 2000; see images of all objects at www.iceman.it). It

TABLE 8.2 Cultural chronology, data from Festi et al. 2014

Bronze Age	2200–1000 cal BC
Copper Age/Late Neolithic	3500–2200 cal BC
Neolithic	6000–3500 cal BC
Mesolithic	9500–5500 cal BC

had been worked—the side facing the archer was evenly rounded and the shoulders tapered from the middle toward the ends—but it was unfinished, as the ends had not been flattened and it lacked bowstring impressions (Spindler 1994). The bow stave was yew, which grows in the region up to 1400 m (Table 8.1). An arrow quiver, a rectangular fur sack (probably deer) stiffened with a hazel rod, was also recovered. It was missing its carrying belt and lid. It contained a 2-m length of coiled cord made of bast fiber (a woody fiber obtained from phloem, the nutrient-carrying tissue of plants) that was likely a bow string (Spindler 1994). There were also two finished arrows (with attached flint heads and fletching), 12 partially smoothed arrow shafts, a bundle of sinews and bast fibers, and antler fragments in the quiver. The arrow shafts were made of long wayfaring tree shoots, which had been evenly smoothed in the two finished arrows. In one case a length of dogwood was glued to form part of one shaft. Birch tar was used to attach the arrowheads and fletching. Interestingly, both finished arrows were broken, whereas all but one of the blank shafts was intact. The fact that Ötzi was carrying materials to make a new bow and arrows and had lost part of his quiver and possessed only broken arrows suggested to Spindler (1994) that Ötzi had suffered a recent misfortune—an accident or violent encounter.

Ötzi also carried an axe and dagger (Spindler 1994). The axe head was copper, cemented in the shafting fork by birch tar and hafted by narrow strips of leather or hide. The handle and shafting fork were formed from a single piece of yew heartwood (Oeggl and Schoch 2000). Loy (2006) found starch residues on this axe. The location and condition of the starch granules (unidentified, but showing optical effects of heating) suggested that the axe was rehafted after Ötzi ate, when he had food residues on his hands. Woody fibers and cellulose were also discovered, consistent with the inferred wood-working function of the axe, and presence of red blood cells and hair indicated that the axe had also been used for butchering. Ötzi carried a small dagger in a scabbard in the region of his right hip, likely fastened to his belt by a leather thong. The dagger was made of a small flint blade, worked on two edges, inserted into a wooden ash handle and held in place by thin animal sinew. The scabbard was plaited from bast, probably lime tree, and sewn with grass thread. Later study confirmed that all bast fibers used for binding materials were from lime (Pfeifer and Oeggl 2000).

Ötzi's carrying belt was made of calf leather and incorporated an elongated pouch that contained three flint implements (blade scraper with sickle gloss, drill, thin broken blade), a bone awl, and a piece of fire-starting tinder (true tinder, a tree fungus) mixed with pyrite crystals (Spindler 1994). Other traditional uses of true timber are cauterization, as an absorbing dressing for wounds and burns, and as a remedy against hemorrhoids and bladder disorders, among other conditions (Grienke et al. 2014). A fire-hardened wooden retouching tool found near the dagger was perhaps also fastened to the belt. This small tool was made from a lime tree branch. Ötzi also carried two pieces of birch fungus on his wrist and a tassel made from a white marble bead and narrow strips of fur in the front of his body. These items were likely medicinal and ornamental/used for repairs, respectively. Birch fungus produces pharmacologically active compounds (Peintner and Pöder 2000). It is also likely Ötzi carried a net made from twisted grass stems, fragments of which were found near the body.

Two short boards split from larch trunk and a hazel rod bent into a U-shape were among the finds and interpreted by Spindler (1994) as the frame of a back pannier or pack frame, which Ötzi would have used to carry loads. The ends of the rod were connected to the boards with grass cord. Scraps of fur found near these wooden objects probably represented a fur sack tied to the pannier. The remains of a birch-bark container were also found near the pannier and had perhaps been tied to it or located inside the fur sack. It was likely a cylindrical box and measured at least 20 cm long.

As mentioned earlier, another birch-bark container was found near Ötzi's head. When first seen it was also cylindrical in shape and contained grass and Norway maple leaves (Spindler 1994). Blackening on the inner side of the birch-bark fragments and flakes of charcoal on the leaves indicated that this was a vessel for carrying live embers. In addition to maple leaves, spruce and juniper needles and fragments of glumes and husks of einkorn and wheat were present in the container. The charcoal recovered from among the leaves represented six taxa: elm, spruce (*Picea/Larix* type), pine (*Pinus mugo* type), green alder, possible juneberry, and alpine willow (*Salix reticulata* type) (Oeggl and Schoch 2000). This represented a mixture of montane (valley bottom to 1,800 m), subalpine (1,800–2,500 m), and alpine (above 2,500 m) species, indicating that embers of several fires had been collected by Ötzi.

The clothing preserved on Ötzi's body represents the first complete set of Neolithic garments recovered in Europe (Spindler 1994). No woven cloth was represented among the clothing, although linen and wool textiles are known in fragmentary form from this time period.

On his legs Ötzi wore loose-fitting fur leggings that reached from crotch to ankle (Spindler 1994; see images of the fragments and reconstructed items at www.iceman.it). They were suspended from his body belt, and each tucked into his shoes by means of an attached fur tongue. The leggings were worn fur side out. Ötzi wore a soft leather loincloth over the belt and leggings. The loincloth was sewn with fine sinew thread from long, narrow strips of leather; the leggings were also sewn from smaller pieces.

The upper part of the Iceman's body was covered by a fur garment that has been interpreted as a cloak (Spindler 1994) or jacket (Oeggl 2009). It was made from numerous small pieces of leather sewn together to create a stripped pattern. There were no sleeves, and the garment was open in the front (a closing mechanism was not preserved). The garment was worn in places and patched. On his head Ötzi wore a bearskin cap in the shape of a blunted cone, held in place by leather chinstraps (Spindler 1994; Oeggl 2009). His shoes had bearskin leather soles with attached fur uppers made of red deer. Inside each shoe was a net knotted from lime bark string that held in place grass stuffed into the shoes for warmth (Oeggl 2009).

Mitochondrial DNA analysis was conducted on nine leather fragments from Ötzi's garments (O'Sullivan et al. 2016). Cattle, sheep, goat, brown bear, and roe deer were identified. Each fragment came from a different individual animal. The jacket/cloak was a combination of at least four hides and two species, sheep and goat. It appears that species selection was based on availability and functionality. Leggings were made of goat, a shoelace was cattle hide, the loincloth sheep, and the hat was confirmed as brown bear. Roe deer was used in the quiver. Interestingly, Ötzi had access to two deer species, because red deer was also identified from hair and in samples from Ötzi's gut (see later).

Finally, over his fur clothes and the equipment he carried, Ötzi wore a cloak made from long grass stems (Spindler 1994). It was plaited at the top by seven or eight horizontally inserted twines and hung in an open fringe at the bottom. The cloak would have shed water and served as a ground cloth or blanket. Grass capes formed part of the traditional clothing of shepherds in central Europe into the early twentieth century, providing warmth and protection from rain.

In addition to being found among the plants used to make Ötzi's equipment and clothing, grasses were commonly recovered during site excavation (Acs et al. 2005). Few flowering or fruiting parts were present, so identifications were based on leaf epidermal cell patterns. These were studied by soaking leaves in an acid solution to detach the epidermis, slide-mounting it, and comparing the cell pattern to a comparative collection of native grasses of the Eastern Alps. In many cases identifications were only possible to broad types, which incorporated several genera and species (i.e., *Agrostis* type, *Festuca* type 1, 3, and 4). Among the findings, the grass cape was made of vertical bundles of *Brachypodium pinnatum*, with minor components of *Molinia caerulea*, *Agrostis* type, other grasses, and sedges. A similar assemblage of grasses was identified on the leather, fur, and hide clothing, suggesting transfer of material from the outer cape to the clothing. Meltwater samples also contained these grasses, indicating that the body was submerged in meltwater at some time. Grass used as thermal insulation in Ötzi's shoes was *Brachypodium pinnatum* and *Agrostis* type, in equal proportions, with minor amounts of *Festuca* types 1, 3, and 4; *Nardus stricta*; and sedge. Grasses recovered from the birch-bark vessel and strings made of lime were predominantly *Molinia caerulea*. *Brachypodium pinnatum*, *Molinia caerulea*, and *Nardus stricta* do not grow in the alpine zone where the body was found, but could have been collected in the subalpine region.

To summarize, Ötzi's clothing and equipment showed that he was familiar with traveling in the mountains, but did not spend all his time in the alpine zone. Parts of his equipment were made with materials from lower elevations. The fact that he kindled fires at different places and collected grasses from the subalpine region to stuff his shoes suggests that he had traveled from a lower elevation in the period before his death. His clothing was functional and mended using scraps of leather at hand, but also decorative. His possession of a copper axe perhaps signified that he was a high-status individual. Ötzi carried the means of repairing his equipment and for staying warm and cooking and had some medicinal plants with him. He had used his axe for butchering, but had few provisions with him (two ibex bones, several einkorn wheat spikelets, and a sloeberry were found associated with his body).

Studies of the Iceman's Body

Health and Cause of Death

Most researchers agree that Ötzi's body was preserved by natural processes operating in the find area; detailed discussions of these processes, subsequent conservation efforts, and determinations of sex, age at death, and other physical characteristics can be found in Spindler (1994) and volumes of the *Man in the Ice* series. Later we'll consider an alternative view, that of Vanzettii et al. (2010), that Ötzi died elsewhere and was taken to the Hauslabjoch for burial.

Ötzi was a man of 40 to 50 years old, who had several healed rib fractures on his left side and unhealed fractures on the right that perhaps impeded his mobility in the last weeks of his life (Spindler 1996). He did not suffer from head lice, but was infested with intestinal whipworms (Aspöck et al. 2000) and fleas (Schedl 2000). Ötzi had a functional, but perhaps painful, dentition: all 28 of his surviving teeth showed severe abrasion, and he had two severe caries, or cavities (one penetrating pulp), and possibly other early caries, as well as extensive bone loss around the teeth (Seiler et al. 2013). The tooth abrasion was consistent with grit in diet—likely from consumption of milled grains—and the caries rate (7 percent) was consistent with a high-carbohydrate diet.

Tattoos created with soot particles were present on different parts of Ötzi's body. There were two types: short lines, either single or in groups, and crosses (Pabst et al. 2009). A complete mapping of tattoos revealed 19 groups, consisting of 61 lines (including crosses) (Samadelli et al. 2015). A number of groups were located on or near traditional acupuncture points, raising the possibility that they represented treatment of pain or inflammation (Dorfer et al. 1998). The back and leg tattoos corresponded directly to locations of likely chronic pain from arthritis and other types of musculoskeletal damage (Kean et al. 2013).

How did Ötzi die? The prevailing early interpretation, based on the position and condition of the body and lack of provisions, was that Ötzi had suffered a personal catastrophe that damaged his equipment, injured him, and led him to flee into the high mountain pastures. He lay down on his left side, froze to death, and was covered by snow (Spindler 1996). The discovery of an arrowhead in his left subclavian region (i.e., under the collarbone), which lacerated the subclavian artery and led to rapid blood loss and death (Pernter et al. 2007), changed this scenario to murder (Gleirscher 2014).

Three types of injuries on Ötzi's body must be distinguished to understand what happened to him: injuries from ice pressure, healed injuries, and unhealed injuries associated with the events leading to his death (Gleirscher 2014). Facial deformation and broken ribs likely occurred from ice pressure. There was a healed abrasion on his left shoulder. An unhealed deep cut on Ötzi's hand indicates he was stabbed about 24 hours before death. It was perhaps during this fight that he lost his bow and damaged his quiver and arrows and fled to higher elevation. Study of gut contents, discussed in more detail later, indicate that Ötzi ate a meal of bread and meat about a half hour before he was shot in the back. A fractured eye socket and fracture to rear of the cranium may also be associated with the struggle that led to his death (Gleirscher 2014). The murderer apparently took the arrow shaft, but left Ötzi's equipment.

There are two opinions about when Ötzi died (Oeggl 2009). Autumn is suggested by the condition of the body—it was rapidly covered by snow, protecting it from insect or predator damage; it became desiccated; the snow was transformed to ice (Spindler 1994). The presence of *Artemisia* pollen in an ice sample and the einkorn and sloeberry finds are consistent with fall. However, foods can be stored, and the ice sample could be from a mixed context (Oeggl 2009). Based on the pollen content of the gut, which included a preserved gametophyte (i.e., living cell) of hop-hornbeam pollen (*Ostrya*-type), Oeggl argued for death in spring or early summer, when this tree pollinates. Examination of Ötzi's skin showed loss of epidermis and transformation of fat into adipocire (a waxy substance produced during decomposition under wet conditions), both indications that the body was submerged in water for several months and desiccated afterward (Bereuter et al. 1996). In this scenario, immersion in cold water in the gully would have preserved the body until snowfall (Oeggl 2000).

To summarize, studies of Ötzi's remains have revealed much about his physical condition, health, and injuries suffered in the weeks and days leading up to his death. Only a brief summary of this extensive literature was possible here, but indications are that Ötzi suffered from a number of chronic complaints, from toothache to intestinal worms to sore joints, and may have sought treatment, including a kind of acupuncture. He died as a result of an arrow shot in the back, most likely in the spring or early summer.

Clues to Ötzi's Diet and Travels

Two studies were made of food residues from Ötzi's colon. In the first, a 40-mg sample was removed from the transverse (crosswise) section of the colon and analyzed for pollen and plant macroremains (Oeggl 2000). The macroremains from the sample were dominated by pericarp and testa tissues (coverings of the fruit/seed) characteristic of wheat and rye (*Triticum/Secale*-type; 63 percent of the sample). Because several einkorn spikelets (part of the cereal fruiting structure) were found on the body and rye was not cultivated in central Europe during the Neolithic, consumption of einkorn was indicated. The size of the tissues suggested a finely ground meal. Charcoal fragments also occurred.

The colon pollen spectrum was much more diverse, with 30 types represented (Oeggl 2000). These included trees of the deciduous forest and nonarboreal taxa from cultivated fields, meadows, and tall forb (broad-leaved herb) communities. Most (23) were interpreted as background pollen—unintentionally ingested on food or in water. The most common of these were hop hornbeam (*Ostrya*-type), birch, hazel (*Corylus* sp.), spruce (*Picea* sp.), and pine. Hop hornbeam is a good indicator of the Iceman's home territory, as it grows only in valleys south of the Alps. The fact that cellular gametophytes were preserved in both the hop hornbeam and birch pollen suggested that Ötzi's last journey took place in spring or early summer.

Pollen of economic plants and taxa associated with crop cultivation was also present in the colon sample: Cerealia (*Triticum* type, from consumed einkorn meal), pulses, goosefoot family, plantain (*Plantago major* type), *Polygonum persicaria* type, sheep's sorrel, and nettle. Although Cerealia was the only confirmed crop plant, the other disturbance indicators can be consumed as greens when leaves are young (Oeggl 2000) or are trapped in cereal bran during crop processing (Oeggl 2009). Diatoms, muscle fibers, charred bone fragments, whipworm eggs, and mineral particles were also observed in the sample.

The pollen assemblage of this colon sample was compared to one derived from the ice in which Ötzi was found and five samples from a transect through the region (alpine, subalpine, and montane zones). It differed significantly from all these comparative samples, lending further support to the evidence that Ötzi came from the valley bottoms south of the main alpine range (Oeggl 2000). Study of diatoms from the colon indicated that Ötzi consumed water from both lower and higher elevations during the last day of his life (Rott 2000).

Additional samples were later taken from Ötzi's colon to expand the dietary study; with the original sample these gave a sequence of five gut samples (from the ileum, the final section of the small intestine, to the rectum) that covered about 33 hours (Oeggl et al. 2007). Marker pollen was used to compute pollen concentrations; absolute counts of macroremains and muscle fibers were made (Figure 8.2). Cluster analysis of pollen results indicated three groups, interpreted as three different meals (ileum and colon 1; colon 3 and rectum; colon 2). This was in agreement with DNA analysis of two samples, which detected red deer *(Cervus elaphus)* meat in the ileum and ibex *(Capra ibex)* meat in colon 3 (sigmoid, or S-shaped, colon) (Rollo et al. 2002).

Wheat pollen (*Triticum* type) and bracken spores occurred in all samples. Chenopods, primrose family, pulses (Papilionaceae), and kingcup (*Caltha* type) may also have been eaten, because those pollen types exceed 2 percent in one or more samples. Macroremains were dominated by cereal bran fragments (likely einkorn) and muscle fibers (meat). Bracken fruiting bodies were also present in all samples. A single chenopod seed was found.

The background pollen identified in four samples (two of the "meals": ileum/colon 1, rectum/colon 3) was quite similar, dominated by taxa characteristic of the alpine and subalpine regions, whereas the fifth (colon 2) was distinctive, dominated by taxa of the valley bottoms (note, for example, the distinctively higher occurrences of *Ostrya* type and *Corylus avellana* in

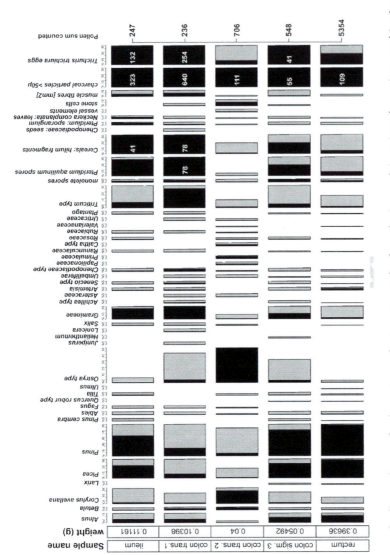

FIGURE 8.2 The content of pollen and macrofossil remains in the ingesta samples from the Iceman's intestines shown in a combined relative and absolute diagram. Only major taxa are considered. The basic pollen sum is established by all arboreal and nonarboreal pollen. Spores, charcoal particles, and *Trichuris trichuria* eggs are taken out and illustrated in percentages relating to the basic pollen sum. Plant macroremains are shown in absolute numbers for the whole sample weight. Muscle fibers are given in the area (mm²) they capture in the slide. Black bars represent percentage or absolute data, grey bars per mille in 10 times exaggerated scale. Numbers in the bars correspond in case of nonpollen microfossils to percentages or in the case of cereal macroremains to absolute numbers of remains per sample. (Figure 3 from Oeggl, Klaus, Werner Kofler, Alexandra Schmidl, James H. Dickson, Eduard Egarter-Vigl and Othmar Gaber. 2007. The reconstruction of the last itinerary of "Ötzi", the Neolithic Iceman, by pollen analyses from sequentially sampled gut extracts. *Quaternary Science Reviews* 26:853–861.)

the colon 2 sample). Taking the gut samples in order, based on the pollen he inhaled/drank in water, Ötzi traveled down from the subalpine zone south to the valley bottoms and then back up to the alpine region to the pass where he died (Oeggl et al. 2007). Given that study of trace elements and strontium, carbon, and oxygen isotopes from two bone samples favor the Ötztal valley to the north of the find site (see Figure 8.1) as Ötzi's home, Hoogewerff et al. (2001) suggested that he traveled between the areas, spending the winter in the southern Vinschgau valley and was perhaps going home in the spring/early summer when he died at the Hauslabjoch Pass.

To summarize, during the last day and a half of his life Ötzi cooked (as indicated by charcoal inclusions) and consumed three meals of ground einkorn meal, meat (red deer or ibex), and greens (pulses, goosefoot family, plantain, *Polygonum persicaria* type, sheep's sorrel, and nettle). He likely traveled from altitude down to the southern Vinschgau valley, then back up to high elevation, where he was killed.

Environmental and Archaeological Studies of the Iceman Site and Region

The start of the Neolithic in the valleys of the Alps is characterized in pollen profiles by appearance of pollen grains of cereals, declines in pollen values of trees of the mixed deciduous forest—most notably elm, ash *(Fraxinus* sp.), and lime—and increases in light-demanding species such as birch and hazel (*Corylus* sp.) (Bortenschlager 2000). Most herb-rich meadows and grasslands are located above valley agricultural lands; today sheep are still driven seasonally from the valleys, across the glaciers, to upland pastures above the tree line (a practice called transhumance). Was this why Ötzi was at the Hauslabjoch Pass, to move flocks to or from upland pastures? Pollen diagrams from the alpine zone show changes in natural species composition under the influence of annual grazing: plants that are better at resisting grazing pressure (for example, by growing close to the ground, like plantains or being unpalatable, like gentians) increase, as do those like docks and goosefoot, which benefit from disturbance and increased nitrogen from animal droppings.

Six pollen profiles were studied from the inner Ötztal region to investigate human impacts on this high alpine region during the Neolithic and Bronze ages, bracketing Ötzi's lifetime (Bortenschlager 2000). Representing a transect from subalpine forest to alpine grasslands above the tree line, over a 5,000-year period the profiles all showed increases in relative and absolute levels of plant species grouped as pasture indicators. For example, as illustrated in the simplified pollen diagram from Am Soon bog, located at 2,620 m (Figure 8.3), pasture indicators increased strongly beginning at 3960 to 3790 cal. BC. The full diagram (not illustrated) showed that this increase was largely due to Umbelliferae (Apiaceae), with lesser contributions from Chenopodiaceae, Ranunculaceae, Rosaceae, and *Rumex*. There was also evidence from increasing charcoal particles in subalpine records that the tree line was lowered through burning to create more grazing lands.

Bortenschlager's (2000) research provided evidence that animals were pastured in the high-elevation Ötz valley before the Iceman's lifetime; further, the discovery site is located on a traditional transhumance route. There was, however, no direct evidence for pasturing in the highlands above the Vinschgau valley (Festi et al. 2014; refer to Figure 8.1 for locations). Using new pasture indicator calibrations developed specifically for the montane and subalpine

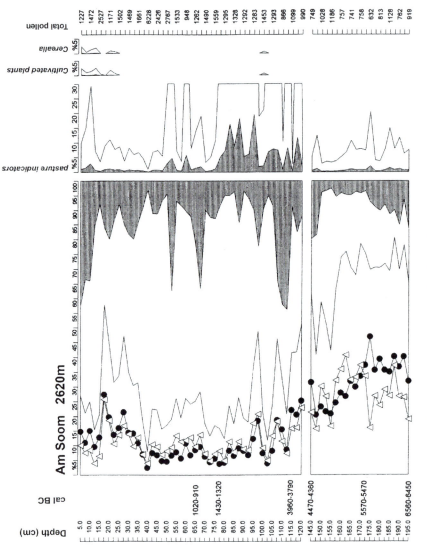

FIGURE 8.3 Simplified relative pollen diagram from the "Am Soom"; for details see the complete relative and pollen concentration diagram in the Appendix. (Figure 6 from Bortenschlager, Signar. 2000. The Iceman's environment. In *The Iceman and his Natural Environment. Palaeobotanical Results. The Man in the Ice, Volume 4*, edited by Sigmar Bortenschlager and Klaus Oeggl, pp. 11–24. Springer-Verlag/Wien, New York.)

Reproduced with permission of Springer Nature. On the left are illustrated the relative occurrences of *Pinus* (black circles) and *Picea* (open triangles) and the summed occurrences of trees and shrubs (white area) and herbaceous plants (black stippled area). On the right are shown the summed occurrences of pasture indicators, cultivated plants, and cereals. Notice the jump in pasture indicators beginning at 3960 to 3790 cal. BC, after a short hiatus in the profile, and the association with increased indicators of other herbaceous plants.

zones of the Iceman study region, Festi and colleagues analyzed new pollen sequences from that region. They identified increases in pasture indicators during the Neolithic and Copper Age (6000–2200 cal. BC) in two of the sequences studied, Lake Vernagt and Lagaun Mire, but the patterns were weak and not sustained (Figure 8.4). These signals were based on few indicators, and the authors felt the increases could be explained by natural variation in vegetation. In the Lagaun Mire diagram, for example, only two or three taxa made up the pasture assemblages early in the sequence, compared to three to five taxa later in time (Figure 8.5).

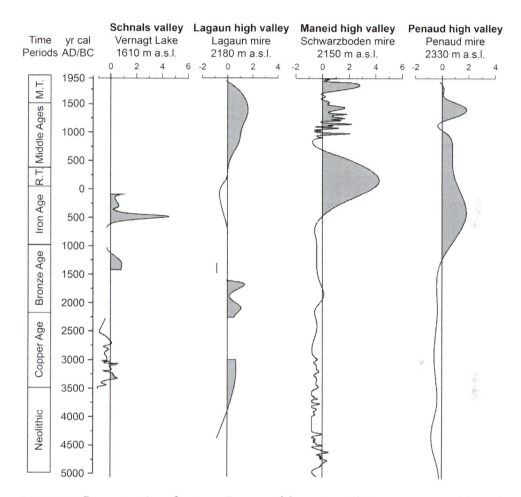

FIGURE 8.4 Reconstruction of pastures. Z–scores of the pasture indicators are presented for each site. Grey areas are potential pasture phases. (Figure 7 from Festi, Daniela, Andreas Putzer and Klaus Oeggl. 2014. Mid and late Holocene land-use changes in the Ötztal Alps, territory of the Neolithic Iceman "Ötzi". *Quaternary International* 353:17–33.)

Reproduced with permission of Elsevier. This graph is a summary of the evidence from four pollen cores for pasturing in the Iceman study region. Grey areas (Z-scores > 0) are potential pasturing phases; open areas (Z-scores < 0) represent natural occurrences of plants. Notice that there is some evidence for Neolithic and Copper Age pasturing, but it is not a sustained pattern like that seen later in time, for instance, during the Iron Age and after.

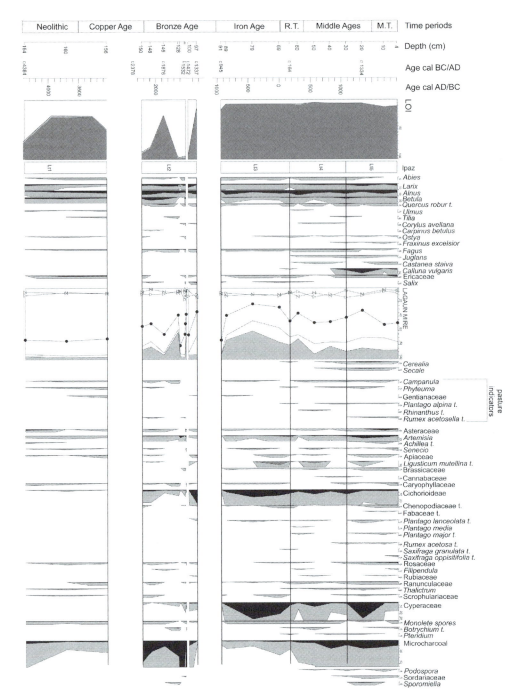

FIGURE 8.5 Lagaun mire pollen diagram, percentage values are shown. In main diagram: open tri-angle = *Picea*; black dot = *Pinus* sp.; Z = *Pinus cembra*; grey filled line = Poaceae; black continuous line indicates AP/NAP proportion. LOI graph (percentage values): dark grey represents organic content; light grey represents carbonate content; white represents silicate content. Time periods: R.T. = Roman Time; M.T. = Modern Time. (Figure 4 from Festi, Daniela, Andreas Putzer and Klaus Oeggl. 2014. Mid and late Holocene land-use changes in the Ötztal Alps, territory of the Neolithic Iceman "Ötzi". *Quaternary International* 353:17–33.)

Because the valley floor was sparsely populated during the Neolithic and Copper Age, there was likely no need for farmers to use higher-elevation lands to pasture animals or to use them only on an occasional basis. Festi and colleagues concluded that their results did not support a scenario in which Ötzi traveled to where he died because he was a shepherd.

Recent archaeological survey in the high altitudes (above 2,000 m) of the Schnals Valley, the largest tributary valley of the Vinschgau, also indicated little interest in the region by Neolithic populations (Putzer, Festi, Edlmair, and Oeggl 2016). Although ample evidence was found for use of higher elevations during the Mesolithic by hunting groups, there was a clear decline in the early Neolithic (to only one site). The Late Neolithic (4000–3700 cal. BC) showed evidence of some reawakened interest in the high alpine landscape. The Iceman's resting place was the only Copper Age site, but this may have been sampling bias, as not all Mesolithic rock shelters were checked for reuse by later populations. The authors attributed this renewed interest in higher-elevation terrain to the prestige of hunting for higher-status individuals, such as the Iceman, or to secure wild protein in the face of deteriorating climatic conditions. Archaeological survey by Putzer, Festi, and Oeggl (2016) in tributaries of the Schnals Valley on the traditional transhumance route also found no evidence for its use as a route during the Copper Age.

Quantities of caprine dung (i.e., from animals in the Caprinae, goat-antelope group) were recovered from the Iceman site. Was this dung derived from livestock (sheep or goat) and thus evidence for transhumance, or was it from game (ibex or chamois) (Oeggl et al. 2009)? Given that pollen and macroremains in dung should reflect diet, Oeggl and colleagues proposed that low-elevation plants would indicate livestock, high-elevation would indicate game. Study of modern analogues, including fresh droppings from sheep being driven up to high pastures from the valley and those from animals in high pastures for the summer did show clear differences corresponding to elevation of pasture. Pollen of dung samples from the Iceman site all grouped statistically with the alpine pasture comparatives. Macroremains were also from alpine species. So all dung was derived from animals that grazed in the alpine region, providing no evidence for transhumance. Although the concentration of dung and the location were suggestive of transhumance, dates on 13 examples ranged from 5400 to 2000 cal. BC, meaning that the concentrations could have represented droppings of wild animals over a long period. The oldest dung samples also seemed too old to support interpretation as transhumance (Oeggl et al. 2009).

Studies of macroremains from the Iceman site have provided evidence relevant to reconstructing Ötzi's travels and identifying his home. For instance, identification of the wood and charcoal remains found with the Iceman documented only two species from the alpine zone, green alder and dwarf willow (Oeggl and Schoch 2000). Most of the other wood belonged to species from forests in the montane zone, and in the case of spruce, larch, and pine, taxa that range sporadically into the subalpine zone. Significantly, the species from which Ötzi's equipment was made all have a montane distribution, growing in humid habitats with warm

---

FIGURE 8.5 (Continued)

Reproduced with permission of Elsevier.) The main diagram referred to earlier is the column labeled Lagaun Mire. Taxa to the left of this column are trees and shrubs, to the right herbaceous taxa. AP/NAP = arboreal/nonarboreal. LOI = loss on ignition, a measure of organic content. Notice that fewer kinds of pasture plants (center column) make up this grouping in the Neolithic and Copper Age, in comparison to later time periods.

summers and mild winters. The montane forest communities nearest the Iceman site are located at the entrances to the north-south–oriented side valleys in the lower Vinschgau and Schnalstal. Taken as a whole, the wood species associated with the Iceman indicated that his home was likely located south of the main alpine chain (Oeggl and Schoch 2000). The same conclusion was drawn by Dickson (2000), based on identification of remains of the woodland mosses *Neckera complanata* and *N. crispa* washed from the Iceman's clothing or equipment.

A large quantity of plant material embedded in the ice and sediments of the Iceman site was excavated in 1991 and 1992. Analysis of this material by Heiss and Oeggl (2009) has identified three new crops associated with Ötzi and provided insight into the formation processes of the find assemblage, especially the issue of potential movement of the body and equipment. The researchers identified 40,612 plant remains from 121 vascular plant taxa. These came from seven plant groups: plants of rocky meadows and rock crevices, anthropogenic/zoogenic heaths and meadows, herbs and scrubs of woodland margins, conifers and heathland, deciduous woods, herbs of disturbed habitats, and crops. These plant groups ranged in elevation from valley bottoms to snow line, but most originated from elevations below the find site (all but the six taxa in the rocky meadows and rock crevices group). In addition to cultivated hulled barley and einkorn found on Ötzi's garments, probable broomcorn millet, opium poppy, and flax were recovered from the site excavation (Heiss and Oeggl 2009).

How did the numerous nonlocal plants come to be deposited at the find site? Heiss and Oeggl (2009) argued that these were not modern intrusions, because fresh snow and ice were removed before ice layers were sampled. Possible depositional processes included wind (e.g., birch and alder nutlets, Asteraceae fruits, larch, spruce, and pine needles), bird droppings (fleshy fruits like bearberry, elder, juniper), caprine droppings (alpine daisy, glacier buttercup, dwarf willow, purple saxifrage were observed in droppings recovered from the site; fragmented juniper, larch, spruce needles, and some grass remains likely also had this source), and other mammals or humans (e.g., spiny fruits transported on fur). Heiss and Oeggl (2009) concluded that only the cultivated plants and plants belonging to Ötzi's equipment could be regarded as being contemporary with him.

One of these items, lime bast used as binding material for much of Ötzi's equipment, was found scattered throughout the excavated area and in two concentrations: in the quadrants where the backpack frame, axe, and bow were found (a slightly elevated, rocky area) and where the body was found (including on Ötzi's clothing) (Figure 8.6). Heiss and Oeggl (2009) argue that this distribution pattern indicates that the body was originally located near the equipment (where it picked up the fragments), then was dislocated by melting snow and/ or water, and submerged for a time before being exposed to drying winds and becoming mummified.

Vanzetti et al. (2010) go a step further, arguing that the spatial analysis supports a different scenario for how the Iceman came to this location—that he was placed on a stone platform with his possessions in formal burial. Cyclical thawing and freezing carried the body and many objects through a natural fissure into the adjoining depression, leaving only the backpack frame on the platform and creating two clusters of finds: the platform and the depression. They suggest that the unfinished weapons make sense as funerary items, the grass cape as a burial shroud, and the accompanying objects as grave goods and question why a valuable object like the copper axe wasn't taken by Ötzi's assailant if he was killed at the site. In their

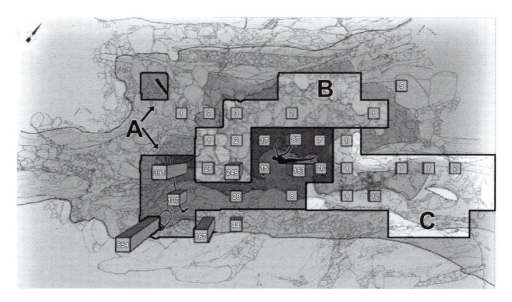

FIGURE 8.6   Distribution of lime bast. The numbers in the bars represent the total fragments. For meanings of colors, see Fig. 2. (Figure 8 from Heiss, Andreas G. and Klaus Oeggl. 2009. The plant macro-remains from the Iceman site (Tisenjoch, Italian-Austrian border, eastern Alps): New results on the glacier mummy's environment. *Vegetation History and Archaeobotany* 18:23–35.)

Reproduced with permission of Springer.) Sectors designated by color coding in the original are labeled as follows: A, area excavated during the 1991 campaign; B, quadrants with undisturbed sediments selected for preliminary assessment of spatial distribution; C, quadrants within the meltwater stream of the 1992 excavation. Notice the high concentrations of bast fragments in the lower left quadrant of sector A, where the backpack frame (under the 654 count bar), bow, and axe (under the 391 and 107 count bars) were located.

view, death in the spring, at lower elevation, followed by preservation in ice for later burial at the pass, would account for the contradictory indicators of seasonality in the pollen assemblages from Ötzi's gut and ice from the find site.

In summary, several avenues of research focused on the Iceman site and its regional context have contributed to ongoing debates about Ötzi's life and times. Pollen records support two different scenarios for the onset of transhumance, the seasonal movement of herds between low- and high-elevation pastures. If transhumance was not being practiced until after Ötzi's lifetime, this decreases the likelihood that he was killed while moving flocks to or from high-elevation pastures; if this practice was in place during the Copper Age, then it is possible Ötzi was a shepherd. In part the debate hinges on how pasturing is identified (different pasture indicators were used in the studies reviewed earlier) and how natural and anthropogenic influences are distinguished. If Ötzi and his Copper Age contemporaries were moving sheep through this region, they had a light impact on regional vegetation and left no settlements that archaeologists have found. Dung of alpine-grazed animals was present at the Iceman site, but from what animals is unknown. Some of the numerous plants from lower elevations present at the site may also have their origin in dung. Whether Ötzi frequented the higher elevation for herding, hunting (recall ibex and deer in meals; elements of wild animals in equipment), or another purpose, he equipped himself using mostly lower-elevation materials. Spatial analysis of macroremains from the find site unambiguously associated with the Iceman's equipment and clothing support a scenario of postmortem movement of the body from the spot where Ötzi first came to rest.

Conclusion: Insights from Paleoethnobotany Into the Life and Times of Ötzi

Ötzi the Tyrolean Iceman was a 40- to 50-year-old man who lived during the Copper Age or final phase of the Late Neolithic and was likely affiliated with a farming community in an alpine valley below the Hauslabjoch Pass where his body was found. We know this from the contents of his last meals, which included cultivated plants and pollen of lower-elevation plants, and the plant and animal species he used to make his equipment and clothing, among other indicators. Can further inferences be made about Ötzi's home community and his life there?

Classification of archaeological finds to cultural group in the central Alps is largely based on ceramics, and none were found with the Iceman (Spindler 1994). Several final Neolithic-phase cultures existed in the central Alpine region; in Spindler's opinion the best contenders for Ötzi's homeland were, north of Alps, the late Altheim or early Cham cultures, and south of the Alps, early Remedello. The Val Venosta (Vinschgau) valley, located within a day's walk south of the Iceman site, was densely inhabited during the Neolithic, with Remedello being the main culture of the final Late Neolithic there. The most convincing evidence linking Ötzi to this cultural group came from his axe, dagger, and arrowheads, which all showed strong similarities to objects found in Remedello graves. Spindler (1994) discussed one Remedello grave that had goods that were almost indistinguishable from Ötzi's, for example.

Do the domesticated plants found with Ötzi (einkorn, hulled barley, broomcorn millet, opium poppy, flax) link him to farming villages from this region? There are relatively few archaeobotanical data sets from Neolithic and Copper Age sites in northern Italy, and unlike at the Iceman site, preservation at those sites is largely by charring (Rottoli and Castiglioni 2009). During the Early Neolithic a highly diverse array of crops characterized Italian sites, including four cereals, five pulses (legumes), and flax. Assemblages were quite similar to crop assemblages from Bulgaria and Greece, but different from the crop mix north of the Alps (see later). Wild plants were relatively abundant and diverse at sites. Barley, emmer, and einkorn appear to have been the main crops, with lentil and pea. There was continuity in food patterns into the Middle/Late Neolithic and Copper Age, although the data set is smaller. Opium poppy was documented at two waterlogged later Neolithic sites. Barley and emmer production continued, with secondary use of einkorn. Broomcorn millet was represented by a few finds at two Copper Age sites; spelt may have been present, but identifications are uncertain. Wild plant use continued. In summary, all the crops found with Ötzi could have come from a village affiliated with a northern Italian culture; the use of a diverse array of wild plants is also consistent.

The fit is weaker between the Iceman botanical assemblage and northern farming villages. The waterlogged Arbon Bleiche 3 site on the southern shore of Lake Constance, north of the main Alpine chain, is contemporary with the Iceman; its well-preserved macroremains, along with remains from other sites, give a detailed picture of daily life in a Late Neolithic lakeside village (Jacomet 2009). Considering the cereals found with Ötzi (einkorn, hulled barley, broomcorn millet), there is a better fit to cereal assemblages from sites south of the Alps (northern Italy) than from sites north of the mountains. Naked barley was the most common cereal found with Ötzi, and it was an important cereal in the north at this time. However, einkorn was the most important wheat identified with Ötzi, and it was the least abundant at northern sites, and considered of minor importance relative to emmer and naked wheat (which was lacking in the Iceman assemblage). Broomcorn millet has not been found in northern sites. Domesticated pea, flax, and opium poppy have been identified at lake-dwelling sites north of the Alps (Jacomet 2009).

Arbon Bleiche 3 likely existed during Ötzi's lifetime and provides an informative model for his home village (Jacomet 2009). The average house was 4 by 8 m, made of wood. In addition to cultivating plants, villagers kept pigs, cattle, sheep, and goats; gathered plants; hunted deer and wild boar (among other species); and fished for pike, perch, carp, and whitefish. Stews of cereals, meat, and greens like dock were cooked. Weeds recovered in samples indicated that fields were likely permanent and intensively cultivated. Cereals were grown and used by all households, but there were differences in the abundance of gathered plants and game among households, suggesting some specialization of labor. High numbers of parasites in human coprolites indicated villagers were likely in suboptimal physical condition. Overall the image is of a self-sufficient society whose members had detailed knowledge of the natural world (Jacomet 2009).

Excavations at Hočevarica, a waterlogged lakeside settlement south of the Alps in Slovenia, provide another assemblage contemporaneous with the Iceman (Jeraj et al. 2009). Cereals, oil crops, pulses, berries (including wild grape), nuts, and edible weeds (especially *Chenopodium album*) and wetland plants like water chestnut were identified. As documented north of the Alps, barley, einkorn, and emmer were important cereals, but wheat appears to have become important earlier in the south than the north. Naked wheat, by contrast, was all but absent in the south but important in the north.

The Late Neolithic crop assemblages of eastern Austria closely resemble contemporary assemblages from the Alps, with the exception of the greater importance of naked wheats in the alpine regions and the cultivation of broomcorn millet in the east (Kohler-Schneider and Caneppele 2009). Barley and einkorn dominated crop assemblages of sites of the Jevišovice culture and were of equal relative abundance, followed by emmer wheat, broomcorn millet, and poppy, with rarer occurrences of spelt wheat, naked wheat, foxtail millet, lentil, pea, and flax. The abundance of broomcorn millet at one site confirmed its status as a regular crop.

To summarize, because there were no ceramics associated with Ötzi, a commonly used means of associating an archaeological find to a cultural group cannot be employed. Characteristics of the axe, dagger, and arrowheads and the presence of probable broomcorn millet suggest Ötzi was affiliated with a cultural group south of the Alps, in what is now northern Italy. Broomcorn millet was also grown to the east, however. In general there were strong similarities in the mixture of crops used in the Late Neolithic throughout the circum-alpine region and in the use of diverse wild species. One can imagine Ötzi feeling at home at the Arbon Bleiche 3 village, for instance.

The assemblage of plants directly associated with Ötzi is less diverse than that recovered from many of the contemporaneous sites discussed by Rottoli and Castiglioni (2009), Jacomet (2009), Jeraj et al. (2009), and Kohler-Schneider and Caneppele (2009). This is in large part the contrast between a single actor and the collective record, but likely also reflects factors of deposition and preservation of archaeobotanical remains at the Iceman site. We might find it interesting, for example, that no pulses were found with Ötzi. Perhaps he didn't like peas or stores of peas had run out by his final journey, but it is also possible that domesticated pulses, ground as flour, contributed to the Papilionaceae pollen found in his colon or the heat-altered starch on his axe.

There is ongoing debate about Ötzi's profession or social status within his group. Spindler's (1994) interpretation, that Ötzi was a shepherd integrated into a farming community, is still commonly held. Oeggl (2009) reviewed the arguments for outlaw, hunter, warrior, shaman, ore prospector, and shepherd and found none convincing; more recently Gleirscher (2014) proposed Ötzi was a clan leader or headman. Part of the challenge in interpreting what role(s) this middle-aged man played in his social group is that status/occupation indicators for the Late Neolithic/Copper Age of this region have not been clearly established or agreed upon. One issue is the copper axe: Did it indicate high status? Spindler (1994) had doubts about this, arguing that copper axes were not especially rare in Remedello graves, whereas Gleirscher (2014) characterized copper axes as not common tools and argued that Ötzi's elaborate shirt (made of alternating strips of different-colored goat skin) was another indication of higher social rank. From his equipment it is clear the Iceman was a hunter; it is unclear how this activity should be interpreted in terms of status. He was also familiar with medicinal plants and a form of acupuncture and adept at maintaining his gear and clothing. Finally, as already discussed, there is disagreement about whether transhumance was an established practice by the Copper Age; this issue is directly relevant to the interpretation of the Iceman as a shepherd.

To conclude, the 1991 discovery of a body emerging from a glacier at 3,200 ft. in the Tyrolean Alps, and the subsequent 25-plus years of study of the Iceman and the find site in regional context, have given us an extraordinary glimpse into the life and death of a man who lived 5,000 years ago. This in turn has enriched our understanding of the Late Neolithic of the central Alps. A diverse array of archaeobotanical studies detailed the plants associated with Ötzi, from the wood he used to make his bow, to the ground meal he ate, to the pollen he inhaled as he traversed the Alps, and informed us of the circumstances of his daily life, his final journey, and his likely cultural affiliation. Archaeological and paleoenvironmental studies of the region provided new insights and stimulated debate about the nature of the environment and human relationships to it during the Copper Age. Spatial analysis of plant remains from the find site helped document postdepositional movement of the Iceman's body after his death (burial?) at the pass. Ultimately, what has challenged researchers in interpreting the Iceman find, and understanding Ötzi's relationship to the natural world, is what challenges us in general in archaeology and paleoethnobotany: understanding depositional processes, dealing with preservation, developing frameworks for drawing inferences about human behaviors, and integrating multiple lines of evidence.

References

Acs, Peter, Thomas Wilhalm and Klaus Oeggl 2005 Remains of grasses found with the Neolithic Iceman "Ötzi". *Vegetation History and Archaeobotany* 14:198–206.

Aspöck, H., H. Auer, O. Picher and W. Platzer 2000 Parasitological examination of the Iceman. In *The Iceman and His Natural Environment: Palaeobotanical Results: The Man in the Ice, Volume 4*, edited by S. Bortenschlager and K. Oeggl, pp. 127–136. Springer-Verlag/Wien, New York.

Bereuter, T. L., C. Reiter, H. Seidler and W. Platzer 1996 Post-mortem alterations of human lipids—Part II: Lipid composition of a skin sample from the Iceman. In *Human Mummies: A Global Survey of Their Status and the Techniques of Conservation*, edited by K. Spindler, H. Wilfing, E. Rastbichler-Zissernig, D. zur Nedden and H. Nothdurfter, pp. 275–278. Springer-Verlag/Wien, New York.

Bortenschlager, Sigmar 2000 The Iceman's environment. In *The Iceman and His Natural Environment: Palaeobotanical Results: The Man in the Ice, Volume 4*, edited by S. Bortenschlager and K. Oeggl, pp. 11–24. Springer-Verlag/Wien, New York.

Bortenschlager, Sigmar and Klaus Oeggl (editors) 2000 *The Iceman and his Natural Environment: Palaeobotanical Results: The Man in the Ice, Volume 4*. Springer-Verlag/Wien, New York.

Dickson, James H. 2000 Bryology and the Iceman: Chorology, ecology, and ethnobotany of the mosses *Neckera complanata* Hedw. and *N. crispa* Hedw. In *The Iceman and His Natural Environment: Palaeobotanical Results: The Man in the Ice, Volume 4*, edited by S. Bortenschlager and K. Oeggl, pp. 77–87. Springer-Verlag/Wien, New York.

Dorfer, L., M. Moser, K. Spindler, F. Bahr, E. Egarter-Vigl and G. Dohr 1998 5200-year-old acupuncture in Central Europe? *Science* 282(5387):242–243.

Egg, Markus and Konrad Spindler (editors) 2009 *Kleidung und Austrüstung der Kupferzeitlichen Gletschermumie aus den Ötztaler Alpen: The Man in the Ice, Volume 6*. Verlag des Römisch-Germanischen Zentralmuseums, Mainz.

Festi, Daniela, Andreas Putzer and Klaus Oeggl 2014 Mid and late Holocene land-use changes in the Ötztal Alps, territory of the Neolithic Iceman "Ötzi". *Quaternary International* 353:17–33.

Fleckinger, Angelika 2011 *Ötzi, the Iceman: The Full Facts at a Glance*. Third ed. South Tyrol Museum of Archaeology, Bolzano, Italy.

Gleirscher, Paul 2014 Some remarks on the Iceman: His death and his social rank. *Praehistorische Zeitschrift* 89(1):40–59.

Grienke, Ulrike, Margit Zöll, Ursula Peintner and Judith M. Rollinger 2014 European medicinal polypores—A modern view on traditional uses. *Journal of Ethnopharmacology* 154:564–583.

Heiss, Andreas G. and Klaus Oeggl 2009 The plant macro-remains from the Iceman site (Tisenjoch, Italian-Austrian border, eastern Alps): New results on the glacier mummy's environment. *Vegetation History and Archaeobotany* 18:23–35.

Hoogewerff, Jurian, Wolfgang Papesch, Martin Kralik, Margit Berner, Pieter Vroon, Hermann Miesbauer, Othmar Gaber, Karl-Heinz Künzel and Jos Kleinjans 2001 The last domicile of the Iceman from Hauslabjoch: A geochemical approach using Sr, C, and O isotopes and trace element signatures. *Journal of Archaeological Science* 28:983–989.

Höpfel, Frank, Werner Platzer and Konrad Spindler (editors) 1992 *Der Mann im Eis, Band 1: Bericht über das Internationale Symposium 1992 in Innsbruck: The Man in the Ice, Volume 1*. Universität Innsbruck, Innsbruck.

Jacomet, Stefanie 2009 Plant economy and village life in Neolithic lake dwellings at the time of the Alpine Iceman. *Vegetation History and Archaeobotany* 18:47–59.

Jeraj, Marjeta, Anton Velušček and Stefanie Jacomet 2009 The diet of Eneolithic (Copper Age, Fourth millennium cal. B.C.) pile dwellers and the early formation of the cultural landscape south of the Alps: A case study from Slovenia. *Vegetation History and Archaeobotany* 18:75–89.

Kean, Walter F., Shannon Tocchio, Mary Kean and K. D. Rainsford 2013 The musculoskeletal abnormalities of the Similaum Iceman ("Ötzi"): Clues to chronic pain and possible treatments. *Inflammopharmacology* 21:11–20.

Kohler-Schneider, Marianne and Anita Caneppele 2009 Late Neolithic agriculture in eastern Austria: Archaeobotanical results from sites of the Baden and Jevišovice cultures (3600–2800 B.C.). *Vegetation History and Archaeobotany* 18:61–74.

Loy, Tom H. 2006 Starch on the axe. In *Ancient Starch Research*, edited by R. Torrence and H. Barton, pp. 178–180. Left Coast Press, Walnut Creek, CA.

O'Sullivan, Niall J., Matthew D. Teasdale, Valeria Mattiangeli, Frank Maixner, Ron Pinhasi, Daniel G. Bradley and Albert R. Zink 2016 A whole mitochondria analysis of the Tyrolean Iceman's leather provides insights into the animal sources of Copper Age clothing. *Scientific Reports* 6, 31279. doi:10.1038/srep31279.

Oeggl, Klaus 2000 The diet of the Iceman. In *The Iceman and His Natural Environment: Palaeobotanical Results: The Man in the Ice, Volume 4*, edited by S. Bortenschlager and K. Oeggl, pp. 89–115. Springer-Verlag/Wien, New York.

———— 2009 The significance of the Tyrolean Iceman for the archaeobotany of Central Europe. *Vegetation History and Archaeobotany* 18:1–11.

Oeggl, Klaus and W. Schoch 2000 Dendrological analyses of artefacts and other remains. In *The Iceman and His Natural Environment: Palaeobotanical Results: The Man in the Ice, Volume 4*, edited by S. Bortenschlager and K. Oeggl, pp. 29–61. Springer-Verlag/Wien, New York.

Oeggl, Klaus, Werner Kofler, Alexandra Schmidl, James H. Dickson, Eduard Egarter-Vigl and Othmar Gaber 2007 The reconstruction of the last itinerary of "Ötzi", the Neolithic Iceman, by pollen analyses from sequentially sampled gut extracts. *Quaternary Science Reviews* 26:853–861.

Oeggl, Klaus, Alexandra Schmidl and Werner Kofler 2009 Origin and seasonality of subfossil caprine dung from the discovery site of the Iceman (Eastern Alps). *Vegetation History and Archaeobotany* 18:37–46.

Pabst, M. A., I. Letofsky-Papst, E. Bock, M. Moser, L. Dorfer, E. Egarter-Vigl and F. Hofer 2009 The tattoos of the Tyrolean Iceman: A light microscopical, ultrastructural, and element analytical study. *Journal of Archaeological Science* 36:2335–2341.

Peintner, U. and R. Pöder 2000 Ethnomycological remarks on the Iceman's fungi. In *The Iceman and His Natural Environment: Palaeobotanical Results: The Man in the Ice, Volume 4*, edited by S. Bortenschlager and K. Oeggl, pp. 143–150. Springer-Verlag/Wien, New York.

Pernter, Patrizia, Paul Gostner, Eduard Egarter Vigl and Frank Jakobus Rühli 2007 Radiologic proof for the Iceman's cause of death (ca. 5300 BP). *Journal of Archaeological Science* 34:1784–1786.

Pfeifer, K. and K. Oeggl 2000 Analysis of the bast used by the Iceman as binding material. In *The Iceman and His Natural Environment: Palaeobotanical Results: The Man in the Ice, Volume 4*, edited by S. Bortenschlager and K. Oeggl, pp. 69–76. Springer-Verlag/Wien, New York.

Putzer, Andreas, Daniela Festi, Sophie Edlmair and Klaus Oeggl 2016 The development of human activity in the high altitudes of the Schnals Valley (South Tyrol/Italy) from the Mesolithic to modern periods. *Journal of Archaeological Science: Reports* 6:136–147.

Putzer, Andreas, Daniela Festi and Klaus Oeggl 2016 Was the Iceman really a herdsman? The development of a prehistoric pastoral economy in the Schnals Valley. *Antiquity* 90(350):319–336.

Rollo, Franco, Massimo Ubaldi, Luca Ermini and Isolina Marota 2002 Ötzi's last meals: DNA analysis of the intestinal content of the Neolithic glacier mummy from the Alps. *Proceedings of the National Academy of Sciences of the United States of America* 99(20):12594–12599.

Rott, E. 2000 Diatoms from the colon of the Iceman. In *The Iceman and His Natural Environment: Palaeobotanical Results: The Man in the Ice, Volume 4*, edited by S. Bortenschlager and K. Oeggl, pp. 117–125. Springer-Verlag/Wien, New York.

Rottoli, Mauro and Elisabetta Castiglioni 2009 Prehistory of plant growing and collecting in northern Italy, based on seed remains from the early Neolithic to the Chalcolithic (c. 5600–2100 cal. B.C.). *Vegetation History and Archaeobotany* 18:91–103.

Samadelli, Marco, Marcello Melis, Matteo Miccoli, Eduard Egarter-Vigl and Albert R. Zink 2015 Complete mapping of the tattoos of the 5300-year-old Tyrolean Iceman. *Journal of Cultural Heritage* 16:753–758.

Schedl, W. 2000 Contribution to insect remains from the accompanying equipment of the Iceman. In *The Iceman and His Natural Environment: Palaeobotanical Results: The Man in the Ice, Volume 4*, edited by S. Bortenschlager and K. Oeggl, pp. 151–155. Springer-Verlag/Wien, New York.

Seiler, Roger, Andrew I. Spielman, Albert R. Zink and Frank Rühli 2013 Oral pathologies of the Neolithic Iceman, c. 3300 BC. *European Journal of Oral Sciences* 121:137–141.

Spindler, Konrad 1994 *The Man in the Ice: This Discovery of a 5000-Year-Old Body Reveals the Secrets of the Stone Age*. Translated by E. Osers. Harmony Books, New York.

———— 1996 Iceman's last weeks. In *Human Mummies: A Global Survey of Their Status and the Techniques of Conservation*, edited by K. Spindler, H. Wilfing, E. Rastbichler-Zissernig, D. zur Nedden and H. Nothdurfter, pp. 249–263. Springer-Verlag/Wien, New York.

Spindler, K., E. Rastbichler-Zissernig, H. Wilfing, D. zur Nedden and H. Nothdurfter (editors) 1995 *Der Mann im Eis: Neue Funde und Ergebnisse: The Man in the Ice, Volume 2*. Springer-Verlag/Wien, New York.

Spindler, K., H. Wilfing, E. Rastbichler-Zissernig, D. zur Nedden and H. Nothdurfter (editors) 1996 *Human Mummies: A Global Survey of Their Status and the Techniques of Conservation: The Man in the Ice, Volume 3*. Springer-Verlag/Wien, New York.

Vanzetti, A., M. Vidale, M. Gallinaro, D. W. Frayer and L. Bondioli 2010 The Iceman as a burial. *Antiquity* 84:681–692.

9

PLANTS AND HEALING/HEALTH

Glossary

Bronze Age   historical/archaeological period following the Neolithic period, characterized by the widespread use of bronze (produced by smelting [heating in the presence of a reducing agent] of copper with tin, arsenic, or other metals) for the manufacture of tools and weapons.

diuretic   a substance that increases the production of urine; in medicine used to treat a variety of conditions, including heart failure.

infusion (of medicinal plants)   the process of extracting chemical compounds or flavors by soaking plant materials in a liquid, such as water or alcohol.

Iron Age   historical/archaeological period following the Bronze Age during which iron, produced from iron ore by smelting, was the dominant tool-making material.

Middle Ages, Medieval Period   historical/archaeological period following the fall of the Roman Empire, dating from the fifth to the fifteenth centuries AD.

Paleolithic, Upper   the third and last subdivision of the Paleolithic, or Old Stone Age, archaeological period, dated approximately 50,000 to 10,000 years ago.

quid   chewed plant matter that is not swallowed.

tonic   a substance with medicinal properties intended to restore or maintain health.

Introduction

For most of the college students who took my "Plants and People" class over the years, "foods" and "medicines" were largely separate domains. I began the semester by asking students to free-list all the interactions they had with plants for a 24-hour period; some would include herbal teas, a few knew that aspirin was developed from a plant, but most lists were made up of foods, everyday items made of natural materials, and plants growing around campus. They learned in class that in many traditional cultures, there was much more overlap among plants consumed to fuel the body, to maintain health, and to restore health and well-being. Such cultural differences in perception and practices surrounding plant use can present challenges for interpreting archaeobotanical data. We can't interview ancient peoples to determine how they classified the plant world (although historical records, ethnographic accounts, ethnobotanical studies, and analyses of therapeutic effects may contain clues), so how do we know whether the plants we have recovered were consumed as foods, medicines, spices, stimulants, or for some/all of these reasons? Does it matter if we know this?

I would argue that if we are interested in understanding past plant–people interrelationships, an essential component is understanding the role played by plants in maintaining health, re-establishing health, or altering the state of the mind or body. Knowledge of what might be called medicinal plants gives us insight into the health status of the population we are studying, the challenges to health and well-being that they were facing, and how these challenges differed over time or among members of the society. Understanding health may in turn provide us with insights into the overall functioning of the society vis-á-vis its subsistence base and environment.

The focus of this chapter, then, is the paleoethnobotany of medicinal plants, that is, plants that were used for their therapeutic effects—alleviating symptoms, promoting healing, and maintaining health. In some cases, therapeutic effects of plants recovered archaeologically have been documented scientifically. This chapter does not include studies based solely on textual sources or studies of ritual or ceremonial contexts that resulted in the recovery of food offerings. Although our focus is not on foods, I end with an example of how assessing the dietary quality of a recovered archaeobotanical assemblage may provide insight into how good health was maintained in a population.

We will look at plants and healing/health from a methodological point of view: the approaches that have been used by paleoethnobotanists and archaeologists (and some other specialists) to investigate medicinal plant use to make convincing arguments. There are five common approaches: 1) interpretation of archaeobotanical remains as medicinal plants is based on ethnographic, ethnobotanical, or historical/textual evidence of their potential medicinal uses; 2) in addition to inferences from the earlier-named sources, remains are recovered from an archaeological context that supports interpretation as medicinal plants; 3) potential medicinal plants are identified in human coprolites or in contexts interpreted as latrines, cesspools, or drains; 4) residues of medicinal plants are recovered from artifact surfaces or identified in preparations; and 5) analysis of human remains reveals an elemental or chemical signature of an active plant agent. As we will see, there is archaeological evidence that ancient cultures around the world *likely* used plants to treat illness and maintain health, but in many cases it is challenging to exclude alternative interpretations. Table 9.1 lists the scientific names of plants mentioned in the chapter.

Interpretation Based on Medicinal Properties of Plants

Most studies focused on investigating the use of medicinal plants by ancient cultures include descriptions of traditional or folk knowledge and practices surrounding potential medicinal plants. The inference that a plant recovered archaeologically was likely used as a medicine sometimes rests solely on the fact that it has medicinal properties or is considered to have such properties in folk medicine. In some cases it may also be possible to argue that other potential pathways into the archaeological record were unlikely for the plant in question (i.e., it is not edible, not weedy, not fed to animals, not used as fuel, and so on).

TABLE 9.1 Scientific names of plants mentioned in the chapter (only plants for which common names were used in the text are listed)

achiote	*Bixa orellana*
acorn	*Quercus* sp.
amaranth	*Amarathus* sp.
aster	Asteraceae, *Aster* type
beans	*Phaseolus* sp.
bedstraw	*Galium aparine, G. odoratum*
belladonna	*Atropa bella-donna*
bird's-foot trefoil	*Lotus* sp.
black cumin/black seeds	*Nigella sativa*
black haw	*Viburnum prunifolium*
black nightshade	*Solanum ptycanthum*
blue tansy	*Tanacetum annuum*
blueberry	*Vaccinium* sp.
bramble/blackberry	*Rubus* sp.
bush clover	*Lespedeza* sp.
cacao	*Theobroma cacao*
cannabis	*Cannabis sativa*
caper	*Capparis spinosa, Capparis* sp.
caper spurge	*Euphorbia lathyris*
chenopod	*Chenopodium* sp.
chickweed	*Cerastium* sp.
chili pepper	*Capsicum annuum*
chocolate	*Theobroma cacao*
coca	*Erythroxylon coca, E. novogranatense*
comfrey	*Symphytum officinale*
common gromwell	*Lithospermum officinale*
common millet	*Panicum miliaceum*
creosote	*Larrea* sp.
elderberry	*Sambucus canadensis*
erect knotweed	*Polygonum erectum*
fig	*Ficus carica*
fly agaric	*Amanita muscaria*
foxtail millet	*Setaria italica*
Franklin tree	*Franklinia alatamaha*
garlic	*Allium sativum*
grapes	Vitaceae, *Vitis* sp.
grass family	Poaceae/Gramineae
greater celandine	*Chelidonium majus*
hemlock	*Conium maculatum*
hemp	*Cannabis sativa*
henbane	*Hyoscyamus* cf. *reticulatus*
hickory	*Carya* sp.
holly	*Ilex vomitoria, I. cassine*
hops	*Humulus lupulus*
horse radish	*Armoracia rusticana*
iris or amaryllis family	Iridaceae or Amaryllidaceae
jimsonweed	*Datura stramonium*
ladanum	*Cistus ladanifer*
lily family	Liliaceae

mace	*Myristica fragrans*
maize/corn	*Zea mays*
maygrass	*Phalaris* sp.
maypops	*Passiflora incarnata*
meadowsweet	*Filipendula* sp.
mesquite	*Prosopis* sp.
mints	Lamiaceae
monk's rhubarb	*Rumex pseudoalpinus*
Mormon tea	*Ephedra* sp.
morning glories	Convolvulaceae
myrtle	*Myrtus communis*
nettles	Urticaceae
olive	*Olea europaea*
onion	*Allium cepa*
opium poppy	*Papaver somniferum*
panic grass	*Panicum dichotomiflorum*
peach	*Prunus persica*
persimmon	*Diospyros virginiana*
pine family	Pinaceae
plum	*Prunus* sp., *P. americana*
pokeweed	*Phytolacca americana*
purslane	*Portulaca oleracea*
qinghao	*Artemisia annua*
Queen Anne's lace	*Daucus carota*
red cedar	*Juniperus virginiana*
rose family	Rosaceae
rosemary	*Rosmarinus officinialis*
sage	*Salvia* sp.
sagebrush	*Artemisia* sp.
savory	*Satureja* sp.
squash	*Cucurbita* sp.
spurges	Euphorbiaceae
St. John's wort	*Hypericum* sp.
strawberries	*Fragaria* sp.
sumac	*Rhus* sp.
sumpweed	*Iva annua*
sunflower	*Helianthus annuus*
sweet basil	*Ocimum basilicum*
sweet flag	*Acorus* sp.
sweet gale	*Myrica gale*
sweet wormwood	*Artemisia annua*
tick trefoil	*Desmodium* sp.
tobacco	*Nicotiana* sp.
valerian	*Valeriana* asp.
vervain	*Verbena* sp.
walnut	*Juglans regia*
weld	*Reseda luteola*
willow	*Salix* sp.
wormwood	*Artemisia* sp.
yarrow	*Achillea* sp.
yaupon	*Ilex vomitoria*

Eastern North America

This approach is demonstrated in Williams's (2000) study of medicinal plants in the paleoethnobotanical records of the American Bottom, Moundville, and Tombigbee regions (Late Woodland through Mississippian periods; see Table 7.2 for the regional chronology). Williams proposed that medicinal plants had a long history of use in Eastern North America, but were not recognized archaeologically because charred macroremains of medicinal plants were rare in any given context. In studies in which the emphasis is on plant foods (e.g., most of those reviewed in Chapter 7), rare, nonfood charred seeds may be dismissed as accidental inclusions. Williams used the ethnobotanical record of Eastern North American Native peoples (compiled by Moerman 1998) to identify potential medicinal plants, then searched for those in macroremain databases large enough to reveal trends in rarely occurring taxa. If medicinal plants could be identified, this might permit changes in health/disease stressors to be tracked over time or reveal the emergence of full-time healing specialists.

Williams defined four use categories of potential medicinal plants from Moerman's (1998) compilation: 1) plants used primarily as medicines by Native groups (for example, spurges, St. John's wort, bedstraw); 2) plants with uses about equally divided between food and medicine (e.g., mints, sumac, black nightshade); 3) plants that were primarily foods but had secondary medicinal use (e.g., purslane, strawberries, maypops); and 4) plants used primarily in rituals, with secondary or related medicinal use (e.g., morning glories, red cedar, tobacco). To be included in a use category, plants had to be used by two or more Native groups, and there had to be commonalities in medical practices using herbal treatments or tonics. A total of 68 potential medicinal plants were identified this way. Williams (2000) argued that it was important to include plants in use categories 2 and 3, because repeated use of a plant as a food might lead to exposure to active chemicals effecting health. Such dual-purpose plants were also more likely to be preserved in domestic settings, which are typically the most commonly sampled areas. Archaeobotanical data for the plants in the four use categories were analyzed using taxon frequency, feature ubiquity, and site/component ubiquity.

I focus here on the major findings for the American Bottom, the focus of Chapter 7. Category 1 plants, those used primarily as medicines, occurred very rarely (Williams 2000). In the American Bottom, 20 Category 1 taxa occurred; of these the more common seeds recovered (by count) were tick trefoil, spurges, bedstraw, St. John's wort, and bush clover. Category 2 plants, those used about equally as foods and medicines, overall were more numerous per taxon than those of Category 1. Plants with edible fruits (sumac, elderberry, black nightshade) were the most common taxa within Category 2. Other commonly occurring taxa were maypops (absent in the American Bottom) and pokeweed. Black nightshade occurred only in American Bottom sites, including in contexts with ritual significance. Plants used as foods, with secondary medicinal use (Category 3), were also generally more numerous per taxon than Category 1 plants. Commonly occurring plants were persimmon, strawberries, plum, purslane, bramble, and grapes. Ritual plants (Category 4) recovered from sites were jimsonweed (at two American Bottom Mississippian sites), morning glory (all regions), yaupon (Moundville), red cedar wood (American Bottom, Moundville), and tobacco (American Bottom). Red cedar wood increased through time in the American Bottom and was associated with elite or ritual contexts (Williams 2000).

In the American Bottom there were 20 medicinal plants in continual use over the Late Woodland, Emergent Mississippian, and Mississippian periods, including seven plants in

Category 1 or Category 4 (tick trefoil, spurges, bedstraw, bush clover, vervain, red cedar, tobacco). These represented cultural commonality in medicinal plants used in the region through time (Williams 2000). There were also changes in medicinal plant use over time, for example, more use of tobacco during the Late Woodland and of red cedar and morning glories during the Mississippian. A wider variety of medicinal plants was used in the Mississippian period, perhaps in response to new health challenges from increased population numbers. Williams argued that of the 68 potential medicinal plants identified from ethnobotanical accounts, a strong case could be made for prehistoric use of spurge, bedstraw, pokeweed, sumac, elderberry, black nightshade, bramble, plum, purslane, morning glory, red cedar, and tobacco, based on their presence in multiple regions and time periods. Further, these plants were used historically for ailments that might have afflicted prehistoric populations.

Another example of this approach to identifying prehistoric medicinal plant use in Eastern North America is Claassen's (2011) reinterpretation of Newt Kash Shelter, Kentucky, as a women's retreat place, based on the presence of potential gynecological and venereal disease remedies in the archaeobotanical assemblage.

Europe and Southwest Asia

Upper Paleolithic-aged sediments (36,000–11,000 cal. BP) from four caves in Georgia revealed evidence for medicinal plant use (Martkoplishvili and Kvavadze 2015). Five medicinal plants that could be identified to species by their pollen were the target of this study: *Centaurea jacea, Artemisia annua, Artemisia absinthium, Achillea millefolium*, and *Urtica dioica*. These plants have a wide variety of therapeutic applications, including as anti-inflammatory and antibacterial agents. Modern pollen samples taken from within and outside the caves revealed a pattern of underrepresentation of all five taxa inside the caves in comparison to outside, indicating that their pollen was rarely deposited through natural means in the caves (Table 9.2). Pollen of medicinal plants was present in cultural sediments of all the caves; the authors argued that the abundances indicated human actions introduced these plants to the caves. In the case of Kotias Klde Cave, for instance, modern samples lacked pollen from the medicinal plants, whereas these were well represented in the Upper Paleolithic layers of the cave (Figure 9.1).

TABLE 9.2 Abundance of pollen in modern pollen spectra. (Table 1 from Martkoplishvili, Inga and Eliso Kvavadze. 2015. Some popular medicinal plants and diseases of the Upper Paleolithic in Western Georgia. *Journal of Ethnopharmacology* 166:42–52. Reproduced with permission of Elsevier.) The table compares modern pollen samples taken inside and outside caves in Georgia. Notice the marked pattern of higher representation of the medicinal plant taxa outside the caves

Caves	Achillea millefolium L.		Centaurea jacea L.		Urtica dioica L.		Artemisia	
	Inside	Outside	Inside	Outside	Inside	Outside	Inside	Outside
Dzudzuana Cave	2	9	1	2		1	1	1
Satsurblia Cave		3		4		7	1	4
Kotias Klde Cave		7		2		2		16
Khvedelidzeebis Cave	11	25	7	11	3	10	1	15
Samertskhle Klde Cave	7	22	1	4		2		3
Datvis Cave		4		5		2		2
Total sum of pollen	20	70	9	28	3	24	3	41

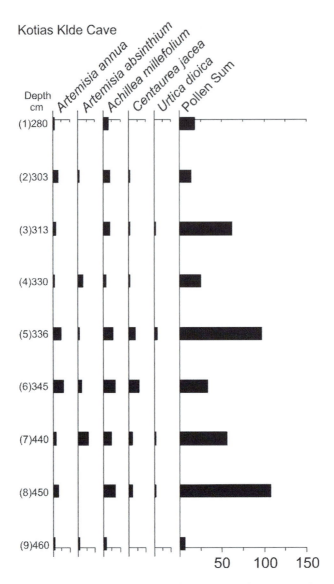

FIGURE 9.1 Absolute abundances of pollen from the investigated species in the Upper Paleolithic layers of Cave Kotias Klde; the right column gives the total sum of pollen grains in the samples. (Figure 5 from Martkoplishvili, Inga and Eliso Kvavadze. 2015. Some popular medicinal plants and diseases of the Upper Paleolithic in Western Georgia. *Journal of Ethnopharmacology* 166:42–52.)

Reproduced with permission of Elsevier.

Textual evidence indicates that tropical spices from South and Southeast Asia were used in antiquity in the Mediterranean region in traditional medicine, ritual (in funeral rites, as offerings), perfumery, and cuisine. Van der Veen and Morales (2015) described new botanical evidence for trade in tropical spices during the Roman (ca. AD 1–250) and Islamic (ca. AD 1050–1500) periods at Quseir al-Qadim and Berenike, two ancient ports on the Red Sea.

Plant remains were well preserved due to hyper-arid conditions at the sites; many thousands of seeds, fruits, grains, and other botanical remains were recovered through systematic sampling of deposits. Among these were 12 imports, including spices (Table 9.3). Black pepper, ginger, turmeric, and cardamom are spices in the modern culinary sense, whereas belleric myrobalan, black myrobalan, emblic myrobalan, and fagara would be considered health supplements today (see Table 9.3 for scientific names). In antiquity all were likely regarded not just as seasonings but also as ingredients in medicines, perfumes, and offerings. Results documented an increase in the variety of spices traded in the Islamic period in comparison to the Roman. If quantity of remains recovered is a reflection of the scale of trade (i.e., the more shipped, the more accidentally spilled), black pepper was traded in larger quantities than other spices (Van der Veen and Morales 2015).

Sweet basil is another culinary spice with medicinal uses. In an analysis of macroremains and pollen from the Iron Age site of Salut in north Oman, Bellini et al. (2011) report recovering *Ocimum* (basil) pollen in many contexts.

Garlic and onion bulbs were recovered from a fifteenth-century shipwreck, named the Copper Wreck for the ingots that it contained, in the southern Baltic Sea (Badura et al. 2013). The position of the bulbs in the wreckage suggested they were not part of the cargo, but of crew provisions. They were preserved by being covered with a layer of tar during a fire on board the ship. Onion and garlic have a significant content of sulfur compounds used in medicine and were likely commonly used for flavoring and as vegetables, but are rarely recovered archaeologically due to preservation issues. The healing properties of onions and garlic were widely known; they were often used to alleviate headaches or snakebites and had a positive impact on health. Symbolism based on the spherical shape and concentric rings of onion held that the plant gave courage and protection in battle. Badura and colleagues argued that this was one reason why onions were in sailors' rations, but significantly, they helped prevent scurvy. Garlic also had magical significance for protection against witchcraft, disease, and shipwreck.

Starch, which has little taste, is the starting point for beer production. Flavoring agents were often added to beer in ancient times, both to improve its taste and to help preserve it, given beer's relatively low alcohol content. Behre (1999) reviewed the archaeobotanical evidence for beer additives, focusing on those species mentioned in written sources in the context of beer making. There have been numerous archaeological finds of sweet gale and hops, generally of uncharred fruitlets from waterlogged contexts. Sweet gale was already in use by the Iron Age, whereas hops became common only in the early Middle Ages. Beer made with sweet gale was sweet, but did not preserve well. Hops beer could be transported and became an important export, eventually replacing sweet gale beer. Behre (1999) found that some 55 other plants were added to beer as flavoring, and the archaeobotanical record contained many of these. According to ancient herbals and medical books some beer additives had medicinal properties and were used to prepare medicinal beers against plague and other diseases. Examples included sweet flag, bedstraw, and St. John's wort.

Africa

Generally, analyses of macroremains in African archaeology do not consider the potential medicinal or ritual uses of plants (Insoll 2015). Insoll argued that there was untapped potential for identifying such uses. He noted, for example, that 11 of the plant taxa identified at the

TABLE 9.3 Spices and other imports found at the two ports. (Table 1 from Van der Veen, Marijke and Jacob Morales. 2015. The Roman and Islamic spice trade: New archaeological evidence. *Journal of Ethnopharmacology* 167:54–63. Reproduced with permission of Elsevier.) Check marks indicate presence. Notice that a much larger variety of plant imports, including spices, was present during the Islamic period (last two columns) compared to the Roman period (first three columns) at the ports of Quseir al-Qadim and Berenike

Spices and other imports			Roman 1–3 c. AD Quseir	Roman 1–2 c. AD Berenike	Roman 4–6 c. AD Berenike	Islamic 11–13 c. AD Quseir	Islamic 14–15 c. AD Quseir
Black pepper, *Piper nigrum* L.	Piperaceae	Fruit (peppercorns)	√	√	√	√	√
Rice, *Oryza sativa* L.	Poaceae	Grain (hulled and naked) and husk fragments	√	√	√	√	√
Coconut, *Cocos nucifera* L.	Arecaceae	Shell fragment (endocarp), fibrous husk (exocarp and mesocarp)	√	√	√	√	√
Mung bean, *Vigna radiata* (L.) Wilczek	Fabaceae	Seed	√	√	–	–	–
Emblic myrobalan (amla), *Phyllanthus emblica* L.	Euphorbiaceae	Fruit fragment (endocarp)	–	√	–	–	–
Belleric myrobalan, *Terminalia bellirica* (Gaertn.) Roxb.	Combretaceae	Fruit stone (endocarp)	√	–	–	√	–
Black myrobalan, *Terminalia chebula* Retz.	Combretaceae	Complete fruit and fruit stone (endocarp)	–	–	–	√	√
Fagara, cf. *Tetradium ruticarpum* (A. Juss.) T.G. Hartley	Rutaceae	Fruit (follicle) and seed	–	–	–	√	–
Cardamom, *Elettaria cardamomum* (L.) Maton	Zingiberaceae	Fruit (seed capsule) and seed	–	–	–	√	–
Turmeric, *Curcuma* sp. (cf. *Curcuma longa* L.)	Zingiberaceae	Rhizome fragment	–	–	–	√	–
Ginger, *Zingiber officinale* L.	Zingiberaceae	Rhizome fragment	–	–	–	√	–
Betelnut, *Areca catechu* L.	Arecaceae	Seed	–	–	–	√	–

medieval site of Oursi hu-Beero in Burkina Faso, West Africa, by Petit et al. (2011, cited in Insoll 2015), were described as ruderal weeds. All also have recorded medicinal uses in West Africa. *Commelina*, for example, was used as a medicinal wash and fever treatment, and *Tribulus terrestris* as a diuretic, tonic, and stomach treatment. Rather than incidental inclusions, finds of weedy plants may indicate the intentional use of encouraged plants. Attention to the contexts of finds, plant parts represented, and kinds of processing would allow more understanding of medicinal plant use (Insoll 2015).

In summary, inferences that archaeobotanical remains represented plants used for medicinal purposes may rely almost entirely on ethnographic, ethnobotanical, or historical/textual evidence for that use. Sometimes this line of argument is supported by scientific evidence of plant efficacy. In the case of macroremains preserved by charring, it is important that we not dismiss rare finds as accidental inclusions without considering potential uses—including as medicinals—that may rarely result in charred remains. Sites with enhanced preservation (i.e., by waterlogging or desiccation) may provide evidence for healing practices utilizing plant parts that are rarely preserved at most sites. In all cases, inferences are strengthened if the pathway that brought remains into a site can be modeled and supported. If ingesting a plant has both caloric and therapeutic benefits/impacts, both should be considered in our interpretations. Inferences based on traditional use or textual evidence are often more compelling if cultural continuity can be demonstrated. However, one can also argue that the therapeutic effect of any given plant taxon could be discovered and rediscovered over time and in many places. Finally, level of identification of remains (i.e., genus versus species level) has an important impact on the strength of interpretations of the nature of ancient plant use, including of medicinals.

Medicinal Plants in Compelling Archaeological Contexts

As we have just seen, there is value in identifying the presence of potential medicinal plants in the ancient sediments of a cave, the wreckage of a ship, or the secondary fill of house floors and storage pits. Recovering medicinal plant parts in situ, whether in special use areas or in association with artifacts used to prepare or administer them, can provide even more compelling evidence for the nature of human behaviors surrounding those taxa.

Central and South America

Such evidence for ancient medicinal practices has been identified at the Monte Verde site, located in the temperate rainforest of southern Chile. The younger component of the site is dated to between 12,800 and 12,400 years ago and represented a late Pleistocene hunter-gatherer settlement (Dillehay 1997b). One area of the site, Stratum MV-5, contained perishable materials preserved by a water-saturated peat layer. Twelve small domestic structures were clustered in one area of Stratum MV-5, and an isolated hut with a wishbone-shaped foundation of gravel and sand in another (Figure 9.2). The wishbone-shaped hut contained an array of artifacts and plant and animal remains distinctive from those recovered from the other structures, suggesting it was a place of specialized activities, including medicinal practices. It was built and used in two phases (Dillehay 1997a).

Evidence for medicinal practices at Monte Verde included the presence of eight quids formed from leaves and stalks of *Juncus procerus, Juncus* sp*., Peumus boldus, Sargassum* sp.,

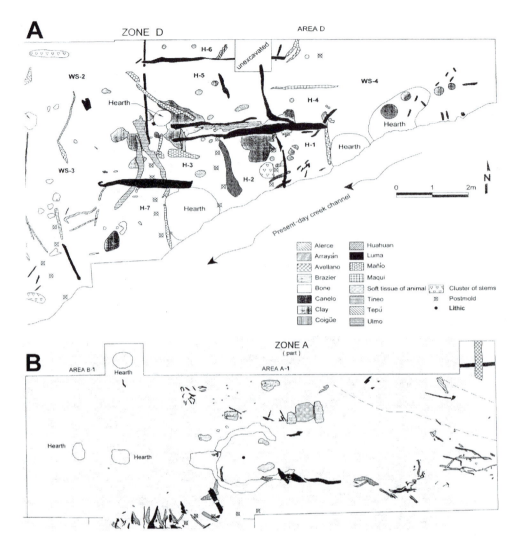

FIGURE 9.2   **A:** Enlargement of structural remains, features, and associated refuse in Area D, Zone
D. In this drawing huts are labeled H-1 to H-12. Workshops are labeled WS-1 to
WS-4; **B:** Enlargement of structural remains, features, and associated refuse in Areas
A-1 and B-1, Zone A. (Figure 8.4 and Figure 8.6 from Dillehay, Tom D. 1997. Hut
remains and associated refuse. In *Monte Verde: A Late Pleistocene Settlement in Chile*,
edited by T. D. Dillehay, pp. 173–220. Smithsonian Institution Press, Washington D.C.)

Reproduced with permission of the author. These images show the remains of structures and associated artifacts and
other remains from Stratum MV-5 at the Monte Verde site, Chile. A: domestic structures; B: wishbone structure.
Figure legends give common names for wood species identified; see the source for scientific names.

Durvillaea antarctica, and an unidentified plant. The local Huilliche people chew a variety of
plants, including *Juncus* and *Peumus*. *Peumus boldus* is a nonlocal plant; its only known use is
as a medicinal. *Sargassum* has both food and medicinal uses; *Durvillaea antarctica* is medicinal
(these are seaweeds) (Dillehay 1997b; Rossen and Dillehay 1997). Other potential medicinal

plants were recovered from the wishbone structure, including *Drosera* (medicine and insect control), *Lycopodium* (medicine and fire starter), *Berberis* (food and medicine), *Escallonia, Anagallis, Myrceugenia exsucca, Myrceugenia* sp., *Polygonum* (all medicines), *Fitzroya* (construction and medicine), *Amomyrtus,* and *Aristotelia* (construction, food, fuel, medicine) (Dillehay and Rossen 1997; Rossen and Dillehay 1997). In all, a third (23) of the plant taxa identified at Monte Verde had well-documented medicinal properties, and more than half of those co-occurred in the wishbone structure. Among these were nonlocal plants, including two seaweeds, *Anagallis, Peumus boldus*, and *Polygonum*. Dillehay and colleagues argued that the association of many medicinals, including nonlocal taxa, in a unique structure, with distinctive artifact and faunal assemblages, strongly supported a specialized function for the wishbone structure that included curing.

Coastal resources were commonly exploited by the people of Monte Verde (Dillehay et al. 2008). The coast was located about 90 km west and 15 km south of the settlement during its occupation. Analysis of previously unstudied sediments from the wishbone structure and a residential tent identified five new species of seaweeds: *Gigartina* sp., *Mazzaella* sp., *Porphyra columbina*, cf. *Sarcothalia crispate*, and *Macrocystis pyrifera*. Many fragments were mixed with other plants in masticated quids and were likely valued as both foods and medicines. All the recovered seaweeds from the site are excellent sources of iodine, iron, zinc, protein, hormones, and a range of trace elements and had medicinal uses, including antibiotic effects.

The Ceren site in El Salvador was buried by a sudden volcanic ash fall 1,400 years ago (Sheets 2006). It was a community of commoners of the Mesoamerican Classic period. Fleeing for their lives, the villagers left virtually everything behind them. There was extraordinary preservation of architecture, plants, and artifacts. Some plant remains were charred or desiccated by the heat of the ash; many were preserved as casts, which when filled with dental plaster by archaeologists preserved the plant as a plaster mold. Food production at Ceren was maize based, with a variety of other crops, including beans, chili peppers, and root and tree crops (Lentz and Ramírez-Sosa 2002). One medicinal plant was identified, cf. *Hamelia patens*, a shrub in the Rubiaceae used by the Maya to treat skin problems. Evidence from two nondomestic buildings suggested special uses for two other plants. An effigy jar of *achiote* seeds was found in a feasting structure in a room used for storage of special-use items (Brown and Gerstle 2002). Achiote is used as a red food coloring by the Maya; in addition to everyday use, it is used to make special ceremonial breads and added to chocolate, a festival drink, as a symbol of human blood, and to make red ceremonial paint. A structure interpreted as a locus for divination contained two small piles of beans, one found within a bench niche with other objects comprising the toolkit of a ritual practitioner, the other on the floor (Simmons and Sheets 2002). Maya shamans use beans and crystals in divination ceremonies (i.e., casting them and interpreting the resulting patterns).

Europe

Organic remains recovered from a storage vat in the cellar of a farmhouse near Pompeii have provided evidence for drug preparation by a Roman-period household (Ciaraldi 2000, 2002). The farmhouse, Villa Vesuvio, was covered by several meters of volcanic pumice during the AD 79 eruption of Vesuvius. It was a modest rural home with a threshing floor, wine press, and cellar. The cellar contained seven large vats, partly embedded in the ground, of a type generally used to store oil or wine. Waterlogged organic deposits were found in each. Vat 2 had especially abundant plant remains: a ca. 30-cm-thick layer of peach stones and walnuts, underlain by a thick organic deposit that was sampled for plant and faunal remains. Ciaraldi identified over 50 plant taxa in this deposit, most of which were represented by seeds and fruits, but including other tissues. Of special interest was the fact that 58 percent of the plants were taxa with medicinal properties, and of those, 77 percent were effective against poisons, both individually and as components of two compounded drugs: *methridatium* and *theriac*. Among plants having medicinal uses were members of the Solanaceae, comfrey, hemp, and opium poppy. In addition to the presence of plants with historically documented medicinal uses, Ciaraldi argued that the presence in the house of a small cooker provided more evidence that the plant assemblage was related to the preparation of medicines: such cookers were associated with medical activities and dye preparation at Pompeii and other Vesuvian sites. Some of the plants could also have been used in creating soap, dyes, or herbal wines.

A comparison of anatomical plant parts found in the Villa Vesuvio storage vat with descriptions from historical sources of parts used for medicines found many consistencies between recovered tissues and medicine preparation practices (Ciaraldi 2000, 2002). In Roman times medicines were commonly prepared as decoctions, infusions, or through soaking in wine. These were less destructive practices—in comparison to grinding or pounding—that potentially produced waste that could be preserved archaeologically. Preparation practices frequently involved plant parts that contained seeds, which were a common component of the vat assemblage. Potential medicinal plants were also found among mineralized remains in the drain system at the House of the Vestals in Pompeii. Seeds of Queen Anne's lace, used as a contraceptive in ancient times and in traditional medicine, were somewhat abundant in those samples, for example.

The burned remains of a medicine made of black cumin seed were found in a flask from the Old Hittite Period (ca. 1650 BC) at Boyali Höyük in north-central Turkey (Salih et al. 2009). Black cumin, or black seeds, is a traditional remedy of some antiquity in Asia. It is used alone or mixed with bee products to treat a variety of conditions (respiratory, stomach, kidney, and liver, among others) and to support general good health. Black cumin has significant pharmacological effects; the main constituents are alkaloids and essential oils, and fat-soluble vitamins are present. Examination of the charred seeds in the flask found that all were black cumin. Chemical analysis showed that waxes, mainly from bees, had been added to the seeds. Salih and colleagues concluded that cleaned black cumin seeds were stored with bee wax in the flask and used as a remedy by the Hittites.

There was evidence for medicinal fumigation using henbane smoke during the Ottoman occupation (fifteenth to seventeenth centuries) of Kaman-Kalehöyük, Turkey (Fenwick and Omura 2015). Henbane produces tropane alkaloids (most importantly atropine and scopolamine), powerful neurotransmitter blockers that produce narcotic and psychotropic effects. Historically, henbanes were used across Eurasia to treat a variety of conditions, but documenting ancient use has been challenging because henbane is a common weedy plant that produces abundant seeds. Finding henbane seed concentrations in a compelling context was thus essential to make a case for its medicinal use. Flotation-recovered macroremain assemblages from Kaman-Kalehöyük included henbane seeds in 18 contexts (pits, hearths, one room) (Table 9.4). As the table shows, henbane was rare in the contexts in which it occurred, making up only 0.82 percent of recovered seeds overall. Only one context, the H37 hearth, contained quantities (8.55 percent) that appeared to be above the level of incidental inclusion of weed seeds. This hearth was a ventilated earth oven, or *tandir*, found in a corner of a room

TABLE 9.4 Macrofossil samples from Ottoman contexts containing *Hyoscyamus* seeds; multiplied-up (x-up) equivalents are rounded to the nearest integer, and subsample percentages to the nearest 0.01 percent. (Table 2 from Fenwick, Rohan S. H. and Sachihiro Omura. 2015. Smoke in the eyes? Archaeological evidence for medicinal henbane fumigation at Ottoman Kaman-Kalehöyük, Kırşehir Province, Turkey. *Antiquity* 89(346):905–921. Reproduced with permission of Cambridge University Press.) Notice the distinctively high proportion of henbane seeds in the H37 hearth sample (middle of the table) at Kaman-Kalehöyük

Flot #	Context	Type	subsample		Total remains		*Hyoscyamus* remains		
			fraction	%	raw	×-up	raw	×-up	raw %
47	P333	pit	$^3/_{16}$	18.75	1022	5451	4	21	0.39
78	H103	hearth	$^{13}/_{16}$	81.25	932	1147	2	2	0.21
89	P749	pit	$^{10}/_{16}$	62.50	1346	2154	1	2	0.07
95	P758	pit	$^{15}/_{64}$	23.44	590	2517	1	4	0.17
131	P826	pit	$^3/_{32}$	9.38	722	7701	1	11	0.14
149	H106	hearth	$^{16}/_{16}$	100.00	464	464	2	2	0.43
161	H35	hearth	$^8/_{16}$	50.00	1192	2384	18	36	1.51
194	P286	pit	$^2/_{16}$	12.50	577	4616	4	32	0.69
226	P366	pit	$^4/_{16}$	25.00	996	3984	3	12	0.30
227	H37	hearth	$^4/_{16}$	25.00	1310	5240	112	448	8.55
645	P1542	pit	$^3/_{16}$	18.75	635	3387	1	5	0.16
1997/019	H62	hearth	$^{11}/_{16}$	68.75	780	1135	2	3	0.26
1998/030	H72	hearth	$^6/_{16}$	37.50	764	2037	2	5	0.26
2003/003	P2622	pit	$^3/_{16}$	18.75	890	4747	7	37	0.79
2005/006	H139	hearth	$^3/_{16}$	18.75	717	3824	1	5	0.14
2006/032	H141	hearth	$^4/_{16}$	25.00	843	3372	1	4	0.12
2009/014	R404	room	$^2/_{16}$	12.50	860	6880	4	32	0.47
2009/022	P3048	pit	$^8/_{16}$	50.00	835	1670	1	2	0.12
Total of contexts containing henbane					15 475	62 710	167	663	1.08

Ubiquity	18
Frequency (%)	43.90
Mean abundance per context (×-up: contexts with henbane *only*)	36.83
Mean abundance per context (×-up: *all contexts*)	16.17
Mean proportion per context (%, ×-up: contexts with henbane *only*)	0.82
As proportion of entire ×-up assemblage estimate ($n = 161,449$)	0.41

in a domestic complex. Other than henbane seeds, the macroremain assemblage from the hearth appeared typical for a rural farming settlement whose inhabitants burned animal dung fuel. Tropane alkaloids are easily dispersed from all parts of henbane by burning, but seeds are especially alkaloid-rich; historic accounts describe fuming the open mouth by sprinkling henbane seeds onto coals. Steam (from a pot of hot water) maximizes the effect. A ventilated underground *tandir* would help draw out the noxious odor. Fenwick and Omura (2015) concluded that the concentration of henbane seeds and the structure of the hearth supported an interpretation of deliberate burning of henbane to produce medicinal fumes.

Many objects were placed with the dead in graves during the Bronze Age, including medicinal plants. Kvavadze and Kakhiani (2010) studied pollen, fibers, and wood from the floor of a burial chamber in Paravani Kurgan, an Early Bronze Age (first half of the third millennium BC) burial mound in Georgia. Excavation of the burial chamber revealed the remains of a ceremonial wagon, in addition to other objects and remains of threads and textiles. Pollen samples were collected from the covering layers of soil and the central chamber of the burial mound, including from among the wagon remains. The study revealed information about the local environment and plants cultivated there. Among the findings relevant to our topic: high concentrations and clumps of pollen from *Filipendula* (meadowsweet), *Lotus* (bird's-foot trefoil), and *Aster* indicated that these flowers were placed in the burial pit and on the ceremonial wagon. Meadowsweet and bird's-foot trefoil have medicinal properties, as well as being decorative, like *Aster*. Textile fibers and pollen of other genera of well-known medicinal plants, *Apium, Valeriana, Achillea, Polygonum,* and *Tilia*, were found associated with a decomposed basket. The basket, likely made of willow, had also held cereal grain. From this evidence, Kvavadze and Kakhiani inferred that a basket of medicinal herbs and grain had been placed on a fabric in the bottom of the burial chamber.

East Asia

Medicinal plants were also placed with the dead in the Yanghai Tombs in Xinjiang Province, China. Among these was caper, a small shrub widely distributed in the Old World and traditionally used as a condiment (flower buds and unripe fruits) and medicinal plant (Jiang et al. 2007). Caper seeds were found in a jar with cannabis fruits, leaves, and shoots. Direct dating of the caper seeds put their deposition in the tomb at 2,800 years ago. There are earlier finds of caper seeds in Southwest Asia, but the Yanghai find is unique in the association with cannabis, another significant medicinal plant, and deliberate deposition in the tomb. A wooden bowl filled with pounded cannabis was recovered from another tomb in the cemetery—that of a male individual of high social status (Russo et al. 2008). Based on associated artifacts, he was inferred to have been a shaman. Phytochemical analysis identified the presence of tetrahydrocannabinol, the psychoactive component of cannabis, in the pounded plant sample. This confirmed that cannabis was cultivated for its psychoactive quality.

A review by Long et al. (2016) of the occurrence of cannabis fibers, pollen, and seeds in archaeological contexts and coring records has suggested that humans began to use cannabis at about the same time in the early Holocene in Europe/Southwest Asia and East Asia. Cannabis is an annual herb that is closely associated with nutrient-rich ground near human settlements; uses include smoking for hallucinogenic effect or as part of ritual or medicine, use in exchange, and hemp-made rope and other products.

Sweet wormwood *(qinghao)* is a strongly aromatic herb utilized in traditional Chinese medicine to treat wounds and fevers (Liu et al. 2013). It is the source of artemisinin, a substance used today to treat drug-resistant malaria. The first archaeological evidence for use of sweet wormwood was found in two tombs at the Shengjindian cemetery, in Xinjiang, China, dating to 2400 to 2000 BP. Whole plants had been placed in the tombs, perhaps to disguise the odor of decay.

In summary, sites with extraordinary preservation of organic materials often provide the opportunity for recovering more kinds of plant tissues, including those rarely preserved by charring. Such sites may also provide more opportunities for recognizing in situ deposits of plants or plant products where they were stored, prepared, or consumed/used. Enhanced preservation and recovery of in situ deposits (including those preserved by charring) enhance our ability to identify medicinal plant use by bringing together a potential medicinal plant(s), evidence for its preparation or mode of delivery (e.g., stored in a flask, chewed as a quid, burned as a fumigant), and compelling contextual evidence (e.g., in association with artifacts used to prepare or store the remedy, recovered in a distinctive location). Recovering medicinal plant remains from primary contexts may further strengthen interpretations by allowing us to eliminate alternative pathways for remains to have entered the archaeological record.

Coprolites and Latrines: Evidence From the Ingestion of Medicinal Plants

A distinctive kind of "primary context" for recovering evidence of medicinal plants taken internally is the human digestive system itself, or preserved feces (coprolites) or latrine deposits.

North America

Coprolites preserved in the dry deposits of Salts Cave, Mammoth Cave, and Big Bone Cave, as well as samples taken from the Salts Cave mummy, have provided direct evidence for ingestion of some of the potential medicinal plants identified by Williams (2000) in sites in the American Bottom, Moundville, and Tombigbee regions. Plants identified as macroremains in coprolites and mummy samples (all samples combined) included chenopod, amaranth, maygrass, erect knotweed, sumpweed, sunflower, gourd, squash, hickory, acorn, **bramble**, **strawberry, grape**, *Ilex*, panic grass, **purslane**, **sumac**, black haw, chickweed, **pokeweed,** and blueberry (Marquardt 1974; Stewart 1974; Yarnell 1969, 1974; Faulkner 1991; plants in bold face are potential medicinals found at sites reviewed by Williams 2000). Chenopod, sumpweed, and sunflower were also potentially represented by pollen in coprolites (i.e., Chenopodineae pollen, Chenopod-Amaranth group; Ambrosieae, sumpweed group; other Compositae [Asteraceae]). Pollen from insect-pollinated plants in coprolites likely represented deliberate ingestion of flowers, buds, or pollen-dusted foliage. In addition to other Compositae, insect-pollinated taxa identified in Salts Cave samples were sweet flag, lily family, iris or amaryllis family, rose family, Caryophyllaceae, and *Polygonum* (Schoenwetter 1974). Considering the Salts Cave macroremains and pollen together, Schoenwetter (1974) proposed a diet of stored seeds and nuts and consumption of fresh plant foods (sweet flag, lily, iris/amaryllis), the latter likely as herbal teas or tonics to combat seasonal vitamin deficiencies. Two mammoth cave coprolites contained high percentages of grass pollen, in one case in association with maygrass macroremains (Bryant 1974). Overall the pollen spectrum in Mammoth Cave samples was similar to that of Salts Cave.

In summary, studies of coprolites from cave sites in the Eastern Woodlands have confirmed ingestion of bramble, strawberry, grape, sumac, purslane, poke, and *Ilex* (yaupon) from the group of potential medicinals reviewed by Williams (2000). A pattern of ingestion of flowers, buds, and/or greens of sweet flag, lily, and iris/amaryllis as tonics was also found. Faulkner's (1991) identification of parasites in eight coprolites recovered from Big Bone Cave in association with potential medicinal plants (purslane, in three samples; sumac, in two), suggests one of the health issues that faced populations.

Studies of coprolites from sites in the southwestern United States have also provided evidence for ingestion of medicinal plants. For example, excavations at Baker Cave, a dry rock shelter in southwestern Texas, recovered coprolites from a buried latrine area near the entrance (Sobolik 1988). The latrine was contemporary with a living floor dated to 1100 BP.

Of 38 coprolites studied, 8 contained very high pollen concentrations (over 100,000 grains/ gm of material). In seven cases most pollen was Brassicaceae (mustard family), and clumps of mustard pollen were observed. Because mustards are an insect-pollinated group, the high concentration and presence of clumps indicated that flowers or seeds were eaten. The other coprolite containing very high pollen concentrations was dominated by sagebrush pollen, which is wind pollinated. It also occurred in clumps in the sample; this and the high concentration suggested that sagebrush flowers were ingested. Both sagebrush and mustards are known medicinal plants and are also eaten as greens.

Analysis of coprolites from Bighorn Cave in western Arizona, a site dating to AD 600 to 900, has provided evidence for use of two other medicinal plants: Mormon tea and willow (Reinhard et al. 1991). These plants are commonly used as medicinals by Native Americans, typically as teas (infusions of plant parts in water). Willow is insect pollinated; Mormon tea is wind pollinated. Nine samples from Bighorn Cave had pollen concentration values greater than 100,000 grains/gm, indicating intentional ingestion of polleniferous foods. Mormon tea occurred in two of these coprolites, willow in three. In all cases, the likely medicinal plant occurred at high frequencies relative to other pollen grains. Although creosote, another known medicinal plant, occurred in a number of samples, it was always at low frequency, suggesting incidental ingestion. In her comment on this study, Dean (1993) argued that creosote was not accidently ingested, given the relatively high concentrations of this insect-pollinated plant in samples.

Study of coprolites from Caldwell Cave in western Texas has demonstrated an association between consumption of Mormon tea and chronic diarrhea (Sobolik and Gerick 1992). Caldwell Cave was occupied from AD 1200 to 1450. Coprolite samples recovered from the cave indicated that chronic diarrhea, probably caused by the high levels of magnesium in the local water, was a prevalent health problem. Thirty-two coprolites were analyzed for pollen and macroremains, including a number that were diarrhetic (Table 9.5). Based on the presence of pollen in high concentrations (over 100,000 grains/gm of sample) in 12 coprolites, grass, cactus, and Mormon tea were intentionally ingested. In many cases aggregates of pollen, indicating ingestion of flower anthers, were found. Two samples contained high frequencies of insect-pollinated mesquite and intermediate concentration values, suggesting mesquite was also likely intentionally ingested. Mormon tea pollen occurred in high frequencies in three samples and at concentrations above 100,000 grains/gm in one of these. All were diarrhetic, leading Sobolik and Gerick (1992) to conclude that Mormon tea—the pollen, leaves, and stems of which are widely used to treat diarrhea—was likely ingested for that reason. Mesquite leaves also have medicinal uses, but ingestion as a food is also possible. Grass seeds and cactus fruits were likely foods.

South America

Coprolites recovered from strata dated 8500 to 7000 BP in the Boqueirão da Pedra Furada rock shelter in semi-arid northeast Brazil have preserved evidence for early to mid-Holocene use of medicinal plants in the American tropics (Chaves and Reinhard 2006). Pollen was extracted from five examples; in total 30 pollen taxa were identified. Among these were 12 from genera that included medicinal species: *Chenopodium, Bauhinia* (anthelmintics, or substances that expel parasitic worms), *Borreria, Terminalia, Alternathera, Anacardium, Caesalpinia* (for treating symptoms of parasitic worms), *Croton, Cecropia* (analgesics, pain relievers),

TABLE 9.5 Major pollen frequencies from the Caldwell Cave coprolites. (Table 1 from Sobolik, Kristin D. and Deborah J. Gerick. 1992. Prehistoric medicinal plant usage: A case study from coprolites. *Journal of Ethnobiology* 12(2):203–211. Reproduced with permission of the Society of Ethnobiology.) Frequencies of individual taxa and total sample concentration values are shown. Coprolite morphological categories are as follows: I, solid, firm, well formed; II/III, soft, well formed or not well formed; IV, soft, paddy-like. Notice the high frequencies of pollen of the medicinal plant Mormon tea *(Ephedra)* in three diarrhetic coprolites (samples 26, 27, 32)

Sample Number	Morph. Category	Ephedra %	Prosopis %	Cactaceae %	Poaceae %	Concentration Values	Count Totals
1	I	0	0	1	91 a	105,805.2	250
2	I	1	0	0	98 a	240,125.0	238
3	II/III	0	0	0	98 a	283,233.8	386
4	II/III	0	0	1	85 a	120,860.9	246
6	II/III	0	0	0	45	4,731.5	204
7	II/III	2	0	0	37	15,281.9	213
8	II/III	0	0	0	20	9,746.3	207
10	II/III	4	0	18	24	5,244.8	200
11	II/III	0	0	0	80 a	77,549.0	210
12	II/III	0	0	0	92 a	154,433.3	205
13	II/III	0	0	0	31	35,123.7	221
14	II/III	0	0	0	91 a	80,440.7	210
15	II/III	0	0	0	98 a	700,376.2	313
16	II/III	0	1	0	93 a	254,684.6	293
17	II/III	0	0	0	87 a	110,684.4	239
18	II/III	0	1	0	89 a	27,775.2	234
19	II/III	4	47	0	18	21,375.8	227
20	IV	0	1	0	96 a	96,857.1	216
21	IV	0	0	2	36	3,550.7	200
22	IV	0	3	1	38	8,999.6	205
23	IV	4	6	2	43	9,658.1	200
24	IV	2	0	0	49	9,783.5	200
25	IV	0	0	0	98 a	300,923.9	245
26	IV	47	0	0	23	67,261.9	200
27	IV	75	1	0	12	303,277.4	416
28	IV	0	2	91 a	2	128,866.4	222
29	IV	0	0	0	86 a	113,758.4	200
30	IV	1	1	0	47	3,705.7	223
31	IV	5	41	1	25 a	67,472.5	206
32	IV	51	0	1	22	96,660.8	211

a = aggregates

Anandenanthera (for sore gums and toothache), *Sida* (for wounds), and *Mansoa* (for sore throats). Traditionally, most remedies were made from these plants by infusing plant foliage or flowers, which would have resulted in the ingestion of pollen. Medicines made of *Bauhinia* and *Anandenanthera* used the bark or resin, and *Sida* was applied externally, reducing the likelihood of pollen ingestion in those cases. With the exception of *Chenopodium* and *Anacardium*, all taxa are insect pollinated, and therefore unlikely to become ingested routinely through contamination of foods by airborne pollen. Chaves and Reinhard used a cut-off of 4 percent for incidental ingestion of pollen from insect-pollinated taxa, and on that basis concluded that *Anacardium, Borreria, Croton, Sida*, and *Terminalia* were intentionally used. Abundances of wind-pollinated *Chenopodium* and *Alternanthera* could have represented intentional use or ambient pollen contamination. Table 9.6 summarizes the case for medicinal use of the 12 taxa; the authors found a strong case could be made for *Anacardium, Borreria*, and *Terminalia* being used as medicinal plants. Further, all three are used to treat maladies of the digestive tract; this correlated well with evidence for hookworm and whipworm in the Boqueirão da Pedra Furada population.

In a literature review of the occurrence of parasites in coprolite and other human fecal samples in archaeological sites worldwide, Leles et al. (2010) found two distinctive patterns. Old World (especially post-Neolithic) and historic North American samples were similar in the co-occurrence of giant roundworm and whipworm, two parasites that almost always co-occur in humans today. By contrast, whereas whipworm occurred in prehistoric South American samples, roundworm was rare. Both parasites were rare in prehistoric North American samples. The authors argued that these patterns could not be explained entirely by environmental factors or differential survival of eggs of the two parasites. They concluded that medicinal plant use likely limited the exposure of prehistoric Americans to fecal-borne

TABLE 9.6 Summary of conclusions concerning the potential that the taxa represent prehistoric medicinal use. (Table 5 from Chaves, Sérgio Augusto de Miranda and Karl J. Reinhard. 2006. Critical analysis of coprolite evidence of medicinal plant use, Piauí, Brazil. *Palaeogeography, Palaeoclimatology, Palaeoecology* 237:110–118. Reproduced with permission of Elsevier.) Notice that only three taxa recovered from Boqueirão da Pedra Furada coprolites met all five expectations for medicinal use

Taxon	Of use to ancient health	Pollen to be expected in preparation	Medicine ingested	Pollination	Pollen abundant in coprolite	Summary of evidence
Alternanthera	Yes	Yes	Yes	Wind	Yes	Problematic
Anacardium	Yes	Yes	Yes	Insect	Yes	Strong case
Anadenanthera	Yes	No	Yes	Insect	No	Weak case
Bauhinia	Yes	No	Yes	Insect	No	Weak case
Borreria	Yes	Yes	Yes	Insect	Yes	Strong case
Caesalpinia	Yes	Yes	Yes	Insect	No	Weak case
Cecropia	Yes	Yes	Yes	Insect	No	Weak case
Chenopodium	Yes	Yes	Yes	Wind	Yes	Problematic
Croton	Yes	Yes	Yes	Insect	Yes	Problematic
Mansoa	Yes	Yes	Yes	˙space.	No	Weak case
Sida	Yes	Yes	No	Insect	Yes	Problematic
Terminalia	Yes	Yes	Yes	Insect	Yes	Strong case

A strong case can be made only for insect pollinated (entomophilous) taxa that have "yes" entered in every space. "Problematic" is entered for any wind pollinated taxon or a taxon that has many non-medicinal species.

parasites: vermifuges (substances that expel worms or other parasites) such as *Chenopodium* expel roundworm more effectively than whipworms. A high-fiber diet also helps eliminate roundworms, which live freely in the gut (whipworms attach themselves).

Southwest Asia and Europe

A yellow organic deposit recovered from a feature from Tel Megiddo, a Late Bronze Age site in Israel, was tested using infrared spectroscopy (a technique used to identify chemical compounds), lipid, and other analyses to determine whether it was fecal in origin (Langgut et al. 2016). These tests indicated that the material was of plant origin, that plant cellular structures had been preserved due to replacement of organic components with phosphate-rich solutions, and that organic compounds related to fecal matter (sterols and stanols) were present. Taken together, these results indicated the deposit likely represented the bottom of a cesspit/ latrine. Pollen was extracted from the yellow deposit, a brown crust covering it, the sediments below it, and from a recent sediment sample (Table 9.7). Most of the pollen from the yellow deposit and the brown crust was from edible plants (60 percent and 75 percent, respectively), and likely represented remains of foods (for instance, olives/olive oil, cereals, figs) and drinks or teas made of mint (*Mentha* sp.), sage, myrtle, and nettle. Most taxa are insect pollinated. Pollen from edible plants was slightly less abundant in the two samples below the deposit, indicating admixture of pollen from consumed plants and background vegetation. The latter was represented by the recent control sample, which was dominated by pollen of wind-pollinated, nonedible taxa. Mint, sage, myrtle, and nettle, as well as wormwood (listed under natural vegetation, because it is wind pollinated), have medicinal properties. Some could also have been used as condiments or spices. The latrine was located in a palatial context, and Langgut and colleagues proposed that it was used by members of the ruling elite. Interestingly, only a single parasite egg was found in the samples.

Pollen samples from four cesspits/latrines were analyzed from two late medieval sites in Flanders, Belgium (Deforce 2006). Three were from a fishing village, and one from a wealthy household. All contained ladanum pollen, among pollen of other useful plants. Ladanum macroremains were lacking. Ladanum is a shrub native to the Mediterranean region and valued since antiquity for its aromatic resin, which is exuded by hairs on the leaves and stems. It is mentioned in medieval herbal books and recipes as an ingredient of medical preparations and perfumes. It is likely that pollen adhered to harvested vegetation that lacked seeds. The lack of other Mediterranean pollen taxa indicated that the source of ladanum pollen was not use of honey from the Mediterranean but from direct use of this aromatic herb.

Intact organic deposits may also be preserved in drains. Dickson (1996) studied fifteenth-century deposits recovered from the drains of Paisley Abbey in Scotland. Macroremains, recovered by wet sieving, revealed a mixture of medicinal plants, cultivated vegetables, fruits, and grains, and a wide array of plants from the local environment. A total of 140 taxa were identified. Because river water was used to flush the drains, leading to silt accumulation in them, many of the wild plant remains recovered were likely transported into the deposit that way. Dickson (1996) argued that six plants with medicinal properties represented remains of plants that were grown in the physic garden of this wealthy abbey: greater celandine, caper spurge, hemlock, opium poppy (medicinal plants), monk's rhubarb, and horse radish (medicinal and culinary). Weld, an introduced plant used for yellow dye, was also present, as was an imported spice, mace, which has medicinal properties.

TABLE 9.7 Pollen results of Locus 12/H/75. (Table 2 from Langgut, Dafna, Ruth Shahack-Gross, Eran Arie, Dvora Namdar, Alon Amrani, Matthieu Le Bailly and Israel Finkelstein. 2016. Micro-archaeological indicators for identifying ancient cess deposits: An example from Late Bronze Age Megiddo, Israel. *Journal of Archaeological Science Reports* 9:375–385)

Plants type	Taxon/description	1 Yellowish material (%)	2 Brown crust (%)	3 1 cm below the yellowish material (%)	4 5 cm below the yellowish material (%)	5 Recent sediment - control sample (%)
Possible edible/drinkable plants[a]	*Mentha* type (mint)	8.0	10.0	2.5	3.8	–
	Salvia type (sage)	–	–	0.6	–	–
	Ficus carica (common fig)	16.0	–	–	–	–
	Myrtus communis (true myrtle)	8.0	–	1.2	–	–
	Gundelia tournefortii (tumbleweed)	4.0	–	0.0	–	–
	Cereal type	16.0	10.0	25.8	22.1	1.3
	Apiaceae (carrot family)	8.0	–	13.5	21.2	1.3
	Vitis vinifera (grape)	–	–	1.2	1.9	–
	Papaver	–	–	–	1.0	–
	Achillea/Matricaria type (chamomile)	–	–	5.5	–	–
	Urticaceae (nettle family)	–	20.0	–	–	–
	Olea europaea (olive)	–	35.0	3.7	1.9	2.5
	Total edible/potable	**60.0**	**75.0**	**54.0**	**51.9**	**5.1**
Plants of natural environments	*Quercus calliprinos* type (evergreen oak)	–	–	0.6	–	–
	Quercus ithaburensis type (deciduous oak)	–	–	–	–	0.3
	Pinus (pine)	–	–	0.6	1.9	29.7
	Cupressaceae (cypress)	–	–	3.1	–	–
	Eucalyptus	–	–	–	–	2.2
	Poaceae (grasses)	8.0	–	2.5	1.0	0.0
	Sarcopoterium spinosum (thorny burnet)	4.0	–	–	–	0.6
	Asteraceae Asteroideae (aster-like)	8.0	–	9.8	16.3	8.9
	Asteraceae Cichorioideae (dandelion-like)	12.0	–	1.2	–	1.6
	Carthamus (distaff thistles)	–	–	6.7	–	–

Taxon				
Xanthium (cocklebur)	–	4.9	1.9	1.3
Echinops (globe thistles)	–	–	–	0.3
Centaurea cyanus type (cornflower)	–	–	1.0	–
Artemisia (wormwood)	5.0	–	1.9	–
Brassicaceae (cabbage family)	–	3.7	6.7	45.9
Arriplex type (saltbush)	10.0	1.8	–	2.8
Polygonaceae (knotweed family)	–	0.6	1.0	–
Scabiosa (scabious)	–	3.7	1.9	–
Knautia (widow flower)	–	3.7	1.0	0.6
Caryophyllaceae (pink family)	8.0	10.0	–	–
Ephedra (Mormon tea)	–	0.6	2.9	0.6
Bellevalia type	–	0.6	3.8	0.0
Crocus (croci)	–	0.6	–	–
Cyperaceae (sedges)	–	0.6	–	–
Rannunculaceae (crowfoot family)	–	–	3.8	–
Valerianaceae (valerian family)	–	–	2.9	–
Total nonedible	**40.0**	**46.0**	**48.1**	**94.9**
Unrecognizable (A.N.)[b]	14	9	9	3
Unidentified (A.N.)	1	–	–	–
Total counted (A.N.)	**41**	**172**	**113**	**319**
Unidentified pollen clump (A.N.)	1	–	–	–
Spores (A.N.)	–	1	5	62
Lycopodium (A.N.)	1,806	1,303	947	399
Weight (g)	0.30	2.55	2.00	3.50
Pollen concentrations values (g/sediment)	681	466	537	2,056

Samples 6 and 7 do not appear in the table since they were almost pollen barren. The division into food/drink (=digested pollen) vs. natural environment plants is not clear-cut since some taxa from the natural environment group may include both edible and nonedible plants such as Asteraceae, Brassicaceae and Caryophyllaceae. Within these families it is difficult to palynologically distinguish to the genus/species levels. However, some of the pollen taxa could also have derived from the nearby surroundings (for instance, Olea europaea, Apiaceae, Urticaceae and cereal pollen type). Yet most of the group of the edible/potable plants is composed of zoophilous (animal pollinated), characterized by low pollen dispersal efficiency and therefore much lower levels of contamination, while the group of the natural plants of the near vicinity is composed of pollen of both zoophilous plants and wind pollinated (anemophilous) taxa. In regard to Samples 1 and 2, some of the pollen grains which belong to the group of the natural environment plants could also be considered edible plants (e.g., wormwood, saltbush, member of the pink family). Only the pollen of Sarcopoterium spinosum (thorny burnet) and Poaceae (grasses) are suggested to be of a different mechanism of penetration into the sediments, unless their flowers were eaten for some yet unknown reason. These pollen grains could have been deposited on top of the yellowish material, when it was still wet, in the same mechanism as dust could have been trapped within this layer.

[a] This group represents digested pollen grains.

[b] A.N. = Absolute numbers.

Reproduced with permission of Elsevier. The total frequency of pollen from edible taxa appears in bold type for each sample from Tel Megiddo.

In summary, coprolites and organic fecal deposits recovered from cesspits, latrines, and drains provide valuable opportunities to recover direct data on plants, including medicinals, ingested by people in the past. Identifying pollen or macroremains from medicinal plants in such contexts provides strong evidence that ingestion was for treating illness; finding independent evidence for the nature of the illness (i.e., chronic diarrhea, intestinal parasites) further strengthens interpretations. Coprolite and latrine studies share several challenges with approaches already discussed. In some cases being able only to identify the plant group (genus) rather than the species of archaeobotanical remains weakens the case for medicinal plant use (e.g., if edible or weedy species are also in the group). In the case of pollen, it may be difficult to distinguish deliberate ingestion of teas made from flowers or palyniferous plant tissues from incidental inclusion of pollen in food or water, depending on the quantities of pollen recovered and the pollination mechanism of the taxa in question. Finding high concentrations of pollen from a medicinal herb typically consumed as a tea brewed from young flowering plants or remains of seeds from a remedy typically prepared from more mature tissues is a strong basis for identifying medicinal plant use.

Analyzing Medicinal Preparations/Residues

As illustrated in earlier chapters, artifacts used in preparing/consuming plant foods or drinks may retain evidence of those uses in the form of residues adhering to surfaces or absorbed into the fabric of artifacts. Similarly, chemical or morphological analyses of medicinal preparations and residues can provide compelling evidence for use of plants with therapeutic effects.

North America

By analyzing absorbed organic residues from pottery, Crown et al. (2015) identified the use of stimulant drinks by prehistoric cultures in the American Southwest and Mexican Northwest (i.e., in the Southwest Culture area). They analyzed samples from ceramic drinking vessels from 18 sites ranging in age from AD 750 to 1400. Included were sites with trade items demonstrating links to Mesoamerica and those lacking such evidence. Identification of stimulant drinks was based on presence of the methylxanthines theobromine, caffeine, and theophylline. There are no plants native to the region known to produce these compounds. The closest possibilities from outside the region are cacao, holly (i.e., Black Drink), and Franklin tree. Samples from six sites contained residues from cacao drinks (identified by the presence of only theobromine, higher theobromine than caffeine, or detected theophylline), and eight sites had ceramics with residues from holly drinks (identified by the presence of caffeine only). Other tested samples contained residues that could have been either or both drinks. Recent contamination from airborne dust (i.e., the concerns of Washburn et al. 2014) was not considered a likely source of the residues because exterior surfaces had been removed prior to sampling. Crown and colleagues concluded from these findings that stimulating drinks were an important part of life in the Southwest Culture area. Ancestral Pueblo groups apparently preferred individual serving vessels, whereas Mimbres people used larger bowls, suggesting communal consumption. It was likely that consumption was used to forge and maintain political and social relationships.

After establishing concentrations of theobromine likely to represent environmental contamination, Washburn et al. (2014) demonstrated that a population of 24 ceramics from Cahokia and other Mississippian centers had contained either cacao or Black Drink. Six of these vessels contained more caffeine than theobromine, which was consistent with Black Drink, whereas 17 contained more theobromine than caffeine, consistent with cacao. These results indicated Mississippian populations acquired cacao by trade from Mesoamerica and consumed it as well as Black Drink. Reanalysis of data from an earlier study of cacao use in the Southwest confirmed cacao consumption there.

Europe and Africa

Chemical analysis of organic compounds absorbed into pottery can also reveal herbal and other inclusions in ancient fermented beverages (McGovern et al. 2009). Residues from two Egyptian jars, representing the earliest and latest stages of ancient winemaking, were studied by McGovern and colleagues (jars from Abydos, ca. 3150 B.C., and Gebel Adda, fourth to early sixth century AD). Tartaric acid/tartrate, the key biomarker for wine and grape products, was identified in both jars using three independent techniques. Pine resin was also found in both. The combination of eight terpenoid compounds identified in the Abydos sample was consistent with the presence of the herbs savory, wormwood, and blue tansy. Other herbs could have contributed to the presence of seven of the compounds. Only rosemary could explain the combination of compounds found in the Gebel Adda sample. From these results McGovern and colleagues concluded that herbal remedies were dispensed in wine from the earliest times of Egyptian wine making.

Among the objects recovered from the Pozzino shipwreck, located off the coast of Tuscany, Italy, and dated 140 to 130 BC, was medical equipment, including numerous small tin containers *(pyxides)*, wooden vials, and tools for bloodletting (Giachi et al. 2013). X-rays showed small tablets inside one *pyxis*; a sample was analyzed to determine tablet composition. Among the findings, zinc compounds were abundant, and likely the active ingredient of the tablets; animal and vegetable lipids, beeswax, and pine resin were present; linen fibers were added to prevent breakage of the tablets; high concentrations of Triticeae starch grains, some heat altered, were found; numerous pollen grains were recovered, including olive, grass (*Avena-Triticum* group), and a diverse group of insect-pollinated taxa, consistent with incorporation of a bee product. The presence of vegetable lipids and olive pollen indicated that oil from pressing unripened olives was part of the medicinal preparation. Wheat flour was likely boiled and then dried as part of preparing the tablets, and pine resin was added to help preserve the compounds. Zinc preparations were used in antiquity to prepare eye medicines.

A plaster made of tar and herbs was recovered during excavation of a grave dating to the early Bronze Age in Szarbia, Poland (Baczyńska and Lityńska-Zając 2005). The plaster, made of wood tar, had been placed while soft and warm over the left clavicle of a 30-year-old woman. Embedded in it were nutlets (fruits) of common gromwell, an herb native to the region. Common gromwell was known in ancient medicine and described by Pliny the second as a remedy for treating kidney stones. The herb, fruit, and root are used in folk medicine; the roots contain tannins and the herb a variety of active substances.

A large cache of sherds from possible medicine pots was excavated from the Touwang site in the Tong Hills of northern Ghana (Fraser et al. 2012). The sherds were found layered under a boulder in a context dated to AD 1463 to 1553. Among the Talensi, who currently occupy the region, pottery is used to prepare and store plant-based medicines, and used pots may be hidden away because they are considered dangerous (Insoll 2011). Four archaeological sherds were analyzed by Fraser and colleagues for organic and compound-specific isotopes to determine whether they were used to prepare plant-based or animal-based medicines. Only two archaeological sherds and a modern medicine pot produced sufficient concentrations of lipids for reliable ∂C^{13} measurements. Values of both archaeological sherds fell in the range of C3 plant oils, and the modern medicine pot was intermediate between C3 and C4 plants. In this case, the C4 contribution was likely from millet, sorghum, and/or introduced maize (all used to make porridge, a staple food). These findings indicated that although the modern medicine pot was used to prepare both food and medicine, there was a conscious choice to separate food from medicine in the past.

In summary, studying medicinal preparations or their residues can provide compelling evidence of plants and other agents used for healing or altering the state of the body or mind for other purposes. Although preservation of actual remedies—herb-infused wine, tablets for treating eye disease, a plaster to relieve shoulder pain—may be rare and limited to sites with extraordinary preservation of organic materials, residues from medicinal preparations absorbed into pottery may be preserved under a wider range of site conditions. Analysis of medicinal preparations or residues may lead to the identification of the active chemical compounds selected by ancient practitioners, as well as inert substances used in preparations.

Identifying Active Plant Agents in Human Remains

Traces of active chemical compounds from medicinal plants or substances ingested to alter the state of the body or mind for purposes other than healing may be preserved in soft body tissues after death.

In 1999 three frozen bodies were found in a stone shrine near the summit of a volcano in northwest Argentina in association with wooden drinking vessels; ceramics; decorated textile bags containing maize, peanuts, and coca leaves; and dried camelid meat (Wilson et al. 2013). The discovery was interpreted as an example of the Inca practice of child sacrifice known as *capacocha*. Diachronic analysis of hair samples for markers of coca and alcohol indicated that all three children had ingested coca and alcohol (most likely in the form of maize beer, or *chicha*, based on carbon isotope data). The older child, a girl of about 13, ingested consistently high levels of coca, beginning with a marked increase 12 months before her death. Peak coca use was about six months before death; peak alcohol use was in her final weeks. The younger boy and girl had markedly lower values for coca and alcohol. Coca and alcohol likely played a dual role at the end of the lives of these sacrificial victims: they produced altered states that were interpreted as sacred and had sedative effects.

Dry conditions of the Chilean coast have preserved numerous human remains and grave goods made of organic materials, including what have been interpreted as kits for preparing psychoactive drugs (snuffing implements such as tubes and tablets). To identify prehistoric drug use more definitively, hair samples from mummified human remains from the Azapa Valley were studied by Ogalde et al. (2009). The hair of 32 mummies from northern Chile was tested for psychoactive alkaloids; the sample included men and women of different ages and three children. None of the mummies tested positive for the alkaloid characterizing *Anadenanthera*. Two samples tested positive for harmine, which characterizes *Banisteriopsis (ayahuasca)*: an infant about one year old, and an adult male. Harmine is not hallucinogenic in its pure form, however, and other alkaloids were absent in samples. Ogalde and colleagues concluded that *Baniseriopsis* was not necessarily used as a hallucinogen in this case, but as a medicinal tea.

Conclusion: Investigating Plants and Healing/Health Through Paleoethnobotany

The focus of this case study has been on exploring approaches used to document medicinal plants, that is, plants that were used for their therapeutic effects—alleviating symptoms, promoting healing, maintaining health—archaeologically. In some of the studies reviewed, the inference that archaeobotanical remains represented medicinals was based largely on ethnographic, ethnobotanical, or historical/textual evidence for that use. This line of argument was sometimes supported by scientific evidence of plant efficacy, cultural continuity between ancient and analogue populations, or demonstration that medicinal use was the most likely pathway for remains to have entered the archaeological record. Whatever the strength of any particular case, these studies demonstrated the importance of not dismissing rare finds as accidental inclusions without considering potential uses—including as medicinals—that may rarely result in such remains and of considering both caloric and therapeutic benefits/impacts of plants that have both qualities. Cases from sites with extraordinary organic preservation demonstrated the great potential for exploring ancient medicinal plant use that exists when a wide variety of plant tissues is preserved.

In a number of studies reviewed here remains of potential medicinal plants were recovered in primary archaeological contexts, that is, in situ where they were stored, prepared, used, or discarded. Association of plant tissues of potential medicinal plants with artifacts used to prepare or store a remedy or with a special-use location strengthens inferences that use was for medicinal purposes. Coprolites and organic deposits recovered from cesspits or latrines are unique primary archaeological contexts in which direct data on plants ingested by people can be preserved. A number of cases demonstrated that identifying pollen or macroremains from medicinal plants in feces/fecal deposits could provide strong evidence for ingestion to treat illness. Documenting independent evidence for the nature of the illness (i.e., chronic diarrhea, intestinal parasites) further strengthened interpretations.

Several studies demonstrated the potential for identifying the active chemical compounds of preserved medicinal preparations and residues absorbed into pottery or preserved in soft body tissues after death. Although preservation of actual remedies may be limited to sites with extraordinary preservation of organic materials, residues from medicinal preparations absorbed into pottery may be preserved under a wider range of site conditions.

Our review of research on medicinal plant use has identified several challenges for understanding this aspect of plant–people interrelationships through the archaeological record. If it is only possible to identify the plant group (genus) rather than the species of recovered macroremains or pollen, then an argument for medicinal plant use may be weakened. Genus-level identifications may be especially problematic if edible or weedy species lacking medicinal properties are also in the group. In the case of pollen from coprolites, it may be difficult to distinguish deliberate ingestion of teas made from flowers or palyniferous plant tissues from incidental inclusion of pollen in food or water, depending on the quantities of pollen recovered and the pollination mechanism of the plants in question. Any inference concerning ancient plant use is stronger if remains were recovered from primary contexts and/or if formation processes affecting contexts (primary or secondary) can be modeled effectively. This is especially important for inferring medicinal plant use, because remains of healing plants may be few in number in absolute terms (overall counts, ubiquity) or in comparison to more abundant remains of foods or fuels. Finally, although it may be possible to make a strong case that a plant was *likely* used to treat illness or maintain health, it may be challenging to exclude alternative interpretations, especially related uses such as foods, drinks, and spices.

Perhaps the most important take-away message from this review is that investigating how people used plants to heal illness, treat injury, maintain health, or alter the state of the mind or body cannot be easily separated from studying the larger web of plant–people interrelationships as revealed in the archaeobotanical record. If our goal is to understand how people lived in the past, how they related to one another and to their environment, then it behooves us to embrace the diversity of ways in which plants affected human health, well-being, and survival.

Let me end with an example of how studying overall diet may reveal a society's strategies for maintaining health. Rowan (2014, 2016) analyzed a broad array of botanical and faunal remains from the Roman town of Herculaneum, which was buried by the eruption of Vesuvius in AD 79. Excavation of the city's Cardo V sewer—a cesspit that collected human and kitchen waste from middle- and lower-class urban dwellers—provided a large sample for evaluating the diet of nonelite individuals. Bioarchaeological materials were recovered by flotation; mineralized, carbonized, and waterlogged materials were present. The mineralized assemblage was made up of weed seeds, common and foxtail millet, and small seeds from fruits and herbs that could be swallowed whole. The carbonized assemblage was dominated by olive stones. Fruit and weed seeds made up the waterlogged assemblage. Overall, diet was based on a limited number of staple foods, but included over 100 types of fruits, herbs, fish, and shellfish, demonstrating that these urban dwellers of modest means could afford a wide range of foodstuffs. None of the recovered plants were characterized as potential medicines by Rowan (but note that opium poppy was present, as were some taxa of plants with healing properties [e.g., chenopod, nettle]). Based on her assessment of the nutrients that would have been provided by the recovered foods, and comparisons to skeletal remains from the site, Rowan (2014) proposed that a healthy and varied diet characterized this middle- to lower-class population. Although childhood illness and poor oral hygiene were documented, there was no evidence that nutrient-deficiency diseases were a problem. Paleoethnobotany played a central role in understanding the basis for the long and healthy lives of the Herculaneum population.

References

Baczyńska, Barbara and Maria Lityńska-Zając 2005 Application of *Lithsopermum officinale* L. in early Bronze Age medicine. *Vegetation History and Archaeobotany* 14:77–80.

Badura, Monika, Beata Możejko and Waldemar Ossowski 2013 Bulbs of onion (*Allium cepa* L.) and garlic (*Allium sativum* L.) from the 15th-century Copper Wreck in Gdańsk (Baltic Sea): A part of victualling? *Journal of Archaeological Science* 40:4066–4072.

Behre, Karl-Ernst 1999 The history of beer additives in Europe—A review. *Vegetation History and Archaeobotany* 8:35–48.

Bellini, Cristina, Chiara Condoluci, Gianna Giachi, Tiziana Gonnelli and Marta Mariotti Lippi 2011 Interpretative scenarios emerging from plant micro- and macroremains in the Iron Age site of Salut, Sultanate of Oman. *Journal of Archaeological Science* 38:2775–2789.

Brown, Linda A. and Andrea I. Gerstle 2002 Structure 10: Feasting and village festivals. In *Before the Volcano Erupted: The Ancient Cerén Village in Central America*, edited by P. Sheets, pp. 97–103. University of Texas Press, Austin.

Bryant, Vaughn M., Jr. 1974 Pollen analysis of prehistoric human feces from Mammoth Cave. In *Archeology of the Mammoth Cave Area*, edited by P. J. Watson, pp. 203–209. Academic Press, New York.

Chaves, Sérgio Augusto de Miranda and Karl J. Reinhard 2006 Critical analysis of coprolite evidence of medicinal plant use, Piauí, Brazil. *Palaeogeography, Palaeoclimatology, Palaeoecology* 237:110–118.

Ciaraldi, Marina 2000 Drug preparation in evidence? An unusual plant and bone assemblage from the Pompeian countryside, Italy. *Vegetation History and Archaeobotany* 9:91–98.

———— 2002 The interpretation of medicinal plants in the archaeological context: Some case-studies from Pompeii. In *The Archaeology of Medicine: Papers given at a session of the annual conference of the Theoretical Archaeology Group held at the University of Birmingham on 20 December 1998*, edited by R. Arnott, pp. 81–85. BAR International Series 1046, Archaeopress, Oxford.

Claassen, Cheryl 2011 Rock shelters as women's retreats: Understanding Newt Kash. *American Antiquity* 76(4):628–641.

Crown, Patricia L., Jiyan Gu, W. Jeffrey Hurst, Timothy J. Ward, Ardith D. Bravenec, Syed Ali, Laura Kebert, Marlaina Berch, Erin Redman, Patrick D. Lyons, Jamie Merewether, David A. Phillips, Lori S. Reed and Kyle Woodson 2015 Ritual drinks in the pre-Hispanic US Southwest and Mexican Northwest. *Proceedings of the National Academy of Sciences of the United States of America* 112(37):11436–11442.

Dean, Glenna 1993 Use of pollen concentrations in coprolite analysis: An archaeobotanical viewpoint with a comment to Reinhard et al. (1991). *Journal of Ethnobiology* 13(1):102–114.

Deforce, Koen 2006 The historical use of ladanum: Palynological evidence from 15th and 16th century cesspits in northern Belgium. *Vegetation History and Archaeobotany* 15:145–148.

Dickson, Camilla 1996 Food, medicinal and other plants from the 15th century drains of Paisley Abbey, Scotland. *Vegetation History and Archaeobotany* 5:25–31.

Dillehay, Tom D. 1997a Hut remains and associated refuse. In *Monte Verde: A Late Pleistocene Settlement in Chile*, edited by T. D. Dillehay, pp. 173–220. Smithsonian Institution Press, Washington, DC.

———— 1997b Introduction. In *Monte Verde: A Late Pleistocene Settlement in Chile*, edited by T. D. Dillehay, pp. 1–24. Smithsonian Institution Press, Washington, DC.

Dillehay, Tom D., Carlos R. Ramírez-Sosa, M. Pino, M. B. Collins, Jack Rossen and J. D. Pino-Navarro 2008 Monte Verde: Seaweed, food, medicine, and the peopling of South America. *Science* 320(5877):784–786.

Dillehay, Tom D. and Jack Rossen 1997 Integrity and distributions of the archaeobotanical collection. In *Monte Verde: A Late Pleistocene Settlement in Chile*, edited by T. D. Dillehay, pp. 351–381. Smithsonian Institution Press, Washington, DC.

Faulkner, Charles T. 1991 Prehistoric diet and parasitic infection in Tennessee: Evidence from the analysis of desiccated human paleofeces. *American Antiquity* 56(4):687–700.

Fenwick, Rohan S. H. and Sachihiro Omura 2015 Smoke in the eyes? Archaeological evidence for medicinal henbane fumigation at Ottoman Kaman-Kalehöyük, Kırşehir Province, Turkey. *Antiquity* 89(346):905–921.

Fraser, Sharon E., Timothy Insoll, Anu Thompson and Bart E. van Dongen 2012 Organic geochemical analysis of archaeological medicine pots from Northern Ghana: The multi-functionality of pottery. *Journal of Archaeological Science* 39:2506–2514.

Giachi, Gianna, Pasquino Pallecchi, Antonella Romualdi, Erika Ribechini, Jeannette Jacqueline Lucejko, Maria Perla Colombini and Marta Mariotti Lippi 2013 Ingredients of a 2,000-y-old medicine revealed by chemical, mineralogical, and botanical investigations. *Proceedings of the National Academy of Sciences of the United States of America* 110(4):1193–1196.

Insoll, Timothy 2011 Substance and materiality? The archaeology of Talensi medicine shrines and medicinal practices. *Anthropology and Medicine* 18(2):181–203.

———— 2015 *Material Explorations in African Archaeology*. Oxford University Press, Oxford.

Jiang, Hong-En, Xiao Li, David K. Ferguson, Yu-Fei Wang, Chang-Jiang Liu and Cheng-Sen Li 2007 The discovery of *Capparis spinosa* L. (Capparidaceae) in the Yanghai Tombs (2800 years B.P.), NW China, and its medicinal implications. *Journal of Ethnopharmacology* 113:409–420.

Kvavadze, Eliso and Kakha Kakhiani 2010 Palynology of the Paravani burial mound (Early Bronze Age, Georgia). *Vegetation History and Archaeobotany* 19:469–478.

Langgut, Dafna, Ruth Shahack-Gross, Eran Arie, Dvora Namdar, Alon Amrani, Matthieu Le Bailly and Israel Finkelstein 2016 Micro-archaeological indicators for identifying ancient cess deposits: An example from Late Bronze Age Megiddo, Israel. *Journal of Archaeological Science Reports* 9:375–385.

Leles, Daniela, Karl J. Reinhard, Martín Fugassa, L. F. Ferreira, Alena M. Iñiguez and Adauto Araújo 2010 A parasitological paradox: Why is ascarid infection so rare in the prehistoric Americas? *Journal of Archaeological Science* 37:1510–1520.

Lentz, David L. and Carlos R. Ramírez-Sosa 2002 Cerén plant resources: Abundance and diversity. In *Before the Volcano Erupted: The Ancient Cerén Village in Central America*, edited by P. Sheets, pp. 33–44. University of Texas Press, Austin.

Liu, Huan, Xiaofei Tian, Yongbing Zhang, Changsui Wang and Hongen Jiang 2013 The discovery of *Artemisia annua* L. in the Shengjindian cemetery, Xinjiang, China and its implications for early uses of traditional Chinese herbal medicine *qinghao*. *Journal of Ethnopharmacology* 146:278–286.

Long, Tengwen, Mayke Wagner, Dieter Demske, Christian Leipe and Pavel E. Tarasov 2016 *Cannabis* in Eurasia: Origin of human use and Bronze Age trans-continental connections. *Vegetation History and Archaeobotany*. 26(2):245–258.

Marquardt, William H. 1974 A statistical analysis of constituents in human paleofecal specimens from Mammoth Cave. In *Archeology of the Mammoth Cave Area*, edited by P. J. Watson, pp. 193–202. Academic Press, New York.

Martkoplishvili, Inga and Eliso Kvavadze 2015 Some popular medicinal plants and diseases of the Upper Paleolithic in Western Georgia. *Journal of Ethnopharmacology* 166:42–52.

McGovern, Patrick E., Armen Mirzoian, Gretchen R. Hall and Ofer Bar-Yosef 2009 Ancient Egyptian herbal wines. *Proceedings of the National Academy of Sciences of the United States of America* 106(18):7361–7366.

Moerman, Daniel E. 1998 *Native American Ethnobotany*. Timber Press, Portland, OR.

Ogalde, Juan P., Bernardo T. Arriaza and Elia C. Soto 2009 Identification of psychoactive alkaloids in ancient Andean human hair by gas chromatography/mass spectrometry. *Journal of Archaeological Science* 36:467–472.

Petit, L. P., M. Von Czerniewicz and C. Pelzer (editors) 2011 *Oursi hu-Beero: A Medieval House Complex in Burkina Faso, West Africa*. Sidestone, Leiden.

Reinhard, K. J., D. L. Hamilton and R. H. Hevly 1991 Use of pollen concentration in paleopharmacology: Coprolite evidence of medicinal plants. *Journal of Ethnobiology* 11(1):117–132.

Rossen, Jack and Tom D. Dillehay 1997 Modeling ancient plant procurement and use at Monte Verde. In *Monte Verde: A Late Pleistocene Settlement in Chile*, edited by T. D. Dillehay, pp. 331–350. Smithsonian Institution Press, Washington, DC.

Rowan, Erica 2014 *Roman Diet and Nutrition in the Vesuvian Region: A Study of the Bioarchaeological Remains from the Cardo V Sewer at Herculaneum*. Ph. D Dissertation, University of Oxford.

——— 2016 Bioarchaeological preservation and non-elite diet in the Bay of Naples: An analysis of the food remains from the Cardo V sewer at the Roman site of Herculaneum. *Environmental Archaeology*.22(3):318–336.

Russo, Ethan B., Hong-En Jiang, Xiao Li, Alan Sutton, Andrea Carboni, Francesca del Bianco, Giuseppe Mandolino, David J. Potter, You-Xing Zhao, Subir Bera, Yong-Bing Zhang, En-Guo Lü, David K. Ferguson, Francis Hueber, Liang-Cheng Zhao, Chang-Jiang Liu, Yu-Fei Wang and Cheng-Sen Li 2008 Phytochemical and genetic analyses of ancient cannabis from Central Asia. *Journal of Experimental Botany* 59(15):4171–4182.

Salih, B., T. Sipahi and E. Oybak Dönmez 2009 Ancient nigella seeds from Boyali Höyük in north-central Turkey. *Journal of Ethnopharmacology* 124:416–420.

Schoenwetter, James 1974 Pollen analysis of human paleofeces from Upper Salts Cave. In *Archeology of the Mammoth Cave Area*, edited by P. J. Watson, pp. 49–58. Academic Press, New York.

Sheets, Payson 2006 *The Ceren Site: An Ancient Village Buried by Volcanic Ash in Central America*. Second ed. Thomson Wadsworth, Belmont, CA.

Simmons, Scott E. and Payson Sheets 2002 Divination at Cerén: The evidence from Structure 12. In *Before the Volcano Erupted: The Ancient Cerén Village in Central America*, edited by P. Sheets, pp. 104–113. University of Texas Press, Austin.

Sobolik, Kristin D. 1988 The importance of pollen concentration values from coprolites: An analysis of southwest Texas samples. *Palynology* 12:201–214.

Sobolik, Kristin D. and Deborah J. Gerick 1992 Prehistoric medicinal plant usage: A case study from coprolites. *Journal of Ethnobiology* 12(2):203–211.

Stewart, Robert B. 1974 Identification and quantification of components in Salts Cave paleofeces, 1970–1972. In *Archeology of the Mammoth Cave Area*, edited by P. J. Watson. Academic Press, New York.

Van der Veen, Marijke and Jacob Morales 2015 The Roman and Islamic spice trade: New archaeological evidence. *Journal of Ethnopharmacology* 167:54–63.

Washburn, Dorothy K., William N. Washburn, Petia A. Shipkova and Mary Ann Pelleymounter 2014 Chemical analysis of cacao residues in archaeological ceramics from North America: Considerations of contamination, sample size, and systematic controls. *Journal of Archaeological Science* 50:191–207.

Williams, Michele L. 2000 *Evidence for Medicinal Plants in the Paleoethnobotanical Record of the Eastern United States During the Late Woodland Through Mississippian Periods*. Ph. D Dissertation, Washington University, St. Louis.

Wilson, Andrew S., Emma L. Brown, Chiara Villa, Niels Lynnerup, Andrew Healey, Maria Constanza Ceruti, Johan Reinhard, Carlos H. Previgliano, Facundo Arias Araoz, Josefina Gonzalez Diez and Timothy Taylor 2013 Archaeological, radiological, and biological evidence offer insight into Inca child sacrifice. *Proceedings of the National Academy of Sciences of the United States of America* 110(33):13322–13327.

Yarnell, Richard A. 1969 Contents of human paleofeces. In *The Prehistory of Salts Cave, Kentucky*, by Patty Jo Watson, pp. 41–54. Illinois State Museum Reports of Investigations No. 16, Springfield.

———— 1974 Intestinal contents of the Salts Cave mummy and analysis of the initial Salts Cave flotation series. In *Archeology of the Mammoth Cave Area*, edited by P. J. Watson, pp. 109–112. Academic Press, New York.

10

CONCLUSION

Investigating Ancient Lifeways Through Paleoethnobotany

Introduction

My goal in *Case Studies in Paleoethnobotany: Understanding Ancient Lifeways Through the Study of Phytoliths, Starch, Macroremains, and Pollen* has been to explore the process of interpretation in paleoethnobotany—in other words, to look at how paleoethnobotanists draw convincing inferences on past plant–people interrelationships from archaeobotanical data and use those insights to investigate ancient lifeways. The points I would like to make in conclusion fall into two broad categories: methodological aspects of interpretation and what can be learned when research questions are approached from different scales of analysis.

Methodological Aspects of Making Convincing Interpretations

In Chapter 1 I described the four common kinds of archaeobotanical remains—starch, macroremains, phytoliths, and pollen—and approaches for studying them. Sound interpretations are based, first and foremost, on well-identified plant remains. At its heart the process of identification is matching of unknown remains—of whatever kind—to known specimens. A charred maize kernel looks very different from a grain of maize starch, for instance, but one goes about identifying them in much the same way. For an experienced analyst, recognition may be immediate, based on the overall appearance of the specimen, the combination of all its features taken together. Such initial recognition may be followed by measurements of key attributes or more detailed examination of diagnostic features, perhaps at higher magnification or in different rotations. Recall in the case of identifying maize (Chapter 6), for example, some of the key attributes that allow separation of pollen, starch, or phytoliths of maize from that of other grasses (e.g., pollen size; cross-shaped phytolith size and three-dimensional morphology; rondel phytolith assemblage characteristics; starch size and morphology), or separation of macroremains of different races of maize (e.g., cupule width, kernel width/length ratio, row number). Sometimes even an experienced paleoethnobotanist will use a check-off list of attributes, a dichotomous key, or other identification aid to narrow down possible matches in the comparative collection.

It is often the case that the starch, seeds, wood, phytoliths, or pollen produced by closely related plants is similar morphologically. Or morphologically distinctive macroremains or microfossils may exist within a group of closely related plants, but diagnostic features may be difficult to discern without the use of advanced techniques such as scanning electron microscopy, which can be impractical to apply to large data sets. The taxonomic level of identification achievable for archaeobotanical remains (i.e., are remains identified to the species, genus, family, or higher taxonomic level?) is a significant component of interpretation. Quality and mode of preservation can also affect identification of archaeobotanical remains, as discussed in Chapter 2. As a reader, one needs to pay attention to the taxonomic level(s) of identifications presented in a study and the impact, if any, of identification level on inferences concerning past plant use.

Archaeobotanical remains do not exist in a vacuum, however, but are recovered from actual sites/tools/lake cores of known temporal and environmental contexts. Paleoethnobotanists collect and study modern plant specimens from their study regions in order to identify archaeological plant remains accurately, but also to learn what plants are present there. Those insights, in combination with published data on plant distributions and uses from floras, historic accounts, ethnobotanical studies, and the like, provide context for interpreting specific assemblages of archaeobotanical remains. Thus a genus-level or family-level identification may be sufficient to make a strong argument for medicinal or edible plant use in a given setting, depending on how many species or genera with overlapping archaeobotanical morphotype(s) grow in the locality, whether all or only some were medicinal or edible, and so on. Some examples from the case studies of contextualized interpretations of archaeobotanical remains identified at various taxonomic levels include the following:

Identifying maize *(Zea mays)* based on phytoliths produced by both maize and teosinte (both *Zea*) outside the range of teosinte (for example, in Ecuador). (Pearsall and Piperno 1990)
Characterizing Ötzi's travels and meals in the days before his death by the genera and families of pollen and seeds characteristic of different altitudes found in his gut. (Oeggl et al. 2007)
Identifying potential medicinal plant use at Cahokia and other American Bottom sites by recovering macroremains from medicinal plant families (e.g., spurges, morning glories) and genera (e.g., St. John's wort). (Williams 2000)

In Chapter 2 I described some of the human behaviors and natural processes through which plant remains become deposited and preserved in natural depositional situations like lake sediments and in localities that will become archaeological sites. Modeling the specific processes and behaviors that produced a given archaeobotanical assemblage is an important aspect of interpretation. Convincing interpretations demonstrate good understanding of the context of recovered archaeobotanical remains and provide support for the inferred pathway(s) that brought those remains into the record. For example, if our research question requires data on the social context and actions surrounding *consumption* of food or drink, understanding how food and drink are potentially represented as pollen, starch, phytoliths, or macroremains in such contexts is essential for identifying the actions. Archaeobotanical data may thus also play an important role in establishing context and associated behaviors. Some examples from the case studies of how understanding deposition, preservation, and context enhance interpretation include the following:

Comparing abundances of pollen of medicinal species in modern samples taken outside and inside caves occupied during the Upper Paleolithic in Georgia supported introduction of plants into the cave by humans, rather than through natural processes. (Martkoplishvili and Kvavadze 2015)

Mapping abundances of lime bast in sediments of the Iceman site and comparing the resulting pattern to the location of Ötzi's body and equipment supported post-depositional movement of the body. (Heiss and Oeggl 2009)

Recovery of maize, but not native seed crops, in association with unusual artifact assemblages in deliberately burned huts at the East St. Louis Mound Center of Greater Cahokia demonstrated the ceremonial significance of maize during a period of significant transformation of Cahokian society. (Pauketat et al. 2013)

Recovering starch and phytoliths from dental calculus from the Shanidar III skeleton provided the first direct evidence for consumption of plant foods (Triticeae, Fabaceae, unknown USO, date palm) by Neanderthals in the Near East. (Henry et al. 2011)

As discussed in Chapter 3, field sampling is a key element of paleoethnobotanical research. In terms of macroremains, recovery of all size classes of remains—by flotation or fine sieving—is crucial for investigating past plant–people interrelationships that result in deposition and preservation of such plant tissues. Equally important is designing a sampling strategy for macroremains and microfossils that leads to the recovery of the diverse kinds of archaeobotanical data—in adequate numbers and well distributed spatially and temporally—that will be needed to address our research questions. Employing a blanket sampling strategy for all archaeobotanical remains is a good first step. There are numerous situations in which sampling in small, precisely located areas is essential. Careful attention to sampling, ideally before the fact, but in some instances by making the best use of what was available, was key to the compelling interpretations discussed in the case studies. Some examples include the following:

Systematic microfossil sampling across a living floor at Tor Faraj rock shelter and mapping of the spatial distribution of identified remains contributed significantly to the finding that the Neanderthals of Tor Faraj organized their activities and living space along the lines of modern hunter-gatherers. (Rosen 2003, Henry 2003)

Comparing macroremains of maize and native crops from Early Mississippian feasting (sub-Mound 51) and domestic (ICT-II tract excavations) contexts at Cahokia indicated that dishes prepared for communal gatherings called for maygrass, chenopod, and knotweed, rather than maize. (Fritz and Lopinot 2003)

Study of pollen in prehistoric woodrat middens in Chaco Canyon recovered significant quantities of maize pollen, which, given its poor dispersal, indicated local cultivation of maize in the alluvial floor of the canyon. (Hall 2010)

Coring of a series of lakes in the montane and subalpine zones above the Vinschgau valley found little evidence that animals were herded at high elevations during the Iceman's lifetime, making it unlikely Ötzi traveled to where he died because he was a shepherd. (Festi et al. 2014)

In Chapter 4 I discussed some of the tried-and-true approaches for interpreting paleoethnobotanical data that have led paleoethnobotanists to strong inferences about past plant–people interrelationships. These approaches fall into two broad types: qualitative (i.e., what is learned from determining that a given plant was present at a site or context) and quantitative (i.e., what is learned from the abundance of remains recovered). The point I'd like to make here is that *any* of the approaches discussed in Chapter 4—documenting the occurrence of plants, raw data tabulation, ubiquity/percentage presence, ratios, diversity or richness, multivariate approaches—can work well and can get the job done, depending on the research question being asked, the strength of the data, and the experience or preference of the analyst. Some examples from the case studies of compelling inferences drawn through qualitative and quantitative approaches to interpretation include the following:

Tabulation of Mousterian plant remains from Kebara Cave demonstrated the breadth of plant taxa that potentially contributed to Neanderthal diet and health. (Lev et al. 2005)

Calculation of richness values (using Menhinick's index) from microfossils recovered from Neanderthal and early modern human dental calculus and tools shed new light on the question of whether Neanderthals had a narrower diet, finding broad similarities in plant food dietary richness. (Henry et al. 2014)

Comparison of mano (handheld grinding stone) grinding surface areas and ubiquity of maize macroremains at sites in the American Southwest found a strong correlation in these measures of agricultural dependence and differences among sites and regions in the timing of the transition to maize as a staple crop. (Hard et al. 1996)

Ratios of maize kernel to maize cob counts calculated by site and phase in the American Bottom measured use of shellable maize (leading to more cob parts) relative to green maize consumption (fewer cob parts preserved), documenting a shift in how maize was used in the late Emergent Mississippian and after. (Lopinot 1992; Pauketat 1994)

Comparison of relative abundances of pollen of edible plants from a suspected latrine deposit in a feature from Tel Megiddo to other sediments in the feature and to a control sample found that the distinctive deposit represented the remains of foods and drinks or teas and was distinguishable from background vegetation. (Langgut et al. 2016)

Approaching Interpretation at Different Scales of Analysis

The second aspect of interpretation in paleoethnobotany I'd like to emphasize concerns insights that can be gained into past plant–people interrelationships when research questions are approached from different scales of analysis. In other words, what can be learned when we sample and analyze archaeobotanical data at the scale of the individual, group, and landscape levels? Archaeobotanical data lend themselves to a multiscalar approach to interpretation, potentially providing us with multiple lines of evidence concerning many aspects of past plant–people interrelationships. Each of the case studies provided examples of insights gained from integrating individual-, group-, and landscape-scale data.

In the Neanderthal case, for example, dental calculus data (microfossils, organic molecules, and DNA) provided insights into the diet or health status of Neanderthal individuals (e.g., K. Hardy et al. 2012, 2016). Limited inferences could also be drawn concerning how foods or remedies were prepared. A second kind of individual-scale data came from artifact residue and functional studies, which provided information on the use histories of tools, including those used for various kinds of plant processing (e.g., B. Hardy 2004). Site-level data have also provided essential insights into Neanderthal lifeways, for instance, in providing "menus" of potential foods, medicines, fuels, and other useful plants available to groups (e.g., Lev et al. 2005) and in documenting how groups organized activities involving plants in the limited space of rock shelters (e.g., Albert et al. 2000). Each of these lines of evidence, among others, contributed to an emerging re-evaluation of the role of plants in Neanderthal life, namely, that few significant behavioral differences existed between Neanderthals and early modern humans in terms of their plant–people interrelationships.

In the maize case we also saw the importance of individual-scale archaeobotanical data in documenting plant–people interrelationships, in this case, the emergence of food systems incorporating domesticated plants. For example, phytoliths and starch recovered from stone tool surfaces and associated sediments provided some of the oldest evidence for the use of maize and other crops in the New World (e.g., Balsas River Valley, Mexico, Piperno et al. 2009; highland Ecuador, Pagán-Jiménez et al. 2016). Starch preserved in human dental calculus and in cooking pot residues provided insights into how maize was prepared and incorporated with other foods into meals (e.g., coastal Ecuador, Zarrillo et al. 2008) and the extent to which consumption varied among individuals (e.g., Caribbean, Mickleburgh and Pagán-Jiménez 2012). At the other end of the spectrum, landscape-scale data—recovered by coring lakes and swamps—were essential in documenting the onset and intensification of plant cultivation: agriculture was undertaken on the landscape and by its nature altered vegetation in ways that were significant and visible in sedimentary pollen, phytolith, and charcoal records, for example, in forested environments in the Amazon (e.g., Bush et al. 1989). Site-level data proved invaluable for providing insights into the relative importance to communities of maize in relationship to other resources, including wild plants and other crops, that is, by assessing relative abundances of archaeobotanical remains by frequency and ubiquity (e.g., Chaco Canyon, Geib and Hietman 2015; Los Naranjos, Honduras, Morell-Hart et al. 2014). Each of these lines of evidence, among others, provided data essential for understanding the changing role(s) of maize in foodways through time and across the diverse environments of the New World, as well as in identifying potential differences in access among members of ancient societies.

In the Cahokia case we saw demonstrated the power of systematic collection and study of group-scale archaeobotanical data for investigating plant–people interrelationships. The flotation program carried out at American Bottom sites provided a broad picture of foodways in communities in the periods leading up to and during the Cahokia chiefdom (e.g., Simon and Parker 2006). These data also allowed comparison of community-, subcommunity-, and household-level patterning across space and time, for example, in changes in the use of maize and native crops of the Eastern Agricultural Complex by elites and commoners, and in ceremonial and domestic settings (e.g., Fritz and Lopinot 2003; Pauketat et al. 2013). Landscape-scale data, like those from Horseshoe Lake near the Cahokia center (Munoz et al. 2015), provided the environmental context for the rise and decline of the chiefdom and documented human impacts associated with crop cultivation. In this case individual-scale data came from stable isotope analyses of absorbed and visible organic residues in pottery, which demonstrated less contribution of maize to meals prepared for elites than nonelites (e.g., Beehr and Ambrose 2007; Reber et al. 2004), and isotope and other studies of human bone, which indicated that gender, social standing, and home location all contributed to the relative contribution to diet of maize and native foods (e.g., Ambrose et al. 2003). These lines of evidence, among others, demonstrated that native crops, wild plants, and maize were important components of Mississippian foodways and that documenting how foods were prepared and consumed by different groups contributed greatly to understanding relationships among people during the emergence of social complexity at Cahokia.

The Ötzi case study focused on an individual, a late middle-aged man who lost his life in the Alps during the Late Neolithic period or Copper Age. The enhanced preservation of the Iceman find and the innovative and painstaking investigations of the body, clothing, artifacts, and recovery site undertaken over more than 25 years resulted in a remarkably detailed picture of Ötzi's physical condition (e.g., Aspöck et al. 2000), gear (e.g., Spindler 1994), and his final days and death (e.g., Gleirscher 2014). Studies of food residues from Ötzi's colon identified the content of his last three meals (einkorn meal, meat, and various greens) and documented his trek from altitude down to the southern Vinschgau valley, then back up to high elevation, where he was killed (Oeggl et al. 2007). Landscape-level data contributed to investigating whether it was likely Ötzi was involved in transhumance (moving herds among pastures at different elevations) (e.g., Festi et al. 2014). Studies of macroremains from the find site identified new crops associated with Ötzi (probable broomcorn millet, opium poppy, and flax) and provided insights into the formation processes of the find assemblage, especially the issue of potential movement of the body and equipment (Heiss and Oeggl 2009). Group-scale archaeobotanical data from the circum-Alpine region, such as that reported by Rottoli and Castiglioni (2009), provided the broader context for Ötzi's life as a member of a Copper Age farming community, most likely in what is now northern Italy.

In the final case study, compelling insights on the role(s) played by plants in maintaining health, re-establishing health, or altering the state of the mind or body came from studies of preserved human fecal remains that documented ingestion of medicinal plants. These included individual-scale data, for example, study of individual coprolites from dry cave deposits (e.g., in Brazil, Chaves and Reinhard 2006), as well as group-scale data from cesspits or latrines (e.g., in Belgium, Deforce 2006). Independent evidence for the nature of the illness (i.e., chronic diarrhea, intestinal parasites) further strengthened interpretations in some cases (e.g., in the American Southwest, Sobolik and Gerick 1992). Although preservation of recognizable fecal remains was largely limited to waterlogged and desiccated contexts, residues from medicinal preparations absorbed into pottery (e.g., Egyptian herbal wines, McGovern et al. 2009) or present in dental calculus (e.g., of Neanderthals, K. Hardy et al. 2016) provided other sources of individual-scale data. In the absence of extraordinary preservation, group-scale data provided valuable insights into potential medicinal plants documented by rare occurrences in the archaeobotanical record (e.g., American Bottom, Williams 2000), or in situ, in special use areas, or in association with artifacts used to prepare or administer them (e.g., Monte Verde shaman hut, Dillehay and Rossen 1997; henbane fumigation hearth, Fenwick and Omura 2015). These lines of evidence, among others, demonstrated the important role played by paleoethnobotany in investigating strategies for maintaining or re-establishing health in ancient societies and the diverse ways plants affected health, well-being, and survival.

Final Thoughts

Paleoethnobotany has its roots in the nineteenth century; its development as a discipline mirrors in many ways the development of its parent discipline, archaeology. Thus paleoethnobotany today is a discipline concerned with formation processes of the archaeological record; testing of hypotheses derived from a broad array of theoretical perspectives; investigating political complexity, social status, and social change; and studying human environmental impacts, management, and land use—in fact, searching out any and all aspects of past plant–people interrelationships using every and all tools and approaches. I hope that the case studies discussed here have illustrated the wide array of issues that are informed through the systematic recovery and analysis of macroremains, pollen, phytoliths, and starch. Put the effort into reading the graphs and tables and evaluating the strength of the inferences—your efforts will be rewarded with an enhanced understanding of ancient lifeways.

References

Albert, Rosa M., Steve Weiner, Ofer Bar-Yosef and Liliane Meignen 2000 Phytoliths in the Middle Palaeolithic deposits of Kebara Cave, Mt. Carmel, Israel: Study of the plant materials used for fuel and other purposes. *Journal of Archaeological Science* 27:931–947.

Ambrose, Stanley H., Jane Buikstra and Harold W. Krueger 2003 Status and gender differences in diet at Mound 72, Cahokia, revealed by isotopic analysis of bone. *Journal of Anthropological Archaeology* 22:217–226.

Aspöck, H., H. Auer, O. Picher and W. Platzer 2000 Parasitological examination of the Iceman. In *The Iceman and His Natural Environment: Palaeobotanical Results: The Man in the Ice, Volume 4*, edited by S. Bortenschlager and K. Oeggl, pp. 127–136. Springer-Verlag/Wien, New York.

Beehr, Dana E. and Stanley H. Ambrose 2007 Reconstructing Mississippian diet in the American Bottom with stable isotope ratios of pot sherd residues. In *Theory and Practice of Archaeological Residue Analysis*, edited by H. Barnard and J. W. Eerkens, pp. 189–199. British Archaeological Reports S1650, Archaeopress, Oxford.

Bush, Mark B., Dolores R. Piperno and Paul A. Colinvaux 1989 A 6000 year history of Amazonian maize cultivation. *Nature* 340:303–305.

Chaves, Sérgio Augusto de Miranda and Karl J. Reinhard 2006 Critical analysis of coprolite evidence of medicinal plant use, Piauí, Brazil. *Palaeogeography, Palaeoclimatology, Palaeoecology* 237:110–118.

Deforce, Koen 2006 The historical use of ladanum: Palynological evidence from 15th and 16th century cesspits in northern Belgium. *Vegetation History and Archaeobotany* 15:145–148.

Dillehay, Tom D. and Jack Rossen 1997 Integrity and distributions of the archaeobotanical collection. In *Monte Verde: A Late Pleistocene Settlement in Chile*, edited by T. D. Dillehay, pp. 351–381. Smithsonian Institution Press, Washington D.C.

Fenwick, Rohan S. H. and Sachihiro Omura 2015 Smoke in the eyes? Archaeological evidence for medicinal henbane fumigation at Ottoman Kaman-Kalehöyük, Kırşehir Province, Turkey. *Antiquity* 89(346):905–921.

Festi, Daniela, Andreas Putzer and Klaus Oeggl 2014 Mid and late Holocene land-use changes in the Ötztal Alps, territory of the Neolithic Iceman "Ötzi". *Quaternary International* 353:17–33.

Fritz, Gayle J. and Neal H. Lopinot 2003–2004 Native crops at Early Cahokia: Comparing domestic and ceremonial contexts. *Illlinois Archaeology* 15 & 16:90–111.

Geib, Phil R. and Carrie C. Heitman 2015 The relevance of maize pollen for assessing the extent of maize production in Chaco Canyon. In *Chaco Revisited: New Research on the Prehistory of Chaco Canyon, New Mexico*, edited by C. C. Heitman and S. Plog, pp. 66–95. The University of Arizona Press, Tucson.

Gleirscher, Paul 2014 Some remarks on the Iceman: His death and his social rank. *Praehistorische Zeitschrift* 89(1):40–59.

Hall, Stephen A. 2010 Early maize pollen from Chaco Canyon, New Mexico, USA. *Palynology* 34(1): 125–137.

Hard, Robert J., Raymond P. Mauldin and Gerry R. Raymond 1996 Mano size, stable isotope ratios, and macrobotanical remains as multiple lines of evidence of maize dependence in the American Southwest. *Journal of Archaeological Method and Theory* 3(3):253–318.

Hardy, Bruce L. 2004 Neanderthal behaviour and stone tool function at the Middle Palaeolithic site of La Quina, France. *Antiquity* 78(301):547–565.

Hardy, Karen, Stephen Buckley, Matthew J. Collins, Almudena Estalrrich, Don Brothwell, Les Copeland, Antonio García-Tabernero, Samuel García-Vargas, Marco de la Rasilla, Carles Lalueza-Fox, Rosa Huguet, Markus Bastir, David Santamaría, Marco Madella, Julie Wilson, Ángel Fernández Cortés and Antonio Rosas 2012 Neanderthal medics? Evidence for food, cooking, and medicinal plants entrapped in dental calculus. *Naturwissenschaften* 99:617–626.

Hardy, Karen, Stephen Buckley and Michael Huffman 2016 Doctors, chefs or hominin animals? Non-edible plants and Neanderthals. *Antiquity* 90(353):1373–1379.

Heiss, Andreas G. and Klaus Oeggl 2009 The plant macro-remains from the Iceman site (Tisenjoch, Italian-Austrian border, eastern Alps): New results on the glacier mummy's environment. *Vegetation History and Archaeobotany* 18:23–35.

Henry, Amanda G., Alison S. Brooks and Dolores R. Piperno 2011 Microfossils in calculus demonstrate consumption of plants and cooked foods in Neanderthal diets (Shanidar III, Iraq; Spy I and II, Belgium). *Proceedings of the National Academy of Sciences of the United States of America* 108(2):486–491.

——— 2014 Plant foods and the dietary ecology of Neanderthals and early modern humans. *Journal of Human Evolution* 69:44–54.

Henry, David O. 2003 Behavioral organization at Tor Faraj. In *Neanderthals in the Levant. Behavioral Organization and the Beginnings of Human Modernity*, edited by D. O. Henry, pp. 237–269. Continuum, London.

Langgut, Dafna, Ruth Shahack-Gross, Eran Arie, Dvora Namdar, Alon Amrani, Matthieu Le Bailly and Israel Finkelstein 2016 Micro-archaeological indicators for identifying ancient cess deposits: An example from Late Bronze Age Megiddo, Israel. *Journal of Archaeological Science Reports* 9:375–385.

Lev, Efraim, Mordechai Kislev and Ofer Bar-Yosef 2005 Mousterian vegetal food in Kebara Cave, Mt. Carmel. *Journal of Archaeological Science* 32:475–484.

Lopinot, Neal H. 1992 Spatial and temporal variability in Mississippian subsistence: The Archaeobotanical record. In *Late Prehistoric Agriculture: Observations from the Midwest*, edited by W. I. Woods, pp. 44–94. Illinois Historic Preservation Society, Springfield.

Martkoplishvili, Inga and Eliso Kvavadze 2015 Some popular medicinal plants and diseases of the Upper Paleolithic in Western Georgia. *Journal of Ethnopharmacology* 166:42–52.

McGovern, Patrick E., Armen Mirzoian, Gretchen R. Hall and Ofer Bar-Yosef 2009 Ancient Egyptian herbal wines. *Proceedings of the National Academy of Sciences of the United States of America* 106(18):7361–7366.

Mickleburgh, H. L. and J. R. Pagán-Jiménez 2012 New insights into the consumption of maize and other food plants in the pre-Columbian Caribbean from starch grains trapped in human dental calculus. *Journal of Archaeological Science* 39(7):2468–2478.

Morell-Hart, Shanti, Rosemary J. Joyce and John S. Henderson 2014 Multi-proxy analysis of plant use at Formative Period Los Naranjos, Honduras. *Latin American Antiquity* 25(1):65–81.

Munoz, Samuel E., Kristine E. Gruley, Ashtin Massie, David A. Fike, Sissel Schroeder and John W. Williams 2015 Cahokia's emergence and decline coincided with shifts of flood frequency on the Mississippi River. *Proceedings of the National Academy of Sciences of the United States of America* 112(20):6319–6324.

Oeggl, Klaus, Werner Kofler, Alexandra Schmidl, James H. Dickson, Eduard Egarter-Vigl and Othmar Gaber 2007 The reconstruction of the last itinerary of "Ötzi", the Neolithic Iceman, by pollen analyses from sequentially sampled gut extracts. *Quaternary Science Reviews* 26:853–861.

Pagán-Jiménez, Jaime R., Ana M. Guachamín-Tello, Martha E. Romero-Bastidas and Angelo R. Constantine-Castro 2016 Late ninth millennium B.P. use of *Zea mays* L. at Cubilán area, highland Ecuador, revealed by ancient starches. *Quaternary International* 404:137–155.

Pauketat, Timothy R. 1994 *The Ascent of Chiefs: Cahokia and Mississippian Politics in Native North America*. The University of Alabama Press, Tuscaloosa.

Pauketat, Timothy R., Andrew C. Fortier, Susan M. Alt and Thomas E. Emerson 2013 A Mississippian conflagration at East St. Louis and its political-historical implications. *Journal of Field Archaeology* 38(3):210–226.

Pearsall, Deborah M. and Dolores R. Piperno 1990 Antiquity of maize cultivation in Ecuador: Summary and reevaluation of the evidence. *American Antiquity* 55(2):324–337.

Piperno, D. R., A. J. Ranere, I. Holst, J. Iriarte and R. Dickau 2009 Starch grain and phytolith evidence for early ninth millennium B.P. maize from the Central Balsas River Valley, Mexico. *Proceedings of the National Academy of Sciences of the United States of America* 106(13):5019–5024.

Reber, Eleanora A., Stephanie N. Dudd, Nikolaas J. van der Merwe and Richard P. Evershed 2004 Direct detection of maize in pottery residues via compound specific stable carbon isotope analysis. *Antiquity* 78(301):682–691.

Rosen, Arlene Miller 2003 Middle Paleolithic plant exploitation: The microbotanical evidence. In *Neanderthals in the Levant: Behavioral Organization and the Beginnings of Human Modernity*, edited by D. O. Henry, pp. 156–171. Continuum, London.

Rottoli, Mauro and Elisabetta Castiglioni 2009 Prehistory of plant growing and collecting in northern Italy, based on seed remains from the early Neolithic to the Chalcolithic (c. 5600–2100 cal. B.C.). *Vegetation History and Archaeobotany* 18:91–103.

Simon, Mary L. and Kathryn E. Parker 2006 Prehistoric plant use in the American Bottom: New thoughts and interpretations. *Southeastern Archaeology* 25(2):212–257.

Sobolik, Kristin D. and Deborah J. Gerick 1992 Prehistoric medicinal plant usage: A case study from coprolites. *Journal of Ethnobiology* 12(2):203–211.

Spindler, Konrad 1994 *The Man in the Ice: This Discovery of a 5000-Year-Old Body Reveals the Secrets of the Stone Age*. Translated by E. Osers. Harmony Books, New York.

Williams, Michele L. 2000 *Evidence for Medicinal Plants in the Paleoethnobotanical Record of the Eastern United States During the Late Woodland Through Mississippian Periods*. Ph. D Dissertation, Washington University, St. Louis.

Zarrillo, Sonia, D. M. Pearsall, J. S. Raymond, Mary Ann Tisdale and J. Quon Dugane 2008 Directly dated starch residues document early Formative maize (*Zea mays* L.) in tropical Ecuador. *Proceedings of the National Academy of Sciences of the United States of America* 105(13):5006–5011.

INDEX

Note: Page numbers in **bold** indicate tables on the corresponding page; page numbers in *italic* indicate a figure on the corresponding page.